SOCIALIST REGISTER 2024

THE SOCIALIST REGISTER

Founded in 1964

EDITOR

GREG ALBO

FOUNDING EDITORS

RALPH MILIBAND (1924–1994)
LEO PANITCH (1945-2020)
JOHN SAVILLE (1916-2009)

ASSOCIATE EDITORS

STEPHEN MAHER
ALFREDO SAAD-FILHO
ALAN ZUEGE

ASSISTANT EDITOR

CHRIS LITTLE

CONTRIBUTING EDITORS

GILBERT ACHCAR
NICOLE ASCHOFF
PATRICK BOND
ATILIO BORON
JOHANNA BRENNER
MICHAEL CALDERBANK
VIVEK CHIBBER
MADELEINE DAVIS
BARBARA EPSTEIN
NATALIE FENTON
BILL FLETCHER JR
ANA GARCIA
SAM GINDIN
ADAM HANIEH
BARBARA HARRISS-WHITE
DAVID HARVEY
JUDITH ADLER HELLMAN
CHRISTOPH HERMANN
URSULA HUWS
RAY KIELY
MARTIJN KONINGS
HANNES LACHER
COLIN LEYS
SASHA LILLEY
LIN CHUN
MICHAEL LOWY
BIRGIT MAHNKOPF
ŞEBNEM OĞUZ
BRYAN PALMER
ADOLPH REED JR
STEPHANIE ROSS
SHEILA ROWBOTHAM
JOAN SANGSTER
MICHALIS SPOURDALAKIS
HILARY WAINWRIGHT

To get online access to all Register volumes visit our website
http://www.socialistregister.com

SOCIALIST REGISTER 2024

A NEW GLOBAL GEOMETRY?

Edited by GREG ALBO

THE MERLIN PRESS
MONTHLY REVIEW PRESS
FERNWOOD PUBLISHING

First published in 2024
by The Merlin Press Ltd
Central Books Building
Freshwater Road
London
RM8 1RX

www.merlinpress.co.uk

© The Merlin Press, 2024

British Library Cataloguing in Publication Data is available from the British Library

ISSN. 0081-0606

Cover images:
SaeedSajjadi_CCA2.0 / KenHodge_CCA2.0 / DavyImage_CCBYSA4.0 Shutterstock_684989755 / AmazoniaReal_CCL2.0 / SESU_CC4.0 Gg1a_CC-BY-SE4.0 / USN Public Domain / Wikimedia Commons_CC-BY-SA4.0

Published in the UK by The Merlin Press
ISBN. 978-0-85036-785-0 Paperback
ISBN. 978-0-85036-786-7 Hardback

Published in the USA by Monthly Review Press
ISBN. 978-1-68590-039-7 Paperback

Published in Canada by Fernwood Publishing
ISBN. 978-1-77363-638-2 Paperback

Printed in the UK by Imprint Digital, Exeter

CONTENTS

Greg Albo	Preface	ix
Jerome Klassen	Liberals to the rescue? Team Biden and the US empire	1
Ingo Schmidt	US capitalism: too big to fail, too weak to lead	34
John Bellamy Foster	The US quest for nuclear primacy: the counterforce doctrine and the ideology of moral asymmetry	58
Andreas Bieler Adam David Morton	Reframing the geopolitics of global capitalism	82
Tanner Mirrlees	The US and China's digital tech war: a new rivalry within and beyond the US empire?	105
Achin Vanaik	Continuity and change in India's foreign policy: realpolitik, Hindu nationalism and Modi	141
Ken C. Kawashima	Japan's 'new pre-war': five dislocations of its historical development	165
Thomas Sablowski	Germany in the new capitalist geometry	186
Alan Cafruny Vassilis K. Fouskas	Europe, the world economy and new imperial Grossraums	206

Eren Duzgun Can Cemgil	Class, state and geopolitics: explaining Erdoğan's Turkey	224
Claudio Katz	The new geopolitical scene in Latin America	247
Lindsey German	Fighting for peace, preparing for war: the British antiwar movement	261
James Meadway	'The first crisis of the Anthropocene': the world economy since Covid	280
Birgit Mahnkopf	From globalization to geopolitics: a way back, not forward	312

CONTRIBUTORS

Andreas Bieler is Professor of Political Economy at the University of Nottingham and Co-Director of the independent Centre for the Study of Social and Global Justice (CSSGJ).

Alan Cafruny is Henry Platt Bristol Professor of International Affairs at Hamilton College in New York State.

Can Cemgil teaches international relations and political economy at Istanbul Bilgi University.

Eren Duzgun is Assistant Professor of Political Science at the University of Cyprus.

John Bellamy Foster is Professor of Sociology at the University of Oregon and editor of *Monthly Review*.

Vassilis K. Fouskas is Professor of International Relations at the University of East London.

Lindsey German is a socialist writer and campaigner in Britain. She is convenor of the Stop the War Coalition and a member of the editorial board of *Counterfire*.

Claudio Katz is an economist and a researcher at Argentina's National Council of Science and Technology who teaches at the University of Buenos Aires.

Ken C. Kawashima is Associate Professor in the Department of East Asian Studies at the University of Toronto.

Jerome Klassen is a Lecturer in Political Science at UMass Boston.

Birgit Mahnkopf is Professor Emeritus of European Politics at the Berlin School of Economics and Law.

James Meadway is Director of the Progressive Economy Forum, and was an adviser to the former Shadow Chancellor John McDonnell.

Tanner Mirrlees is an Associate Professor in the Faculty of Social Science and Humanities at Ontario Tech University.

Adam David Morton is Professor of Political Economy at the University of Sydney.

Thomas Sablowski is Senior Research Fellow for the Political Economy of Globalization at the Institute for Critical Social Analysis of the Rosa Luxemburg Foundation Berlin.

Ingo Schmidt is a Professor of Labour Studies at Athabasca University in Canada and a columnist for the German monthly *Sozialistische Zeitung*.

Achin Vanaik is a writer, social activist, former Professor at the University of Delhi and an Associate Fellow of the Transnational Institute.

PREFACE

Preparing the 2024 *Socialist Register* presented several challenges. This year's volume was the last of a quintet planned out with the late Leo Panitch, in collaboration with comrades in London and Toronto, with the intent of surveying the configuration of global capitalism and geopolitical alignments after the long period of turmoil stretching from the Great Financial Crisis to the 'pandemic shutdown'. We had only sketched the barest of outlines of the issues to tackle in the volume before he died, but the intent was clear – to elaborate on key themes we had begun to explore in earlier volumes, notably 2019's *A World Turned Upside Down* investigating the forces that were redrawing the map of global capitalism. Since then, the contradictions and stresses in world order have only intensified, leaving the buttresses of the neoliberal policy regime straining under the pressure. Geographically, the fissures in the globalization project stretch from Europe and across Eurasia to East Asia, spread across the Middle East, and extend further to any number of points in the Global South. Meanwhile, the most pressing social issues of global governance seemed to exceed the capacities of existing multilateral institutions to address them with any coherence or resolve: the greenhouse gas emissions breaching climate change targets; the inequalities of global health provisioning exposed by the Covid pandemic; the marginalization of the WTO and the erosion of other regimes in the management of global trade; the resurgence of the global arms race encompassing nuclear weapons and new military technologies and systems capable of unimaginable destruction; the outbreak of several major wars of attrition involving multiple regional and global powers; and the escalating global contestation over control of frontier technologies and geopolitical zones of influence between the US and China, the world's leading economic and political powers. In his last comments on the *Register*'s editorial plans, Leo reiterated the need for a comprehensive study of this 'new global geometry' (invoking Giovanni Arrighi's classic text revisiting questions of imperialism). But with such an agenda, Leo's distinctive abilities to take stock of the 'actually-existing' political and economic terrain confronting socialists, and to harness a 'revolutionary optimism of the intellect' in finding new openings for struggle (as he framed his outlook in the 2017 *Socialist Register*), were sorely missed.

There was, indeed, much merit in his insistence of carrying on with this project. In Washington, the world's leading capitalist power was outlining its own concerns. In October 2022, US President Joe Biden launched the new National Security Strategy, which warned that the world was at an 'inflection point', declaring that the 'post-Cold War era was definitively over, and a competition is underway between the major powers to shape what comes next'. American leadership would be needed more than ever, the document declared, to define 'the future of the international order' by marshalling its unparalleled economic, military and diplomatic resources to confront America's geopolitical rivals. The US Chamber of Commerce came to a similar conclusion a year earlier, in its 'Understanding U.S.-China Decoupling' report, which posited that '[c]omprehensive decoupling is no longer viewed as impossible: if the current trajectory of U.S. decoupling policies continues, a complete rupture would in fact be the most likely outcome'.

As economic and political fissures have deepened, ideals of universal global integration have succumbed – if unevenly – to new global flashpoints. The nature of the changes to the world order are still hard to discern and require sustained examination and debate. But a proliferating range of international tensions and conflicts, and the rising bellicosity of states wishing to alter the international order, in ways small and large, appear to mark the end of the American 'unipolar moment' that was pivotal to the globalization project. China has long since inherited the mantle as the primary perceived challenger to the American state's global dominance. As the size of the Chinese economy has come to rival the heft of America's, it has played a growing role in developing the commercial and military technologies of the future, as well as in determining the parameters of global standards. More aggressive US support for Taiwan, and military deployments and actions in the South China Sea, have been met with increasingly forceful and confident Chinese responses. Meanwhile, Russia's invasion of Ukraine has, for some, rekindled an old Cold War rivalry, while demonstrating the substantial capacity of the Russian state to wage conventional war with little regard for the all-out US effort to impose consequences for flagrantly violating the 'rules-based international order' (as interpreted through the lens of NATO). At the same time, a string of embarrassing failures American defence procurement, from the F-35 fighter aircraft to various white elephants of the US navy, have even begun to cast doubt upon the mythic invincibility of American military might.

While continued setbacks for Ukrainian forces have given that conflict all the signs of a quagmire – and raised the possibility of significant concessions by the beleaguered Zelensky government – the Middle East has erupted into a cauldron of conflicts centred on Israel and the Palestinian struggle against ethnic-cleansing and for the realisation of statehood, but also criss-crossing that central axis of division with other national divides of religion, ethnicity, authoritarianism and American military outposts. The uncontrolled descent of Israel into a hard right politics inclusive of fascist elements and the ensuing political chaos has jeopardized the logic that cemented its place at the centre of US policy. Since the overthrow of the US's other most important ally, the Shah of Iran, in 1979, Israel has served as a uniquely reliable base for American interests in the most strategically significant region of the world – at least until now. Israel's genocidal war on Gaza, launched after Hamas's desperate and brutal assault on Israeli military forces and villages in October 2023, has failed to attain its stated goal of 'eliminating' Hamas, or even its major leaders, but has encouraged the most violent elements of the settler movement to further their project of cleansing the West Bank of Palestinians. These developments have broken the more than a decade long phase in which the US and its allies abandoned even the chimerical 'peace process' begun in the late 1990s, thereby fully neglecting the oppression of Palestinians while turning instead to an attempt to normalize Israel's relations with the Arab states. The dramatic and violent end to this long period of diplomatic neglect has compounded the dilemmas for US regional power (and that of other Western states) presented by the increasing autonomy of the Saudi regime. The latter was a pivotal fount of the American empire throughout the fossil fuel age, classified since 1945 by the US State Department (in an oft-repeated phrase) as 'a stupendous source of strategic power, and one of the greatest material prizes in world history' on account of the leverage afforded by control over the energy supplies necessary to fuel all advanced industrial economies. Moreover, as the global mix of energy sources begins to shift in the context of a worsening ecological crisis, so too do the territories which contain the necessary energy supplies – driving new resource conflicts and shifting relations of global power, not least in the contested spaces of the Middle East.

The capacity of the American state to dictate and enforce – on its own or in concert with its Western allies – the rules of international order is facing unprecedented difficulties. Challenges have accumulated to such a degree that even the catastrophe for American power represented by the 2003 Iraq War (with its horrendous human cost) has all but faded from view, along with the subsequent, highly destructive Obama-era venture in Libya. In this context, it is entirely understandable that there is considerable debate, on all sides of the political spectrum, as to whether the American empire is entering a phase of inexorable decline. Yet, the post-1980s globalization of capitalism since, overseen and anchored by the American state, has proven remarkably resilient, due as much to the US's still dominant economic and diplomatic capacities as to its military power. Despite the potential for challenges over the longer-term from the emergence of regional hub currencies, the dollar retains its primary position as world money backed by the prominence and breadth of US financial markets. Cross-border flows of investment and trade remain foundational to global order, as does the overall commitment of states and capitalist classes to protecting this. If the corporate pageantry of international economic forums can no longer be relied upon to serve up the glowing paeans to the inexorable progress of global liberalization and prosperity, the institutional infrastructure of individual nation-states continues to reflect the 'constitutionalization' of free trade and private property regimes shaped across the neoliberal period.

In part, this resilience stems from the structural constraints of global capitalism in a deeply unequal world still marked by the legacies of uneven development. States compete to solicit investment from multinational corporations by implementing and leveraging the institutional and social arrangements desired by the owners of global capital, predominantly located in the states of the global core. And multinational corporations, in turn, find the competitive struggle by states for investments to be highly profitable. If hard-right rhetoric challenging 'globalism' is a daily part of their organizing discourse, less apparent is the extent to which these nationalist forces are capable of – or truly interested in – significantly altering these dynamics, grounded as they are in the firmament of relations between interstate forces, class interests, and economic structures and logics. The internationalization of capital that is at the core of globalization is integral to the logic of capital, expressing the need to constantly seek out new markets. Despite globalization's general unpopularity and association with domestic austerity in wages and social provisioning, any projects of 'decoupling' or 'de-globalization' thus entail a challenge to the interests of the dominant sections of ruling classes, as well as the state structures to which their power is tied. Despite growing social, ecological and geopolitical contradictions, globalization remains part of *what states are* as well as *what they do*. Yet, it is impossible to miss the contradictions and tensions in the global order, as the confident predictions of universal global inclusion of the 1990s and 2000s – especially around China – have given way to state politics of containment and rivalry amidst the erosion of US unilateralism and ideological hegemony. Further, the shifting economic and military correlation of global social forces, including pressures from ecological and social crises, are being augmented by a rising tide of 'anti-globalist' hard-right forces – including within the US state itself.

All this makes the task of taking stock of the contradictory and uneven evolution of the contemporary interstate system as perplexing as it is difficult. A growing bloc of geo-strategists have parsimoniously defined the emerging structure of world order as evolving from US dominated unipolarity to tripolarity – with the US, Europe and a Russia-China alliance as the three major players engaging on what Zbigniew Brzezinski memorably termed the 'Grand Chessboard'. Others have gone further, suggesting that a multipolar order may be emerging, structured around the interaction of a wider range of powers, like the BRICS, and the new multilateral institutions and fora emerging outside the UN system which are not hostage to the Washington Consensus.

The former position of the geo-strategists within the ministries for international affairs and the vast array of military strategy think tanks betrays a desire to resurrect Cold War notions of a stable balance of power at the expense of drastically oversimplifying complex relations among the constituents within these supposed 'poles' – to say nothing of the tremendous power imbalances between such poles. The latter multipolarity framing raises the question of how such a complex order could emerge at all given the capitalist economic rivalries that form between these fixed poles of state power and the hierarchy among states in the world system that exists. This could in fact only amount to a remaking of global capitalism within new forms of global political accommodation and regulation, while allowing greater autonomy for institutions of regional governance. Any other agenda would require a fundamental anti-capitalist rupture of the international state system that is nowhere imminent in the balance of state and class forces today.

What seems clear is that the American state is no longer capable of the unilateralism it brandished in the early 2000s in imposing the 'war on terror' as the line of demarcation in international relations. While still possessing primacy (in the sense of being the leading state) in the international relations between states, there is a notable erosion of American political authority and economic dominance within an increasingly fragmentary interstate order. In their 2019 *Register* essay, 'Trumping the Empire', Leo Panitch and Sam Gindin had already noted, 'The question that is posed in this context is whether the American state still has the capacity to manage global capitalism. This in turn entails new contradictions for every other capitalist state, and not only because of the pressures to accommodate to US demands, and the internal tensions this generates. It is also because of the implications for all states if the American state cannot play the leading facilitating, superintending, and crisis-containing roles it heretofore has … Trump has not only led the attack on free trade but at the same time overseen the erosion of institutional capacities essential to managing the global capitalist economy.' It is doubtful already that the Biden Administration could claim to have reversed these developments and re-established American leadership and institutional capacities to defend the 'logic of global capitalism'.

This volume is an attempt to grapple with this emerging world order, and to assess its implications for socialist strategy and the overlapping forms of national and geopolitical crises we are confronting today. This was the remit we gave our contributors in soliciting their essays: 'Against this backdrop, voices are growing louder within economic and foreign policy circles lamenting the exhaustion of neoliberal globalization, even if only vaguely gesturing toward an alternative characterized by local economic resilience, re-shoring and 'friend-shoring' of supply chains, managing global social pressures from migration to climate change, and renewing attention to national and regional security priorities … While it is clearly premature to speak of the development of a multipolar international system, let alone the end of the liberal economic order, it is not too early to take stock of how these momentous changes, even if not spelling the end of globalization, might alter its historical trajectory, or point toward a new global geometry. And, from there, to assess potential vulnerabilities, contradictions, and resistances from socialist movements (with their historical demands for a democratic and equalizing world order) in this context.'

We want to thank this year's contributors for their essays and for lending a long-term perspective to events that continue to unfold in unexpected directions at a relentless pace. Needless to say, writing under such pressures is demanding, and none of us will agree with all the contentions argued across the essays in this volume. That is expected and encouraged, and within the comradely spirit of debate that helps all of us think through this difficult period for the socialist movement. Such thanks also must be extended to Adrian Howe and Tony Zurbrugg of Merlin Press for their guidance and patience in pulling this volume together. Editorial and production flows for an annual volume can easily be thrown off course, and they have been crucial in holding things together. Once again, Louis Mackay provided us with inspired design work for the cover that so well captures the global tensions that the volume set out to investigate. Alan Zuege and Steve Maher, both associate editors of the *Register*, were indispensable. Their political and editorial insights were crucial in pulling the volume together. We were further assisted by contributing editors Colin Leys, Alfredo Saad-Filho, Sebnem Oguz and Sam Gindin. In addition, Chris Little joined the *Register* as assistant editor this year, and has already more than proven his worth with his editorial skills and political acuity.

Finally, it is necessary but with great regret that we note the passing of John Saul. John was a regular contributor to the *Socialist Register*, with the unmatched record of publishing over every decade since its founding under the editorship of Ralph Miliband and John Saville in the 1960s. John's essays on decolonization, development and revolution in Southern Africa were always highly anticipated and became some of the most important and widely cited contributions, read by both academics and political activists alike. From the 1980s on, he was a colleague and constant collaborator with Leo at York University, and from the 1990s on with Greg Albo as well. John also maintained close ties with Colin Leys dating back to their joint experiences in Africa early in their careers. These strong ties continued during Colin's period as co-editor of the *Register* and their joint book on *Namibia's Liberation Struggle*. John's death leaves an enormous loss for the *Register* and its readers, but also for the Canadian and South African lefts where John was always one of the fiercest advocates for the necessity and possibilities of socialism.

GA with SM, AZ, CL
January 2024

LIBERALS TO THE RESCUE? TEAM BIDEN AND THE US EMPIRE

JEROME KLASSEN

The year 2023 was a watershed for the politics and economics of world order. As a multiplicity of armed conflicts and economic transformations escaped the control of 'Team Biden' in the White House, the unrivaled dominance of the United States in the global political economy was open to question, if not approaching an end. The limits of American power were not simply exposed for sober senses, but were resisted by a welter of actors, including geopolitical rivals, multilateral agencies, social movements, and armed resistance groups. For the 'new mandarins' of the liberal establishment in Washington – whose return to the White House was premised on restoring the 'sources of American power' after the Trump presidency – 2023 was a reality check.[1] The markers of global power – economic, political, military, and ideological – had shifted inexorably, and strategic reckoning was in order.

The year opened, however, not with American genuflection to a changing world-system, but with a sequence of strategic initiatives by other aspirants of influence. It commenced with the People's Republic of China's (PRC) efforts to reframe and reorient the politics of world order. To begin, on 20-21 February 2023, China's Ministry of Foreign Affairs published two landmark documents. The first, 'US Hegemony and its Perils', detailed 'the US abuse of hegemony in the political, military, economic, financial, technological and cultural fields', and drew 'attention to the perils of [such] practices to world peace and stability and the well-being of all peoples'. It stated, in short, an open rejection of US primacy.[2] On this foundation, the second document, 'The Global Security Initiative Concept Paper', proposed an alternative vision of 'world peace and development', based on core principles of cooperative security, respect for state sovereignty and international law, and peaceful diplomacy and conflict resolution. China signalled clear intention 'to conduct bilateral and multilateral security cooperation with all countries' and to 'actively promote coordination of security concepts and convergence of interests'.[3]

This inflection point in Chinese foreign policy – its strategic vision, norm promotion, and problem-solving efforts – informed three subsequent initiatives. On 24 February 2023, China delineated broad principles for ending the crisis in Ukraine, focusing centrally on the 'equal and uniform application of international law', and opposing a 'Cold War mentality' of 'bloc confrontation' and 'the pursuit of one's own security at the cost of others' security' – a clear critique of the 'European security architecture' since 1990.[4] Then, turning to the Middle East, on 6 March China hosted negotiations in Beijing on the restoration of diplomatic ties between the Islamic Republic of Iran and Saudi Arabia. In the process, China overturned the US strategy of 'coercive diplomacy' towards Iran, defined by the Trump administration as a 'rogue state' and 'sponsor of terrorism', which warranted 'tough sanctions' and its political isolation from other states in the region.[5] Eight months later, as Israel waged genocide on Palestinians in Gaza, China once again asserted diplomatic initiative, hosting Arab and Islamic leaders in Beijing on 20 November and issuing clear statements on the right of Palestinians to self-determination, the need to uphold international law and the urgent need for a ceasefire and delivery of humanitarian aid. In each case, China's foreign policy of conflict-resolution and multilateral security cooperation directly challenged US policies of conflict-*escalation* and geopolitical *division*. In doing so, China stood with the majority of the international community, as reflected in several United Nations General Assembly votes.

By contrast, in spring 2023, US foreign policy seemed so diminished beyond the realm of the 'West' that key analysts of the Anglo-American establishment were forced to reckon with the new strategic realities. On the eve of the G7 meetings in May of that year, for example, Martin Wolf of the *Financial Times* penned an obituary to Western global leadership, declaring that, 'both the "unipolar" moment of the US and the economic dominance of the G7 are history'. For Wolf, the declining share of the G7 in world economic activity, the rise of China as a manufacturing and trade colossus, the emergence of the BRICS as an institutional alternative to the G7 and G20, and the impasse of International Monetary Fund and World Bank development financing, meant that the US and its allies 'cannot run the world' as they had in the past.[6]

Then, in July, as the much-anticipated Ukrainian counter-offensive was burned on the 'Surovikin line' in Zaporozhye, Richard Haass, the long-time President of the Council on Foreign Relations, delivered a paradigm-shattering interview to the *New York Times*. He averred that the greatest threat to international security was neither climate change nor the revisionist powers of China or Russia – 'it's us', he admitted. According to the *Times*, for Haass, 'instead of being the most reliable anchor in a volatile world ... the United States has become the most profound source of instability and an uncertain exemplar of democracy'.[7]

Facing this gamut of critique from within and without, the liberal technocrats of the Biden presidency were forced to respond. Across a choreographed sequence of keynote speeches, strategy documents, and featured publications, Team Biden laid out a new defence of the 'rules-based international order' under US leadership. This strategy centred on four themes: strategic competition with Russia and China; ideological conflict between democracy and autocracy; alliance systems through which US power is augmented; and the domestic foundations of American power, including the capital-labour relation as well as federal assistance for innovation and infrastructure, to correct 'market failures'.

As a package, the riposte of Team Biden – that is, of the liberal power elite[8] – was unequivocal: the US would struggle for comprehensive primacy vis-à-vis systemic challenges at home and abroad. With the American empire on the line, however, will Team Biden's strategy mitigate or reverse the crisis dynamics and transformative vectors of world politics today? Or, will the sober senses of Wolf and Haass prove accurate, presaging new departures in the balance of power and global political economy?

To answer these questions, it is vital to trace the origins of US global power and the grand strategy of 'armed primacy' which flowed from it. On that basis, the crosswinds of US empire and multipolarity can be measured, along with Team Biden's gambit for another 'American century'.

ARMED PRIMACY: THE POLITICAL ECONOMY OF US EMPIRE

World War II was the turning point for US global power. Although the US commanded the world's largest economy by 1900 and had become a creditor nation as a result of World War I, the global balance of power, and the domestic capacities and political alignments of the federal state, were not yet primed for an external strategy of world-making. President Roosevelt's New Deal 'synthesis', which mollified the class struggle and built new state capacities, coupled with the wreckage of the European empire-states in World War II, created the conditions for a new global order under US hegemony.[9]

From the earliest days of the war, US elites drawn from Wall Street banks, blue chip industrial firms, Ivy League schools and the military worked closely with the State Department and the Council on Foreign Relations to devise plans for a new world system under US direction.[10] The first strategy – devised after the Nazi conquest of France – was known as the 'quarter sphere', a plan for US hegemony over Canada, Mexico, Central America and the northern portion of South America, all of which would be economically integrated and militarily defended. However, the quarter sphere strategy fell short of encompassing and defending approximately two-thirds of existing US global trade relations, and so planners devised a new vision dubbed the 'Grand Area', which would incorporate the Western hemisphere, the former British Empire, and much of Asia and Africa into a US-defended free-trade zone. Only an Axis-dominated Europe and a neutral Soviet Union were envisioned, at first, to fall outside the zone of US dominance. As a planning memorandum stipulated, the Grand Area was an 'integrated policy to achieve military and economic supremacy for the United States within the non-German world'. The Grand Area would thus bolster the economic interests of US capitalism with a geopolitical and military strategy of 'armed primacy', to quote Stephen Wertheim.[11]

To these ends, US defence officials articulated a new military scheme for the postwar order. During 1943-44, an extensive overseas basing system was envisaged to meet two strategic imperatives: 'defence-in-depth' and 'power-projection' against any potential adversary, both of which 'presupposed American hegemony over the Atlantic and Pacific Ocean'. For American defence officials, the corollary of armed primacy was that no prospective enemy could monopolize the landmass, resources, and markets of Eurasia. Indeed, as Melvyn Leffler reveals, 'strategic thinkers and military analysts insisted that any power or powers attempting to dominate Eurasia must be regarded as potentially hostile to the United States'. The reason was that 'long-term American prosperity required open markets, unhindered access to raw materials, and the rehabilitation of much – if not all – of Eurasia along liberal capitalist lines'.[12] As Walter LaFeber elaborates:

> Washington officials believed another terrible economic depression could be averted only if global markets and raw materials were fully open to all peoples on the basis of equal opportunity, or the open door, for everyone. American domestic requirements, moreover, dictated such a policy. The world could not be allowed to return to the 1930s state of affairs, when nations tried to escape depression by creating high tariff walls and regional trading blocs that dammed up the natural flow of trade. If that recurred, Americans could survive only through massive governmental intervention into their society. If the government dominated the economy, however, it

would also regulate individual choice and perhaps severely limit personal freedom.[13]

After slaying the spectre of isolationism and winning the battle for 'internationalism'-*cum*-armed primacy in the domestic political arena, the 'architects of globalism' in the US establishment were forced to confront the question of international organization.[14] In particular, how would US primacy be reconciled with global demands for multilateral governance and an international security organization? In 1941, the conception of the Grand Area – a US-led free-trade global empire supported by the British – precluded an 'effective international organization', a formulation of Churchill's that FDR struck from the Atlantic Charter.[15]

In late 1941 and into 1942, however, US planners were impelled to rethink and embrace the principle of multilateral organization, for several reasons. First, the prospect of Soviet survival and advance on the eastern front would render immaterial US plans for unilateral dominance. Soviet interests would have to be acknowledged, and hopefully tamed, through institutional means. Second, US planners were concerned with domestic support for an external strategy of hegemony, which they came to believe could only be legitimated through a universal organization – that is, through a collective security institution. Third, they recognized that trade and investment relations between states – and the creation of a world market – required universal rules of the sort that only multilateral processes and institutions could provide. Fourth, decolonization as a means of integrating the capitalist world economy – a key desideratum of US wartime agreements with the British – would inevitably create demand for global representation by postcolonial states, which would have to be placated to avoid radical challenges. Finally, American elites came to believe that multilateral organization, if structured according to US interests and prerogatives, could project US power with international legitimacy.[16] Given US power-capacities at the time, a collective security organization would be inextricable from, and reinforcing of, US global primacy.

The resulting 'rules-based international order' was premised, therefore, on strategic calculations of material importance, namely, completing the world market for capital, pre-empting great power rivalry, and mitigating foreign and domestic opposition to US global primacy.[17]

With this understanding, President Roosevelt enlisted Allied support for a new international security organization, the United Nations (UN), founded at the San Francisco Conference in 1945 under heavy US influence. Indeed, 'it was Americans who designed the body, writing the UN

Charter within the State Department, using as their inspiration President Woodrow Wilson's League of Nations, the US offering to the international community in 1918. Washington also prepared an elaborate spying scheme in San Francisco to guarantee its control over the conclave and to assure its favourable outcome.'[18] While the UN Charter embodied liberal values of sovereign equality, self-determination and collective security, it ensconced a great power dictatorship in the Security Council, which assumed 'primary responsibility for the maintenance of international peace and security' and afforded a veto power to the 'Big Five' permanent members. Thus, from conception, the UN would not '[take] away the independence of the US in any shape, manner or form', as FDR put it. The General Assembly would serve, in the words of Sumner Welles, as a 'sop for smaller states', or an annual assembly for 'small countries' to 'blow off steam', according to President Roosevelt.[19]

American hegemonic interests also permeated postwar agreements on world economic management. The Bretton Woods Agreement of July 1944 created a new international monetary system for trade and investment. To this end, the US dollar was anchored to gold at $35 an ounce, fixed exchange rates were planned for other national currencies, and capital controls would minimize short-term financial flows so that states could exercise fiscal powers without fear of capital flight. In addition, two institutions – both based in Washington, DC – were established: the International Monetary Fund (IMF), which governed the fixed exchange-rate regime and provided loans to countries experiencing balance-of-payments crises; and the World Bank, which sold bonds to private capital for large-scale infrastructure funding, primarily in war-torn Europe. The Bretton Woods system reinforced the global role of the US dollar in trade and investment, accentuated Wall Street as the nexus of global finance, and implanted US power in multilateral economic governance, the latter being secured by dominating IMF and World Bank voting-shares based on financial contributions. In the process, the US state assumed responsibility for governing global capitalism.[20]

For leading international relations scholars such as John Ikenberry, postwar US strategy resulted in a 'liberal international order', based on principles of open markets, social bargains, human rights, multilateral cooperation and collective security backed by US leadership and direction. In this reading, the postwar order was institutionalized and rules-based, and US hegemony was 'built in critical respects around consent'.[21] US global power, then, was benign hegemony; it provided public goods for all nations, resulting in a liberal world-system of peace and prosperity. Armed primacy and universal order were natural and necessary complements.

THE RULES-BASED ORDER: CONTRADICTIONS AND CRISES

Without doubt, US grand strategy supported the decades of economic growth and political transformation amongst advanced capitalist countries after World War II. Across the 1950s and 1960s, for instance, the 'advanced capitalist nations as a whole grew three times as fast as in the interwar years, and twice as fast as before World War One'. Multiple factors supported this expansion. To begin with, the Marshall Plan overcame the dollar gap in postwar Europe, contributed to rapid capital formation, revived production and exports, and pre-empted the spectre of socialist governments coming to power in Italy, France, and Belgium. Similarly, the Dodge Plan revived and remilitarized Japanese capitalism in response to rising class conflict in Japan and the revolutionary 'threat' emerging from China. More broadly, the General Agreement on Tariffs and Trade resulted in liberalized exchange within the advanced capitalist world and triggered an export boom. Although the Bretton Woods Agreement restricted cross-border portfolio flows, foreign direct investment by multinational corporations grew rapidly, primarily by US industrial firms. Capital controls also allowed for public sector spending to rise as a share of GDP across Europe and North America, thus augmenting the welfare state and diminishing social inequality. For liberals, then, the 'golden age' of postwar capitalism seemed to show that, 'modern industrial societies could be committed simultaneously to generous social policies, market capitalism, and global economic integration'.[22]

But the liberal world order under US hegemony was not without contradictions and crisis tendencies, both of which triggered a myriad of opposition and resistance. First, the US imperial order rested on a fundamental contradiction. On the one hand, US strategy demanded the liberalization of trade and investment and, to support this, the 'internationalization' or policy harmonization of states along free-market lines. Against this demand for limited state power vis-à-vis the market and globalizing corporate actors, US strategy also asserted 'exceptional' powers for itself: in essence, the right to act as a global hegemon, unfettered by rules and laws which hindered US interests. As Stephen Gill explains, this 'central political contradiction of the US role in world order – one that involves both a justification of limited government and its direct repudiation by arbitrary state power – is crucial to an understanding of the nature and limits of US power, and resistance to that power'.[23]

Second, the logic of armed primacy drove the US into a pattern of global interventionism. In their seminal work, Joyce Kolko and Gabriel Kolko explain that the essential aim of the US 'was to restructure the world so that American business could trade, operate, and profit without restrictions everywhere'. However, 'American business could operate only in a world of politically reliable and stable capitalist nations, and with free access to raw materials. Such a universal order precluded the Left from power and necessitated conservative, and ultimately subservient, political control throughout the globe.' As a result, US strategy 'internationalized' domestic class struggles universally, making them a US national security interest, and paving the way for permanent, global interventionism.[24]

The primary flashpoints of US foreign policy are well known. In Western Europe, US strategy focused on preserving capitalist markets, dismantling colonial empires, regionalizing West Germany, containing the socialist left, and preventing 'neutralism' in the Cold War. To these ends, NATO was established to 'keep the Americans in, the Russians out, and the Germans down', as Lord Ismay, the first Secretary General of NATO, put it. For US planners, reconstruction in Western Europe was to be supported by the food and resource supplies, including oil, of Eastern Europe – a plan obstructed, firstly, by Soviet victory in World War II, and, secondly, by US and British initiatives to divide Germany after the war.[25] As LaFeber reveals, the source of the Cold War was 'not the threat of Soviet invasion of Asia or Europe'. Rather, 'the problem lay in Eastern Europe, where Stalin militarily roped off the region – and thus directly challenged the Atlantic Charter principles and the growing belief in Washington that the American system could only work globally'.[26] Thus, for Leffler, the roots of the Cold War are in 'the breadth of the American conception of national security that ... emerged between 1945 and 1948'.

> This conception included a strategic sphere of influence within the Western Hemisphere, domination of the Atlantic and Pacific oceans, an extensive system of outlying bases to enlarge the strategic frontier and project American power, an even more extensive system of transit rights to facilitate the conversion of commercial air bases to military use, access to the resources and markets of most of Eurasia, denial of those resources to a prospective enemy, and the maintenance of nuclear superiority.[27]

Although the Cold War featured rival social systems, it became centrally important – and massively over-inflated – because of the political economy of US imperialism. Simply put, no region of the world economy could be walled off to US capital, and US National Security Council Paper 68 (1950) was clear: the fundamental aim of US foreign policy was a 'world environment' for the 'American system'.[28] Hence the strategies of containment, roll-back, and regime change towards Soviet communism.[29]

In Asia, initial US strategy was to leverage China under the Nationalists as a means of supporting US exporters. After the Communists won the civil war, the 'reverse course' of US foreign policy included reviving Japanese industry and linking it to regional resource chains in Southeast Asia, backed by US militarism. In this political-economic context, the US internationalized the Korean civil war, backing the former collaborators with Japanese imperialism versus nationalist, leftist, and popular social forces, in what Bruce Cumings calls a 'dirty' war that killed four million people.[30] The same logic unfolded in Vietnam.

US Middle East policies were a subset of the grand strategy of globalizing capitalism and US hegemony. National Security Council Paper 5428 (1954) declared that 'United States policy is to keep the sources of Middle East oil in American hands'. For US planners, achieving that would conserve domestic supplies of oil, and control access to oil for any competitors.[31] Under such imperatives, Operation AJAX ousted Prime Minister Mossadegh in Iran, Saudi Arabia was roped into the US strategic orbit, and Israel became a tool of regional discord and dependence, aligned with US oil interests.[32]

In Latin America, the major postwar intervention of US foreign policy occurred in Guatemala, where President Arbenz had launched social welfare programs and industrialization measures, which included nationalizing assets of the United Fruit Company, a US corporation. In June 1954, Arbenz was overthrown in a military coup that was armed and directed by CIA operatives in Nicaragua and Honduras. Over the next decade, the resulting dictatorship received more US aid than any other Latin American nation.[33]

The upshot of this history is that the liberal world order was 'built with blood', as journalist Vincent Bevins puts it.[34] The class conflicts of, and American interventions in, the Third World were not, as Ikenberry believes, 'peripheral' to that order but were instead constitutive of it.[35] In fact, armed primacy was manifest as savage violence against any perceived challenge to US strategic interests, whether economic or geopolitical. Similarly, the ideological framing of the Cold War as a global struggle between 'freedom' and 'totalitarianism' was contradicted by Washington's constant 'connection to Third World fascism', as Noam Chomsky documented repeatedly.[36]

The final contradiction of the 'rules-based international order' surfaced as a crisis of the Bretton Woods system. With access to lower-cost labour, advanced technologies, and preferential access to US consumers, Japan and the West European capitalist states quickly recovered economically and began to seize world market shares, based on investment-led, export-oriented growth strategies. In 1965, the US began to run trade deficits with West Germany, and in the following year the same occurred with Japan.

In 1971, the US registered trade deficits with the rest of the world, a sign of declining US competitiveness in productive circuits of capital.[37] As US trade balances moved negative, US dollars began to accumulate in central banks globally. The greenback glut put downward pressure on the dollar-gold standard and a run on US gold supplies commenced as central banks converted dollars to gold under Bretton Woods allowances. However, to avoid domestic austerity and military retrenchment, in August 1971 President Nixon abrogated the dollar-gold peg and with it the Bretton Woods international monetary regime. The US refused any return to a fixed exchange-rate system and asserted the dollar as de facto world money, unfettered by any commodity basis. Here, then, was another contradiction between US hegemony and multilateral organization, the supersession of which had major consequences for global capitalism and US strategy in the decades which followed.

THE UNIPOLAR FAILURE

The end of the Cold War seemed to vindicate the US strategy of armed primacy and was greeted with rapturous applause by foreign policy elites. For Francis Fukuyama, the demise of the Soviet Union meant an 'end of history as such', as free-market capitalism and liberal democracy would endure on a global scale.[38] The end of the Cold War also left the balance of power in favour of one state, the US, and in this context, new theories of a 'unipolar moment' emerged. Charles Krauthammer, for instance, claimed that 'American pre-eminence is based on the fact that it is the only country with the military, diplomatic, political, and economic assets to be a decisive player in any conflict in any part of the world it chooses to involve itself'. As a consequence, other major powers would not challenge US dominance, but align their foreign policies 'behind that of the United States'.[39] American realists, such as William Wohlforth, concurred, arguing that unipolarity was 'not only peaceful but durable' and that the 'chief threat' was 'US failure to do enough'.[40] Similarly, academic liberals like Michael Ignatieff theorized US primacy as an 'empire lite, a global hegemony whose grace notes are free markets, human rights, and democracy, enforced by the most awesome military power the world has ever known'.[41]

The unipolar moment was underpinned by a particular structure of world economic relations. Under the post-Bretton Woods dollar standard, the US was able to run structural trade deficits and to pay for imports with US dollars, which would accumulate in central banks globally. Unable to use US dollars at home, central banks would lend them back to the US, either to Wall Street institutions or to the US Treasury Department in exchange for government bonds. Through the latter, the US government could run annual budget deficits and thus pay for military spending, bases, and wars. Through the former, Wall Street became awash with dollars, which were recycled to US corporations for research and development, foreign direct investments, mergers and acquisitions, and financial speculation. In the 1990s, the stock market boom, the wave of R&D in computer technology and biotech, and the further globalization of US corporate capital were supported by this structure of global finance, which Peter Gowan dubbed the 'Dollar-Wall Street Regime'.[42]

In this context, US grand strategy reflected the underlying balance of power as well as the mechanisms of accumulation through which US capitalism operated. For the George Bush senior administration, the US had 'a vital interest to prevent any hostile power or group of powers from dominating the Eurasian land mass' and should pre-empt other states 'from challenging our leadership'.[43] For the Clinton administration, US policy was to 'sustain American global leadership' and secure 'uninhibited access to key markets, energy supplies, and strategic resources'.[44] Similarly, the George W. Bush administration aimed to 'dissuade potential adversaries from pursuing a military build-up in hopes of surpassing, or equaling, the power of the United States'.[45] Likewise, the National Security Strategy of the Obama administration argued that US military force must 'underwrite global security'.[46] Perpetuating economic advantage through armed primacy, then, was the programmatic consensus of the US foreign policy establishment.

Several contradictions sundered this ambition. First, the absence of a peer rival unfettered US militarism which, after 1990, was unleashed in far-flung and seemingly never-ending wars, from the Balkans to Iraq and Afghanistan.[47] According to Stephen Walt, the 'forever wars' failed 'because US leaders exaggerated what American power – especially its military power – could accomplish'. Indeed, 'every major case of US military intervention after 1992 – in Afghanistan, Bosnia, Iraq, Kosovo, Libya, Somalia, and Yemen – took significantly longer and cost substantively more than US leaders expected while achieving much less than they promised. *Every single one*'.[48] For realists, the failed wars were emblematic of foolish strategy. Armed primacy, for Barry Posen, led to 'hard' (military) and 'soft' (diplomatic) balancing by revisionist powers like China and Russia and nurtured 'reckless driving' by 'free-riding' allies whose security was paid for and provided by Washington.[49] Inevitably, armed primacy became associated with divide-and-conquer tactics and unequal security structures in most regions of the world, and US foreign policy seemed to lie behind every festering global flashpoint.

Second, in 2008, the Great Financial Crisis damaged the economic fount of US supremacy. To understand the crisis, it is necessary to grasp how abstract tendencies of capitalist crisis unfolded through the institutional forms of the 'neoliberal' US economy. The story begins, though, with the stagflation crisis of the 1970s. That crisis was rooted in the falling rate of profit in advanced capitalist countries, resulting from over-capacity and over-production in world markets.[50] The OPEC oil embargo, alongside US military spending and Keynesian stimulus measures, produced inflation alongside stagnation. Starting in 1979, the Volcker interest-rate 'shock' was critical for restoring profits and accumulation through imposing recession, bankrupting inefficient firms, raising unemployment and thus taming inflation and working-class militancy. Neoliberalism – the political economy of free-market capitalism – emerged from this context and, in the US, assumed a particular institutional form. First, the circuits of capital in the US were restructured in favour of finance over industry, as evident in the rising share of finance, insurance and real estate in the US economy; the rising portion of financial profits in US corporate accounts; and the rising share of financial profits for US industrial firms.[51] These dynamics of financialization were compounded by structural US trade deficits and the recycling of global savings to Wall Street, resulting in a perverse pattern of negative net financial transfers for developing economies.[52] The new American empire rested, then, on financial expropriation, at home and abroad.

Second, neoliberalism involved a reorganization of class relations in the US economy, to the detriment of working-class incomes and quality of life. President Reagan's defeat of the air traffic controllers' union set in motion a long-term decline in collective bargaining and unionization rates. President Clinton's embrace of NAFTA and the World Trade Organization further diminished manufacturing employment and pushed workers into low-wage, unbenefited, non-unionized and precarious service-sector jobs. Clinton's welfare reforms further introduced a 'whip' to US labour markets, while mass incarceration served as discipline and punishment for the millions, particularly African Americans, made functionally irrelevant by the 'new economy'. To compensate for stagnant real wages and declining saving rates, US workers were offered cheap goods at Walmart as well as escalating debt for houses, cars, college tuition, and overpriced healthcare. Neoliberalism, then, involved a 'restoration of class power' for capital, while 'vanishing' the middle class.[53]

The Great Financial Crisis must be viewed in this light. Neoliberal restructuring raised the rate of profit for US industry from the early 1980s until approximately 1999, after which accumulation and stock prices were maintained by low interest rates and, as a corollary, the housing market and highly leveraged asset valuations. When interest rates rose after 2005, sub-prime borrowers began to default on mortgages, triggering financial losses and insolvency for Wall Street, which had shared and spread the 'fictitious capital' of mortgage-backed securities and credit default swaps.[54] The Great Financial Crisis was a systemic crisis of capitalism, manifest through the institutional forms of financialization and neoliberal class formation in the US economy.

As such, the crisis threatened the material and ideological bases of US hegemony in their entirety. At the UN General Assembly meetings in the fall of 2008, French President Nicolas Sarkozy declared that the 'world is no longer a unipolar world with one superpower, nor is it a bipolar world with the East and West. It's a multipolar world now.' Likewise, Argentina's President Christina Kirchner criticized how the crisis had 'emanated from the first economy of the world' and argued that it 'was a historic opportunity to review' the notion that 'the market would solve everything'.

Such demands for an alternative political economy were supported by China's development in the wake of the crisis. China's massive post-crisis stimulus focused on state-of-the-art infrastructure and public services, resulting in a 9.1 per cent growth rate in 2009. As a result, 'for the first time in the modern era', according to Adam Tooze, 'it was the movement of the Chinese economy that carried the entire world economy'. While US capitalism languished, 'China's combined fiscal and financial stimulus was the main force counteracting the global crisis'.[55]

AMERICAN CARNAGE AND TRUMP'S NEW REALISM

Donald Trump's election as US president must be grasped in the context of these economic and geopolitical setbacks. First, in the wake of the Great Financial Crisis, the US economy returned to growth at the slowest rate in US history,[56] while neoliberal patterns of social inequality worsened.[57] Second, a rebalancing of world economic activity towards developing economies – what the UN called the 'Rise of the South' – proceeded rapidly in the form of industrialization, merchandise trade competitiveness and increased 'south-south' trade among 'emerging economies'.[58] American geopolitical debacles in Ukraine, Syria, Iraq, Libya, and Afghanistan were only offset by Obama's nuclear deal with Iran, which was designed in part to extricate the bulk of US forces from the Middle East in order to 'pivot to Asia'. This was part of what then Secretary of State Hillary Clinton called a 'global effort to secure and sustain America's global leadership'.[59]

Against the strategy of 'liberal hegemony', candidate Trump announced a framework of 'America First', implying that US foreign policy had sacrificed national interests in pursuit of military occupations and 'rebuilding' nations abroad. He condemned 'bad trade deals' such as NAFTA and criticized 'free-riding' allies.[60] These themes were echoed in his inauguration speech, in which he also blamed 'American carnage' on 'a small group in the nation's capital', which 'reaped benefits while the people bore the costs'. In putting 'America first', he asserted, trade 'protection will lead to great prosperity and strength'.

In 2017, these arguments were synthesized in Trump's National Security Strategy, which called for the 'America First' approach to be enacted through 'principled realism that is guided by outcomes, not ideology'. It declared that 'great power competition' had returned, and that China and Russia 'are contesting our geopolitical advantages and trying to change the international order in their favour'. In this world of 'continuous competition … the United States must retain [military] overmatch … and restore the readiness of our forces for major war'.[61]

The Trump Doctrine of 'principled realism' was deeply contested amongst the foreign policy commentariat. For realists like Randall Schweller, Trump's strategy was fully rational: the pursuit of better trade deals, the critique of free-riding and outdated alliances, the replacement of multilateralism with transactionalism, and the tariff war on China matched the fact that the 'unipolar era, if not already over, is beginning to wind down'.[62]

By contrast, American liberals were repelled by Trump's attacks on free-trade theory and long-term alliances, as well as by his diplomacy with Russian President Vladimir Putin and North Korean leader Kim Jong Un. Trump's agreements with North Korea, and his orders to withdraw troops from Syria and Afghanistan, were all obstructed or slow-walked by neoconservatives in his administration, by Pentagon and foreign policy officials, Congress and corporate media. However, praise for Trump by the military and foreign policy elite did come when he launched cruise missiles at Syria, assassinated Iranian General Qassem Soleimani in Iraq, relocated the US embassy in Israel to Jerusalem, withdrew from the Intermediate-Range Nuclear Forces Treaty, announced the nuclear submarine deal with Australia, revived the 'Quad' security alliance against China, and deepened US involvement in Ukraine's counter-insurgency in Donbas. These instances of praise aside, establishment liberals such as Paul Krugman feared that 'the loss of trust in America will gradually have a corrosive effect'. The Pax Americana will fade because 'no matter how good a global citizen America becomes in the next few years, everyone will remember that we're a country that elected someone like Donald Trump, and could do it again'.[63]

PRE-EMINENCE IN QUESTION

Team Biden occupied the White House at this inflection point for US empire. Not since the Korean War had an American administration faced such a panoply of crises, limits to power, and opposition forces – and the need to strike back urgently and strategically. The American power elite – the dominant class forces of big tech, finance, the military-industrial complex and corporate media – faced a spectrum of challenges to US global power. Team Biden – a political amalgam of 'deep state' liberals and neoconservatives – was the vehicle for transcendence. The Black Lives Matter protests of 2020 and the amateur 'coup' of 6 January 2021 only added to the panic. The prestige and power of the American state was at stake.

The totality of this crisis has yet to be theorized but includes the following trends and vectors. First, on the eve of the Biden Presidency, the US economy faced *macroeconomic exhaustion*, or what Keynesian economists such as Robert Gordon and Lawrence Summers call 'secular stagnation'.[64] This was evident in declining rates of profit for productive capital, save for the largest industrial firms; low growth rates vis-à-vis China and other emerging markets; corporate concentration in finance and big tech; rising corporate debt and numbers of 'zombie companies'; and stagnant levels of business investment and productivity.[65] Although the US economy had outpaced that of the European Union since the Great Financial Crisis (in nominal terms, US GDP was one-third larger than that of the EU in 2022),[66] the US model of neoliberalism was contested by alternative systems of 'political capitalism' which, for Branko Milanovic, demonstrate 'efficient administration' and 'faster economic growth'.[67]

Second, economic stagnation had renewed tendencies of *financial turbulence*. US national debt – the result of tax-cutting, low growth rates, and excessive military spending – is currently $34 trillion and interest payments on that debt are approaching $1 trillion per year. Rating agencies have downgraded US government bonds, the buyers for which have shrunken internationally, leaving domestic elites and the Federal Reserve as 'consumers of last resort' for Treasury bills. Despite the risk of an American debt crisis, Congress has been unable to escape the fiscal and monetary 'dilemmas' of raising interest rates and taxes versus gutting entitlement programs versus military retrenchment.[68] These domestic dynamics, coupled with US financial warfare against Russia and Iran, have impelled dynamics of de-dollarization in global capitalism. The US dollar share of world foreign exchange reserves has fallen from 71 per cent in 2000 to 58 per cent in 2022; the proportion of US national debt held by foreigners has dropped from 49 per cent in 2008 to 30 per cent in 2022; and Russia, China, Brazil and India have sharply increased their central bank gold reserves.[69] Core actors in the world economy are thus lessening their reliance on the dollar. In addition, transactions in yuan now account for half of Chinese trade, while Saudi Arabia and the United Arab Emirates have established currency swaps and energy trade in yuan with China, further challenging dollar hegemony.

Third, *social decay* increasingly stalks American capitalism. Life expectancy has fallen from nearly 79 years in 2019 to 76.4 years in 2022;[70] poverty, homelessness, and food insecurity rates have risen;[71] and the homicide rate is more than seven times greater than in other high-income countries.[72] Chronic health problems, drug addiction and violent crime are structural features of American life, as are gun violence and mass shootings. Rising patterns of psychological anxiety and mental illness express deep alienation in the social fabric.[73] Increasing suicide rates indicate the sad hopelessness of capitalist existence for many.[74] Related to all this, the US labour force participation rate has dropped from 67 per cent in 1999 to 62 per cent in 2022, evidence of millions of working-age Americans dropping out of socially productive employment.[75]

Fourth, US capitalism faces unprecedented competition in the *war of technology*. In 2020, a major study by the Harvard Kennedy School found that 'China has become a serious competitor in the foundational technologies of the 21st century: artificial intelligence, 5G, quantum information science, semiconductors, biotechnology, and green energy. In some races, it has already become No. 1. In others, on current trajectories, it will overtake the US within the next decade.'[76] These findings were amplified in a 2023 State Department-funded study, which found that China has a commanding lead in 37 out of 44 critical emerging technology fields 'spanning defense, space, robotics, energy, the environment, biotechnology, artificial intelligence, advanced materials and key quantum technology areas'.[77]

Fifth, the US is experiencing a *military-technical and geo-strategic* crisis of power. In 2022, the US spent more on defence than the next highest 11 countries combined. The US operates hundreds of overseas military bases and depot storages, and 'commands the commons' of critical sea lanes for trade and defence.[78] It leads in satellite-based intelligence, reconnaissance and surveillance systems, while operating the greatest number of aircraft carriers and nuclear-powered submarines. Despite these advantages, the US has lost the arms race in key fronts, including missile technology. Russian hypersonic missiles, including Zircon and Kinzhal, afford Russia conventional escalation-dominance, as well as long-range strike capabilities, for which US missile defence systems are technologically inadequate.[79] Indeed, according to *Science*, '[t]he United States is largely defenseless against such weapons, at least for now, in part because it can't track them'.⁸⁰ Furthermore, US efforts to produce and test hypersonic missiles have repeatedly failed. Beyond this, RS-24 Yars, RS-28 Sarmat, and RSM-56 Bulava – key examples of Russian nuclear ICBM and SLBM modernization – are now combat deployed, while US efforts at nuclear modernization are over budget and delayed.⁸¹ Further setbacks for US nuclear modernization – including for the LGM-35 Sentinel ICBM – portend strategic danger, given expiry dates for existing infrastructure, delivery platforms and weapons, as well as recent test failures of Minuteman III ICBMs. US fantasies of 'nuclear primacy' have thus been pre-empted.⁸²

China's military modernization adds a quandary to US primacy strategies. Between 2000 and 2016, China increased its defence budget annually by approximately 10 per cent, and President Xi Jinping has articulated a vision of the People's Liberation Army becoming a 'world-class military by the middle of the century'. However, as Taylor Fravel explains, 'the notion of building a world-class military does not reflect a global military strategy or illuminate China's global ambitions'.⁸³ More rationally, 'China's strategic goals are keyed to the defence of a continental power with growing maritime interests as well as to Taiwan's unification and are largely conservative, not expansionist. China is developing internal control, peripheral denial, and limited force-projection capabilities consistent with these objectives.'⁸⁴ The US Department of Defense acknowledges that China is the 'top ship-producing nation in the world by tonnage, [and] is increasing its shipbuilding capacity for all naval classes'. Furthermore, 'China produces a wide range of ballistic, cruise, air-to-air, and surface-to-air missiles, many comparable in quality to those of other international top-tier producers'. Moreover, 'China has the world's leading hypersonic arsenal and has dramatically advanced its development of both conventional and nuclear-armed hypersonic missile technologies'.⁸⁵ Although nuclear weapons play a limited role in Chinese military strategy, US policies are 'fueling' China's nuclear expansion of ICBMs and SLBMs to 'bolster its second-strike capability' and guarantee 'assured retaliation'.⁸⁶

To address these new security dilemmas, the US will have to correct structural problems in its defence industrial base, including cost and schedule overruns; financial mismanagement; a paucity of skilled workers for engineering, manufacturing and maintenance; reliance on Chinese supply chains; and a lack of surge capacity for industrial-scale warfare.⁸⁷ The problems associated with signature defence projects, including the F-35, the Littoral Combat Ship, and several hypersonic missile prototypes, signify military-technical decline vis-à-vis extant security risks. More broadly, US military strategy is over-reliant on carrier strike groups and air supremacy, both of which are unobtainable vis-à-vis Russia and China's air defence, anti-shipping, electronic warfare, submarine, air-to-air missile and satellite-killing systems. In short, fundamental US power in military science, technology, strategy and force structure have been balanced, neutralized or surpassed by rival states. After failures in Iraq and Afghanistan, the US military also faces record shortfalls in recruitment. If, as A.J.P. Taylor put it, 'the mark of a great power is the ability to prevail in war', US pre-eminence is now open to question.[88]

Finally, the US has been displaced from – and become obstructionist toward – key forums of *global governance and diplomacy*. At the UN, data shows that 'Sino-Russian positions enjoy much broader global support than those of the United States'.[89] The US has blocked the appointment of World Trade Organization appellate judges (for fear of losing tariff cases to China) and refuses to join – and indeed threatens – the International Criminal Court.[90] Under Trump, the US did not just rework NAFTA, but withdrew from the Paris Climate Treaty, the World Health Organization and the UN Human Rights Council. The US has been responsible for ending key arms control agreements, such as the Anti-Ballistic Missile Treaty, the Intermediate-Range Nuclear Forces Treaty and the Open Skies Treaty – all of which were cornerstones of international security. Finally, the US is absent from what Amitav Acharya calls the new 'multiplex' of global governance, which in Asia features the Regional Comprehensive Economic Partnership, the Asian Infrastructure Investment Bank, the Chiang Mai Initiative, the Asian Bond Initiative, the Association of Southeast Asian Nations Plus-Three, the ASEAN Surveillance Process, the Shanghai Cooperation Organization and the Northeast Asia Trilateral Cooperation Secretariat, not to mention China's Belt and Road initiative.[91] By contrast, the US withdrew from the Trans-Pacific Partnership, another sign that US centrality in the political economy of Asia has diminished.

TEAM BIDEN TO THE RESCUE?

Team Biden thus faced an unprecedented challenge – saving empire from systemic crises at home and abroad. Recalling the 'global offensive' of Truman and Acheson in 1950, Team Biden has launched a full-spectrum campaign for US primacy, with three strategic pillars.[92] First, according to the 2022 National Security Strategy, the world is at an 'inflection point'; it is living through a 'decisive decade', which will 'determine the direction of our world and impact the security and prosperity of the American people for generations to come'.[93]

Second, the global crisis stems from 'strategic competition'. World order is 'more divided and unstable' and 'the need for American leadership is as great as it has ever been'. In particular, the US is locked in great power competition with China and Russia and their 'revisionist foreign [policies]'. As the National Security Strategy explains, China and Russia are entirely to blame for the new world disorder: 'it is their behaviour that poses a challenge to international peace and stability – especially waging or preparing for wars of aggression, actively undermining the democratic political processes of other countries, leveraging technology and supply chains for coercion and repression, and exporting an illiberal model of international order.' Team Biden thus amplifies the Trump Doctrine of great power competition. In this framework, Russia is an 'acute threat' to the 'free and open international system, recklessly flouting the basic laws of the international order'. By contrast, the PRC is 'the only competitor with both the intent to reshape the international order and, increasingly, the economic, diplomatic, military, and technological power to advance that objective'.

Third, strategic competition turns on a 'great battle for freedom: a battle between democracy and autocracy, between liberty and repression, between a rules-based order and one governed by brute force'.[94] The global fissure, in other words, is an ideological rift between different models of governance. According to Secretary of State Antony Blinken, 'democracy is under threat around the world right now' and 'we're making the argument that our system – the democratic one – is the better one'.[95] In sum, 'the most pressing strategic challenge facing our vision is from powers that layer authoritarian governance with a revisionist foreign policy'.[96]

On this strategic foundation, Team Biden advances three lines of attack: investing in domestic foundations of strength, including technological advantage and social reform; aligning efforts with US allies and partners; and projecting military supremacy.

The first line of attack is premised on a new political economy: while the 'private sector and open markets have been, and continue to be, a vital source of ... national strength and a key driver of innovation ... markets alone cannot respond to the rapid pace of technological change', and so strategic public investment is necessary for a 'strong industrial and innovation base'. Hence, the US will pursue a 'modern industrial and innovation strategy', for example, in semiconductors, artificial intelligence and other emerging technology fields.[97] According to National Security Advisor Jake Sullivan, this will involve protecting 'the United States' advantages and security through new export controls and investment rules, in partnership with allies', the aim being to 'sustain ... core advantages in geopolitical competition'.[98]

Renewing the domestic foundations of US power also requires a rebalancing of the capital-labour relation, against the grain of neoliberal class formation. Team Biden's 'foreign policy for the middle class' is premised on 'inclusiveness to ensure a strong, vibrant American middle class and greater opportunity for working people around the world'. To address economic inequality, 'decades of trickle-down economic policies – policies like regressive tax cuts, deep cuts to public investment, unchecked corporate concentration, and active measures to undermine the labour movement that initially built the American middle class' must be rectified.[99]

The second line of attack involves bolstering US alliances. Breaking with the Trump Doctrine of 'America First', the 2022 National Security Strategy asserts that US 'alliances and partnerships around the world are our most important strategic asset and an indispensable element contributing to international peace and stability'. According to Sullivan, US power 'rests on its alliances'.[100] The 2022 National Defense Strategy incorporates these tenets, claiming that US alliances and partnerships are of 'global strategic advantage', and that the US will 'strengthen major regional security architectures'.[101]

For Team Biden, the final line of attack involves military modernization, in two key manners. First, the US will invest in 'a range of advanced technologies including applications in the cyber and space domains, missile defeat capabilities, trusted artificial intelligence, and quantum systems'. Second, the US will modernize its 'nuclear Triad, nuclear command, control, and communications' alongside 'nuclear infrastructure' and strengthen 'extended deterrence commitments to [its] Allies'.[102]

In sum, Team Biden's strategy is to double-down on armed primacy and US hegemony. In theory, this means great power rivalry *cum* strategic competition with Russia and China; ideological warfare against alternative forms of domestic governance and political economy; and asserting state power over technological innovation, international trade and investment, and domestic class relations, all in pursuit of US global dominance.

From a socialist standpoint, this strategy will be torn asunder by systemic contradictions, many of which are already evident. For example, ideologically, the framing of strategic competition in terms of 'democracy versus autocracy' is incommensurate with the governance structures of many US security partners. The conflation of the US political economy with 'democracy' also fails to capture the reality of 'economic elite domination'.[103] Furthermore, if the US embraces a new industrial policy of de-coupling and de-risking, then what will remain of US imperial free-trade theory, as captured in Cordell Hull's maxim that 'if goods don't cross borders, soldiers will'? If the US fades further as a nexus of global trade, the contradictions between US national interests and world market governance will heighten, US productivity will be compromised by a dearth of competition, and economic conflicts will morph into geopolitical and military ones – the opposite of a 'free, open, prosperous, and secure international order', the bromides of Team Biden's National Security Strategy.

On the economic front, the Biden administration has maintained Trump's tariff policies, which have had no effect on US trade deficits. It also imposed technology export rules to 'eradicate, root and branch, China's entire ecosystem of advanced technology', according to the *New York Times*.[104] This 'act of war' aimed to trap China in lower value-added goods and services production, maintain US chokepoints in existing technology sectors and position the US for dominance in future technologies, such as AI. Here, too, contradictions are evident. For example, Huawei and SMIC's production of the 7-nanometre Kirin 9000 5G chip for Huawei's Mate 60 Pro smartphone demonstrates China's ability to outflank US technological warfare in short order. In this case, US strategy was not just misinformed but counterproductive to extending legacy monopolies, which in Apple's case now face genuine competition. China's subsequent parries against Micron and Foxconn should alert Team Biden to the fact that China will increasingly compete from a position of technological autonomy, if not advantage. Furthermore, in the field of green technology, China commands a lead in solar panel, wind turbine, electric battery and electric vehicle markets, and so a broader tech war on China can only mean a delay in carbon emission reductions globally and another mark of US strategic failure, this time on climate change.

The limits of 'Bidenomics' also contradict the 'foreign policy for the middle class'. Biden's signature Build Back Better Act failed in the Senate, as Republicans and Democrats refused to countenance massive public investment in social welfare, infrastructure and climate transition. Meanwhile, Team Biden requested $886.4 billion for military spending in 2024, an increase of $28 billion from the previous year, at a time when poverty, hunger and homelessness rates are rising. While labour markets remain tight, US nominal wage gains have trailed inflation rates, meaning declining standards of living for working-class Americans. According to the Federal Reserve, between 2019 and 2022 'increases in income were experienced across the income distribution but were largest at the top, consistent with some increase in income inequality over this period'.[105] In 2022, the unionization rate in the US economy fell to 10.1 per cent, the lowest on record. Bidenomics has thus failed to dent the class structures of neoliberalism.

US alliance and partnership systems are replete with contradictions as well. Behind the 'liberal zone of peace' lies a reality of hegemony, dependence, and economic languor. To cite a few examples, allies and partners are pressured into buying US weaponry, from F-35s to Patriot missile batteries, of questionable utility. Similarly, they are prevented from incorporating cutting-edge and cost-friendly Huawei technology into their information and communication networks. Furthermore, they must abide by unilateral US sanctions against third parties and thus lose sovereignty over basic national interests. In the case of Meng Wanzhou, for example, 'officials at the top levels of the US government orchestrated [her] arrest', without informing Canadian Prime Minister Justin Trudeau, the result of which 'threw Canada-China relations into a deep freeze'.[106] Under Team Biden, the 'vassalization of Europe' is evident in the passive uniformity of political elites on foreign policy crises and in critical dynamics of de-industrialization and economic stagnation, caused in part by the loss of cost-competitive Russian gas.[107] For US allies and partners in Asia, including Japan, South Korea, and Taiwan, the consequences of the trade and tech war on China are a mix of economic torpor and lost export markets.[108] Thus, the US alliance and partnership system is becoming, tendentially, a self-enclosed and less-prosperous bloc.

As the balance of power and political economy of world order has shifted, and as US military power has proven unable to win 'decisive' battles in the core of Eurasia, US strategy has shifted to leveraging allies and partners as proxies. Under the mantra of strategic competition, Team Biden aims to impose geopolitical walls around Russia, China and the Resistance Axis in the Middle East. Yet, unable to achieve this directly, the US has been forced to enlist proxies – most notably, Ukraine, Israel, and Taiwan – in frontline flashpoints. In all of these cases, US strategy is to divide and conquer regions through unequal security balances and exclusive economic bloc formations, resulting in systemic conflict escalation on the part of Washington.

In Asia, Team Biden is waging a comprehensive containment strategy against China. US Ambassador to China, Nicholas Burns, has bragged that 'the US is staying in this region – we're the leader in this region in many ways'.[109] Similarly, Biden has declared that 'China has an overall goal … to become the leading country in the world, the wealthiest country in the world, and the most powerful country in the world … [but] that's not going to happen on my watch'.[110] While the Biden administration has declared that it does not seek a 'new Cold War' with China, it has maintained Trump's tariffs, expanded sanctions on Chinese government officials and led efforts of the Quad military alliance. It has also threatened to defend Taiwan militarily in the event that China moves to incorporate its island province. According to the *BBC*, the US is currently 'arming Taiwan to the teeth', against the One China Policy and the 1982 Communique, which says that 'the United States Government states that it does not seek to carry out a long-term policy of arms sales to Taiwan'.[111] Meanwhile, the US is trying to enlist allies and partners in Asia to host missile bases, aimed at China, and has as part of a broader containment strategy mobilized NATO, as evident in NATO's 2022 Strategic Concept, which states that China's 'ambitions and coercive policies challenge our interests, security and values'.[112] In addition, the US has encouraged the territorial claims of the Philippines and Vietnam in the South China Sea vis-à-vis China, while refusing to sign the UN Convention on the Law of the Sea.[113]

US strategy, then, is to 'encircle China with a compelling series of de facto or de jure military alliances with China's neighbours, encouraging and aiding their rearmament and ratcheting up local disputes with China so as to constrain and pressure it. The endgame is a pro-US military, economic, and diplomatic noose around China that can be tightened to veto, punish, pressure or threaten China and narrow its options on a range of issues.'[114] This containment effort, however, confronts the fact that China is much more integrated regionally and globally in production and trade than the US, and that the politics of Asia are overwhelmingly against conflict with China, and favour peaceful commerce and development.[115] US war games also indicate that a military clash over Taiwan is not one the US would necessarily win.[116] In short, US aggression, by proxy, alliance or unilateral action against China faces strong headwinds in the region.

With respect to Russia, the US broke promises to not expand NATO eastward beyond unified Germany and, in doing so, aimed to revise the balance of power on Russia's western and southern flanks.[117] To this end, Ukraine became a critical proxy, with the US participating in the unconstitutional coup of 2014; arming and training Ukrainian security forces to liquidate Donbas autonomists; refusing to implement the Minsk 2 Accords; and, after Russia's invasion of February 2022, forcing Ukraine to walk away from negotiations on neutrality and security guarantees in favour of war to inflict 'strategic failure' on Russia. Whether Team Biden used Ukraine cynically, or actually believed that Ukraine could prevail against Russia, the result has been the opposite: Russia destroyed multiple iterations of the Ukrainian army; outproduced and depleted the arsenals of the Western bloc; deflected 'sanctions from hell' and oil price-caps; maintained robust ties with global majority states; and utilized echeloned air defence systems to progressively counter US and NATO precision-strike weapons, including ATACMS, HARMS, JDAMS, GMLRS fired from HIMARS, and Storm Shadow cruise missiles. In summer 2023, Russia defeated US and NATO armour and strategic and operational planning for Ukraine's counter-offensive. As a result, Team Biden's proxy war is tending towards failure.

Facing defeat in Eastern Europe, the US rushed impulsively to Israel's defence after Operation Al-Aqsa Flood commenced on 7 October 2023. As Israel engaged in what Juan Cole called a 'colonial revenge genocide',[118] the US provided intelligence, surveillance, and massive arms shipments to Israel; vetoed UN Security Council resolutions on pausing and stopping the Israeli bombing; refused to call for a ceasefire; insisted that no 'red lines' would be applied to Israel's use of US weaponry; maligned domestic protests in favour of a ceasefire, including by Jewish peace activists, as 'malignant' and 'disrespectful'; and deliberately lied about 7 October and the legality of Israel's bombing of civilian infrastructure, including al-Shifa hospital. As the genocide in Gaza progressed, the US deployed two carrier strike groups and a nuclear submarine as deterrence to regional resistance forces, which nevertheless attacked US bases in Iraq, Israeli-linked ships in the Red Sea, Israel's port city of Eilat, and Israeli settlements and military bases along the Lebanese border. Biden's energy security advisor, Amos Hochstein, was also dispatched to Israel to consult about developing natural gas fields off Gaza's shore. However, Biden's call for Hamas to be eliminated failed to materialize,[119] and the initial prisoner exchange was mediated by Qatar, not the US, on terms offered by the Palestinian side from the start.

US policy, then, was not just escalatory for hegemonic reasons but complicit in genocide and crimes against humanity. That complicity, though, tore off the mask of US imperialism, revealing a skull of racism, murder, criminality, and hypocrisy. The Palestinian resistance thus shattered the liberal illusions of US power.

With this in mind, the worldwide eruption of pro-Palestine solidarity protest is a harbinger of anti-racist and anti-imperialist resistance to come, in myriad forms. For example, one consequence of Al-Aqsa Flood may be the end of US-led 'normalization' schemes, such as the Abraham Accords, and the stillbirth of US fantasies of an India-Saudi-Israel trade corridor to rival the Belt and Road Initiative. Beyond such concerns, a senior G7 diplomat lamented that, because of US and Western support for Israel, 'We have definitely lost the battle in the Global South … All the work we have done with the Global South has been lost … Forget about rules, forget about world order. They won't ever listen to us again.'[120]

CONCLUSION

One conclusion of this analysis is that US empire is foundering on systemic contradictions and crisis tendencies. On the one hand, the US still commands the second largest national economy (on a purchasing power parity basis), remains the core nexus of global finance, dominates the rankings of corporate profitability, and competes at the peak of scientific and technological development.[121] Geopolitically, the aggregate power of the US military and the depth and breadth of US security partnerships remain dominant globally. As part of this, US hegemony in Europe has deepened throughout the Ukraine crisis, taking the form of increased energy and weapons sales, NATO expansion to Sweden and Finland, and consent granted to the proxy war. In Asia, US geopolitical linkages remain significant, particularly with Japan, South Korea, Taiwan and the Philippines being roped – symbolically if not materially – into a US-led anti-China coalition. At both ends of Eurasia, US geopolitical dictates have trumped the economic interests of allies and partners, which must abide by Washington's tech war on China and sanctions on Russia. These deep lines of control are enduring features of American empire today.

On the other hand, analysis shows that US supremacy is increasingly delimited. As foreign policy debacles add up, the US appears to lack the assets to be a decisive player in any conflict in any part of the world it chooses to involve itself – the definition of unipolarity. Geopolitical and strategic balancing are undeniable vectors of contemporary world politics and the global political economy is no longer beholden to neoliberalism, US-style. Political-economic alternatives and key networks of trade, investment, production, and innovation exist beyond the confines of US empire. In this context, the current conjuncture approximates what Emma Ashford and Evan Cooper call 'unbalanced multipolarity': the US and China – and Russia to a lesser extent – compete in multiple registers of global power, but 'emerging' and 'middle' powers such as Iran, Brazil, India, South Africa, Turkey, Saudi Arabia, and Indonesia are gaining traction and shaping regional and global futures accordingly.[122]

If the unipolar moment is over and US hegemony diminished, Team Biden's gambit for primacy will likely engender contradictions and crises. In fact, 'attempts by the United States to build large coalitions in opposition to China are unlikely to be successful in a more multipolar system, and the risk of direct conflict may be higher if the United States engages in a Biden-style "bloc-building" strategy', as Ashford and Cooper elaborate. To list a few examples, Team Biden's strategy of bloc confrontation may isolate the US-led alliance system from more dynamic centres of capital accumulation;

accelerate the arms race and great power militarism; encourage 'free-riding' and 'reckless-driving' by US allies and partners; infect all matters of global politics with zero-sum rivalries; undermine international law and multilateral institutions; and infringe upon smaller states and their right to sovereignty, multi-alignment, and post-neoliberal strategies of development.

From a socialist standpoint, Team Biden – the political amalgam of capitalist class and national security state interests in the White House – offers no solution to working-class needs at home or abroad, and so left activism in the US must break with the Democratic Party and forge a political vehicle for socialism. In fact, on several strategic planks, including the framing of great power competition and trade policy, Team Biden has accepted and augmented the Trump Doctrine of 'America First'.

For this reason, the US empire is still, as in the words of Martin Luther King, 'the greatest purveyor of violence in the world', threatening any state or actors who resist exploitation and subordination. As a result, the strategic task of anti-imperialist forces globally, both state and non-state, is to contain and deter US militarism. The requisite alliances for this task will be complex and often contradictory, and the evolving multipolar world will feature regressive politics as well. A further complication is that, at the top of world politics, 'the emerging powers by themselves neither represent nor exhaust the possibility of an alternative, or post-hegemonic, global governance structure'.[123] However, as the global solidarity movement with Palestine demonstrates, a politics of anti-imperialism and anti-racism can open spaces for convergent social actors to challenge ruling classes everywhere. In the process, the politics of socialism will find a wider base of support, as resistance movements are forced to locate 'American carnage' in the class relations of capitalism. The end of history, then, is yet to come.

NOTES

1. Jake Sullivan, 'The Sources of American Power: A Foreign Policy for a Changed World', *Foreign Affairs*, November/December 2023.
2. Ministry of Foreign Affairs of the People's Republic of China, 'US Hegemony and Its Perils', February 2023, available at: www.fmprc.gov.cn.
3. Ministry of Foreign Affairs of the People's Republic of China, 'The Global Security Concept Paper', 21 February 2023, available at: www.fmprc.gov.cn.
4. Ministry of Foreign Affairs of the People's Republic of China, 'China's Position on the Political Settlement of the Ukraine Crisis', 24 February 2023, available at: www.mfa.gov.cn.
5. Donald Trump, 'Remarks by President Trump on Iran Strategy', 13 October 2013, available at: http://trumpwhitehouse.archives.gov.

6   Martin Wolf, 'The G7 Must Accept That It Cannot Run the World', *Financial Times*, 23 May 2023.
7   Peter Baker, 'To Foreign Policy Veteran, the Real Danger is at Home', *New York Times*, 1 July 2023.
8   Key Democratic operatives drawn from Wall Street, Silicon Valley, Ivy League universities, the Central Intelligence Agency, the National Security Agency, Congress and the Departments of State and Defense. On the social-science concept of the power elite, see: C. Wright Mills, *The Power Elite*, Oxford: Oxford University Press, 1956.
9   Thomas Ferguson, 'From Normalcy to New Deal: Industrial Structure, Party Competition, and American Public Policy in the Great Depression', *International Organization*, 38(1), 1984, pp. 31-44; Melvin P. Leffler, *A Preponderance of Power: National Security, the Truman Administration, and the Cold War*, Redwood City, CA: Stanford University Press, 1992; Leo Panitch and Sam Gindin, *The Making of Global Capitalism: The Political Economy of American Empire,* London: Verso, 2013.
10 Laurence H. Shoup and William Minter, *Imperial Brain Trust: The Council on Foreign Relations & United States Foreign Policy*, New York: Authors Choice Press, 1977.
11 Stephen Wertheim, *Tomorrow, the World: The Birth of US Global Supremacy*, Cambridge, MA: Harvard University Press, 2020, ch 2, especially pp. 69 and 104.
12 Melvyn P. Leffler, 'The American Conception of National Security and the Beginnings of the Cold War, 1945-48', *The American Historical Review*, 89(2), 1984, pp. 349, 351, 356, 358.
13 Walter LaFeber, *America, Russia, and the Cold War 1945-1992,* Seventh Edition, New York: McGraw-Hill, 1993, p. 9.
14 Patrick J. Hearden, *Architects of Globalism: Building a New World Order During World War 2,* Fayetteville, AR: University of Arkansas Press, 2002.
15 Wertheim, pp. 110, 114.
16 Wertheim, pp. 118-19, 122, 133, 142.
17 By contrast, liberal theories of US grand strategy and postwar institution-building focus on the domestic values of American politics. See: G. John Ikenberry, *Liberal Order and Imperial Ambition: Essays on American Power and International Order,* Oxford: Polity, 2006; John Gerard Ruggie, 'Multilateralism: The Anatomy of an Institution', *International Organization*, 46(3), 1992, p. 568.
18 Stephen C. Schlesinger, *Act of Creation: The Founding of the United Nations*, Cambridge, MA: Westview Press, 2009, p. 2.
19 Peter Gowan, 'US:UN', *New Left Review*, 24(November-December), 2003; Wertheim, p. 142; Jerome Klassen, *Joining Empire: The Political Economy of the New Canadian Foreign Policy,* Toronto: University of Toronto Press, 2014, p. 68.
20 Jeffry A. Frieden, *Global Capitalism: It's Fall and Rise in the Twentieth Century,* New York: W.W. Norton, 2006, p. 260.
21 G. John Ikenberry, *Liberal Leviathan: The Origins, Crisis, and Transformation of the American World Order,* Princeton, NJ: Princeton University Press, 2011, p. 15.
22 Frieden, pp. 281, 300, and ch. 12.
23 Stephen Gill, 'The Contradictions of US Supremacy', in Leo Panitch and Colin Leys, eds, *The Empire Reloaded: The Socialist Register 2005*, New York: Monthly Review Press, 2005, p. 24.

24 Joyce Kolko and Gabriel Kolko, *The Limits of Power: The World and United States Foreign Policy, 1945-54,* New York: Harper and Row, 1972, p. 2.
25 Carolyn Woods Eisenberg, *Drawing the Line: The American Decision to Divide Germany, 1944-49,* Cambridge: Cambridge University Press, 1996.
26 LaFeber, p. 28.
27 Leffler, 'The American Conception of National Security and the Beginnings of the Cold War', p. 379.
28 United States, National Security Council Paper 68, 'United States Objectives and Programs for National Security', Washington, DC, 7 April 1950.
29 Gregory Mitrovich, *Undermining the Kremlin: America's Strategy to Subvert the Soviet Bloc, 1947-56,* Ithaca, NY: Cornell University Press, 2000.
30 Bruce Cummings, *The Korean War: A History,* New York: Random House, 2011, pp. xviii, 35.
31 United States, Foreign Relations of the United States, Diplomatic Papers, 1944, The Near East, South Asia, and Africa, the Far East, Volume V, 'Memorandum by the Inter-Divisional Petroleum Committee of the Department of State – Foreign Petroleum Policy of the United States', 11 April 1944, available at: history.state.gov.
32 Ervand Abrahamian, *The Coup: 1953, the CIA and the Roots of Modern US-Iranian Relations,* New York: The New Press, 2013; Irene Gendzier, *Dying to Forget: Oil, Power, Palestine and the Foundations of US Policy in the Middle East,* New York: Columbia University Press, 2016.
33 Greg Grandin, *The Blood of Guatemala: A History of Race and Nation,* Durham, NC: Duke University Press, 2002; Stephen Schlesinger and Stephen Kinzer, *Bitter Fruit: The Story of the American Coup in Guatemala,* Revised and Expanded Edition, Cambridge, MA: Harvard University Press, 2005.
34 Vincent Bevins, 'The "Liberal World Order" was Built with Blood', *New York Times,* 29 May 2020.
35 G. John Ikenberry, *A World Safe for Democracy: Liberal Internationalism and the Crisis of Global Order,* New Haven: Yale University Press, 2020, p. 186. See also: Richard Saull, 'Locating the Global South in the Theorization of the Cold War: Capitalist Development, Social Revolution and Geopolitical Conflict', *Third World Quarterly,* 26(2), 2005, pp. 253-80.
36 Noam Chomsky and Edward S. Herman, *The Washington Connection and Third World Fascism,* Boston: South End Press, 1979.
37 Robert Brenner, *The Economics of Global Turbulence,* London: Verso, 2006.
38 Francis Fukuyama, 'The End of History', *The National Interest,* 16(Summer), 1989, p. 4.
39 Charles Krauthammer, 'The Unipolar Moment,' *Foreign Affairs,* 70(1), 1990/91, pp. 24-5.
40 William C. Wohlforth, 'The Stability of a Unipolar World', *International Security,* 24(1), 1999, p. 8.
41 Michael Ignatieff, 'The American Empire; The Burden', *The New York Times Magazine,* 5 January 2003.
42 Peter Gowan, *The Global Gamble: Washington's Faustian Bid for Global Dominance,* London: Verso, 1999.
43 United States, *National Security Strategy of the United States of America,* Washington,

DC: The White House, 1990, p. 1; United States, *Defense Planning Guidance, FY1994-1999*, 16 April 1992.
44 William S. Cohen, *Report of the Quadrennial Defense Review*, Washington, DC: Office of The Secretary of Defense, 1997, pp. v, 8.
45 The White House, *The National Security Strategy of the United States of America*, Washington, DC: The White House, September 2002, p. 30.
46 The White House, *National Security Strategy*, Washington, DC: The White House, May 2010, p. 1.
47 Nuno P. Monteiro, 'Unrest Assured: Why Unipolarity is Not Peaceful', *International Security*, 36(3), 2011/12, pp. 9-40.
48 Stephen M. Walt, *The Hell of Good Intentions: America's Foreign Policy Elite and the Decline of US Primacy*, New York: Farrar, Straus, and Giroux, 2018, p. 76. Emphasis in original.
49 Barry R. Posen, 'Pull-Back: The Case for a Less Activist Foreign Policy', *Foreign Affairs*, January/February 2013.
50 Brenner, *Economics of Global Turbulence*.
51 Greta R. Krippner, 'The Financialization of the American Economy', *Socio-Economic Review*, 3(2), 2005, pp. 173-208.
52 United Nations, *World Economic and Social Survey 2005*, New York: United Nations, Department of Economic and Social Affairs, 2005, p. 75.
53 David Harvey, *A Brief History of Neoliberalism*, Oxford: Oxford University Press, 2007, p. 31; Peter Temin, *The Vanishing Middle Class*, Cambridge, MA: MIT Press, 2017.
54 David McNally, 'From Financial Crisis to World Slump: Accumulation, Financialization, and the Global Slowdown', *Historical Materialism*, 17(2), 2009, pp. 35-83; James Crotty, 'Structural Causes of the Global Financial Crisis: A Critical Assessment of the "New Financial Architecture"', *Cambridge Journal of Economics*, 33(4), 2009, pp. 563-80.
55 Adam Tooze, *Crashed: How a Decade of Financial Crises Changed the World*, New York: Penguin Books, 2018, p. 251.
56 Josh Bivens, 'Why is Recovery Taking So Long – and Who's to Blame?' *Economic Policy Institute*, 11 August 2016, available at: www.epi.org.
57 Erik Sherman, 'Three Graphs Show How Income Inequality Got Worse After the Crash', *Forbes*, 29 December 2019.
58 United Nations Development Programme, *Human Development Report 2013: The Rise of the South: Human Progress in a Diverse World*, New York: United Nations Development Programme, 2013.
59 Hillary Clinton, 'America's Pacific Century', *Foreign Policy*, 11 October 2011.
60 For analysis, see: Walt, pp. 1-12.
61 The White House, *The National Security Strategy of the United States of America*, Washington, DC: The White House, 2017, pp. 1, 27, 28.
62 Randall Schweller, 'Three Cheers for Trump's Foreign Policy: What the Establishment Misses', *Foreign Affairs*, September/October 2018.
63 Paul Krugman, 'Killing the Pax Americana: Trump's Trade War is About More Than Economics', *New York Times*, 11 May 2019.
64 Robert J. Gordon, 'Secular Stagnation on the Supply Side: US Productivity Growth

in the Long-Run', *Digiworld Economic Journal*, 100(4), 2015; Lawrence Summers, 'The Age of Secular Stagnation: What It Is and What To Do About It', *Foreign Affairs*, March/April 2016.

65   Berardino Palazzo, 'Corporate Profits in the Aftermath of COVID-19', *FEDS Notes*, 8 September 2023, available at: www.federalreserve.gov.

66   Gideon Rachman, 'Europe Has Fallen Behind America and the Gap is Growing', *Financial Times*, 19 June 2023.

67   Branko Milanovic, *Capitalism, Alone*, Cambridge, MA: Harvard University Press, 2019, pp. 118, 121.

68   Christopher Layne, 'This Time It's Real: The End of Unipolarity and the 'Pax Americana', *International Studies Quarterly*, 56(1), 2012, pp. 203-213.

69   Carol Bertaut, Bastian von Beshwitz, and Stephanie Curcuru, 'The International Role of the US Dollar – Post-Covid Edition', *FEDS Note*, 23 June 2023; 'Yuan settlements in global trade reach record high of 24%: central bank data', *Global Times*, 3 September 2023.

70   'What's Behind "Shocking" US Life Expectancy Decline – And What to Do About It', Harvard T.H. Chan School of Public Health, 13 April 2023, available at: www.hsph.harvard.edu.

71   Aimee Picchi, 'America's Poverty Rate Soared Last Year. Children Were Among the Most Hit', *CBS News*, 12 September 2023; Khristopher J. Brooks, 'Homelessness Rose in the US After Pandemic Aid Dried Up', *CBS News*, 21 June 2023; Matthew P. Rabbitt et al, 'Household Food Security in the United States in 2022', United States Department of Agriculture, Economic Research Report 325, October 2023.

72   Erin Grynshteyn and David Hemenway, 'Violent Death Rates in the US Compared to Those of the Other High-Income Countries, 2015', *Prev Med*, June 2019.

73   Renee D. Goodwin et al, 'Trends in Anxiety Among Adults in the United States, 2008-2018: Rapid Increases Among Young Adults', *J Psychiatr Res*, 130(November), 2020, pp. 441-446.

74   Center for Disease Control, 'Provisional Suicide Deaths in the United, 2022', 10 August 2023, available at: www.cdc.gov.

75   Federal Reserve Bank of San Francisco, 'How Far is Labor Force Participation From its Trend', 14 August 2023, available at: www.frbsf.org.

76   Graham Allison et al, 'The Great Tech Rivalry: China vs the US', Cambridge, MA: Belfer Center, Kennedy School, Harvard University, December 2021.

77   Jamie Gaida et al, 'ASPI's Critical Technology Tracker: The Global Race for Future Power', Australian Strategic Policy Institute, Policy Brief Report Number 69, 2023.

78   Barry Posen, 'Command of the Commons: The Military Foundation of US Hegemony', *International Security*, 28(1), 2003, pp. 5-46.

79   According to the *2022 Missile Defense Review*, US homeland missile defence architecture 'is neither intended for, nor capable of, defeating the large and sophisticated ICBM, air-, or sea-launched ballistic missile threats from Russia and the PRC'. United States, Department of Defense, *2022 Missile Defense Review*, p. 6.

80   Richard Stone, '"National Pride is at Stake": Russia, China, United States Race to Build Hypersonic Weapons', *Science*, 8 January 2020.

81   United States Government Accountability Office, 'National Nuclear Security Administration – Assessments of Major Projects', August 2023.

82   Keir A. Lieber and Daryl G. Press, 'The Rise of US Nuclear Primacy', *Foreign Affairs*,

85(2), 2006, pp. 42-54.
83 M. Taylor Fravel, 'China's "World-Class Military" Ambitions: Origins and Implications', *The Washington Quarterly*, 43(1), 2020, p. 86.
84 M. Taylor Fravel, 'China's Search for Military Power', *The Washington Quarterly*, 38(3), 2008, p. 126.
85 United States, Department of Defense, *Military and Security Developments Involving the People's Republic of China: Annual Report to Congress*, 2023, pp. 166-67.
86 M. Taylor Fravel, Henrik Stålhan Hiim and Magnus Langset Trøan, 'China's Misunderstood Nuclear Expansion: How US Strategy is Fueling Beijing's Growing Arsenal', *Foreign Affairs*, 10 November 2023; Henrik Stålhane Hiim, M. Taylor Fravel and Magnus Langset Trøan, 'The Dynamics of an Entangled Security Dilemma: China's Changing Nuclear Posture', *International Security*, 47(4), 2023, pp. 147-87.
87 For example, see: Alex Vershinin, 'The Return of Industrial Warfare', *RUSI*, 17 June 2022, available at: www.rusi.org; Interagency Taskforce in Fulfillment of Executive Order 13806, 'Assessing and Strengthening the Manufacturing and Defense Industrial Base and Supply Chain Resiliency of the United States', Report to President Donald Trump, September, 2018; Paul McLeary, and Joe Gould, 'Pentagon: US Arms Industry Struggling to Keep Up with China', *Politico*, 2 December 2023, available at: www.politico.com.
88 Taylor, cited in: Joseph S. Nye Jr. and Jack Landman Goldsmith, 'The Future of Power', *Bulletin of the American Academy of Arts and Sciences*, 64(3), 2011, p. 47.
89 Dimitriy Nurulayev and Mihaela Papa, 'Bloc Politics at the UN: How Other States Behave When the United States and Russia-China Disagree', *Global Studies Quarterly*, 3(3), 2023.
90 Human Rights Watch, 'Q&A: The International Criminal Court and the United States', 20 September 2020, available at: www.hrw.org.
91 Amitav Acharya, *The End of American World Order*, Second Edition, Cambridge, UK: Polity, 2018, p. 8.
92 On Truman, Acheson and the globalization of 'containment', see: LaFeber, p. 106.
93 The White House, *National Security Strategy*, Washington, DC: The White House, 2022.
94 The White House, 'Remarks by President Biden on the United Efforts of the Free World to Support the People of Ukraine', Warsaw, Poland, 26 March 2022, available at: www.whitehouse.gov.
95 Antony J. Blinken, 'Domestic Renewal as a Foreign Policy Priority', Remarks to University of Maryland, 9 August 2021, available at: www.state.gov.
96 The White House, *National Security Strategy*, Washington, DC: The White House, 2022.
97 The White House, *National Security Strategy*, 2022. Emphasis added.
98 Sullivan, 'The Sources of American Power'.
99 The White House, 'Remarks by National Security Advisor Jake Sullivan on Renewing American Economic Leadership at the Brookings Institution', 27 April 2023, available at: www.whitehouse.gov.
100 Sullivan, 'The Sources of American Power'.
101 Department of Defense, *2022 National Defense Strategy of the United States of America*, Washington, DC: Department of Defense, 27 October 2022.
102 The White House, *National Security Strategy 2022*.

103 Martin Gilens and Benjamin I. Page, 'Testing Theories of American Politics: Elites, Interest Groups, and Average Citizens', *Perspectives on Politics,* 12(3), 2014, pp. 564-581.
104 Alex W. Palmer, '"An Act of War": Inside America's Silicon Blockade Against China', *New York Times,* 12 July 2013.
105 Aditya Aladangady, *et al., Changes in U.S. Family Finances from 2019 to 2022: Evidence from the Survey of Consumer Finances.* Washington: Board of Governors of the Federal Reserve System, October 2023.
106 Robert Fife and Steven Chase, 'Inside the Final Hours that Led to the Arrest of Huawei Executive Meng Wanzhou', *Globe and Mail,* 30 November 2019.
107 Jeremy Shapiro and Jana Puglierin, 'The Art of Vassalization: How's Russia's War on Ukraine has Transformed Transatlantic Relations', Policy Brief, European Council on Foreign Relations, 4 April 2023, available at: www.efcr.eu.
108 Thompson Chau, 'Taiwan GDP Down 3.02% in Q1 as Economy Sinks into Recession', *Nikkei Asia,* 28 April 2023; Choonsik Yoo and Jihoon Lee, 'South Korean Economy Averts Recession But Faces Tough Headwinds', *Reuters,* 24 April 2023; Tetsushi Kajimoto, 'Japan's Export Growth Slows as China, Global Downturn Risks Loom', *Reuters,* 15 November 2023.
109 'Powerless and Ridiculous for US to Cry for its Recognition as Regional Leader', *Global Times,* 2 March 2023.
110 Jarrett Renshaw, Andrea Shalal and Michael Martina, 'Biden Says China Will Not Surpass US as Global Leader on His Watch', *Reuters,* 25 March 2021.
111 Rupert Wingfield-Hayes, 'The US is Quietly Arming Taiwan to the Teeth', *BBC News,* 5 November 2023.
112 North Atlantic Treaty Organization, *NATO 2022 Strategic Concept,* 29 June 2022, p. 5.
113 According to Kishore Mahbubani, 'China is right in saying that it did not start the process of reclaiming land around the rocks and reefs of the South China Sea. The other four claimants started this game. China had exercised great restraint for a long time. Unfortunately, it suddenly decided to sharply increase its reclamation after the global financial crisis. As a result, the anti-China voices in America found the South China Sea a useful propaganda tool to use against China'. Kishore Mahbubani, *Has China Won? The Chinese Challenge to American Primacy,* New York: PublicAffairs, 2020, p. 35.
114 Jude Woodward, *Asia's New Cold War: The US vs China.* Manchester: Manchester University Press, 2017.
115 Acharya, *The End of American World Order,* p. 33.
116 Kyle Mizokami, 'The US Military "Failed Miserably" in a Fake Battle over Taiwan', *Popular Mechanics,* 2 August 2021.
117 Joshua R. Itzkowitz Shifrinson, 'Deal or No Deal? The End of the Cold War and the US Offer to Limit NATO Expansion', *International Security,* 40(4), 2016, pp. 7-44; John J. Mearsheimer, 'Why the Ukraine Crisis is the West's Fault: The Liberal Delusions that Provoked Putin', *Foreign Affairs,* September/October 2014; Richard Sakwa, *Frontline Ukraine: Crisis in the Borderlands,* Updated Edition, London: I.B. Tauris, 2016; Stephen Cohen, *Soviet Fates and Lost Alternatives: From Stalinism to the New Cold War,* New York: Columbia University Press, 2011, Ch. 7.
118 Juan Cole, 'Israel's Colonial Revenge Genocide in Gaza is Only the Latest in a Long

History of Such Massacres', *Informed Comment Blog*, 14 October 2023, available at: www.juancole.com.

119 Nandita Bose and Katherine Jackson, 'Biden Says Hamas Must be Eliminated, US Officials Warn of Escalation', *Reuters*, 16 October 2023.

120 Henry Foy, 'Rush by West to Back Israel Erodes Developing Countries' Support for Ukraine', *Financial Times*, 18 October 202.

121 Stephen G. Brooks and William C. Wohlforth, 'The Myth of Multipolarity: American Power's Staying Power', *Foreign Affairs*, May/June, 2023.

122 Emma Ashford and Evan Cooper, *Assumption Testing: Multipolarity is More Dangerous Than Bipolarity for the United States*, 2 October 2023, Washington, DC: The Stimson Center, available at: www.stimson.org.

123 Acharya, *The End of American World Order*. p. 6.

US CAPITALISM: TOO BIG TO FAIL, TOO WEAK TO LEAD

INGO SCHMIDT

Invoking a great American past has paid off electorally. Not only for Donald Trump, who recycled Ronald Reagan's 1980 campaign slogan 'Make America Great Again', but also for Joe Biden who promised an ecologically-amended version of Franklin D. Roosevelt's 1930s New Deal. Both Trump and Biden raised expectations, however, that they couldn't fulfill.

Roosevelt represented the welfare state consensus that enabled the US to forge an international order based on Keynesian policies combined with welfarism in the capitalist centres and developmentalism in the peripheries, integrated by increasingly open markets and fixed exchange rates anchored to the US dollar. This first US hegemony was shattered by social unrest and economic crises in the 1960s and 1970s. Reagan represented the making of a second US hegemony based on fashioning market populist consensus at home and the free flow of goods, services, and capital internationally. The collapse of the Soviet Union, and the world-market turn of the Chinese Communists, marked the triumph of US-led efforts to globalize neoliberalism. This second hegemony was undermined by the rise of economic powers, most significantly China, that had developed within the US-shaped international order but were able to retain a degree of sovereignty that allowed them to escape total control by the US and its allies. Economic crises and stagnation threw the twin hegemony of the US and neoliberalism into a full-blown crisis.[1]

Responding to this second crisis of US hegemony, Trump and Biden promised, in partly different and partly overlapping ways, that they would restore US leadership. However, neither was capable of building domestic consensus around a new political project that would also serve as role model for other countries and thereby help to remake a US-centred international order. A look at the crisis of New Deal-based US hegemony and the trajectory of neoliberal hegemony helps explain why US capitalism is today at an impasse. Culture wars and a paralyzed political system stand in the way of forming a new historical bloc domestically and internationally. However, the inability to forge such a bloc does not mean that capitalism, the reproduction of which has been reliant on US leadership since the end of World War II, breaks down – no matter how many ecological, economic, and social challenges emerge.

The national and international institutions that sustained US hegemony in the past are, at one and the same time, preconditions for the reproduction of world capitalism and its current stagnation. The growing number of international institutions outside of US-centred governance structures and rising economic powers aren't anywhere near forming a historical bloc that could take the place that the US and its allies have held since the end of World War II. Escalating Cold War-style rhetoric that counterposes a 'good democratic West' to a 'bad authoritarian rest' disguises the fact that non-Western countries are far from being a unified bloc. Some of these countries cooperate bilaterally and form alternative governance structures some of the time, but they also cooperate with Western countries individually and operate within US-dominated governance structures most of the time. However, the return of Cold War rhetoric, despite all the jingoism that comes with it, also indicates a retreat from the global ambitions that marked US politics after the collapse of the Soviet Union. Holding its old Cold War alliance together and preventing the convergence of all the social forces in the world that might overcome US dominance is the best the American ruling class can do. US capitalism is too weak to lead. But it is also too big to fail.

MADE IN AMERICA: NEOLIBERAL HEGEMONY

The US has been in a similar position before. In the 1970s, the New Deal-based hegemony was called into question by many social groups. US capitalists complained about a productivity slowdown, foreign competition – notably from Japanese and West German companies – and the taxes and public deficits used to pay for the welfare state.[2] Organized workers fought against capitalist efforts to speed-up work and defend profit margins in the face of overcapacities and decreasing productivity growth. Unorganized workers fought against their second-class status in fragmented labour markets. Black and Latino people protested against discrimination and racism, women challenged the male-breadwinner model, and students protested against the use of scientific knowledge for social engineering purposes and the development of military equipment.[3] Inflation, driven by struggles over the distribution of income between (organized) labour and capital, was further fuelled by two oil-price hikes in 1973 and 1979. Occurring just shortly after the US became a net oil importer, rising energy prices added to the current account deficits that originated in growing imports of manufactured goods. After a few depreciations of the dollar, in 1973 the US abandoned the Bretton Woods system of fixed exchange rates for good in an effort to stop escalating current account deficits. At the time, this move was widely seen as the end of the dollar's role as international reserve currency.

Dollar supremacy wasn't the only pillar of US hegemony that was shaken in the 1970s. The retreat from Vietnam, the Iranian revolution and the coming to power of anti-imperialist regimes in southern Africa marked significant cracks in the neocolonial order the US had crafted in the 1950s and 1960s. In Europe, policies of détente undermined the anti-communism that had served as ideological glue for the US-led bloc since the end of World War II. On the margins of society, environmentalists challenged fossil-based industrialism in the capitalist West and the communist East. Warnings against the depletion of natural resources, coupled with rising oil prices, added to widespread worries about the future. At the same time, the government couldn't sustain prosperity by Keynesian means. By the mid-1970s, it looked as if Keynesian demand management was incapable of avoiding economic crises and unemployment. If anything, measures towards this end seemed to fuel inflation rather than stabilizing production and employment in the face of declining private investment.

Table 1: Accumulation, Productivity and Inflation, United States, 1970-85.[4]

	GDP growth	Capital formation (% of GDP)	Capacity utilization (% of GDP)	Labour productivity growth	Unemployment	Inflation
1970	-0.3	N/A	79	N/A	6.1	5.8
1971	3.3	N/A	81	2.0	6.0	4.2
1972	5.3	22	87	4.1	5.2	3.2
1973	5.6	22	88	4.6	4.9	6.1
1974	-0.5	22	79	-1.5	7.2	11.0
1975	-0.2	21	78	-1.2	8.2	9.1
1976	5.4	21	82	4.4	7.8	5.7
1977	4.6	22	84	3.6	6.4	6.5
1978	5.5	24	87	4.4	6.0	7.6
1979	3.2	24	84	2.0	6.0	11.1
1980	-0.3	24	81	-1.4	7.2	13.5
1981	2.5	23	77	1.5	8.5	10.3
1982	-1.8	23	71	-2.6	10.8	6.1
1983	4.6	22	78	3.6	8.3	3.2
1984	7.2	23	80	6.2	7.3	4.3
1985	4.2	24	79	3.2	7.0	3.5

Table 2: Monetary and Financial Indicators, United States, 1970-85.[5]

	Real interest rate	Market-capitalization to GDP	Government debt to GDP	Household debt to GDP	Current account to GDP
1970	N/A	76.0	35.7	43.9	0.2
1971	N/A	79.5	35.6	44.3	-0.1
1972	N/A	81.9	33.7	45.0	-0.4
1973	-2.4	58.3	31.8	44.9	0.5
1974	-5.6	36.8	30.8	45.0	0.1
1975	-1.2	44.4	32.7	44.7	1.1
1976	0.4	49.2	33.8	44.8	0.2
1977	0.3	41.0	33.2	46.5	-0.7
1978	0.5	37.2	31.8	48.0	-0.7
1979	-2.1	40.3	31.0	49.3	0.0
1980	1.7	46.9	31.2	50.0	0.1
1981	5.3	39.1	31.3	47.6	0.1
1982	5.2	42.3	35.2	47.8	-0.3
1983	4.2	45.3	37.2	48.4	-1.3
1984	3.5	40.9	40.1	49.0	-2.5
1985	3.7	48.0	43.8	53.7	-2.9

There was no shortage of left alternatives to New Deal policies when they lost public support and didn't yield expected results. These alternatives ranged from moderate to revolutionary. Moderate proposals were aimed at the integration of women and ethnic minorities into the New Deal and amending the Keynesian policy toolbox by adding long-term employment programs, perhaps accompanied by price controls, and higher taxes on profits and high incomes, all potentially embedded in a 'New International Economic Order'. Revolutionary proposals suggested the replacement of US capitalism with Soviet, Chinese, Cuban or any other brand of actually existing or utopian socialism. Moderate proposals came from various think-tanks and publications but were lacking an organizational centre. They also suffered from widespread suspicion that they boiled down to more of the same policies that had produced the economic and social crises of the 1970s. The revolutionary left had a myriad of miniature parties and an array of networks. It could also claim that it had pointed to the impossibility of endless prosperity already at a time when the long post-World War II boom was still in full swing. However, the revolutionary left could not consolidate mass mobilizations into anything remotely resembling a historical bloc capable of challenging, let alone overcoming, capitalist class power.

Moreover, revolutionary organizations, particularly those of Black and Latino people, faced massive state repression. Capitalists and political elites, figuring that revolution wasn't imminent, were actually more concerned with moderate proposals which, if put into practice, would reinforce the profit squeeze they were already bemoaning in the face of overcapacities, a productivity slowdown and escalating strike activity. They also feared that policies of détente and a New International Economic Order would limit the privileged access to world markets they enjoyed while New Deal hegemony was intact. More and more capitalists were convinced that New Deal liberalism, once an unloved but convenient set of policies to contain challenges from the old left, had turned into a breeding ground for a new left that might converge with a resurgent old left. It had to be replaced by something new: a liberalism that would shelter private property rights from democratic interference but look democratic from the outside.

Freedom became a watchword for various progressive movements of the 1960s and 1970s, but also the ideological cornerstone for the remaking of US capitalism and hegemony, Ronald Reagan its right-wing messenger.[6] After protracted ideological battles, the meaning of freedom shifted from overcoming the exploitation of workers by capitalists and gender and racial discrimination to the freedom of individuals to exercise their property rights without state interference. This (neo-)liberal picture painted the state as victim of the special interests of unions as well as women's and civil rights groups, who imposed undue taxes on hardworking people and turned hard earned savings into unsustainable public deficits. This picture translated the dry economic theories of Hayek, Friedman, Schumpeter and other thinkers of the right into a market populist ideology that served as the glue for a neoliberal bloc in the making, first in the US but also, with more or less delay, in other countries around the world.[7] Its political promise was the restoration of individual freedom, exercised at the ballot box and in the market, from organized interests that had misused democratic rights to capture the state and impose their interests onto everyone else. Its economic promise was to enable everyone to buy and sell whatever they wish without being bothered by the state – the pursuit of happiness exercised in the marketplace.

Wrapped in free market individualism, the various business associations of capital launched a campaign to restore capitalist class power. The first targets of the neoliberal campaign to restore capitalist class power in the name of free market individualism were inflation, taxes and the Soviet Union. Jacking up prices was a convenient way for industrial capitalists to maintain their profits in the face of overcapacities and a productivity slowdown. But it included the danger of falling behind international competitors if the latter restrained themselves from price increases. Finance capitalists worried that inflation would weaken the dollar and international investments in the US. They were anxious about the real value of their assets. Organized workers were able to defend their real wages but were concerned with the negative effect inflation had on their savings. Unorganized workers and welfare recipients could only hope political decision makers would eventually adjust their incomes to inflation. Only debtors, not least the state, enjoyed the advantage of repaying their outstanding debt with devalued money.

This was exactly the Archimedean point to forge cross-class consensus against inflation. Inflation was portrayed as the result of special interest groups forcing governments to increase public spending and thereby stifle private investment, growth and employment. As a result, rising prices boost nominal incomes while real incomes would remain unchanged at best or decrease at worst. The anti-inflation consensus was easily amended by opposition to taxes. The market populist appeal to individual freedom rendered differences in incomes and wealth, and the ability to pay taxes related to these inequalities, invisible. Keynesian efforts to balance equality and efficiency were replaced by the claim that rising taxes – enforced by special interest groups of course – strangled individuals' incentive to work, study and save as well as companies' incentive to invest, no matter how rich or poor the individual, no matter how big or small the company.[8] Nurtured by the state, the rent-seeking behaviour of special interest groups, crowds out productive work and investments. On the other hand, markets, unhindered by the state, create equal opportunities for everyone and prosperity for all.

Within the ideological apparatuses mobilized by the market populists, freedom was cleansed from all the left meanings associated with it, from the French Revolution to the American New Left, and became another word for market liberation. It was the watchword for policies that would create equal opportunities for everybody to live according to their individual time and consumer preferences. Markets would serve both as enablers of entrepreneurialism and impartial judges of economic activities. The first domestic steps towards market liberation were the fight against inflation and unbearable taxes.

Internationally, market liberation meant fighting the Soviets, who were presented as an actually existing counterexample to the free market utopia: a bureaucratic system that left no room for economic prosperity or individual freedom. Rekindling the anti-communism that had played such an important ideological role in forging New Deal hegemony in the 1950s, unions and civil rights groups, lumped together with state bureaucrats, were portrayed as Moscow's fifth column. Market liberation required the rollback of this fifth column and its Kremlin masters. It came with the reassertion of American imperial ambition: starting another arms race with the Soviet Union, forcing European allies to abandon their policies of détente in favour of a new anti-Communist crusade, and rolling back anti-imperialist regimes in the Global South.[9] Logically, anti-communism, calling upon the American nation to close ranks against its internal and external enemies, was incompatible with neoliberal individualism. Politically, it was convenient, as it recreated an imagined community that was shaken by the economic crises, social unrest and political setbacks of the 1970s. Once poor(er) and powerless people found out that they would not be on the receiving end of the benefits of neoliberal policies and prosperity for all was not to be had, anti-communism and nationalism turned into convenient ideologies to plaster over cracks in the neoliberal consensus.

The tandem of neoliberal policies and imperial ambition soon revealed why, despite the waning of New Deal hegemony, the US was still in a unique position that allowed it to rebuild hegemony on neoliberal terms. Friedmanite policies aimed at curbing inflation sent interest rates skyrocketing and thereby produced a severe recession and unemployment: the infamous Volcker Shock. Tax cuts, meant to induce higher private investment, consumer expenditure and labour supply, produced larger public deficits instead. Increased military spending further contributed to these deficits. George Bush senior would later label the policies of his predecessor 'voodoo economics' and turn to a more moderate mix of tax and spending cuts.

However, Bush arguably reaped the fruits sown during the Reagan presidency. Under the pressure of an unwinnable arms race, the Soviets had signed major agreements on arms control and embarked on a path of domestic reform that soon saw them hand the keys to the Kremlin to post-communist rulers and neoliberal shock therapists from the West. As the winner of the Cold War, the US could lower its military spending without giving up its dominant position in world politics. Moreover, the twin deficit in public budgets and current accounts, one of market populists' favourite scarecrows, turned out to be a cornerstone of neoliberal hegemony: the world economy became addicted to US deficits, US consumers became the world's consumers of last resort, US finance became the safe haven for surplus capital from around the world and the dollar's role as international reserve currency was reinforced. It retained that position, despite considerable exchange rate turbulence, over the entire neoliberal wave of accumulation and even into the crisis of neoliberalism beginning with the world economic and financial crises 2007-09.

Capitalist classes in other Western countries had to impose austerity, and secure consent from subordinate classes, to regain international investors' trust. Comprador bourgeoisies in the peripheries, in many cases lacking consent at home, collaborated with the IMF, the World Bank and, if necessary, the CIA to globalize neoliberal hegemony. Only the US, as a country, was exempt from fiscal austerity, because its ruling class had established itself as guarantor of capitalist class rule at a time when this rule was shaken by economic crises and social unrest. It had done this not only by confronting the Soviet Union but also through imposing austerity in social provisioning and wages on the American working class, thereby demonstrating to capitalists in other countries that the forward march of labour could be halted. However, other countries' capitalists, no matter how determined they were in fighting labour, didn't enjoy the privileges of the world's hegemon. For the US, running deficits became an extension of the exorbitant privilege associated with the dollar's role as reserve currency.[10] It also became a necessity in order to keep accumulation on a world scale going. As long as the US economy served as the world's engine of growth, its hegemony was unchallenged. After leading the remaking of world capitalism along neoliberal lines, any such challenge seemed unthinkable.[11]

GLOBALIZING NEOLIBERAL CAPITALISM

The collapse of the Soviet Union and the opening of China to the world market, under the leadership of the Chinese Communist Party, seemed to validate everything market populists ever said about the superiority of markets over states. And not only that. The Cold War victory of the US and its allies freed them from the burden of great power competition. The radical wing of liberalism saw states withering away in a world market offering equal opportunities to everybody.[12] Even President Bush, firmly committed to what he saw as the American national interest, talked about a peace dividend and continued the cuts in military spending that Reagan had already begun after the Reykjavik summit with Mikhail Gorbachev. However, his claim that American leadership remained indispensable for governing the new world order was markedly different from multilateral, if not entirely borderless, conceptions of globalization.

Tensions between American imperial ambition and utopic visions of globalization without a hegemon marked the neoliberal era, from the end of the Cold War between the US and the Soviet Union to the New Cold War between the US and China. Theoretically, globalization had its attractions for every state other than the hegemon as it promised an alternative to subordination, be it in the privileged role as the hegemon's junior partner or in a (semi-)peripheral role. However, in the absence of a coalition of states able to contain American imperial ambition, globalization relied on

American willingness to surrender some of its sovereignty to supranational bodies. As it turned out, this willingness was quite limited. Sometimes, the US presented itself as a benevolent hegemon, at other times, it displayed a naked imperialism.[13] Soft and hard versions of imperial policies relied on the US' ability to promote accumulation through a regime that was, compared to the New Deal era, less prone to interference from organized labour, welfare spending, or developmental states.

One key element of that new regime was a new role for the US military. The wars against Iraq in 1991 and Yugoslavia in 1999 demonstrated the ability and willingness of the US to project military power throughout the world, notably in the former communist East and the Middle Eastern centres of oil production. If necessary, the US was able to enforce market access on its own terms and conditions. Capitalists from around the world were invited to conduct business under the new rules as long as they left US supremacy, including the bulk of imperial rents flowing to the US, untouched. The new rules applied to energy, manufacturing and finance, and their roots stretched back to the crisis of New Deal hegemony.

In the 1970s, OPEC was often considered an example of Third World solidarity. Cartels for other primary products were hoped by many Third World advocates – and feared by capitalists in the imperialist centres – to potentially be an effective means of redistributing wealth from centres to peripheries. Yet OPEC oil price hikes in 1973 and 1979 drove a wedge between oil exporting and importing countries in the Global South. The former recycled huge amounts of petrodollars through the purchase of US Treasury securities and deposits in American banks, thereby helping the government to finance its deficits and banks to lend money to oil-importing countries – until the Volcker Shock, which was a response to the combination of high oil prices and union militancy. After the shock, oil prices went down and stayed low because Iran and Iraq sold plenty of oil to pay for their 1980-88 war. As before the 1970s stagflation, cheap energy fuelled accumulation, even if the growth levels of the post-World War II boom were not reached again.[14]

While energy was cheap again, skyrocketing interest rates pushed many debtor countries of the Global South into the debt crises that offered the IMF and World Bank the leverage they needed to enforce the turn from developmentalist import-substitution to export-oriented integration into the world market, effectively reinstating the neocolonialism that developmentalist regimes had tried to escape. This helped make cheap labour available for production processes catering to, and controlled by, companies headquartered in the imperialist centres.

The first steps towards a new international division of labour aimed at sourcing cheap industrial labour at a global scale in order to counter rising wages in the centres were already taken by US companies in the 1950s, when they moved some of their production to Western Europe where wages, by US standards, were low.[15] Although import-substitution still dominated the policies of post-colonial regimes, multinational companies from the centres had already established pockets of export-oriented production in the 1970s.[16] After the 1980s debt crisis and the structural adjustment that came in its aftermath, these relocations spread to many parts of the Global South.[17] But the real take-off occurred in the 1990s. Though global production networks kept on spreading, there was a clear focus on China, which attracted the vast majority of foreign direct investments from Western countries.

If there ever was a sign of global governance that might constrain even the US, it was the founding of the World Trade Organization (WTO) in 1995. Left protestors, such as those taking to the streets of Seattle during the 1999 WTO summit, saw the WTO, and other so-called free trade agreements, as another step from democratic control of economic processes toward a global empire of capital. The American right, on the other hand, saw US membership in the WTO as a sell-out of American interests and Chinese membership in 2001 as a betrayal of freedom. This was at a time when large parts of the American ruling class lined up behind Bill Clinton's bid to use international organizations like the WTO as a means to sign the entire world up to playing by the American-made rules of the game.[18]

If anything attracted more attention in the 1990s than world trade, it was finance. Unlike the cautious steps towards global governance that the WTO represented, finance, though global in reach, was clearly centred in Wall Street with support from the US Treasury and Federal Reserve. Wall Street banks, the stock market and credit rating agencies helped funnel the profit surge enabled by the new international division of labour into shareholders' accounts, allocate capital to investment projects and set benchmark profit rates.[19] The latter pressured managers to continuously seek cheaper labour. Rising asset prices reinforced the push for higher profits and lower wages. Information technology, widely used to manage ever longer supply chains and international finance, propelled profit expectations even further. Gone were the days when a productivity slowdown, a real or perceived profit squeeze and twin deficits risked scaring investors away from the US.

With the restructuring of production and the defeats of the working classes, especially in the US, productivity growth partially recovered in the 1990s, and profit rates, due to the rollback of wages and longer working hours, recovered particularly strongly.[20] The twin deficits of budget and current accounts that confronted the US in the 1980s disappeared in the 1990s. However, at the same time, private households depleted their savings and took out more and more credit. In other words, public deficits were replaced by private household deficits. Current account deficits once again soared. US deficit spending, in the unlikely form of a privatized Keynesianism,[21] remained what it already was in the 1980s – an engine of accumulation – while the rest of the world was more or less bogged down by austerity. Running deficits, while imposing austerity on others through various combinations of hard and soft power, was central to US neoliberal hegemony. In the end, along with the political conflict between American national interests and visions of globalization beyond nation-states, this was a key contradiction that would lead to the cracks in a US hegemony that had looked unshakeable in the 1990s.

The American privilege of running deficits while austerity reigned in the rest of the world slowly turned into a burden. This was not because other governments revolted against the US way of mitigating the neoliberal onslaught on welfare and the developmental state with privatized Keynesianism, nor was it because international investors withdrew their money from the US. Rather, it was because of the way the popular classes in the US were integrated into neoliberal hegemony. As consumers, they benefited from the import of cheap consumer goods. For workers, whose wages and benefits had been rolled back by neoliberalism at home, the super-exploitation of workers in the Global South (notably in China, as the new workshop of the world) offered some relief.[22] But not much, as the costs of housing, health, and education were rising even while general inflation rates, due to cheap imports of manufactured goods and energy, remained low. As long as rising asset prices created a wealth illusion, these rising costs could be covered by credit, the private deficit spending that fuelled global accumulation and produced ever larger current account deficits.[23]

During the 1990s boom, more and more people – not just the rich but increasingly even those with only modest savings (in the US and beyond) – joined the stock-market game and helped to keep asset prices rising. While this was happening, some investors (notably large-scale ones) began realizing that profit expectations outpaced the potential for profit realization, despite the fact that wages continuously lagged behind productivity growth and thereby kept realized profits growing. Investors also began worrying about private households' ability to pay back their loans. After all, generally stagnant wages, alongside falling wages at the lower end of the labour market, didn't bode well for the ability to service outstanding debt.

IT companies were at the centre of the stock-market mania in the 1990s, and the dot-com bubble was the first to burst, sending a warning that the entire model of consumer-debt driven accumulation tended towards unsustainable gaps between the accumulation of fictitious and productive capital.[24] Yet, there was no alternative. The anti-WTO protests in Seattle in 1999 had shown that discontent with neoliberal globalization was growing. But the unrest also revealed that the groups organizing these protests were far from forging a counter-hegemonic bloc. Neoliberal accumulation restarted after the dot-com crash and the associated recession, although weaker than before and lacking the 'New Economy' hype that had surrounded the 1990s boom. Instead of tech stocks, rising real estate prices and mortgage debt became the drivers of the 2000s upturn.

In a desperate response to the tensions in the neoliberal consensus, George W. Bush embarked on the War on Terror. The invasions of Afghanistan in 2001 and Iraq in 2003 were equally efforts to close ranks among Western allies, but instead revealed divisions. If anything, neoconservative complaints that 'old Europe', i.e. France and Germany, were not up to the 'new' Eastern European standards of subservience to the US reinforced such divisions. Clinton had been careful enough to couch claims to US supremacy in multilateral rhetoric. He had also benefited from the New Economy boom that made it easy to present the US as a role model for other countries. Good Gaullist that he was, French president Jacques Chirac always kept a distance from both the US and neoliberalism without offering any clear alternative. German chancellor Gerhard Schröder, on the other hand, alongside British prime minister Tony Blair, had been an enthusiastic follower of Clinton's Third Way politics, but sensed after the boom that joining Bush's 'coalition of the willing' against Saddam Hussein would cost him dearly. Yet, if anti-WTO protestors didn't represent a counter-hegemonic bloc, neither did Chirac and Schröder, despite cheers from millions of anti-war protestors.[25] The cracks in the transatlantic alliance that the war against Iraq had produced didn't last. But they did show that European subservience couldn't be taken for granted. If this wasn't bad enough for the US, the war also showed that while it had no trouble toppling regimes it disliked, it lacked the ability to install friendly and functioning regimes at will.

The troubles sustaining the twin hegemony of the US and neoliberalism didn't end there. The War on Terror turned much of the Middle East into a potential battlefield, and contributed to a commodity-super-cycle which, after the dot-com bubble had burst, offered an alternative field of investment other than US real estate. In tandem with government concerns about energy sovereignty, it also helped US energy companies who wanted to boost production in the US but couldn't do so profitably at the prices prevailing before the super-cycle due to the high cost of fracking oil and gas compared to conventional energy production.[26] However, what was good for US oil companies and the government wasn't good for US consumers who, on top of the rising costs of housing, health and education, had to pay higher energy prices. Moreover, rising prices generated massive extra profits for the low-cost producers of conventional energy, including those in countries the US considered adversaries, notably Iran, Russia and Venezuela. Although rising prices lifted many fracking projects above the break-even point, oil production in the US continued the long-term decline that had begun in the early 1970s, just before the first OPEC oil price shock. This downward trend was only reversed after the world economic and financial crises of 2007-09.

MADE IN AMERICA 2.0: HEGEMONIC DECAY

Through the 1980s and 1990s, a string of debt and financial crises shook countries all over the world. These were part of the ascendency of neoliberalism and the restoration and triumph of US hegemony. Not surprisingly, each of these crises sparked a certain amount of anti-American sentiment, but all of them ended with the deeper integration of crisis shaken countries into the American-made international order. The end of the New Economy boom in 2000, triggered by the Nasdaq crash which spilled over to all of Wall Street before going global, was a warning sign that there was worse to come if the neoliberal regime of accumulation remained in place. In 2006, instead of IT stock prices, it was falling housing prices causing a general financial and economic crisis. The 2007-09 crisis that then erupted was both much deeper and wider than the 2000-01 crisis.[27] If both crises were American-centred, they were caused by the specific forms that the internal contradictions of the capitalist mode of production had taken during the neoliberal wave of accumulation, not by international or domestic challenges.

Internationally, the BRICS (Brazil, Russia, India, China, South Africa) had morphed from a Goldman Sachs acronym identifying profitable investment opportunities into a loose association of countries, but their cooperation was, and still is, far from representing a counter-hegemonic bloc to the US-led bloc of the old imperialist centres. The members of Latin America's ALBA (Alianza Bolivariana para los Pueblos de Nuestra América) might harbour the ambition to form such an economic and political bloc, but are much too weak to do so. The European Union might be strong enough, sometimes even portraying itself as a more socially-inclined alternative to the US's unfettered market capitalism. But the EU has failed to develop as a strategic centre that might have elevated it beyond junior partner status to the US. If anything, the EU helped spread and institutionalize neoliberalism.[28] Within countries, unions never recovered from the setbacks they had suffered at the hands of governments and employers since the Reagan presidency. For a brief moment, the movement against neoliberal globalization served as a rallying point for various groups, including unions, organizing around a range of issues. However, unable to respond to the turn from Clintonite globalization to the naked imperialism of Bush junior, the movement faded away without ever becoming a social force that might have challenged neoliberalism in either its more free-trade or more military-oriented varieties.

It was the reliance on credit that led neoliberalism into crises in its American homeland from which it never recovered. During the neoliberal boom, investors assured – and deceived – themselves and others that debt-financed investment would lead to lasting prosperity and that debt repayment would be easy. Rising asset prices represented prosperity, both for the present and the future, and provided the collateral to buy homes and take out consumer credit. However, asset purchases were increasingly financed by credit, turning the US economy into a quasi-Ponzi scheme. Ironically, everything neoliberals said about Keynesianism in the 1970s turned out instead to be true with regards to neoliberalism some thirty years later.

To avoid the accumulation of runaway debt, liberal Keynesians prescribed government deficit spending as an anti-cyclical measure so that debt could be repaid during the next upswing. Left Keynesians, on the other hand, assumed that capitalism possesses a long-term tendency towards stagnation that would render counter-cyclical measures ineffective. Instead, they argued for a long-term expansion of public spending, financed by taxation so as to avoid the accumulation of unpayable public debt. In an ironic turn of history, it was neoliberalism which fostered just such an unpayable public debt burden (or debtor states). At the same time, various rounds of tax cuts kept up the pressure to restrain public spending. Escalating current account deficits before the crises stimulated accumulation on a global scale. Yet when the crises hit, the sharp contraction of effective demand in the US dragged the entire world economy down, a challenge to neoliberal and US hegemony alike.

The mandate to reign in these multiple imbalances fell on Barack Obama. By signing on to grandiose designs for a 'New American Century', George W. Bush had managed to push concerns about increasing social insecurity and economic inequality into the background. By the time of the 2008 presidential elections, such concerns were back with a vengeance. The failure to turn Afghanistan and Iraq into shiny outposts of this New American Century had been obvious already before the 2006-08 crises.

Yet, running for president under the slogan 'Change You Can Believe In', Obama instigated hope across several layers of US society. But others were troubled by his electoral success and took refuge in open and increasingly violent expressions of racism not seen since the heyday of the Civil Rights Movement in the 1950s and 1960s.

White supremacy, religious fundamentalism, conservative family values and the insistence on American exceptionalism played an indispensable role in the construction of the neoliberal bloc before and during the Reagan presidency. The emergent neoliberal right represented themselves as the true counterculture against a Keynesian liberalism that had allegedly sold out to rent-seeking special interest groups, many of them self-styled counter-culturalists, and thereby corroded the Protestant work ethic on which American capitalism had been built. Neoliberalism, then, was not just about restoring the allocative efficiency of markets, but also about repairing the moral basis on which markets rely. Clinton's 'New Democrats' supplemented this right-wing moral economy with a liberal cosmopolitanism.[29] By retaining the neoliberal economic policies established under Reagan and consolidated under Bush senior, the Clintonites fostered the cultural universalization of neoliberalism. After that, the culture wars that had already been part of the making of a neoliberal bloc under Reagan could be continued, but alternative economic policies were no longer available. There still were some academic blueprints for alternative policies,[30] but certainly no counter-hegemonic bloc. Far from being the face of an emerging new bloc, as Roosevelt had been for the New Deal and Reagan had been for neoliberalism, Obama ended up using 'big government' to bail out 'big money' during the Great Financial Crisis of 2007-09. The firms and families who had advanced neoliberalism for their own benefit were not willing to bear losses once the neoliberal boom went bust.

Generous infusions of government money, some of it to sustain effective demand and lots of it to bail out big money, supplemented by an unlimited supply of money from the US Federal Reserve, held off the spectre of another Great Depression.[31] Whereas the Great Depression had incubated the hegemony of the New Deal, the financial crisis led to the fracturing of the neoliberal bloc and a shift of the lead role as the engine of global accumulation from the US to China.

An unbridgeable rift in the neoliberal bloc opened up as many of the poorer supporters of neoliberalism watched in indignation as the Obama Administration and the Federal Reserve came to big money's rescue yet had nothing to offer to them. Meanwhile, Occupy Wall Street's defiant slogan 'We are the 99%' captured a widespread sentiment that would fuel Bernie

Sanders' 2016 and 2020 socialist-tinged presidential campaigns. At the other end of the political spectrum, a radicalized right paved Trump's way to the White House in 2016. For the right, everything bad neoliberals ever said about big government was confirmed by Obama's bailing out of the 1%. However, finding themselves among the losers of neoliberal capitalism, they didn't ask for further cuts to welfare, Medicare or Medicaid. Rather, they transplanted neoliberalism's survival of the fittest principle from markets into race and demanded state action to defend white supremacy against the inside threat of Black people and the outside threats of immigrants from Latin America and China's theft of American jobs. They hated Obama for his handing government money over to the banks and their perception that he had sold out America to non-whites. It didn't interest them that Obama had made the containment of China the main goal of his foreign policy.

To be sure, the American right has been obsessed with China for a long time. It fiercely opposed Chinese WTO membership and had nothing but disdain for Clinton's efforts to bring the country into an American-shaped global order. Complaints about the relocation of jobs from the US to China were neither new nor were they the monopoly of right-wingers. Many unionists and some currents in the Democratic Party, before its New Democratic transformation, shared these views. No matter that the new international division of labour that came with the neoliberal remaking of US capitalism integrated many countries other than China, alongside right-to-work states within the US.[32] If rampant Sinophobia had a rational core, it was the fact that China was one of the few countries whose world market integration had the growth effects neoliberals had predicted. Arguably, because the Chinese government retained substantial control over the economy and defied subordination to American supremacy, it grew into a position where it could claim, with some credibility, to be advancing an alternative to the neoliberal Washington Consensus in its authoritarian statism.[33]

As if this wasn't bad enough for Americans, for the elites and popular strata alike, who considered US hegemony a natural or divine right, the Great Financial Crisis and its management came as a real shock. The US combination of big bailouts, little deficit spending and endless money supply had little effect on effective demand, production or employment. Good enough to overcome the recession, these measures nevertheless left the US economy in stagnation. Effective demand was so weak that the infusion of interest-free money didn't lead to inflation beyond the central bank target rate – contrary to monetarist orthodoxy. This was despite the fact that energy prices rebounded as fast as they had dropped during the recession, while real estate prices rose strongly and continuously with just a little time-lag. Stock markets also recovered quickly, but the much-vaunted wealth effect on economic growth, referring to stock market gains channelled into consumer spending and productive investments, was already waning before the crisis.[34]

Table 3: Accumulation, Productivity and Inflation, United States, 2005-22.[35]

	GDP growth	Capital formation (% of GDP)	Capacity utilization (% of GDP)	Labour productivity growth	Unemployment	Inflation
2005	3.5	23	81	2.4	4.9	3.4
2006	2.8	23	81	1.8	4.4	3.2
2007	2.0	22	81	1.0	5.0	2.9
2008	0.1	21	72	-0.8	7.3	3.8
2009	-2.6	19	70	-3.5	9.9	-0.4
2010	2.7	18	75	1.8	9.3	1.6
2011	1.5	19	77	0.8	8.5	3.1
2012	2.3	20	77	1.5	7.9	2.0
2013	1.8	20	78	1.1	6.7	1.5
2014	2.3	20	79	1.4	5.6	1.6
2015	2.7	20	76	1.9	5.0	0.1
2016	1.7	20	75	0.9	4.7	1.3
2017	2.2	21	78	1.5	4.1	2.1
2018	2.9	21	80	2.3	3.9	2.4
2019	2.3	21	77	1.8	3.6	1.8
2020	-2.8	21	76	-3.1	6.7	1.2
2021	5.9	21	79	5.8	3.9	4.7
2022	2.1	N/A	79	1.7	3.5	8.0

Meanwhile, massive stimulus programs in China triggered not only a strong recovery of the Chinese economy but also turned the country into the engine of global accumulation.[36] Seeing this role that had been a key pillar of US hegemony shift to China caused panic in some and relief in others. It didn't help that Japan, the US' closest Asian ally, and considered a potential economic rival in the 1970s and 1980s, had been mired in stagnation since the 1990s. Nor did it help that the Mediterranean members of the EU were squeezed between a sovereign debt crisis and an austerity-imposing Troika, or that Britain opted for exit from the EU in 2016.

Table 4: Monetary and Financial indicators, United States, 2005-22.[37]

	Real interest rate	Market-capitalization to GDP	Government debt to GDP	Household debt to GDP	Current account to GDP
2005	0.9	94.6	61.3	93.0	-5.6
2006	2.4	101.4	61.8	97.1	-5.9
2007	-0.9	101.7	62.7	99.1	-5.1
2008	-2.3	63.5	73.2	96.3	-4.7
2009	-2.4	79.9	84.0	97.1	-2.6
2010	-1.2	87.7	91.6	92.1	-2.9
2011	-2.8	83.6	96.1	88.0	-2.9
2012	-1.4	93.7	100.1	84.1	-2.6
2013	-1.4	115.6	99.8	82.3	-2.0
2014	-0.5	122.6	101.3	79.9	-2.1
2015	-0.3	116.7	102.6	78.0	-2.2
2016	-1.2	122.6	104.6	78.1	-2.1
2017	-0.4	138.2	102.3	77.8	-1.9
2018	1.0	121.6	105.0	76.0	-2.1
2019	-0.9	152.0	105.9	75.3	-2.1
2020	-1.3	175.1	126.0	79.3	-2.9
2021	-6.7	196.2	120.1	77.0	-3.6
2022	-1.7	146.7	119.0	74.4	-3.7

A sense of decline at home, weak allies in Asia and Europe, and the rise of China to economic powerhouse status with substantial political sovereignty were the background against which Trump presented himself as the leader who was called upon to pull the country out of the rut, to 'Make America Great Again' as Reagan had done in the 1980s. Trump built his support base around the same blend of America-first, racist, religious and family ideologies that Reagan had used to forge a bloc against New Deal liberalism. Reagan also pursued a neoliberal agenda of tax cuts and deregulation at home, and free trade across the world, and Trump also signed on to tax cuts and deregulation. Trump posed, however, a rhetorical challenge to free trade, even if his USMCA (United States – Mexico – CanadaAgreement), the so-called 'new NAFTA', looked rather similar to the old one and was embraced by those who had supported NAFTA in Congress.[38] And while he claimed that his embrace of tariffs and sanctions would bring jobs back from China, it was not clear how the unfolding 'tech war' this initiated would do anything to effect employment in the US rust-belt, as this pertained entirely to the vicissitudes of international corporate competition over property rights.[39] Reagan's Cold War adversary, the Soviet Union and its Eastern European allies, represented a state-owned and bureaucracy-run world of its own, sealed off from the capitalist world market almost entirely but engaged in ideological warfare, proxy wars and an arms race with the US that it couldn't win. Whatever the characterization of the Chinese social formation – socialist, state-capitalist or a particularly brutal form of neoliberal capitalism – instead of being sealed off from markets shaped by the US, it is a key player in those markets. Supply chain disruptions during the Covid-19 pandemic made clear that de-coupling would hurt the US just as much as it would hurt China. Already before the pandemic, it had become obvious that that relatively limited protectionist measures wouldn't make America great again, and a full-on de-coupling from China wasn't on the cards either with trade too intertwined and the Chinese market too massive for US capital to exit from. Unlike Reagan, whose politics connected the Cold War against the Soviets with the project of creating a US-dominated world market, Trump fell into a growing gap between jingoistic rhetoric needed to mobilize his support base and an incoherent protectionism that didn't offer a vision for an America great enough to shape the world after its own vision and for the benefit of its own people.

The Biden administration has offered a different vision of sorts.[40] While toning down anti-Chinese rhetoric, he nevertheless acted more decisively against China than Trump had done, tying protectionist measures imposed in the name of national security to a mild industrial policy aimed at creating industrial jobs in the US and fostering the transition from fossil fuels to solar and wind energy. This allowed Biden to distance himself from the neoliberal policies more coherently than Trump had done and win over Sanders supporters who suspected that Biden, given his history as Vice-President under Obama, would continue the New Democrat version of neoliberalism established by Clinton. Taking office in the midst of the Covid-19 recession offered him the chance, though fiercely opposed by Republican opposition in Congress, to propose the largest public spending program since Lyndon Johnson.[41] Unfortunately for him, the end of the recession went hand in hand with rates of inflation close to those that were instrumental in bringing about the turn from Keynesianism to neoliberalism under Reagan.

Not surprisingly, neoliberals jumped at the chance to lay the blame for the return of inflation, which they had wrongly predicted in response to Obama's management of the Great Recession, at Biden's doorstep, even though inflation had little to do with a government triggered demand pull or a wage-push dynamic. After all, the economy was in deep recession when the Biden spending began. Inflation in fact had a lot to do with the strain induced by the breakdown of supply-chains connecting the international division of labour under the reign of neoliberalism. This breakdown was precipitated in the short-term by the Covid-19 lockdowns and in the long-term due to the escalation of protectionist measures. It also had to do with companies, unsure about the future of the low-cost production networks they had set up over decades, increasing their profit-margins after the recession. Henceforth, Biden was under pressure from Trumpites who were convinced that Biden had stolen the 2020 election from their 'Führer' and from neoliberals anxious to defend their lives' work against a state-interventionist turn of any kind. Meanwhile, market populism had lost too much of its currency to be revived by an inflation scare 1970s-style, when it had helped to forge the neoliberal bloc. However, together with Trump's right-wing identity politics, itself a response to the discontent produced by neoliberal praxis, the new inflation scare stood in the way of forging any imagined Green New Deal-bloc.

In light of weak support for his domestic policies, Biden jumped at the chance to reinvent himself as leader of the democratic world against growing authoritarianism following Russia's invasion of Ukraine. The authoritarian world included not only Vladimir Putin and Xi Jinping but also his domestic rival Trump. While European allies, some more enthusiastically than others, and Japan closed ranks behind Biden, domestic support for US reinforcement of Ukraine was modest from the outset and has shown signs of decline as the war of attrition drags on. Biden's stance certainly didn't offer him the popularity boost he needed to become the face of a historical bloc, as Reagan had been the face of the emergent neoliberal bloc and Clinton the face of neoliberal triumph. Biden's enthusiastic turn to great power politics and war, moreover, triggered a fossil-fuel counterrevolution, from the oil companies to suburban commuters, that contrasts sharply with his rhetorical commitment to a green transition.

Underlying Biden's difficulties in drawing different layers of society into a historical bloc is the limited nature of his vision for a green transition. Relatively modest spending increases and industrial policies don't add up to a new regime of domestic accumulation, let alone one that could drive global accumulation and serve as a model for other countries, as had been the case with the Keynesian and neoliberal regimes, respectively. This incompleteness extends to the lack of designs for a replacement international economic order. Roosevelt's New Deal only became hegemonic once it adopted Keynesianism domestically and inserted this approach into a set of international organizations that facilitated the recovery of world trade and investment after its collapse at the onset of the Great Depression. Despite commitments to restore free trade and create room for developmentalism, this also meant that Keynesianism became part of a neocolonial order. The efforts of postcolonial regimes to overcome this order by creating the New International Economic Order, or to de-link from the capitalist world market entirely, were, along with domestic unrest and economic crises, a key factor inspiring capitalist classes to embrace the making of a neoliberal world order under US leadership.

The inability to rebuild US leadership after neoliberalism's fall into economic and legitimation crises over the current phase is not only obvious from Biden's problems forging a new historical bloc at home but also internationally. While the old imperialist centres and their new peripheries in Eastern Europe lined up behind Biden's leadership claims, a significant number of countries in the Global South, large and small, did not. This is indicative of the US failure to create a world after its own image as it did under New Deal and neoliberal hegemony. The reason the US is still on top is not a unique leadership ability but the fact that no alternative hegemonic bloc is in the making. Whatever the discontents of oppositional social layers within countries outside the US-dominated core, they are nowhere near forming such a bloc.

NOTES

1 Gary Gerstle, *The Rise and Fall of the Neoliberal Order: America and the World in the Free Market Era*, Oxford: Oxford University Press, 2022; Ingo Schmidt, 'Capital Accumulation and Class Struggles from the '"Long 19th Century" to the Present: A Luxemburgian Interpretation', *International Critical Thought*, 4(4), 2014, pp. 457-73; Ingo Schmidt, 'US-Kapitalismus von Reagan bis Trump', *SPW- Zeitschrift für Sozialistische Politik und Wirtschaft*, 242(1), 2021, pp. 37-46.

2 Robert Brenner, *The Economics of Global Turbulence*, London: Verso Books, 2006; Robert Eisner, *The Misunderstood Economy: What Counts and How to Count It*, Boston: Harvard Business School Press, 1994; Robert J. Gordon, *The Rise and Fall of American Growth*, Princeton, NJ: Princeton University Press, 2016; Thomas I. Palley, *Plenty of Nothing: The Downsizing of the American Dream and the Case for Structural Keynesianism*, Princeton, NJ: Princeton University Press, 1998; Leo Panitch and Sam Gindin, *The Making of Global Capitalism: The Political Economy of American Empire*, London: Verso Books, 2012; Robert Pollin, *Contours of Descent: US Economic Fractures and the Landscape of Global Austerity*, London: Verso Books, 2003.

3 Aaron Brenner, Robert Brenner and Cal Winslow, eds, *Rebel Rank and File: Labor Militancy and Revolt from Below During the Long 1970s*, London: Verso Books, 2010; Jefferson Cowie, *Stayin' Alive: The 1970s and the Last Days of the Working Class*, New York: The New Press, 2010, pp. 21-209; Nancy F. Gabin, *Feminism in the Labor Movement: Women and the United Auto Workers, 1935-1975*, Ithaca, NY: Cornell

University Press, 1990, pp. 188-228; Gerd-Rainer Horn, *The Spirit of '68: Rebellion in Western Europe and North America, 1956-1976,* Oxford: Oxford University Press, 2007; Jeremi Suri, *Power and Protest: Global Revolution and the Rise of Détente*, Cambridge, MA: Harvard University Press, 2003.

4 GDP Growth data from World Bank, available at: https://data.worldbank.org; Capital formation data from World Bank, available at: https://data.worldbank.org; Capacity utilization data from Macrotrends, available at: https://www.macrotrends.net; Labour productivity growth data from OECD, available at: https://stats.oecd.org; Unemployment data from Macrotrends, available at: https://www.macrotrends.net; Inflation data from Federal Reserve Bank of St Louis, available at: https://fred.stlouisfed.org.

5 Real interest rate and market capitalization to GDP data from Longtermtrends, available at : https://www.longtermtrends.net; Government debt to GDP data from Federal Reserve Bank of St Louis, available at: https://fred.stlouisfed.org; Household debt to GDP data from International Monetary Fund, available at: https://www.imf.org; Current account to GDP data from World Bank, available at: https://data.worldbank.org.

6 Fritz Bartel, *The Triumph of Broken Promises: The End of the Cold War and the Rise of Neoliberalism*, Cambridge, MA: Harvard University Press, 2022, pp. 110-33.

7 Thomas Frank, *One Market Under God: Extreme Capitalism, Market Populism and the End of Economic Democracy*, New York: Anchor Books, 2000; Ingo Schmidt, 'Market Populism, Its Right-Wing Offspring and Left Alternatives', in S. McBride, B. Evans and D. Plehwe, eds, *The Changing Politics and Policy of Austerity*, Bristol: Policy Press, 2021, pp. 195-212.

8 Arthur M. Okun, *Equality and Efficiency: The Big Trade-Off*, Washington, DC: Brookings Institution Press, 2015 (original publication 1974); Anne Krueger, 'The Political Economy of the Rent-Seeking Society', *American Economic Review*, 64(3), 1974, pp. 291-303.

9 Richard Saull, *The Cold War and After: Capitalism, Revolution and Superpower Politics*, London: Pluto Press, 2007, pp. 119-54; Odd Arne Westad, *The Global Cold War: Third World Interventions and the Making of Our Times*, Cambridge: Cambridge University Press, 2007, pp. 331-63.

10 Barry Eichengreen, *Exorbitant Privilege: The Rise and Fall of the Dollar and the Future of the International Monetary System*, Oxford: Oxford University Press, 2012.

11 Michael Cox, 'Whatever Happened to American Decline? International Relations and the New United States Hegemony', *New Political Economy*, 6(3), 2001, pp. 311-40.

12 Kenichi Ohmae, 'Managing in a Borderless World', *Harvard Business Review*, May-June 1989.

13 Stephen G Brooks, 'Can we identify a benevolent hegemon?', *Cambridge Review of International Affairs*, 25(1), pp. 27-38, 2012; John Bellamy Foster, *Naked Imperialism: The U.S. Pursuit of Global Dominance*, New York: Monthly Review Press, 2006.

14 Matthieu Auzanneau, *Oil Power and War*, London: Chelsea Green Publishing, 2018, pp. 319-88; John G. Clark, *The Political Economy of World Energy*, Chapel Hill, NC: University of North Carolina Press, 1990, pp. 230-356.

15 Raymond Vernon, 'International Investment and International Trade in the Product Cycle', *Quarterly Journal of Economics* 80(2), 1966, pp. 190-207.

16 Folker Fröbel, Jürgen Heinrichs and Otto Kreye, *The New International Division of Labour: Structural Unemployment in Industrialised Countries and Industrialisation in Developing Countries*, Cambridge: Cambridge University Press, 1980.

17 Eric Toussaint, *Your Money of Your Life: The Tyranny of Global Finance*, Chicago: Haymarket Books, 2005.

18 William K. Tabb, *Economic Governance in the Age of Globalization*, New York: Columbia University Press, 2004, pp. 289-330.

19 Leo Panitch and Sam Gindin, *The Making of Global Capitalism: The Political Economy of American Empire*, London: Verso Books, 2012, pp. 172-183.

20 Michel Husson, 'Riding the Long Wave', *Historical Materialism,* 5(1), 1999, pp. 77-102.

21 Colin Crouch, 'Privatised Keynesianism: An Unacknowledged Policy Regime', *The British Journal of Politics & International Relations*, 11(3), 2009, pp. 382-99.

22 John Smith, *Imperialism in the 21st Century: Globalization, Super-Exploitation, and Capitalism's Final Crisis*, New York: Monthly Review Press, 2016.

23 William J. Baumol, *The Cost Disease: Why Computers Get Cheaper and Health Care Doesn't*, New Haven, CT: Yale University Press, 2012, pp. 3-32; Richard D. Wolff, *Capitalism Hits the Fan: The Global Economic Meltdown and What to Do About It*, Northampton, MA: Olive Branch Press, 2010, pp. 135-48.

24 Doug Henwood, *After the New Economy*, New York: The New Press, 2003, pp. 187-226.

25 Frank Deppe, 'Habermas' Manifesto for a European Renaissance: A Critique', in Leo Panitch and Colin Leys, eds, *Socialist Register 2005*, London: Merlin Press, 2005, pp. 313-23.

26 William Ginn, 'World Output and Commodity Price Cycles', *International Economic Journal*, 37(4), 2023, pp. 530-54.

27 John Bellamy Foster and Fred Magdoff, *The Great Financial Crisis*, New York: Monthly Review Press, 2009.

28 Patrick Bond, 'East-West/North/South – or Imperial-Subimperial? The BRICS, Global Governance and Capital Accumulation', in: *Human Geography* 11(2), 2018, pp. 1-18. Martin Hart-Landsberg, ALBA and the Promise of Cooperative Development, *Monthly Review* 62(7), 2010, pp. 1-17; Ingo Schmidt, 'New Institutions, Old Ideas – The Passing Moment of the European Social Model', *Studies in Political Economy*, 84(1), 2009, pp. 7-28.

29 Andrew Hartman, *A War for the Soul of America: A History of the Culture Wars*, Chicago: University of Chicago Press, 2015.

30 Paul Krugman, *The Conscience of a Liberal*, New York: W.W. Norton Publishing, 2007; Robert Reich, *Aftershock: The Next Economy and America's Future,* New York: Alfred E. Knopf, 2010.

31 Fred Magdoff and Michael D. Yates, *The ABCs of the Economic Crisis: What Working People Need to Know*, New York: Monthly Review Press, 2009, pp. 89-104.

32 Kim Moody, *On New Terrain: How Capital is Reshaping the Battleground of Class War*, Chicago: Haymarket, 2017, pp. 37-57.

33 Jenny Clegg, *China's Global Strategy: Towards A Multipolar World,* London: Pluto Press, 2009. Ho-fung Hung, *The China Boom: Why China Will Not Rule the World*, New York: Columbia University Press, 2015.

34 Shawn Sprague, 'The US Productivity Slowdown: An Economy-wide and Industry-Level Analysis', *Monthly Labour Review*, April 2021, available at: www.bls.gov.
35 For data sources, see endnote 4.
36 Minqi Li, *China and the 21st Century Crisis*, London: Pluto Press, 2016, pp. 4-6.
37 For data sources, see endnote 5.
38 Sarah Lazare, 'Biden Continues Trump's Devastating Sanctions – Yellen's Treasury Department Misses a Chance for Reform', *The American Prospect*, 21 October 2021, available at: www.prospect.org; Philip A. Wallach and Kelly Kennedy, *Examining Some of Trump's Deregulation Efforts: Lessons From the Brookings Regulatory Tracker*, 8 March 2022, available at: www.brookings.edu.
39 Leo Panitch and Sam Gindin, 'Trumping the Empire', in Leo Panitch and Greg Albo, eds, *Socialist Register 2005*, London: Merlin Press, 2005, pp. 2-25.
40 Sam Gindin, 'Bidenomics and the Left', *The Bullet*, 29 October 2023, available at: www.socialistproject.ca; Samir Sonti, 'The Crisis of US Labour, Past and Present', in Greg Albo and Alfredo Saad-Filho, eds, *Socialist Register 2005*, London: Merlin Press, 2005, pp. 135-58.
41 Greg Iacurci, 'How Biden's $3.5 trillion economic plan compares to LBJ's Great Society and FDR's New Deal', *CNBC*, 2 October 2021, available at: www.cnbc.com.

THE US QUEST FOR NUCLEAR PRIMACY: THE COUNTERFORCE DOCTRINE AND THE IDEOLOGY OF MORAL ASYMMETRY

JOHN BELLAMY FOSTER

When I come to study in detail some of the arguments of these new military writers about nuclear war, I will necessarily have to adopt many aspects of their own methods and terminology, that is, I will have to meet them on the methodological ground of their own choosing. I want therefore to apologise in advance for the nauseating inhumanity of much of what I have to say. P.M.S. Blackett[1]

The demise of the Union of Soviet Socialist Republics (USSR) in 1991 resulted in Washington declaring at that very moment that a new unipolar world order was being ushered in with the United States now the sole superpower. The United States, supported by its NATO (North Atlantic Treaty Organization) allies, immediately initiated a grand strategy of regime-change or 'naked imperialism' in the Balkans, the Middle East, northern Africa, and along the entire perimeter of the former Soviet Union. This was accompanied by the rapid expansion of NATO itself eastward into the former Warsaw Pact countries and regions previously part of the USSR.[2] The pivotal goal in this expansion, as explained by former US National Security Adviser Zbigniew Brzezinski in *The Grand Chessboard*, was to incorporate Ukraine into NATO, which would create the geopolitical and geostrategic conditions for the final overpowering and forced breakup of the Russian Federation.[3]

Underlying this imperial design for the formation of a unipolar world order was Washington's effort to reestablish its absolute nuclear dominance of the early Cold War years, when it had an absolute nuclear monopoly (1945-49), followed by a period of quantitative nuclear superiority (1949-53) – prior to the Soviet Union achieving effective nuclear parity with the United States.[4] Attempts were made in the early 1960s during the John F. Kennedy administration to shift to *counterforce* (the targeting of Soviet nuclear weapons and command systems) as a means of re-establishing US nuclear hegemony. This, however, was soon abandoned as impractical at the time, and the US nuclear deterrence posture in the decades from the 1960s to the 1980s remained one of mutual assured destruction (MAD), in which nuclear weapons were targeted primarily at enemy cities, or *countervalue* targets. But with the disappearance of the USSR from the world stage in 1991, Washington abruptly abandoned MAD as its nuclear strategy, replacing it with counterforce, sometimes referred to as NUTS (after nuclear use theories or Nuclear Utilization Target Selection).[5] Ironically, the demise of the Soviet Union led in the United States (and NATO) to the triumph of the *maximum deterrence posture*, despite various strategic arms agreements, and to the seeming final defeat of those who had long argued for a *minimal deterrence posture*.[6]

Counterforce has as its objective nuclear primacy or first-strike capability, that is, the use of nuclear weapons for 'decapitating' the enemy's nuclear weapons before they can be launched (sometimes referred to as a 'true first strike').[7] Moreover, counterforce also lends itself to the idea of limited nuclear war and can therefore be seen as operating within a continuum that also includes nonstrategic or tactical nuclear weapons and conventional weapons, thus representing the full integration of nuclear weapons into military strategy at every level. Under MAD, resting on countervalue targeting, nuclear weapons were seen as *unusable* in promoting political and military ends (only to be employed in the case of massive retaliation), while the counterforce revolution initiated by Washington in the post-Cold War era was aimed precisely at making nuclear weapons *usable*.[8]

The long-running nuclear deterrence debate between *minimalists* (sometimes referred to as 'nuclear revolutionaries') such as Patrick Blackett, George Kennan, Bernard Brodie, and *maximalists* such as Albert Wohlstetter, Herman Kahn, Henry Kissinger, and Thomas Schelling, in what is sometimes referred to as the 'golden age' of nuclear deterrence strategy, rested primarily on the question of countervalue versus counterforce targeting.[9] For the minimalists, MAD, based on countervalue targeting and nuclear parity was the most stable condition of deterrence since no side could then hope to benefit from a nuclear war, creating a lasting nuclear stalemate. In contrast, *maximalists* argued for the development of a counterforce strategy aimed at nuclear primacy of the United States (and NATO) as the only stable solution to the problem of nuclear deterrence. The maximalist argument, as Blackett, the celebrated British socialist, Nobel prize-winning physicist, and founder of military operational research, demonstrated, derived its coherence from the assumption of 'moral asymmetry' between East and West, a position that represented the failure of reason.[10] It was Blackett's early critique of the maximum deterrence posture that constitutes the most penetrating theoretical challenge to the counterforce doctrine up to the present day.[11]

The coincidence of declining US hegemony in the world economy, with the US attempt to secure unipolar dominance by military means, in line with its current policy of maximal deterrence by means of counterforce and nuclear primacy, has all come to a head in the current proxy war in Ukraine between the United States/NATO and Russia, and in the increasing tensions over Taiwan between the United States and the People's Republic of China. The ongoing conflicts over Ukraine and Taiwan constitute the main hot spots in the New Cold War emanating from Washington, involving actual and potential proxy war on the very borders of superpowers. This has enormously increased the likelihood of global thermonuclear war. This in turn poses the threat of global omnicide with the onset of nuclear winter, as smoke and soot from all-encompassing fires in 100 cities blocks solar radiation, lowering global temperatures, resulting within a couple of years in the effective annihilation of the global population.[12]

THE CRITIQUE OF MAXIMUM DETERRENCE

With the demise of the Soviet Union the maximalists were able to achieve complete dominance over the minimalists within establishment circles, marked by the first US 'Nuclear Posture Review' in 1994.[13] Nevertheless, the critique of maximum deterrence that arose in the preceding decades, and which has been closely tied to the world peace movements, needs to be unearthed and resurrected in the nuclear crisis of our times.

The greatest critique of the doctrine of maximum deterrence in the 'golden age' of nuclear deterrence was launched by Blackett in his 1948 book, *Fear, War, and the Bomb: Military and Political Consequences of Atomic Energy*, which appeared almost simultaneously with the announcement of his receiving the Nobel Prize in physics for his experimental work in nuclear physics.[14] That book was followed by two others on nuclear weapons strategy: *Atomic Weapons and East-West Relations* (1956) and *Studies of War: Nuclear and Conventional* (1962).

Blackett was a leading British socialist thinker, part of the social relations of science movement associated with J.D. Bernal, and a close colleague of British socialists including Bernal, J. B. S. Haldane, C. H. Waddington, and Solly Zuckerman.[15] Blackett was president of the left-wing Association of Scientific Workers from 1943-1947. He was also a close friend of the physicist Robert Oppenheimer in the United States, who headed the Manhattan Project.[16] In his 1935 essay 'The Frustration of Science', in a book by the same name – a volume to which Bernal also contributed, and which had a foreword by Frederick Soddy – Blackett argued for 'complete socialism' and declared that capitalism was a 'retrograde movement' that shaded over into fascism. He had great admiration for the achievements of the Soviet Union in the realms of science and industry.[17]

Like a number of other left scientists – notably Bernal, Haldane, and Zuckerman – Blackett, who had served in the British navy, was a leading figure in the formation of British military strategy during the Second World War. He was the 'father' of the field of military operational research. He played a critical role in developing the radar chain that was to prove the key weapon in the air war, known as the Battle of Britain, and in organizing anti-aircraft defences. His greatest achievement in the war, however, was in 'helping devise the convoy system to deal with the [German] U-boat offensive in the Atlantic'.[18]

In August 1945, British Prime Minister Clement Attlee appointed Blackett to the newly established Advisory Committee on Atomic Energy. He was also appointed to the Chief of Staff Committee on Future Weapons. Blackett strongly opposed British development of nuclear weapons and supported a policy of neutrality toward the Soviet Union. With the termination of the Advisory Committee in 1947, he engaged publicly in the debate over the use of nuclear weapons.[19]

In *Fear, War, and the Bomb* Blackett dealt with the decision of the United States to drop the atomic bombs on Hiroshima and Nagasaki. Here it was argued for the first time that 'the dropping of the atomic bombs was not so much the last military act of the Second World War, as the first major operation of the cold diplomatic war with Russia now in progress'. The Japanese had already offered to negotiate peace terms, while a US invasion of Japan was still in the planning stage and was not to take place for some time. Rather than a result of the need 'to save American lives', as is commonly claimed, the haste in dropping the bomb on Hiroshima on 6 August 1945, and then a second bomb on Nagasaki three days later, had to do with the fact that the Soviet Union was preparing to enter the war against Japan on 8 August, commencing their offensive in Manchuria, on 9 August. The US objective, Blackett explained, was thus to force an unconditional Japanese surrender before the Soviets could advance very far into Manchuria, and to ensure that the Japanese surrender was to the United States alone.[20]

Blackett's analysis was subjected to heavy criticism in a forum on the book in the *Bulletin of Atomic Scientists*, but received support from the Manhattan Project physicist Philip Morrison, who indicated that the scientists responsible for making the bomb were pushed to meet a 'mysterious' deadline in which it was to be ready by 'a date near August tenth'.²¹ The proposition that the dropping of the atomic bombs was not, in reality, the last act of the Second World War, but rather the first act in the Cold War was to be verified in later historical studies by figures such as Gar Alperovitz and Robert Jay Lifton.²²

Blackett showed in *Fear, War and the Bomb* that there was strong sentiment initially in strategic circles in the United States for using the atomic bomb on Soviet cities in a first strike, since the USSR did not at that time have the bomb and was not expected to develop it and have a stockpile until 1953. In 1948 Winston Churchill had argued for threatening the Soviet Union with a preventative nuclear war. Nevertheless, Blackett, seeking to promote sanity, argued at the time that from a military standpoint atomic bombs, however devastating, could not defeat the Soviet Union, any more than strategic bombing had been effective against Germany. The Soviet Union had a large conventional military, and in the event of a US/NATO nuclear first strike, would almost certainly overrun Europe.

By the time Blackett wrote *Atomic Weapons and East-West Relations* the situation had changed entirely. The Soviet Union had its first atomic weapons test in August 1949, a mere four years after the US atom-bombed Hiroshima and Nagasaki. In August 1953, the USSR carried out its first hydrogen bomb test, less than a year after the United States. At that time, the Soviet Union had achieved effective nuclear parity with the United States in everything but delivery. It was at this point that the nuclear deterrence debate took off in earnest. Blackett insisted on the importance of the strategic stalemate between the United States and the Soviet Union:

> Today strategical atomic weapons have not only cancelled themselves out and so made all-out total war exceedingly unlikely, but have finally abolished the possibility of victory by air power alone against a great power ... I think we should act as if atomic and hydrogen bombs have abolished total war and concentrate our efforts on working out how few atomic bombs and their carriers are required to keep it abolished.

Recognizing that NATO was relying on tactical nuclear weapons as a response to the Soviet Union's larger conventional force, together with the European disinclination to go to the expense of equalling it, Blackett saw such nonstrategic nuclear weapons as a major problem. His answer was to consider a policy of using 'no atomic bombs at all—not even on the battlefield'.²³ He came out firmly against US maximalist doctrine of 'graduated deterrence' or the notion of the *use* of nuclear war at various levels of escalation, stretching from battlefield use all the way to a true first strike, in order to achieve political and military objectives.[24]

Blackett was strongly supportive of Oppenheimer, who by that time had come under attack in the McCarthyite atmosphere in the United States. He explained that Oppenheimer's initial concrete opposition to the hydrogen bomb had been based on its poor design. But Oppenheimer's subsequent deeper opposition, and that of the Manhattan Project scientists more broadly, was a response to the way in which the atomic bomb had been used, unnecessarily, in the war. As Blackett pointed out, 'There is a little-noticed passage in the Hearings. When Oppenheimer was asked when his opposition to the H-bomb started, he replied, "I think it was when I realized that this country would tend to use any weapon they had"'.[25]

Despite his enormous prestige as a Nobel laureate in physics and as the founder of military operational research, Blackett's attempt to promote a rational, minimalist deterrence strategy and for downplaying or even removing nuclear weapons resulted in Cold War-style attacks on him as a Communist fellow traveller. He was 'the most outspoken and the most vilified of British scientists who opposed American and British nuclear policies from the mid-1940s to around 1960'.[26] George Orwell put Blackett on his secret blacklist of crypto communists, though he apparently did not know who Blackett was, characterizing him incorrectly as a 'scientific populariser'. The Cold War sociologist Edward Shils wrote an article for the *Bulletin of the Atomic Scientists* entitled 'Blackett's Apologia for the Soviet Position', calling Blackett's careful analysis in *Fear, War and the Bomb* 'a gift to Soviet propaganda'.[27] Both MI5 in Britain and the FBI in the United States had him under surveillance, with MI5 recording all of his phone calls but discovering nothing. Blackett was attacked in *Scientific American* for having a 'pro-Soviet prejudice'.[28] Nevertheless, it was impossible to ignore Blackett or to set him entirely aside due to his enormous credibility both in scientific and military circles, his cogent arguments on nuclear deterrence, and his direct confrontation with nuclear maximalists such as Wohlstetter, Kahn, and Henry Kissinger.

The first part of Blackett's *Studies of War* on nuclear deterrence consisted of essays that he had written between 1948 and 1962, the earlier ones overlapping with his first two books on the subject. However, *Studies of War* also included essays written on nuclear strategy between 1958 and 1962. During this period, between the Soviet launching of Sputnik in 1957 and the Cuban Missile Crisis of 1962, the nuclear debate had intensified. Especially notable was Blackett's 1961 article 'Critique of Some Contemporary Defence Thinking' which constituted his most important contribution to what is known as the Blackett-Wohlstetter debate, representing the minimalist versus maximalist views on nuclear war.[29] Although Blackett's earlier work on nuclear deterrence had caused him to be characterized as an 'atomic heretic', *Studies of War*, appearing around the time of the Cuban Missile Crisis, was received favourably in higher circles in the West as well as the general public and was seen as representing the nuclear consensus of the time.[30] Maximalists in subsequent years therefore set the overturning of Blackett's analysis as one of their principal objects in their campaign to make nuclear weapons usable.

In 'Critique of Some Contemporary Defence Thinking' and in other essays in *Studies of War*, Blackett offered a classic *critique* in the sense of German philosophy and Marxian theory, in which the inner logic and contradictions of the maximalist position on nuclear weapons were shown to represent the irrationalist destruction of reason. He argued that Soviet nuclear parity with the United States had created a nuclear stalemate in which the use of nuclear weapons against another similarly armed nuclear nation was unthinkable 'by any nation that wanted to survive'.[31] His argument was directed against three of the main maximalist thinkers: Kissinger, Kahn, and Wohlstetter. Kissinger's *Nuclear Weapons and Foreign Policy* (1957) argued against then current policy of reliance on MAD, and instead advocated that the United States develop nonstrategic or tactical nuclear weapons that could be used for limited nuclear war and would be available as an extension of politics.[32]

Kissinger's position was strongly rejected by Blackett and by the leading US minimalist thinker, George Kennan, best known as the developer of the US Cold War 'containment' strategy. Blackett pointed out that Kissinger's argument was predicated on the West unilaterally deploying tactical nuclear weapons that could be directed against Soviet conventional forces, with Europe East and West as the battleground. According to Kissinger, NATO could use tactical nuclear weapons in a first strike with the expectation that the Soviets would not respond with massive retaliation, and thus endanger their own country. Moreover, in such a limited nuclear war, Kissinger argued, Western soldiers would be superior in their use of tactical nuclear weapons, as compared with the Soviets, even if the latter were to develop such capabilities – a view that Blackett referred to as 'plain poppycock'. Indeed, 'the initiation by the West of tactical nuclear war might either hasten military defeat, or lead to the destruction of Europe by H-bombs—or both'.[33] Blackett opposed those like Kahn, who, in works such as *On Thermonuclear War* (1960) and *Thinking About the Unthinkable* (1962), argued that a nuclear war could be won and survived through such measures as civil defence. Blackett retorted that civil defence in a nuclear war was impracticable.[34]

Kahn coined the distinction between 'countervalue' and 'counterforce'.[35] With the emergence of nuclear parity between the United States and the Soviet Union and the dominance of MAD, which declared nuclear weapons unusable, the maximalists devoted all their efforts to arguing that any nuclear balance was unstable and that the only answer for the United States was the development of counterforce weapons aimed at a first-strike capability or nuclear primacy. The leading advocate of this position in the early 1960s was Wohlstetter who, like Kahn, Schelling, and other maximalists, was employed by the RAND Corporation.

The key work launching the case that MAD was unstable and arguing for the United States to switch to a counterforce strategy was Wohlstetter's 'The Delicate Balance of Terror', published in the Council on Foreign Relations' publication *Foreign Affairs* in 1959.[36] Wohlstetter heavily criticized Blackett and others who argued that 'mutual extinction' was 'the only outcome' of a general nuclear war, thus adopting the MAD position. Instead, Wohlstetter argued that counterforce attack or first strike could theoretically eliminate the ability of the other side to carry out a second strike, thus raising the question of the 'survivability' of the nuclear second-strike capability in the nation attacked. A first strike could thus be seen, in Wohlstetter's view, as a 'sane' policy for an attacker. This then required the United States to pursue first-strike capability or nuclear primacy, and the modernization of nuclear weapons for greater accuracy and maximum deterrence. Subtly built into Wohlstetter's argument, but constituting the whole basis for his claim that the current nuclear parity was unstable, was the presumption the Soviets would not be deterred by ten million or even more deaths since they had suffered 20 million deaths in the Second World War. Moreover, Wohlstetter's whole case relied on the assumption that there was what Blackett labelled in his critique a 'moral asymmetry' between the United States and the Soviet Union, in which US nuclear primacy represented no danger to the USSR, while Russian nuclear parity represented a very real threat of a nuclear attack on the United States.[37]

Blackett's response to Wohlstetter was devastating. The noted British military historian Michael Howard called it a 'ferocious critique'.[38] Using arithmetical examples he pointed to the fact that true first-strike capability would require the destruction, not simply of 90 per cent of the nuclear weapons on the other side – itself an impossibility given the technical problems involved, the number of targets, the near-automatic push-button responses of the other side, and the immense intelligence difficulties – but would in fact require a 99 per cent destruction of the opposing nuclear forces, and even that would not be enough if mega-deaths were to be avoided on the side of the attacker as well as the attacked. Hence, increased accuracy would not obviate 'the essential insanity of a first-strike policy'. Blackett pointed out that Wohlstetter believed that a US first strike on the Soviet Union would have been sane at the time that the United States had a nuclear monopoly or even when it simply had nuclear superiority. For those like Wohlstetter, the goal was to reestablish the basis for such a 'sane' first strike.[39]

Most important was Blackett's criticism of Wohlstetter's notion of the 'moral asymmetry' between the United States and the USSR. As Wohlstetter wrote, 'they [the Soviets] make sensible strategic choices and we do not', meaning they would undoubtedly use nuclear superiority (or even nuclear parity) as a basis for a nuclear attack to achieve their ends, but the United States would not, due to its higher morality.[40]

In response, Blackett stated, 'Wohlstetter's doctrine seems to be that the West must plan on the enemy's capability, but the USSR should plan on the West's intentions', which are assumed to be benign. By 'introducing a large and arbitrary degree of moral asymmetry between the two contestants' as a 'methodological device', Wohlstetter, according to Blackett, saw 'the period 1954 to 1957 [when Russia "had no effective power of hitting America at all" with missiles] ... to be a safe period because, though America had a large nuclear superiority, she was pacific, while the present time is dangerous because this superiority is less and the USSR is aggressive'.[41] It was this kind of dangerous logic, Blackett insisted, that was behind demands of the maximalists that the United States should attempt 'to regain a first counter-force capability by improved missiles and reconnaissance satellites'.[42]

Arguing strenuously for 'the policy of the minimum deterrence', Blackett insisted that 'enough is enough'.[43] However, if the maximalists were to have their way and get Washington to pursue counterforce or first-strike capability, the Soviet Union and China would have to respond at a certain point by taking actions to ensure the survivability of their deterrence as a matter of pure defence, which would then set off an endless nuclear arms race and increase the dangers of a nuclear war.[44] He was sharply critical of those at RAND, like Schelling, who used game theory as a way of creating false scenarios of limited nuclear warfare and counterforce strategies in the irrational pursuit of continuing nuclear modernization spending. In 1962, Blackett again raised the issue of nuclear disarmament, which, he suggested, would have to be done on an extremely large scale or would be ineffective.[45]

In the 1980s, the Jimmy Carter and Ronald Reagan administrations attempted to place nuclear-armed cruise missiles and Pershing II missiles in Europe, ostensibly in response to the Soviet SS-20 – a more survivable intermediate-range missile that was seen as reducing NATO's first-strike capability.⁴⁶ The US response was introducing new counterforce missiles with Europe as the base of operations. This was coupled with the US plan to introduce the Strategic Defense Initiative (SDI), better known as Star Wars, an overall missile defence system. This too was only meaningful in terms of a first strike or counterforce attack. The result was the development of an enormous anti-nuclear movement in Europe, in which the Marxist historian E. P. Thompson played a major role as the leading spokesperson for European Nuclear Disarmament (END).⁴⁷ In the United States, these developments generated the nuclear freeze movement. In this context, Wohlstetter once again sought to criticize Blackett, who had died in 1974, for his criticisms of maximum deterrence and game theory. Zuckerman responded by referring back to Blackett's issue of moral asymmetry embedded in the work of Wohlstetter and all the other US counterforce strategists.⁴⁸

THE US PURSUIT OF NUCLEAR PRIMACY: FROM 1991 TO NOW

It is one of the great ironies of our time that the demise of the Soviet Union and the end of the Cold War led to the immediate triumph of the maximum deterrence doctrine in Washington and the pursuit of nuclear primacy through the development of counterforce capabilities. Despite nuclear arms agreements initially put into place and reductions in nuclear warheads, the basic structure of nuclear forces was left intact, while Washington saw this as a chance to secure global nuclear primacy or true first-strike capability, and thus absolute nuclear dominance. 'Minimum deterrence', according to Lawrence Freedman and Jeffrey Michaels in their classic work *The Evolution of Nuclear Strategy*, 'still had its supporters but they constituted a minority', and were greatly weakened.⁴⁹ The way was then open to the initiation of a full counterforce strategy. As Janne E. Nolan of the Arms Control Association declared, 'counterforce remains the sacrosanct principle of American nuclear strategy'.⁵⁰

Since the US nuclear strategy is based on counterforce, building the capability for a first strike arriving as a 'bolt from the blue', with anti-missile systems picking off the few weapons that survive, it requires the unification of 'offensive' and 'defensive' nuclear weapons.⁵¹ The overall goal is ensuring the *non-survivability* of command-and-control centres and nuclear weapon systems on the other side. Anti-ballistic missile systems, which are regarded as practically useless in defending against a full-scale first strike, are not mainly defensive weapons, but are meant to ensure that those few nuclear weapons in the country attacked that manage to survive in the face of a first strike are picked off before they can reach their targets. Hence, nuclear missile defence systems are chiefly intended to enhance first-strike capability.[52]

Faced with the prospect of a first strike, there are only four ways in which a nuclear power can protect its deterrent: (1) *redundancy* of such weapons since the more targets there are the more difficult it is for an attacker to carry out a successful first strike; (2) *hardening* missile silos to protect the strategic deterrent from incoming missiles; (3) *hiding* the nuclear weapons, by means of submarine-based nuclear weapons and mobile ground-based missiles/missile launchers; and (4) (most questionable of all) reliance on *doomsday machines* where a massive retaliation can be set off at a moment's notice, almost automatically, with only bare human intervention.[53]

With these conditions in mind, it is possible to understand the otherwise seemingly contradictory actions of Washington with respect to nuclear arms control and development since the demise of the Soviet Union. A big emphasis has been placed by all US presidents, from Reagan to Joe Biden, on developing nuclear missile defence systems, seen as crucial to an effective counterforce strategy. The George H. W. Bush administration, while moving away from Reagan's Star Wars, chose to promote the 'Global Protection Against Limited Strikes' program. This was pushed forward by the Bill Clinton administration, which offered a scheme for National Missile Defense. However, missile defence systems could not be put into operation while the United States remained bound to the 1972 Anti-Ballistic Missile Treaty, which led to the George W. Bush administration's unilateral withdrawal from the treaty in 2002. In 2007, the Bush administration decided to expand its two missile defence sites in California and Alaska and add a 'Third Site' in Europe, under the cover of protecting Europe from Iran (a non-nuclear power), but the Russians naturally understood this as directed at them. In 2008, this system was integrated with the general NATO defence missile system. The Barack Obama administration revised this plan by placing missile defence systems aimed at longer-range ballistic missiles (yet also capable of launching offensive nuclear-armed missiles) in Poland and Romania.[54]

At the same time, as missile defence systems were being introduced in Europe, stockpiles of nuclear warheads held by the United States and Russia were reduced.[55] Nevertheless, in 2023 the United States still had 5,244 strategic nuclear warheads, France 290, the United Kingdom 225, and Russia (seeking to match all three NATO nuclear powers) 5,889. China, meanwhile, had 410.[56]

Washington's reductions in the number of nuclear warheads, in line with parallel reductions by Moscow, although seemingly reducing nuclear tensions conformed to its overall counterforce strategy, given that redundancy in the sheer numbers of such weapons is one of the main means of ensuring the survival of a nuclear deterrent. Coupled with the modernization of its nuclear weapons systems for greater accuracy, and enhanced means of detection of nuclear submarines and mobile ground-based missiles, the United States was able to move rapidly toward its goal of nuclear primacy. According to Cynthia Roberts of the Saltzman Institute of War and Peace at Columbia University, 'Russians perceive further US improvements to strategic forces, both conventional and nuclear, as part of a continuous effort to stalk Russia's nuclear deterrent and deny Moscow a viable second-strike option', with the objective of effectively eliminating its nuclear deterrent through 'decapitation'.[57]

In 2006 nuclear analysts globally were startled by the appearance in *Foreign Affairs*, the flagship publication of the Council of Foreign Relations, of an article by Keir A. Lieber and Daryl G. Press entitled 'The Rise of U.S. Nuclear Primacy'.[58] Lieber and Press indicated that the United States had been in pursuit of true first-strike capability since the end of the Cold War and was now 'on the verge of attaining nuclear primacy ... Unless Washington's policies change or Moscow and Beijing take steps to increase the size and readiness of their forces, Russia and China—and the rest of the world—will live in the shadow of US nuclear primacy for many years to come'. Indeed, 'the weight of the evidence', they wrote, 'suggests that Washington is, in fact, deliberately seeking nuclear primacy'.[59]

The United States, Lieber and Press contended, had already obtained nuclear primacy in relation to China, which could not then protect either its hardened missile silos or its nuclear submarines (due to noise level, though this was being reduced), and was near to having a credible first-strike capability in relation to Russia as well. Weapons such as nuclear-armed cruise missiles, nuclear submarines able to fire their far more accurate missiles with low-yield warheads near the shore, and low-lying B-2 stealth bombers and stealth fighters carrying cruise missiles and nuclear gravity bombs could more effectively eliminate hardened missile silos. More advanced remote sensing technology, in which the United States had the lead, had greatly enhanced its ability to detect and target mobile land-based missiles and nuclear submarines.[60] The extension east of NATO made it possible to place nuclear weapons systems (including missile defence systems) much closer to Moscow. The increased accuracy of US missiles and guided gravity bombs, moreover, means that the nuclear weapons of target countries are increasingly vulnerable to conventional weapons with non-nuclear warheads.[61]

The announcement that the United States was, at least theoretically, on the verge of having first-strike capability set off alarms in Russia and

China, leading to massive new efforts to protect the survivability of their nuclear weapons and measures to defend against a counterforce strategy through the development of new hypersonic missile technology, which could elude anti-ballistic missile systems. China has referred to this as an 'assassin's mace', a weapon chiefly advantageous to those challenging a more powerful opponent.[62] In 2007, alarmed by the US attempt to obtain nuclear primacy and the related expansion of NATO, Russian President Vladimir Putin unequivocally declared that there would be no unipolar world.[63] Nevertheless, NATO in 2008 both declared that it intended to bring Ukraine into NATO and went forward with its plans to place missile defence systems in Poland and Romania. The Aegis Ballistic Missile Defense facilities that were installed in these countries are also potential offensive weapons capable of launching nuclear-armed tomahawk cruise missiles.[64]

The United States, through NATO, has always relied on a first-strike strategy based on both nonstrategic and strategic nuclear weapons, forming the core of NATO's defence, first against the Soviet Union's conventional forces, and then against those of Russia, under the umbrella of US 'extended deterrence'.[65] Although the Soviet Union, like China today, had a no-first-strike policy, while post-Soviet Russia has declared that it will only use nuclear weapons in a first strike if the Russian state/territory is directly threatened, all US presidents down to the present office-holder have reconfirmed US first-strike policy.[66] For Washington, nuclear weapons (both strategic and tactical) are 'on the table' all over the world, even in some cases against non-nuclear powers, a policy reinforced by the imperial outreach of the United States, which maintains at least eight hundred military bases abroad.[67] Although Obama had declared in his race to the presidency that he intended to seek 'a world in which there are no nuclear weapons', he adopted a more maximalist position upon entering the White House, while rejecting a no-first-strike pledge.[68] The deputy assistant secretary for nuclear and missile defence policy in the Obama administration placed in charge of writing the 2010 'Nuclear Posture Review' was Brad Roberts, a nuclear hawk deeply committed to a strategy of nuclear first use. The 2010 'Nuclear Posture Review' 'reaffirmed a doctrine of counterforce and rejected changing to focus on counter-value targets'. Shortly after leaving the administration, Roberts published *The Case for U.S. Nuclear Weapons in the 21st Century*, which argued that the United States should be ready and willing to engage in nuclear warfighting at every level. The Obama administration initiated a thirty-year $1 trillion upgrade in US nuclear weapons in line with counterforce strategy.[69]

In 2014, the United States backed the Maidan colour revolution/coup in Ukraine, which removed the democratically elected president Viktor

Yanukovych. This led to a civil war in Ukraine between the government in Kyiv controlled by NATO-backed Ukrainian nationalists, on the one hand, and Russian-speaking separatists in the Donbas region, supported by Russia, on the other. In 2022, Russia, after NATO continually ignored its red lines, firmly intervened on the side of the separatists. Faced with a US/NATO proxy war in Ukraine, Russia was to put its nuclear forces on alert.[70] Suddenly, a global thermonuclear exchange endangering the entire global population with annihilation (via nuclear winter) became an imminent threat.

The Trump administration, meanwhile, had unilaterally withdrawn from the Intermediate Nuclear Forces Treaty in 2019 and from the Open Skies Treaty in 2020. Unilateral withdrawal from these treaties was favourable to Washington in allowing it to further develop its counterforce capabilities. Louisiana Tech Research Institute's *Guide to Nuclear Deterrence in the Age of Great Power Competition* (2020), written by nuclear arms experts for the around 30,000 members of the US Air Force Global Strike force and 700,000 airmen all told, declared that 'the United States has never been content with a mere second-strike capability', and was prepared for a first strike and winning a nuclear war as part of its maximum deterrence posture.[71]

In early January 2023, the United States cleared the C-17A Air Force transport plane for shipping B61-12 nuclear bombs to Europe in a more rapid introduction of the bombs than originally scheduled.[72] The B61-12 nuclear bomb has been designated by *National Interest* as 'the most dangerous nuclear weapon in America's arsenal', because it is the *most usable*, serving the dual purposes of a strategic nuclear weapon capable of a counterforce first strike against hardened missile silos while also doubling as a tactical nuclear battlefield weapon.[73]

The B61-12, although part of the B61 class of nuclear bombs first introduced after the Cuban Missile Crisis, is a new weapon in that, in the words of Hans Kristensen, a nuclear weapons expert at the Federation of American Scientists, is 'the first U.S. guided nuclear gravity bomb', with a guided tail kit assembly that gives it much greater accuracy (a warhead twice as accurate and eight times more lethal). Existing US nuclear bombs have circular error probabilities (CEP) of between 110–170 metres, while the B61-12 has a CEP of 30 metres. It is considered a 'low-yield' nuclear weapon. However, it has an upper-level yield three times that of the atomic bomb the United States dropped on Hiroshima. It also has an earth-penetrating capability, meaning that it can explode underground. Launched against an underground target, its destructiveness in relation to its target, according to the International Campaign to Abolish Nuclear Weapons is 'the equivalent of a surface-burst weapon with a yield of 1,250 kilotons—[i.e.,] the equivalent of 83 Hiroshima bombs', making it an extraordinarily powerful first-strike weapon.[74]

The B61-12 is also a 'dial-a-yield' weapon where the explosive yield can be dialled down to 0.3 kilotons or up as high as 50 kilotons, hence being considered a 'tactical' as well as 'strategic' nuclear weapon to be delivered to its targets by fighter jets, such as the F-35 stealth fighter, as well as by strategic bombers. The United States is using it to replace its current nuclear weapons in Europe. As a more 'usable' nuclear weapon, which is also considered a battlefield weapon, the B61-12 is altering the nuclear threshold in Europe. According to Russia, the B61-12 is particularly threatening due to proximity to Russian targets. Although Russia has 2,000 tactical nuclear weapons, these are all currently in storage, while the new B61-12 bombs are to be deployed (representing the only deployed tactical nuclear weapons anywhere in the world) and located in Italy, Germany, Turkey, Belgium, and the Netherlands, 'just a short flight from Russia's borders'. Poland, which has just obtained the F-35 fighter, is now requesting that B61-12 bombs also be located on its territory.[75] In the event of war, according to NATO's nuclear sharing agreement, the United States could release the nuclear weapons to the individual nations.

The Trump administration's 2018 US 'National Defense Strategy' was written largely by the anti-China hawk Elbridge A. Colby, then deputy assistant secretary of defense for strategy and force development. It focused on China as the principal strategic threat to the United States (a position later adopted by the Biden administration) and stipulated that US first-strike policy would allow nuclear weapons to be used against an undetermined cyber-attack. Moreover, for the first time ever, the preparation for limited nuclear war was formally integrated into US nuclear grand strategy. Colby is most famous for his ultra-aggressive 'strategy of denial' toward China, promoted by his Marathon Initiative think tank. This includes scenarios for the US use of counterforce nuclear weapons in a conflict over Taiwan. The logic of US policy with respect to Taiwan, including that of both of the dominant political parties, thus points to crossing China's red lines, again threatening the entire world.[76]

Since its first nuclear test in 1964, China has had an unambiguous position that it 'will never at any time under any circumstances be the first to use nuclear weapons'.[77] Unlike the United States and Russia, China's nuclear weapons are kept on off-alert status, with the warheads not mated with the missiles, although it now has one nuclear submarine at sea at all times.[78] Its nuclear weapons are deliberately geared to MAD without the accuracy needed for counterforce. According to Benjamin C. Jamison, currently a lieutenant colonel in the US Air Force, serving in the nuclear enterprise division of the US European Command, China's nuclear 'arsenal exclusively includes large megaton and inaccurate weapons that are best suited for a countervalue targeting strategy'. It has not sought nuclear parity with the United States and Russia. China's 'goal remains the preservation of a survivable second-strike option. Technologically and resource wise, there is no reason China could not build a nuclear force to rival the United States or Russia, but they just choose not to'.[79] Consistent with this, China has refrained from developing an arsenal of tactical nuclear weapons.[80] China insists that no nation should place nuclear weapons in another state. Nevertheless, with the US focused on first-strike capability, China has recently entered into modernization and expansion of its nuclear arsenal aimed at the survivability of its second-strike capability. The most recent US defence documents indicate that China has managed to retain a lean, survivable second-strike nuclear deterrent.[81]

None of this, however, has altered the West's quest for nuclear primacy. 'At the nuclear level, missile defences and precision strike', Norwegian political scientist Even Hellan Larsen wrote June 2023, 'render total pre-emption of nuclear retaliation a realistic prospect'. In other words, committing itself to a strategy of a first strike against other nuclear powers can be seen as a 'rational' policy on the part of the main counterforce power, the United States/NATO.[82]

US HEGEMONIC DECLINE AND THE THREAT OF NUCLEAR ARMAGEDDON

US nuclear strategists and military planners, nearly all of whom today are maximalists, do not, as a rule, refer in any of their analyses to the full effects of global thermonuclear exchange, even when a full-scale nuclear war is contemplated. Thus, there is no mention of nuclear winter, which would annihilate almost the entire global human population, even though this has been affirmed over and over in scientific studies.[83] More often, US military planners today contend that a first-strike counterforce strategy with relatively 'low-yield' strategic nuclear weapons (though generally greater in yield than the atomic bombs dropped on Hiroshima and Nagasaki) can decapitate the second-strike capability of the other side, through a bolt from the blue, eliminating the possibility of a massive retaliation. Accompanying this are plans for limited nuclear war that presume that the country being attacked will be able to distinguish between a partial attack and a true first strike and can be counted on to respond in a similarly 'limited' manner, without a threat of escalation. Again and again, however, these assumptions, though governing US nuclear strategy, have been shown to be false and irrational. The dangerous reality that maximalist nuclear analyses conveniently ignore is best depicted by Daniel Ellsberg, himself once a nuclear strategist for RAND Corporation:

> The United States and Russia each have an actual Doomsday Machine. It is not the same relatively cheap system that Herman Kahn envisioned (or Stanley Kubrick portrayed) ... But a counterpart nevertheless exists for each country: a very expensive system of men, machines, electronics, communications, institutions, plans, training, discipline, practices, and doctrine—which, under conditions of electronic warning, external conflict, or expectations of attack, would with unknowable but possibly high probability bring about the global destruction of civilization and nearly all human life on earth.[84]

Today, the US proxy war in Ukraine on the Russian border and Washington's threatening behaviour towards Beijing over Taiwan (recognized by the entire world as part of China, but with a different government) have brought the issue of a general thermonuclear exchange to the forefront of world concern. As Robert S. McNamara wrote in 2005 in 'Apocalypse Soon', 'to launch weapons against a nuclear-equipped opponent would be suicidal. To do so against a nonnuclear enemy would be militarily unnecessary, morally repugnant, and politically indefensible.' The idea that 'nuclear weapons could be used in some limited way' is 'fundamentally flawed, since the effects on civilians cannot be contained, while 'there is no guarantee against unlimited escalation once the first nuclear strike occurs'.[85]

Blackett, however, remains the single greatest critic of the maximalist nuclear strategy. For Howard, writing in 1984:

> [Blackett's] views would now be labelled by [Western] strategic theorists as 'minimal deterrence' or MAD (mutually assured destruction) and considered so primitive as to be hardly worth taking into account. To my mind, however, they remain as valid today as they were 20 years ago: the only basis on which both an acceptable defence policy and a credible arms-control policy can be based.[86]

Five elements of Blackett's critique stand out: First, a counterforce first-strike against other major nuclear nations is strategically, operationally, and mathematically impossible to accomplish without megadeaths on both sides. Hence, all dreams of nuclear primacy are dangerous illusions. Second, limited nuclear war using tactical or nonstrategic nuclear weapons would soon escalate out of control. Third, all Western arguments for maximum nuclear deterrence, rejecting the idea of a nuclear stalemate, rely on notion of moral asymmetry in order to justify the pursuit of nuclear primacy. Fourth, all nations need to adopt a no-first-strike posture. Fifth, nuclear weapons should be restricted to countervalue targets, which is also the only basis from which nuclear disarmament can proceed.

It is significant that today the only major nuclear nation that has implemented all of Blackett's precepts is the People's Republic of China. The very fact that China, both in its nuclear doctrine and practice, has adhered strictly to a minimalist line on nuclear weapons suggests that this is also possible for other nuclear nations.

In contrast, the US maximalist nuclear strategy, going against all of Blackett's precepts, is justified today in nuclear deterrence circles in terms of a supposed moral asymmetry that places the United States uniquely above other nations. It is commonly argued by US nuclear strategists that the powerful 'taboo' created by the US dropping of the atomic bombs on Hiroshima and Nagasaki makes it 'unlikely that the United States would employ a countervalue nuclear attack even in response to an attack on mainland America. Therefore, countervalue nuclear threats are no longer credible for American deterrence.' This is attributed to the presumed higher moral values of the United States relative to other states, and its greater reluctance to use nuclear weapons on cities and against civilian populations, with the result that the United States has no choice but to orient its nuclear strategy to counterforce first-strike, or nuclear primacy. 'Countervalue targeting, however, [we are told,] remains valid for other nuclear states', such as Russia and China, which are not so subject to the taboo on the use of nuclear weapons, since lacking the high moral values of the United States and Western countries more generally, with the result they would not balk at massive retaliation against civilian targets.[87]

The irony of all such arguments based on moral asymmetry, is that the one nation that has actually employed nuclear weapons, killing hundreds of thousands of people – as Blackett demonstrated, not as the last military act of the Second World War but as the first political act of the Cold War – the nation, moreover, responsible for the deaths of some eighteen million people in wars and interventions since 1945 alone, sees itself (and NATO) as so morally above other major nuclear states (such as Russia and China) that it is compelled to pursue a counterforce or first-strike capability.[88] Such a strategy is aimed at *starting* and *winning* a nuclear war, not simply relying on nuclear weapons for massive relation. It is supplemented by plans for limited nuclear war and domination at every step in the escalation ladder.

The US maximalist nuclear strategy, rooted in the assumption that the United States can dominate at all stages of conventional and nuclear escalation and even win a nuclear war, is a major factor in inducing a false sense of power on the part of decision-makers, leading to Washington's aggressiveness toward Beijing and Moscow in the present New Cold War. The most likely result of the current Western view that nuclear weapons *can be used* to achieve political and military ends is that they will indeed end up *being used*, with the destruction of virtually all of humanity.[89] The fact that the entire Western nuclear strategy since 1991 has been based on counterforce targeting, first-strike capability, nuclear primacy, and limited nuclear war, viewing thermonuclear weapons as useful instruments in the struggle to secure a unipolar world order, means that the United States/NATO today constitutes the single greatest existential threat to humanity via a Third World War (that is, outside of the planetary ecological crisis). Only a minimalist, as opposed to maximalist, approach to nuclear arms can put humanity on the road to nuclear disarmament. Ultimately, however, the answer lies in a worldwide shift away from a dying capitalism to what Blackett called *complete socialism*.

NOTES

1   P. M. S. Blackett, *Studies of War: Nuclear and Conventional*, New York: Hill and Wang, 1962, p. 130.
2   'Excerpts from the Pentagon Plan: Preventing the Emergence of a New Rival', *New York Times*, 8 March 1992; General Wesley K. Clark, *Don't Wait for the Next War*, New York: Public Affairs, 2014, pp. 37-40; John Bellamy Foster, *Naked Imperialism*, New York: Monthly Review Press, 2006; Editors, 'Notes from the Editors', *Monthly Review*, 73(11), 2022.
3   Zbigniew Brzezinski, *The Grand Chessboard*, New York: Basic Books, 1997, pp. 46, 92-96, 103; Grey Anderson, 'Weapon of Power, Matrix of Management: NATO's Hegemonic Formula', *New Left Review*, 140/141 (March-June), 2023, pp. 16, 21-22.
4   P. M. S. Blackett, *Atomic Weapons and East-West Relations*, Cambridge: Cambridge University Press, 1956, pp. 27-33; Keir A. Lieber and Daryl G. Press, 'The Rise of U.S. Nuclear Primacy', *Foreign Affairs*, 85(2), 2006, pp. 42-54; Lawrence Freedman and Jeffrey Michaels, *The Evolution of Nuclear Strategy*, London: Palgrave Macmillan, 2019, pp. 649-63.
5   John T. Correll, 'The Ups and Down of Counterforce', *Air and Space Forces Magazine*, 1 October 2005; Daniel Ellsberg, *The Doomsday Machine: Confessions of a Nuclear War Planner*, New York: Bloomsbury, 2017, pp. 120-23; 178-79; Spurgeon M. Keeny and Wolfgang K. H. Panofsky, 'MAD vs. NUTS: Can Doctrine or Weaponry Remedy the Mutual Hostage Relationship of the Superpowers?', *Foreign Affairs*, 60(2), 1981, pp. 287-304; William D. Hartung, 'Bush's Nuclear Doctrine: From MAD to NUTS?', Institute for Policy Studies, 1 December 2000, available at: www.ips-dc.org.

6   Freedman and Michaels, *The Evolution of Nuclear Strategy*, p. 649.
7   Freedman and Michaels, *The Evolution of Nuclear Strategy*, p. 668.
8   Nina Tannenwald, *The Nuclear Taboo*, Cambridge: Cambridge University Press, 2008, p. 22.
9   Michael Joseph Smith, 'Nuclear Deterrence: Behind the Strategic and Ethical Debate', *Virginia Quarterly Review* 63(1), 1987, available at: www.vqronline.org; Freedman and Michaels, *The Evolution of Nuclear Strategy*, pp. 666, 672; Michael Howard, 'Brodie, Wohlstetter and American Nuclear Strategy', *Survival: Global Politics and Strategy*, 34(2), 1992, pp. 107-16.
10 P. M. S. Blackett, *Studies of War: Nuclear and Conventional*, New York: Hill and Wang, 1962, p. 138.
11 Rajesh Basrur, 'Nuclear Deterrence: The Wohlstetter-Blackett Debate Revisited', S. Rajaratnam School of International Studies, Nanyang Technological University, Singapore, RSIS Working Paper, no. 271, 15 April 2014, available at: www.files.ethz.ch/isn/179110/WP271.pdf/; Mary Jo Nye, *Blackett: Physics, War, and Politics in the Twentieth Century*, Cambridge, MA: Harvard University Press, 2004, pp. 65-99.
12 See: John Bellamy Foster, '"Notes on Exterminism" for the Twenty-First Century', *Monthly Review*, 74(1), 2022, pp. 1-17.
13 Freedman and Michaels, *The Evolution of Nuclear Strategy*, 649-50.
14 P. M. S. Blackett, *Fear, War and the Bomb: Military and Political Consequences of Atomic Energy*, New York: McGraw Hill, 1949. The subtitle of the book was the title of the 1948 British edition; the title 'Fear, War and the Bomb' was added for the US edition.
15 On the British Marxist scientists and the social relations of science movement see: John Bellamy Foster, *The Return of Nature*, New York: Monthly Review Press, 2020, pp. 367-73, 457-76.
16 Blackett, *Atomic Weapons and East-West Relations*, p. 73.
17 P. M. S. Blackett, 'The Frustration of Science', in Daniel Hall, et. al., *The Frustration of Science*, New York: Books for Libraries Press, 1935, pp. 137, 140-44.
18 'Counsels of War: An Exchange: Gregg Herken, Albert Wohlstetter, and Thomas Powers, reply by Lord Zuckerman' *New York Review of Books*, 21 November 1985, available at: https://www.nybooks.com/; Nye, *Blackett*, pp. 67-85.
19 Blackett, *Fear, War and the Bomb*, p. v-vi; Bernard Lovell, 'Blackett in War and Peace', *Journal of the Operational Research Society*, 39(3), 1988, p. 228.
20 Blackett, *Fear, War and the Bomb*, pp. 131-39.
21 Philip Morrison, 'Blackett's Analysis of the Issue', *Bulletin of the Atomic Scientists*, 5(2), 1949, p. 40; Nye, *Blackett*, p. 91. Morrison was a columnist for *Monthly Review: An Independent Socialist Magazine* from 1956-61.
22 Gar Alperovitz, *The Decision to Use the Atomic Bomb*, New York: Vintage, 1996; Robert Jay Lifton and Greg Mitchell, *Hiroshima in America,* New York: Harper, 1996; Ben Norton, 'Atomic Bombing of Japan Was Not Necessary to End WWII: US Government Documents Admit It', *Geopolitical Economy*, 7 August 2023, available at: www.geopoliticaleconomy.com.
23 Blackett, *Atomic Weapons and East-West Relations*, pp. 99-100.
24 Michael Howard, 'Blackett and the Origins of Nuclear Strategy,' *Journal of the Operational Research Society*, 36(2), 1985, p. 92.

25 Blackett, *Atomic Weapons and East-West Relations*, p. 78; *In the Matter of J. Robert Oppenheimer*, Transcript of Hearing Before Personal Security Board, April 15, 1954-May 6, 1954, Washington, D.C.: U.S. Government Printing Office, 1954, p. 250.
26 Nye, *Blackett*, p. 66.
27 Nye, *Blackett*, pp. 2-4, 66, 90-93; Edward Shils, 'Blackett's Apologia for the Soviet Position', *Bulletin of the Atomic Scientists* 5(2), 1949, pp. 34-37.
28 Camille Rebouillat-Sarti, 'MI5 and Atomic Scientists (1945-1958): The Case of Patrick Blackett', 11 September 2022, available at: www.byarcadia.org; Nye, *Blackett*, p. 92; Freedman and Michaels, *The Evolution of Nuclear Strategy*, p. 72.
29 Blackett's essay 'A Critique of Defence Thinking' was first published in *Encounter* magazine in April 1961 and was reprinted along with most of his other articles on nuclear deterrence in his *Studies of War*. *Encounter* was a publication of the social democratic, anti-Communist left, and was one of a number of publications secretly funded by the CIA. Blackett, as a Nobel laureate, was clearly sought out for the publication. But unlike others who published in *Encounter* he did not engage in attacks on the left but devoted his article entirely to the critique of the nuclear establishment.
30 Blackett, *Studies of War*, pp. 73-77.
31 Blackett, *Studies of War*, p. 77.
32 Henry Kissinger, *Nuclear Weapons and Foreign Policy*, New York: Harper Brothers [for the Council on Foreign Relations], 1957.
33 Blackett, *Studies of War*, pp. 58-63.
34 Nye, *Blackett*, pp. 95-97, 218; Herman Kahn, *On Thermonuclear War*, New Brunswick, New Jersey: Transaction Publishers, 2007.
35 See: Carl Sagan and Richard Turco, *A Path Where No Man Thought: Nuclear Winter and the End of the Arms Race*, New York: Random House, 1990, p. 215.
36 Albert Wohlstetter, 'The Delicate Balance of Terror', *Foreign Affairs*, 37(2), 1959, pp. 211-34.
37 Wohlstetter, 'The Delicate Balance of Terror', pp. 212, 217, 222, 226; Blackett, *Studies of War*, pp. 128-46.
38 Howard, 'Blackett and the Origins of Nuclear Strategy', p. 94.
39 Blackett, *Studies of War*, pp. 131-34.
40 Wohlstetter, 'The Delicate Balance of Terror', p. 222.
41 Blackett, *Studies of War*, p. 162.
42 Blackett, *Studies of War*, pp. 135-41.
43 Blackett, *Studies of War*, p. 153.
44 Blackett, *Studies of War*, p. 157.
45 Blackett, *Studies of War*, pp. 144, 163-64.
46 Freeman and Michaels, *The Evolution of Nuclear Strategy*, pp. 415-16.
47 See: E. P. Thompson and Dan Smith, ed., *Protest and Survive*, New York: Monthly Review Press, 1981; E. P. Thompson, *Beyond the Cold War*, New York: Pantheon, 1982; Steve Breyman, *Why Movements Matter: The West German Peace Movement and U.S. Arms Control Policy*, Albany: State University of New York Press, 2001; Christos Efstathiou, *E. P. Thompson: A Twentieth-Century Romantic*, London: Merlin Press, 2015, pp. 116-65.
48 Wohlstetter and Zuckerman in 'Counsels of War'. Wohlstetter wrote a highly polemical essay attacking Blackett principally, but also Zuckerman and C. P. Snow for their criticisms of, in Wohlstetter's ironic language, 'the excessively sophisticated

theory of the American' game theorists in the development of nuclear deterrence strategy which had come to 'corrupt' the 'intuitive common sense of English thinkers', forgetting perhaps that he was criticizing in the case of Blackett, in particular, both one of the world's greatest physicists and also the founder of military operational research. Albert Wohlstetter, 'Sins and Games in America', in Martin Shubik, ed., *Game Theory and Related Approaches to Social Behavior,* New York: John Wiley and Sons, 1964, pp. 209-25.

49 Freedman and Michaels, *The Evolution of Nuclear Strategy,* pp. 649, 671.
50 Janne Nolan quoted in Correll, 'The Ups and Downs of Counterforce'.
51 Freedman and Michaels, *The Evolution of Nuclear Strategy,* p. 651.
52 Steven Pifer, Andrey Baklitskiy, and James Cameron, 'Missile Defense and the Offense-Defense Relationship', Freemann Spogli Institute for International Studies, 28 October 2021, available at: https://fsi.stanford.edu; Keir A. Lieber and Daryl G. Press, 'The New Era of Counterforce', *International Security,* 41(4), 2017, pp. 12, 49.
53 Lieber and Press, 'The New Era of Counterforce', pp. 16-17; 'The Rise of U.S. Nuclear Primacy', pp. 44-45; Ellsberg, *The Doomsday Machine,* pp. 306, 323.
54 Freedman and Michaels, *The Evolution of Nuclear Strategy,* pp. 657-61, Jack Detsch, 'Putin's Fixation with an Old-School U.S. Missile Launcher', *Foreign Policy,* 12 January 2022.
55 Hans M. Kristensen, 'How Presidents Arm and Disarm', Federation of American Scientists, 15 October 2014, available at: www.fas.org.
56 Hans Kristensen, Matt Korda, Eliana Johns, and Kate Kohn, 'Status of World Nuclear Forces', Federation of American Scientists, 31 March 2023, available at: www.fas.org.
57 Cynthia Roberts, 'Revelations About Russian Nuclear Deterrence Policy', *War on the Rocks,* Texas National Security Review, 19 June 2020, available at: www.warontherocks.com.
58 Lieber and Press, 'The Rise of Nuclear Primacy'.
59 Lieber and Press, 'The Rise of Nuclear Primacy', pp. 43, 50.
60 Lieber and Press, 'The Rise of Nuclear Primacy', p. 45; Lieber and Press, 'The New Era of Counterforce', pp. 18-19; Kris Osborn, 'US Air Force Stealth Bomber Missions Deploy Over Europe,' Warrior Maven, August 22, 2023, https://warriormaven.com/air/us-air-force-b-2-stealth-bomber-missions-to-deploy-over-europe/.
61 Ian Bowers, 'Counterforce Dilemmas and the Risk of Nuclear War in East Asia', *Journal for Peace and Nuclear Disarmament* 5(supl 1), 2022, pp. 9, 14.
62 Richard Stone, 'National Pride Is at Stake: Russia, China, United States Rush to Build Hypersonic Weapons', *Science,* 8 January 2020, pp. 176-96. As Bowers notes, Chinese submarines are also vulnerable due to the fact that China's 'access routes to the Pacific are difficult to traverse without detection, as the Chinese vessels must transit through Japanese- and U.S.-controlled choke points … There is data that China's emphasis on controlling the South China Sea is in part driven by the need to create a protected patrol area where its SSBN fleet could securely operate'. Bowers, 'Counterforce Dilemmas and the Risk of Nuclear War in East Asia', p. 12.
63 Diana Johnstone 'Doomsday Postponed?', in Paul Johnstone, *From MAD to Madness: Inside Pentagon Nuclear War Planning,* Atlanta, GA: Clarity, 2017, p. 277.
64 NATO, Bucharest Summit Declaration, 3 April 2008, available at: https://www.nato.int/cps/en/natolive/official_texts_8443.htm; Detsch, 'Putin's Fixation with an Old-School U.S. Missile Launcher'.

65 Freedman and Michaels, *The Evolution of Nuclear Strategy*, pp. 640-45, 678; Anderson, 'Weapon of Power, Matrix of Management', p. 112.
66 Octavio Bellomo, 'Russian Tactical Nuclear Weapons Use and Deterrence Over Ukraine', Finabel: The European Army Interoperability Centre, January 2023, available at: www.finabel.org; Gregory Kulacki, 'Would China Use Nuclear Weapons First in a War with the United States?' *The Diplomat*, 27 April 27 2020, available at: www.thediplomat.com.
67 David Vine, *The United States of War: A Global History of America's Endless Conflicts from Columbus to the Islamic State*, Berkeley: University of California Press, 2020, pp. 2, 279-97.
68 Freedman and Michaels, *The Evolution of Nuclear Strategy*, pp. 652-54.
69 Freedman and Michaels, *The Evolution of Nuclear Strategy*, p. 654.
70 John Bellamy Foster, John Ross, and Deborah Veneziale, *Washington's New Cold War*, New York: Monthly Review Press, ND, pp. 81-83; Shannon Bugos, 'Putin Orders Russian Nuclear Weapons on Higher Alert', Arms Control Association, March 2022, available at: www.armscontrol.org/.
71 Louisiana Tech Institute, *Guide to Nuclear Deterrence in the Age of Great-Power Competition*, 2020, available at: www.atloa.org, p. 37; Alan Kaptanoglu and Stewart Prager, 'US Defense to Its Workforce: Nuclear War Can Be Won', *Bulletin of the Atomic Scientists*, 2 February 2022, available at: www.thebulletin.org; Stewart Prager and Alan Kaptanoglu, 'Rebuttal: Current Nuclear Weapons Policy Not Safe or Sane', *Bulletin of the Atomic Scientists*, 24 May 2022, available at: www.thebulletin.org.
72 This paragraph and the following two paragraphs draw on 'Editors' Notes', *Monthly Review*, 75(1), 2023, written by the author.
73 Zachary Keck, 'Why the B-61-12 Bomb Is the Most Dangerous Nuclear Weapon in America's Arsenal', *The National Interest*, 9 October 2018.
74 Hans Kristensen, 'The C-17A Has Been Cleared to Transport B61-12 Nuclear Bomb to Europe', Federation of American Scientists, 9 January 2023, available at: www.fas.org; 'B61-12: New US Nuclear Warheads Coming to Europe in December', ICAN, December 22, 2022; Hans Kristensen, 'Video Shows Earth-Penetrating Capability of B61-12 Nuclear Bomb', Federation of American Scientists, 14 January 2016, available at: www.fas.org; 'B61-12: New US Nuclear Warheads Coming to Europe in December', ICAN, December 22, 2022.
75 Hans Kristensen and Robert S. Norris, 'The B61 Family of Nuclear Bombs', *Bulletin of the Atomic Scientists*, 70(3), 2014, pp. 82-83; Guy Faulconbridge, 'Russia Says U.S. Lowering "Nuclear Threshold" with Newer Bombs in Europe', *Reuters*, 29 October 2022; Len Ackland and Bert Hubbard, 'Obama Pledged to Reduce Nuclear Arsenal, Then Came This Weapon', *Reveal*, 14 July 2015, available at: www.revealnews.org; Military Watch Magazine Editorial Staff, 'Poland Wants American Nuclear Warheads for its New F-35 Stealth Fighters: Will Nuclear Sharing Expand to Warsaw?', *Military Watch Magazine*, 1 July 2023, available at: www.militarywatchmagazine.com.
76 Elbridge A. Colby, 'America Must Prepare for a War Over Taiwan', *Foreign Affairs*, 10 August 2022; Elbridge Colby, *The Strategy of Denial*, New Haven: Yale University Press, 2021; Elbridge A. Colby and Yashar Parsie, 'Building a Strategy for Escalation and War Termination', The Marathon Initiative, November 2022, 23, available at: www.themarathoninitiative.org; Manpret Sethi, 'The Idea of Limited Nuclear War', *Indian Foreign Affairs Journal*, 14(3), 2019, pp. 235-47. When applied to

nuclear weapons, the term 'strategy of denial' is a euphemism for counterforce. 'A counterforce first strike is a denial strategy.' Benjamin C. Jamison, 'The Counterforce Continuum and Tailored Targeting: A New Look at United States Nuclear Targeting Methods and Modern Deterrence', Wright Flyer Papers, Air Command and Staff College, 2022, p. 6.

77 David Logan, 'The Dangerous Myths About China's Nuclear Weapons', *War on the Rocks* (Texas National Security Review), 18 September 2020, available at: https://warontherocks.com.

78 Luke Caggiano, 'China Deploys New Submarine-Launched Balistic Missiles,' *Arms Control TODAY*, May 2023, https://www.armscontrol.org/act/2023-05/news/china-deploys-new-submarine-launched-ballistic-missiles.

79 Jamison, 'The Counterforce Continuum and Tailored Targeting', pp. 6, 13; see also: Benjamin C. Jamison, 'Nuclear Targeting Methods and Modern Deterrence', *Æther: A Journal of Strategic Airpower and Spacepower*, 1(2), 2022, pp. 43-56.

80 Logan, 'The Dangerous Myths About China's Nuclear Weapons'.

81 Kulacki, 'Would China Use Nuclear Weapons in a War with the United States?'; US Department of Defense, *Military and Security Developments Involving the People's Republic of China*, 2022, p. 98, available at: www.navyleaguehonolulu.org; Brad Marvel, '4 New Developments in China's Nuclear Deterrent', Asia Pacific Advanced Network, available at: https://community.apan.org; Bowers, 'Counterforce Dilemmas and the Risk of Nuclear War in East Asia', pp. 6-23.

82 Even Hellan Larsen, 'Deliberate Nuclear First Use in an Era of Asymmetry: A Game Theoretical Approach', *Journal of Conflict Resolution*, 17(16), 2023.

83 See Steven Starr, 'Turning a Blind Eye Towards Armageddon—U.S. Leaders Reject Nuclear Winter Studies', *Public Interest Report*, Federation of American Scientists, 69(2), 2016-17, p. 24; Alan Robock, Luke Oman, and Georgiy L. Stenchikov, 'Nuclear Winter Revisited With a Modern Climate Model and Current Nuclear Arsenals', *Journal of Geophysical Research: Atmospheres*, 112(D13), 2007, pp. 1-14; Joshua Coupe, Charles G. Bardeen, Alan Robock, and Owen B. Toon, 'Nuclear Winter Responses to Nuclear War Between the United States and Russia in the Whole Atmosphere Community Climate Model Version 4 and the Goddard Institute for Space Studies ModelE', *Journal of Geophysical Research: Atmospheres*, 124(15), 2019, pp. 8522-43; Alan Robock and Owen B. Toon, 'Self-Assured Destruction: The Climate Impacts of Nuclear War', *Bulletin of the Atomic Scientists*, 68(5), 2012, pp. 66-74; Steven Starr, 'Nuclear War, Nuclear Winter, and Human Extinction', Federation of American Scientists, 14 October 2015, available at: www.fas.org.

84 Ellsberg, *The Doomsday Machine*, p. 339.

85 Robert S. McNamara, 'Apocalypse Soon', *Foreign Policy*, May-June 2005, pp. 29-35.

86 Howard, 'Blackett and the Origins of Nuclear Strategy', p. 95.

87 Jamison, 'The Counterforce Continuum and Tailored Targeting', pp. 2-13; Jamison, 'Nuclear Targeting Methods and Modern Deterrence', 47; Tannenwald, *The Nuclear Taboo*, p. 16.

88 David Michael Smith, *Endless Holocausts*, New York: Monthly Review Press, 2023, pp. 208-09, 256-57.

89 Jamison, 'The Counterforce Continuum and Tailored Targeting', p. 20.

REFRAMING THE GEOPOLITICS OF GLOBAL CAPITALISM

ANDREAS BIELER AND ADAM DAVID MORTON

Russia's invasion of Ukraine on 24 February 2022 finally ended post–Cold War hopes for a peaceful international order. Of course, there had been earlier warning signs of heightened geopolitical conflict. The list could include the 2003 invasion of Iraq by the US and its coalition of the willing (seeking an access to diesel over the axis of evil)[1] coupled with the permanent war on terror, as well as Russia's earlier military interventions – be it the wars in Chechnya in the 1990s, the war with Georgia in 2008, heavy involvement in the war in Syria since 2015, or the intervention in the Nagorno-Karabakh conflict in 2020. The signs have been there for some time that a peaceful world order is an illusion within a permanent arms economy.[2] Of course, it was the 2014 annexation of Crimea by Russia which really started the war in Ukraine. Equally, heightened tensions over Taiwan between China and the US do not bear well for the future. While China carries out extensive military manoeuvres close to the island, the US is increasing the presence of its naval forces in the region. The purpose of our essay is twofold. First, we contribute to discussions on how best to assess current geopolitical dynamics. We argue that a historical materialist focus on the *content of the form* allows us to conceptualize best the internal relations between the contemporary states-system (form) and capitalism (content) within the geopolitics of global capitalism. Second, drawing on this conceptualization, we then analyze the dynamics underpinning the current war in Ukraine and tensions over Taiwan, revealing how intensified capitalist competition against the background of the crisis of fossil fuel-based capitalism has spilled over into geopolitical confrontation.

In a passage at the very beginning of *Studies in the Development of Capitalism* – seemingly skipped over by many in preference for his more crucial insights on the *fons et origo* of capitalist development – Maurice Dobb usefully sums up much of the state-of-the-art on economic theory since World War II.

There are those who refuse 'to recognize that capitalism as a title for a determinate economic system can be given an exact meaning'.[3] Economists model capitalism out of existence through their severely simple abstractions that strive for parsimony but at the cost of reifying or violently abstracting from history. Historians alternately avoid reference to any capitalist totality striving instead for an emphasis on a multiplicity of contingent social factors that results in mystifying economic development. This form of nihilism emphasizes 'the variety and complexity of historical events, so great as to reject any of those general categories which form the texture of most theories of historical interpretation'.[4] Fast forward to contemporary political economy debates and social constructivism fits this description very neatly with 1) its constant emphasis on varieties of capitalism at the expense of the category of totality; and 2) a methodological bias that avoids dialectics in preference for reifying isolated parts that are, at best, intersectionally associated. Indicative here is the view that, rather than focusing on global capitalism, we need 'to ask what political economic scholarship would look like if it were more attuned to the complex and often-contradictory intersection of a range of global structural forces'.[5] There is an allergy to capitalist totality as well as historical materialism that still grips both the 'science' of economic theory and the constructivist ideas-centred accounts of historical and contemporary change based on contingency.

These frontier lines of thinking configure a suite of present approaches to the geopolitics of global capitalism. Our argument is that contemporary approaches to geopolitics are trapped within a binary opposition between the *form* of ideology and the *content* of materiality. One can repeatedly witness a dualist opposition between the form of geopolitics (the states-system) and its contemporary socio-historical content (capitalism) in theorizing on the international.[6] Instead, we propose a rejuvenation of dialectics to overcome this dualist opposition to offer fresh insights on competition and confrontation within the present-day conditions of capital accumulation. The reframing we propose rejects the binary dilemma of form and content marring alternative theoretical perspectives, namely realist statecraft, constructivist idealism, and the discursivity of poststructuralism (or radical constructivism). Our reframing, to be developed below, asserts a focus on the *content of the form* as a philosophical and dialectical departure point for understanding the internal relation of the geopolitics of the states-system and global capitalism. Is there something peculiar in terms of the content of the capital relation that means that the states-system contingently came into being but has become the necessary form of geopolitics? How is the internal relation of the *content of form* represented most starkly in the modern condition of the geopolitics of global capitalism? This reframing of content and form is then extended from a theoretical discussion in the first section to an analysis of geopolitics in the second section, offering insights on the internality between the form of geopolitics (the states-system) and its contemporary socio-historical content (global capitalism) regarding the war in Ukraine and tensions between the US and China over trade and Taiwan. Across this section, the spillover from capitalist competition into geopolitical confrontation is traced, uniting a dialectical focus on the *form* of geopolitics in terms of the states-system and its internal relation to the socio-historical *content* of contemporary global capitalism. The content of the form of the geopolitics of global capitalism is thus unveiled in this reframing. This conjuncture is a crucial moment to look afresh on the form and content of world order to chart ways out of a crisis of thinking as well as the deep crisis that threatens the future of humanity.

DIALECTICAL VENTURES

In assisting us to clarify differences between the forms of appearance of value (such as profit, money, interest, revenue, or wages) and its essential form (labour-power), Marx admitted, very soon after completing *Capital* and with reference to the general formula of capital that, 'it cost me much hard toil to ascertain *the things themselves*, i.e. their *interconnection*'.[7] Understanding the connections of capital through a philosophy of internal relations is now commonly present across various commentaries on the analytic foundations of historical materialism.[8] In our own work the philosophy of internal relations has been inspirational for some time in addressing concrete class struggles within the uneven and combined development of global capitalism as well as theoretically critiquing the deficits of discourse theories.[9] As Bertell Ollman clarifies, the philosophy of internal relations maintains connections between parts in a relational sense as elements of a whole, giving rise to the dialectical method. In contrast, a philosophy of external relations takes the world as logically made up of things external to each other, often as independent, isolated, and static variables. For Ollman, 'what was a thing for the philosophy of external relations becomes a relation evolving over time (or a process in constant interaction with other processes)' within the relational and dialectical method of historical materialism.[10] The former framing identifies spheres as separate entities in a relationship of *ontological exteriority*.[11] The reframing of dialectics proposed by a philosophy of internal relations takes processes as ontologically interior.

This section unpacks the contribution of a relational approach in two ways. First, through critique, a stark contrast is revealed with some examples of those international theories that attempt to grasp *inter*connections between structures of power but reside within a dualist understanding of *inter*-acting spheres. Second, in rejuvenating dialectics, an advance is made by drawing on the internality of form and content and asserting the relevance of such terms to assess competing claims within international theory. Assistance from Fredric Jameson is necessary in our reframing here to argue that 'the problem of content and form largely transcend their merely aesthetic reference and in the long run come to haunt all the corners and closets of the social itself'.[12] Rather than a binary opposition, or perspectival dualism, that contrasts ideational form versus materialist content, or retreats into one pole, our purpose in this first main section is to advance on Marx's statement that 'form is of no value unless it is the form of its content'.[13] We do so through a focus on the *content of form* as a dialectical solution to the binary dilemma of content and form marring present theories of world order. As worked through for us by Antonio Gramsci, the analysis we are proposing is one 'in which precisely material forces are the content and ideologies are the form, though this distinction is purely didactic since the material forces would be inconceivable historically without form and the ideologies would be individual fancies without the material forces'.[14] We now delve into these dialectical ventures some more to reveal the weaknesses of wider international theorizing. The aim is to highlight a reliance on binary oppositions as a primary form of ideology that can be best detected through a revitalization of the dialectical method.

The binary opposition between form and content can only be overcome, or held in a productive tension, not by doing away with one of the terms but by complicating the relations. This is Fredric Jameson's argument who introduces the term of the *content of the form* to challenge and rebuke the dualism of form and content. He does so by taking us through a set of distinctions on form and content that is heuristically presented and adapted accordingly.[15]

Table 1: Transcending the Dualism of Form and Content

	Form	**Content**
Content	form of content [constructivism]	content of content [structural realism]
Form	form of form [poststructuralism]	content of form [dialectics]

The first referential point on the dualism of form and content is a category of structural realism that presents an objective version of reality and can be identified as a theoretical position emphasizing the *content of the content* in the historical process. To illustrate, the structural realism of Kenneth Waltz most tellingly separates theory as an enterprise from reality to claim that we can understand phenomena through isolation and severely simple processes of abstraction based on principles of parsimony.[16] The purpose of theory here is to aim for 'elegance' by isolating a few elements on the basis of science envy and striving for explanatory and predictive power. The structural concept of anarchy is the foundational content of this international theory held in binary separation from national forms. 'The theoretical separation of domestic and international politics need not bother us unduly', admits Waltz, '... students of international politics will do well to concentrate on separate theories of internal and external politics until someone figures out a way to unite them.'[17] What we have, then, with the power fetishism of structural realism is a vulgar materialism that has a most extreme focus on state material capabilities – the content of the content – separate from any other forces in play. As Robert Cox most compellingly revealed, structural realism appears 'ideologically to be a science at the service of big power management of the international system'.[18] It legitimises a technology of state power that has clearly silenced paralleling Marxist theorizations of anarchy, and race, based on the fusion of capitalist competition and militarist geopolitical conflict.[19] As Marx intimated, the anarchy of the market induces in industry a state of war and it is in 'opposed forces that science seeks order and equilibrium: *perpetual war*, according to it, is the sole means of obtaining peace; that war is called competition'.[20] Unsurprisingly, current geopolitical confrontations have resulted in a revival of realist analyses.[21]

The second referential point on the dualism of form and content is the *form of the content* that, according to Jameson, 'can be said to encompass everything called ideology in the most comprehensive acceptation of the word'.[22] For us, the form of the content is best represented by social constructivist perspectives that deliver an ideas-centred conception of political economic change.[23] Indicative here is John Hobson's attempt to reveal the making of modern world politics through 'Eastern agency' and how he abstracts out intersecting ideas, institutions, and technologies as different elements of 'resource portfolios'. The constituent parts of these resource portfolios are regarded as separate, connected only in exterior relation to each other, to account for the making of modern world politics. Emblematic is his statement that 'materialist causes must be factored in alongside the role of identity if we are to craft a satisfactory explanation of the rise of the West'.[24]

But note that the content of the material and the form of the ideational are held in separation through their a priori ontological exteriority. Likewise, cognate arguments on the origins of international norm dynamics and the role of norm entrepreneurs (as generators of norms with platforms within states, international organizations, and networks) collapse into an ideational emphasis on the form of the content. Martha Finnemore and Kathryn Sikkink are unable to answer their own question on 'where do norms come from' in their attempt to trace the origins of ideational causation through norm emergence (based on the persuasion of norm entrepreneurs); norm cascading (linked to the socializing-, legitimatizing-, and conformity-inducing actions of norm entrepreneurs); and norm internalization (leading to a taken-for-granted universalization of norms).[25] Without recourse to the obvious Marxist alternative of organic intellectuals, social constructivist approaches to norms and values remove intersubjective ideas from the social relations of production in which they cohere. As a result, the form of the content gains priority so that form and content are posed as always-already separate and then combined entities. To draw from our work in *Global Capitalism, Global War, Global Crisis*, social constructivist perspectives fail to ascertain recurring questions: *Which* agents shape the core intersubjective beliefs of underlying social and world orders? *How* have their values and beliefs become embodied in state identities and interests and the relevant constitutional structure of the international society of states? *Why* does a particular form of ideas become part of the structural content and not another?[26] Elsewhere, defining the rise of China within a series of multiple orders all with different simultaneously emergent properties – rather than a single liberal international order – may seem to offer variation, but still reduces norm preferences to the dominant state in the system.[27] That said, as Jameson reminds us, 'we cannot do without these two initial moments of the form-content position, and must always acknowledge the claims these first two perspectives inevitably have on us'.[28]

Jameson's third referential point on the dualism of form and content is the *form of form* or 'the perspective of form on itself; of a formalistic production of forms',[29] which we link to the discourse of poststructuralism (also referred to as radical constructivism). One route to the discursive logic of the form of the form is, of course, the theorizing of total contingency by Ernesto Laclau and Chantal Mouffe. In *Hegemony and Socialist Strategy*, they reject the distinction between discursive (form) and non-discursive (content) practices on the basis that there is no object outside of a discursive condition of emergence. This is rendered so:

The fact that every object is constituted as an object of discourse has *nothing to do* with whether there is a world external to thought, or with the realism/idealism opposition … What is denied is not that such objects exist externally to thought, but the rather different assertion that they could constitute themselves as objects outside any discursive condition of emergence.[30]

Within poststructuralist approaches in international theory, this stance was taken as a departure point for rewriting security that, along the way, revelled in the 'evisceration of political economy' that was levelled against such provocations on identity.[31] Rather than maintaining a dualism of form/content, then, the poststructuralist vulgate retains only one of the two terms in the form of discourse to claim transcendence of the material world. Of course, as Gramsci pointed out, with this extreme stance on ideational discourse (form) and material practices (content), 'it is easy to impart the impression of having transcended a certain position by demeaning it, but this amounts to mere verbal sophistry: the transcendence has taken place only on paper, and the scholar will face the difficulty again in a frightening form'.[32] Unambiguously, Charlotte Epstein's focus on contingency and indeterminacy as the defining features of theorising the social from a radical constructivist standpoint is indicative. 'There are as many constructed worlds', she argues, 'as there are cultures and even individualities. Constitutive theorising, then, requires ways of theorising with the unfixity that the focus on contingency sets into play.'[33] This emphasis on constitutive construction is then writ large to focus on 'how the state and the subject were constructed all the way down' in the crafting of modern politics.[34] The problem, as anticipated by Perry Anderson, is the complete *randomisation of history*: 'Language as a system furnishes the formal *conditions of possibility* of speech, but has no purchase on its actual *causes*.'[35] The hegemony of discourse therefore becomes a phagocytic essence, absorbing and engulfing everything within the discursive, so that radical social construction never has any other basis than itself.[36] Epstein's stating that 'how the invention of the state and of territory, understood as the spatial expression of the state, was enabled by the invention of modern space', clearly reveals such circular logic at the core of radical constructivism.[37] One result of this emphasis on the pure form of form is thus a rendering of capitalist exploitation and domination into a shapeless and contingent world, of fetishized self/other differences, in constructing the spatial and temporal matrix of the modern state. Focusing on the form of the form may allow us to analyse the discursive production of the rise of China, linked to a reassertion of US identity/difference, similar to the 'discursive economy' of the Cold War.[38] However, what is missed is a way of understanding the dialectical interplay of discursive conditions of emergence within a broader capitalist totality.

The three preceding moments on the dualism of form and content each constitute a certain perspective that can be radically and dialectically transformed by a fourth perspective that registers the insufficiency of the preceding three. 'This is not a vicious circle ... because the new one is also the only perspective from which the usefulness and indeed the indispensability of the other three could be appreciated,' writes Jameson.[39] He continues:

> It also constitutes the only productive coordination of the opposition between form and content that does not seek to reduce one term to the other, or to posit illicit syntheses and equally illicit volatilizations of an opposition whose tensions need to be preserved at the same time that we become aware of how philosophically incompatible each of these terms is with respect to the other one.[40]

The significance here of the dialectic, writes Ludovico Silva, is that 'the formal and logical relations into which Marx places verbal *signs/signifiers* constitute a plastic gesture', which are internally related, 'to the material and historical relations of *signifieds*'.[41] Hence historical materialism is, according to Gramsci, 'conceived as an integral original philosophy that initiates a new phase of history and a new phase in the development of world thought ... it surpasses both traditional idealism and traditional materialism,' or form and content, while retaining their 'vital elements' within an internal relation.[42] Comprehending this 'revolutionary dialectic' proposed by historical materialism entails moving away from the separation or binary dualism of form and content and appreciating their internality, crafted as a 'dialectic of distincts', or as a relational, 'unity of opposites and of distincts'.[43] For Gramsci, the dialectic is an expression of social contradictions and not simply a pure conceptual dialectic.[44] Equally, for Robert Cox, the dialectic was valued at both the level of logic (exploring contradictions within the processes of theorizing itself arising from competing perspectives) and at the level of history (seeking alternative forms of development arising from class struggles generated by changing production processes).[45] For historical materialism, then, the content of the form stands as a philosophical and dialectical solution to the initial binary dilemma of content and form. Our movement is now from the moment of historically informed theory to the moment of theoretically informed history to address the content of the form and the internal relations of the contemporary states-system (form) and capitalism (content) within the geopolitics of global capitalism.

GEOPOLITICAL ECONOMY VENTURES

Considering how capitalist production is organised around wage labour and the private ownership or control of the means of production, it is a very dynamic mode of production with capitals in constant competition with each other over market share within a social formation, while also crisis-prone due to the repeated contradictions of overproduction.[46] Hence the underlying structural pressure towards constant, relentless outward expansion produces conditions of uneven and combined development.[47] Collective class agency takes place within these structuring conditions. In this section, we first analyze the structuring conditions of capitalist expansion since the 1990s, before assessing potential class agency within the current moment of global capitalist crisis and geopolitical confrontation.

Capitalist crisis and the break-up of world order

To unravel the current internal relations between capitalist competition and geopolitical rivalry, it is important to go back to the 1990s. The formal end of the Cold War in the 1990s was precisely a moment of renewed capitalist outward expansion along uneven and combined developmental lines in that it offered enormous opportunities for capital to flow into new areas. The global workforce doubled through the intake of 3 billion workers as a result of states in Central and Eastern Europe (CEE) transitioning to market economies, India's neoliberal turn, and China's integration into the global political economy. Newly available cheap labour further intensified the transnationalization of production along global value chains, underpinning the rise of transnational capital as the hegemonic class fraction within a neoliberal global political economy. Albeit with variegations, neoliberal policy priorities became internalised within the expanding European Union (EU) as well as in Russia, China, and the global economy more generally. The 1990s were a moment when neoliberal economic priorities became hegemonic within the global political economy.

In Europe, Western European manufacturing companies – especially German corporations – benefited from cheap, but skilled labour in CEE. Integrating low-wage suppliers in their value chains increased their competitiveness on the global market.[48] Additionally, privatisation programmes across CEE offered western capital cheap opportunities to buy up highly profitable assets in banking and telecommunications, for example.[49] A number of CEE countries were granted EU membership, but they were not provided with the same benefits as existing members.[50] In practice, they were integrated in a subordinated, peripheral position within the European political economy. Eastern European countries outside the EU did not fare better. The EU's neighbourhood programme and association agreements extended neoliberal restructuring further, in Tuomas Forsberg and Heikki Patomäki's view combining 'neoliberal economic policy and a narrow liberalist view of human rights and democracy'.[51] In the words of Yuliya Yurchenko, 'structural adjustment programmes and loans (SAPs and SALs) exported the neoliberal transnationalization model ... since the 1990s, to the post-Soviet states, including Russia and Ukraine,' with dramatic consequences in both countries.[52] 'Ukraine's GDP in 2019 was lower than in 1989 and life expectancy for men was 67', note Alan Cafruny and Vassilis K. Fouskas.[53] In turn, integration with Western financial capitalism came at a high cost for Russia during the 1990s, as detailed by Pawel Wargan:

> Its GDP collapsed by 40 percent. Its industrial inputs fell by half, and real wages dropped to half of what they were in 1987. The number of poor people increased from 2.2 million in 1987-88 to 74.2 million in 1993-95—from 2 percent of the population to 50 percent in just over five years. Life expectancy decreased by five years for men and three years for women, and millions died under the regime of privatization and shock therapy between 1989 and 2022.[54]

Ultimately, Russia was integrated with global capitalism mainly as an exporter of primary commodities and here especially gas and oil.[55] China too became integrated into global production structures during the 1990s in a peripheral position of uneven and combined development. Depending very much on foreign direct investment by transnational corporations, it was especially cheap labour in the electronics sector which caught foreign attention.[56] Admittedly, partly thanks to its large domestic market and partly due to its state-led capitalist model, the Chinese political economy benefited more from global production structures. Developmental catch-up, however, continues to remain elusive. As Sam King illustrates, it is especially the 'grip over the high-end of the labour process – in particular over microchips – that the United States is now wielding against China in the "trade war"', and which indicates China's continuing subordinated position.[57]

Capitalist expansion in both CEE as well as China occurred at the expense of working people. In CEE, post-communist labour was subjected to double exploitation. Aggressive deregulation and liberalization of labour markets at home resulted in a highly precarious labour market and downward pressure on wages and working conditions. In search for better opportunities abroad, workers from CEE migrated in large numbers to Western Europe, where they were often employed at the very bottom of value chains such as fruit pickers in agriculture, or in low-paid jobs in the hospitality and catering as well as care sectors.[58] The experience of migrant workers in Foxconn factories in China demonstrates a similar fate – underneath a rhetoric of a bright global future lurked capitalism's most exploitative dynamics.[59] In fact, Western European and North American prosperity was built on the backs of workers in Eastern Europe, China and elsewhere in the Global South, as capitalism staved off tendential crisis conditions by expanding into new territories and incorporating more wage labour.

Capitalist expansion was internally related to an increasingly assertive military-security stance. In Europe, after some initial years of uncertainty, NATO was slowly transformed into an increasingly belligerent alliance. As described by Wargan, 'the alliance's expansion coincided with the creeping spread of neoliberalism, helping secure the dominance of US financial capital and sustain the rapacious military-industrial complex that underpins much of its economy and society'.[60] Direct interventions in former Yugoslavia, culminating in a campaign of sustained air strikes in Kosovo in 1999, was followed by a mission in Afghanistan from 2003 onwards. In Europe, military interventions were complemented with Eastward expansion. In 1999, Poland, the Czech Republic and Hungary became the first new members. Russia's leadership became slowly alienated as the country's security interests were not taken into account.[61] The most dramatic step of Eastward expansion was taken at the 2008 NATO summit in Bucharest, when future membership was promised to Ukraine and Georgia,[62] admittedly against opposition by France and Germany.[63] Interestingly, the promises at the Bucharest summit occurred precisely at the moment when the global financial crisis (GFC) threw world order into crisis, described by Forsberg and Patomäki as 'a new nodal point, paving the way for regressive developments involving the rise of nationalistic-authoritarian populism across the world'.[64] More recently, NATO has also become embroiled in the tensions over China, declaring in its 2022 Strategic Concept that the 'People's Republic of China's (PRC) stated ambitions and coercive policies challenge our interests, security and values'.[65] As Susan Watkins affirms, 'NATO's truly chilling 2022 "Strategic Concept" document brigades its thirty-odd member states behind Washington in the stand-off against Beijing'.[66] These heightened geopolitical tensions did not result immediately in war between the West and Russia. In the heydays of globalization during the 1990s and early to mid-2000s, rival capitalist interests between the West and Russia could be easily accommodated. Investment by Russian oligarchs were welcomed with open arms and without questions about the origin of the finance. In the UK, for example, a 'Golden Visa' scheme allowed millionaires to bypass lengthy immigration queues in exchange for at least £2m of investment into the UK economy.[67]

This recent heyday of capitalist expansion came to an abrupt halt in 2007 and 2008 when the global financial crisis hit, reinforced by the Covid-19 pandemic just over ten years later. While the worldwide economic crisis of the 1970s had been temporarily overcome during globalization in the 1990s and early 2000s, capitalism's propensity for crisis reappeared towards the end of the 2000s. As William Robinson points out, the global political economy is gripped by a crisis of overaccumulation, in which accumulated surplus value is increasingly unable to find profitable investment opportunities. Surplus capital and surplus labour can no longer be brought together in a profitable way: 'The total cash held in reserves of the world's 2,000 biggest non-financial corporations increased from $6.6 trillion in 2010 to $14.2 trillion in 2020 ... as the global economy stagnated.'[68] Against the background of this crisis, capitalist competition has spilled over into geopolitical confrontation. This does not mean that capitalist competition directly causes geopolitical confrontations, nor does it justify the Russian attack on Ukraine. Rather, global capitalist competition has a tendency to increasingly fragment world order creating the opportunities for tensions and the contingent possibility for an outbreak of violence and war. As Robinson identifies:

> There are mounting fissures within the ruling groups over how to manage the crisis and stabilize global capitalism. Infighting within their ranks is escalating as the global capitalist historical bloc constructed in the heyday of neoliberalism from the 1990s until 2008 unravels and as the post-WWII international system collapses.[69]

With the lack of effective transnational structures capable of mediating between the different interests of various class fractions, world order has increasingly splintered. The war in Ukraine is a reflection of this, as are the heightened tensions between China and the US over Taiwan. 'Following China's lead in massive infrastructure investment through its Belt and Road Initiatives,' Robinson asserts, 'the US government approved in 2021 a nearly two-trillion-dollar infrastructure bill.'[70] The European Union (EU), in turn, has shifted towards an open strategic autonomy course, trying to chart an independent strategy.[71] And yet, it is Europe which has lost out most. As Cafruny and Fouskas point out, Europe's geopolitical dependence on the US has been deepened as a result of war in Ukraine and economic sanctions.[72]

Instead of Russian oil and gas, Europe now has to import Liquefied Natural Gas (LNG) at great expense from the Middle East and the US, with the latter being mainly extracted by fracking, a practice which is banned in many EU member states.[73] In sum, 'the combination of US subsidies, inflation, and the costs involved in the re-routing of energy supplies threatens the competitiveness of European corporations and risks mass de-industrialization in Europe while re-industrializing the USA'.[74]

What position is left?

Any class agency at this point in time has to be understood within these structuring conditions of the content of the form and the internal relations of the contemporary states-system (form) and capitalism (content) within the geopolitics of global capitalism. There are a number of different positions on the left regarding the current state of affairs in the global political economy. First, some observers compare the current situation with the late 1930s. Paul Mason, for example, argues for a major re-think on defence by the left in view of not only Russian but also Chinese totalitarian, authoritarian regimes: 'For the first time since the 1930s, we face an overt, violent and existential rejection of any form of rules-based order—not just by Russia but by its moral supporter in Beijing.'[75] Mason thus asks for all-out support of Ukraine and a general British rethinking of defence spending. Industrial policy on defence is, thereby, regarded as a kind of military Keynesian programme, or advocacy for a permanent arms economy, in which drastic increases in defence spending go hand-in-hand with a re-industrialisation and re-skilling of the British political economy: 'A new political economy of defence would see defence spending as an investment, with positive spin-offs across society, in terms of growth, skills and social cohesion.'[76] Europe's future security would depend on a massively strengthened conventional military force, re-establishing manufacturing and skills clusters along the way.

A second left position regards the US as the only hegemonic power in the world and, thus, as the main enemy. This stance does not necessarily support Russia in its war efforts, but the war is viewed as a response to Western, NATO-led expansion. More importantly, this position deems China as a non-imperialist alternative to Western capitalism. For Vijay Prashad, for example, the responsibility for global tensions and the war resides with the US due to the pressure it has put on Russia and China via NATO expansion and naval exercises in the South China Sea. Commercially, this included a strategy of cutting Europe off from Russian gas supplies and re-directing it to LNG supplies from the Arab Gulf states and the US. 'There is no doubt', he argues, 'that the Russian government violated international law by invading Ukraine. But this is not a war that is only about Russia and Ukraine. It is a war that is driven by the attempt by the fragile US to maintain its position of primacy in the world.'[77] Here, hope is especially based on China as part of an emerging multi-polar order replacing US hegemony. According to the editors of *Monthly Review*, 'it is precisely the collective security approach offered by China's Global Security Initiative that currently holds out the most hope for world peace through its rejection of the "Cold War mentality" and military blocs'.[78] China then becomes a serious contender to US rule, opening up space for (progressive) alternatives. In Wargan's account, 'multipolarity is a step, in other words, toward the articulation of alternative political projects outside the sphere of monopoly capitalism's accumulating drive'.[79]

Both positions, in our view, resemble closely the state-centric structural realist perspective and its extreme focus on state material capabilities, i.e., the content of the content. Different states are assessed according to their material capabilities in the discussion of a potential transition from hegemony to multi-polarity. Mason argues in favour of increasing British material capabilities in order to counter increased Russian material capabilities. The second position, though politically from the opposite side, also only focuses on state capabilities. Moreover, while China does exhibit different traits of state capitalism, to treat it like a promising alternative is rather dubious. This is partly because of the human rights abuses against Uyghurs and other ethnic and religious minorities in Xinjiang, partly because of the extreme exploitation of Chinese migrant workers, and partly because, as Robinson details:

> Chinese capitalism now shows many of the telltale structural signs of crisis: a hypertrophied financial sector, including banking assets that ballooned to some $50 trillion in 2021, not including shadow finance; a runaway spiral of household and corporate debt that went from 178 percent of GDP in 2010 to 287 percent in 2021; overcapacity; a slowdown in growth rates; and social polarization.[80]

A third position treats the war in Ukraine as a war of independence, which must be supported with militarization as much as possible. In her excellent *Ukraine and the Empire of Capital,* Yurchenko initially assessed the build-up to and outbreak of hostilities in 2014 in Ukraine with analysis of competing transnational capitalist class fractions, the Dnipropetrovsk and Donetsk blocs, which have shaped Ukraine's post-Soviet history. The transnationalization of the state in Ukraine thus ensued as a result of a concentration of capital between these competing blocs. Hence 'Russia's manipulation toolbox is not dissimilar to that of Ukraine's Western partners as both groups pursue their economic imperialist interests', through, 'a pronounced intensification of transnational class struggles and East-West geopolitical tensions'.[81] Nevertheless, with the scale of the war spreading in February 2022, this position has seemed to shift towards an identification of the conflict as a war of liberation. Understandably, then, it has more recently become cast as an existential fight for survival. 'Russia has triggered a resistance that is deeply rooted in a centuries-old fight of Ukrainians against Russian imperialism,' she argues. Regarding the war as an inter-imperialist conflict between the East and West, by contrast, would deny Ukraine and Ukrainians their agency in the conflict. Yes, there is an inter-imperialist dimension, but this 'should not prevent us from recognizing the centrality of Ukraine's fight for independence from both Russian and Western Imperial domination. And the imperial competition should not prevent us from seeing the common international class interests that cut across the conflict.' Victory in this war of independence is then regarded as the basis for a future joint class struggle against capitalist exploitation. In short, 'the international left must be in solidarity with Ukraine as an oppressed nation and our fight for self-determination. That includes our right to secure arms for our fighters and volunteers to win our freedom.'[82] Gilbert Achcar indicates a similar position. He too makes reference to inter-imperialist rivalry and likens what he calls the New Cold War to the pre–World War I geopolitical situation. His opposition to all forms of imperialism does not preclude, however, military support of Ukraine:

> In the same way that the only true anti-imperialism during the First World War was that which equally rejected both imperialist sides, the only consistent anti-imperialism nowadays consists in equally rejecting both sides of the New Cold War. However, this does not in the least imply a neutral attitude towards Russia's invasion of Ukraine: no anti-imperialist can remain neutral in a situation where a subaltern nation is attacked by an imperialist power. Solidarity with the victims of imperialist aggressions is the elementary duty of anti-imperialists.[83]

By contrast, advocating for peace without providing Ukraine with weapons for its military defence would ask for its capitulation.

Finally, a fourth stance argues that we need to analyze the war in Ukraine within the broader context of inter-imperialist rivalry against the background of a deep crisis in global capitalism. As Tomáš Tengely-Evans writes, 'the Eastern European country is a battleground for United States and NATO ambitions to reassert their hegemony in the world and for Russia's failing hopes to stamp its authority over its "near abroad"'.[84] It is acknowledged that Ukraine defends its independence, yet 'that is neither the totality nor the dominant characteristic of the war. Rather, Ukraine is the keystone in an arc of inter-imperialist competition that stretches across the Eurasian landmass. Rivalry between the West and Russia has driven the war and now sees NATO's and Russia's guns thundering on Ukrainian soil.'[85] Drawing on classic theories of imperialism, this position defines imperialism as a capitalist phenomenon including war between capitalist states.[86] Western support of Ukraine with weapons is as much part of this war of inter-imperialist rivalry as is the economic warfare through sanctions imposed by the West on Russia. In short, the current situation in this analysis resembles the pre-World War I situation in 1914 with working people on all sides of the conflict losing out.[87] As we see it, this position captures best the content of the form, the internal relations between the contemporary states-system (form) and capitalism (content) within the geopolitics of global capitalism. Or, in Nikolai Bukharin's recognition, how the anarchic structure of capitalism finds expression in both economic competition and militarism.[88] Of course, today's situation is not exactly the same as the past. Capitalism has become transnationalized with production increasingly organized in global value chains and the transnational capitalist class emerging as the dominant international actor. Moreover, as highlighted by Joseph Choonara, China's production structure is 'highly integrated into global circuits of capitalism'.[89] And yet, states have retained their crucial role as nodal points for the organization of capitalist accumulation within the global political economy,[90] while the transnational capitalist class itself is increasingly fragmenting. Hence, the shift from global capitalist competition to geopolitical confrontation. The war in Ukraine is a war of independence, we agree. However, it is nested within wider inter-imperialist conflict.[91] It has been transformed into a proxy war between the US and its allies against Russia, fought with Ukrainian personnel on Ukrainian soil. Such a position does not deny Ukrainian agency. Rather, it provides space for the multiple Ukrainian voices, which are in danger of being subsumed into a monolithic vision of 'the Ukrainian voice' by regarding the war purely as a war of independence by a homogenous people, overlooking for example the difficult position of many Russian speaking Ukrainians, who find themselves in the middle between a Western nation-building project and their opposition to Putin's war.[92] The hopes for an anti-capitalist project after a Ukrainian victory are slim in our view. For example, an international

Ukraine Recovery Conference took place in London on 21 and 22 June 2023 with a heavy emphasis on raising private capital investment secured by government insurance schemes in addition to direct governmental aid.[93] As Volodymyr Ishchenko points out, 'despite the objective imperatives of the war, Ukraine is proceeding with privatizations, lowering taxes, scrapping protective labour legislation and favouring "transparent" international corporations over "corrupt" domestic firms'.[94] Reconstructing Ukraine will be another growth opportunity for (transnational) capital, in a new 'bomb-and-build' strategy, akin to reconstruction in post-war Iraq.[95] This would not be the first time that left forces after a successful struggle for national independence were pushed aside at the moment of victory. Too often independent national movements have become the 'playthings' of imperialist powers.[96]

A DIALECTICAL RUDDER

The war in Ukraine and heightened tensions between the US and China over Taiwan have brought any remaining hopes for a peaceful world to an end. The permanent arms economy remains regnant. In this chapter, we have highlighted the importance of a focus on the content of the form as a philosophical and dialectical departure point for understanding the internal relations of the geopolitics of the states-system and global capitalism to unravel the dynamics underpinning the current historical conjuncture. Returning to our rebuking of the dualism of form and content (see Table 1 above), our dialectical reframing of the geopolitics of global capitalism can be made by taking two extremes to emphasize our points. First, G. John Ikenberry extends the position that we have outlined in this essay as the form of the content, in his case in the form of the ideology of liberal internationalism. In an attempt to capture the discontents of the liberal international order, in 2010 Ikenberry declared that 'in the decades ahead, the United States and Europe and rising states – many of which are in Asia – will have more reasons and not fewer reasons to cooperate in open and rule-based ways'. His view, as a precis of his subsequent book *Liberal Leviathan*, was that the future would still belong to liberal international order and that 'the violent forces that have overthrown international orders in the past do not seem to operate today'. In rejecting imperialism as an argument for addressing crisis in world order, Ikenberry declared that after liberalism there would only be more liberalism.[97] The contemporary geopolitics of the Russo-Ukrainian War clearly reveals how moribund such liberal internationalism and the ideology of an ideas-centred conception of political economic change actually is. Second, our dialectical venture into the content of the form can be extended by contrasting such liberal internationalism with the geopolitical antagonisms traced within historical materialism. Alex Callinicos, in *The New Age of Catastrophe,* outlines how the geopolitics of the Russo-Ukrainian War should be addressed as a 'conflict *within* global capitalism', one perhaps based on the formation of shifting polarities. 'Only the abolition of an imperialist system driven by economic and geopolitical competition,' he argues, 'can make the world and humankind safe from predators like Putin and Bush.'[98] Emphasising the content of the form in this sort of manner assists in advancing what Gramsci identified as regional situations that are at the same time part of a 'differentiated geo-economic organism'.[99] A dialectical rudder does not provide finality on such issues but does offer a guiding red thread on the primacy of the category of capitalism as a totality, rather than separate parts, and how to relate internally theory and history as moments of the whole. We argue that war in Ukraine is an inter-imperialist conflict between the US and its Western allies against Russia, which also needs to be understood as a warning signal against China.

The fact that capitalist crisis has spilled over into geopolitical confrontation indicates the severity of the crisis, but it does not imply that capitalism is close to collapse. There are yet still further expansionary rounds of capital possible, creating the terrain for ever more dramatic crises. For one, the war in Ukraine and the heavy militarization which goes hand-in-hand with it across the world – fuelling a permanent arms economy through a Keynesian-style military industrial programme – is a major new growth point for capital. As Cafruny and Fouskas point out, 'the war has provided a windfall for the German and US military-industrial complexes. US arms sales to NATO allies doubled in 2022.'[100] Unsurprisingly, arms manufacturers made super profits the moment the war started, as detailed by Robinson: 'Two weeks into the conflict, shares of Raytheon were up 8 percent, General Dynamics up 12 percent, Lockheed Martin up 18 percent, and Northrop Grumman up 22 percent.'[101] Another strategy for further capitalist expansion is based on increasing digitalization of the global economy as part of the second information age based on a fusion between the digital economy with transnational financial capital. In the long run, however, even if this form of expansion can counter capitalist crisis for a while, 'absent redistributive and regulatory reforms or state intervention to generate public or alternative forms of employment, digitally driven global transformation will aggravate the structural crisis of overaccumulation'.[102] Third, the move towards 'green capitalism' is often pushed as a new outlet for profitable capital investment. There is the belief that as long as the state provides the right incentives, the market will address the climate crisis successfully. Alternatively, others put their hope in the active state providing a Keynesian Green New Deal. Ultimately, these are false alternatives as they do not change the underlying capitalist social relations of production and the structuring conditions which come with it.[103]

As 'death rides out' in Ukraine,[104] it is yet again everyday lives on all sides that suffer. When capitalist states go to war with each other in inter-imperialist confrontations, workers are always on the losing side. Only if capitalism and its permanent arms economy is overcome can there be hope for a more peaceful world order. Transnational solidarity in opposition to all types of capitalist imperialism is a fundamental starting point in this respect.

NOTES

We would like to thank Shahar Hameiri, Chris Hesketh, Heikki Patomäki, and Adam Swain for guidance and feedback.

1   Andreas Bieler and Adam David Morton, 'Axis of Evil or Access to Diesel? Spaces of New Imperialism and the Iraq War', *Historical Materialism*, 23(2), 2015, pp. 94-130.
2   Michael Kidron, 'A Permanent Arms Economy', *International Socialism*, 28, 1967, pp. 8-12.
3   Maurice Dobb, *Studies in the Development of Capitalism*, London: Routledge, 1946, p. 1.
4   Dobb, *Studies in the Development of Capitalism*, p. 1.
5   Jacqueline Best, Colin Hay, Genevieve LeBaron and Daniel Mügge, 'Seeing and Not-Seeing Like a Political Economist: The Historicity of Contemporary Political Economy and its Blind Spots', *New Political Economy*, 26(2), 2021, p. 226. See also: Genevieve Le Baron, Daniel Mügge, Jacqueline Best and Colin Hay, 'Blind Spots in IPE: Marginalized Perspectives and Neglected Trends in Contemporary Capitalism', *Review of International Political Economy*, 28(2), 2021, p. 290.
6   For an engagement with the contending contributions by David Harvey, Alex Callinicos, William Robinson, and Leo Panitch and Sam Gindin on the territorial and capital logics of geopolitics, see: Andreas Bieler and Adam David Morton, *Global Capitalism, Global War, Global Crisis*, Cambridge: Cambridge University Press, 2018, pp. 109-23 and 191-201.
7   Karl Marx to Friedrich Engels (24 August 1867), in Karl Marx and Friedrich Engels, *Selected Correspondence*, Moscow: Progress Publishers, 1975, p. 180, original emphasis.
8   Bertell Ollman, *Alienation: Marx's Conception of Man in Capitalist Society*, Second edition, Cambridge: Cambridge University Press, 1976; and Derek Sayer, *The Violence of Abstraction: The Analytic Foundations of Historical Materialism*, London: Basil Blackwell, 1987.
9   Andreas Bieler and Adam David Morton, *Global Capitalism, Global War, Global Crisis*; and Andreas Bieler and Adam David Morton, 'The Deficits of Discourse in IPE: turning base metal into gold?', *International Studies Quarterly*, 52(1), 2008, pp. 103-28.
10 Bertell Ollman, 'Marxism and the Philosophy of Internal relations; or, How to Replace the Mysterious "Paradox" with "Contradictions" that can be studied and Resolved', *Capital & Class*, 39(1), 2015, p. 10.
11 Adam David Morton, 'The Limits of Sociological Marxism?', *Historical Materialism*,

21(1), 2013, pp. 129-58.
12   Fredric Jameson, *The Modernist Papers*, London: Verso, 2007, p. xix.
13   Karl Marx, 'Debates on the Law on Thefts of Wood', *Rheinische Zeitung*, No. 298 (25 October 1842), in Karl Marx and Friedrich Engels, *Collected Works*, Vol. 1, London: Lawrence and Wishart, 1975, p. 261.
14   Antonio Gramsci, *Prison Notebooks*, Vol. 3, Joseph A. Buttigieg, ed. and trans., New York: Columbia University Press, 2007, Q7§21, p. 172.
15   Jameson, *Modernist Papers*, pp. xv-xix.
16   Kenneth N. Waltz, *Theory of International Politics*, New York: Random House, 1979, p. 10.
17   Kenneth N. Waltz, 'Reflections on *Theory of International Politics*: A Response to My Critics' [1986], in Kenneth N. Waltz, *Realism and International Politics*, London: Routledge, 2008, p. 51.
18   Robert W. Cox, 'Realism, Positivism, Historicism' [1985], in Robert W. Cox with Timothy J. Sinclair, *Approaches to World Order*, Cambridge: Cambridge University Press, 1995, p. 57.
19   Adam David Morton, 'Mainstreaming Marxism: On the Anarchic Structure of World Economy', *International Affairs*, 99(3), 2023, pp. 1253-72.
20   Karl Marx, *Economic and Philosophic Manuscripts of 1844* [1844], Moscow: Progress Publishers, 1977, p. 35, original emphasis. See also: Justin Rosenberg, *The Empire of Civil Society: A Critique of the Realist Theory of International Relations*, London: Verso, 1994, pp. 142-58.
21   John Mearsheimer, 'Why the Ukraine Crisis Is the West's Fault: The Liberal Delusions That Provoked Putin', *Foreign Affairs* (September/October) (2014), pp. 1-12 and John Mearsheimer, 'The Causes and Consequences of the Ukraine War', Lecture at the European University Institute, 6 June 2022, available at: www.youtube.com/watch?v=qciVozNtCDM.
22   Jameson, *Modernist Papers*, p. xvi.
23   For a critique, see Damien Cahill, *The End of Laissez-Faire? On the Durability of Embedded Neoliberalism*, Cheltenham: Edward Elgar, 2014.
24   John M. Hobson, *The Eastern Origins of Western Civilization*, Cambridge: Cambridge University Press, 2011, pp. 25-6.
25   Martha Finnemore and Kathryn Sikkink, 'International Norm Dynamics and Political Change', *International Organization*, 52(4), 1998, pp. 887-917.
26   Bieler and Morton, *Global Capitalism, Global War, Global Crisis*, pp. 53-60.
27   Alastair Iain Johnston, 'China in a World of Orders: Rethinking Compliance and Challenge in Beijing's International Relations', *International Security*, 44(2), 2019, pp. 9-60.
28   Jameson, *Modernist Papers*, p. xvi.
29   Jameson, *Modernist Papers*, p. xvii.
30   Ernesto Laclau and Chantal Mouffe, *Hegemony and Socialist Strategy: Towards a Radical Democratic Politics*, 2d edition, London: Verso, 2001, p. 108, emphasis added.
31   David Campbell, *Writing Security: United States Policy and the Politics of Identity*, Minneapolis: University of Minnesota Press, 1998, pp. 6, 219; and, for the critical reception, see: Gearóid Ó Tuathail, 'Dissident IR and the Identity Politics Narrative: A Sympathetically Skeptical Perspective', *Political Geography*, 15(6-7), 1996, p. 652.
32   Antonio Gramsci, *Prison Notebooks*, Vol. 2, Joseph A. Buttigieg, ed. and trans., New York: Columbia University Press, 1996, Q4§16, p. 158.

33 Charlotte Epstein, 'Constructivism or the Eternal Return of Universals in International Relations: Why Returning to Language is Vital to Prolonging the Owl's Flight', *European Journal of International Relations*, 19(3), 2013, p. 501.
34 Charlotte Epstein, *Birth of the State: The Place of the Body in Crafting Modern Politics*, Oxford: Oxford University Press, 2021, p. 6.
35 Perry Anderson, *In the Tracks of Historical Materialism*, London: Verso, 1983, p. 48.
36 Nicos Poulantzas, *State, Power, Socialism*, trans. Patrick Camiller, London: Verso, 1978, p. 151.
37 Epstein, *Birth of the State*, p. 3.
38 Campbell, *Writing Security*, pp. 6-7.
39 Jameson, *Modernist Papers*, p. xvii.
40 Jameson, *Modernist Papers*, p. xvii.
41 Ludovico Silva, *Marx's Literary Style* [1975], Paco Brito Nuñez, trans., London: Verso, 2023, p. 30, original emphasis.
42 Gramsci, *Prison Notebooks*, Vol. 3, Q7§29 p. 179.
43 Gramsci, *Prison Notebooks*, Vol. 3, Q7§29, p. 179 and Q8§61, p. 271.
44 Gramsci, *Prison Notebooks*, Vol. 3, Q7§35, p. 187.
45 Robert W. Cox, 'Social Forces, States, and World Orders: Beyond International Relations Theory' [1981], in Cox with Sinclair, *Approaches to World Order*, p. 95.
46 On theorizing modes of production within the differential space of social formations, see: Chris Hesketh, 'Finding Space in the Mode of Production Debate: The Value of Latin America', *Environment and Planning F: Philosophy, Theory, Models, Methods and Practice*, online first, 2023.
47 Bieler and Morton, *Global Capitalism, Global War, Global Crisis*, pp. 36-50. See also: Radhika Desai, *Geopolitical Economy: After US Hegemony, Globalization and Empire*, London: Pluto Press, 2013.
48 Dorothee Bohle and Béla Greskovits, *Capitalist Diversity on Europe's Periphery*, Ithaca, NY: Cornell University Press, 2012, pp. 161-72.
49 Andreas Bieler and Jokubas Salyga, 'Baltic Labour in the Crucible of Capitalist Exploitation: Reassessing "Post-Communist" Transformation', *The Economic and Labour Relations Review*, 31(2), 2020, pp. 194-5.
50 Dorothee Bohle, 'Neoliberal Hegemony, Transnational Capital and the terms of the EU's Eastward Expansion', *Capital & Class*, 30(1), 2006, pp. 57-86.
51 Tuomas Forsberg and Heikki Patomäki, *Debating the War in Ukraine: Counterfactual Histories and Future Possibilities*, London: Routledge, 2022, p. 35.
52 Yuliya Yurchenko, *Ukraine and the Empire of Capital: From Marketization to Armed Conflict*, London: Pluto Press, 2018, pp. 6, 203.
53 Alan Cafruny and Vassilis K. Fouskas, 'Ukraine, Europe, and the re-routing of Globalization', *Journal of Balkan and near Eastern Studies*, DOI: 10.1080/19448953.2023.2197635, 2023, p. 5.
54 Pawel Wargan, 'NATO and the Long War on the Third World', *Monthly Review*, 74(8), 2023; available at www.monthlyreview.org.
55 Joseph Choonara, 'The Devastation of Ukraine: NATO, Russia and Imperialism', *International Socialism*, 174, 2022, p. 12.
56 Bieler and Morton, *Global Capitalism, Global War, Global Crisis*, pp.166-71; and Jane Hardy, 'China's Place in the Global Divisions of Labour: An Uneven and Combined

Development Perspective', *Globalizations*, 14(2), 2017, pp. 189-201.
57 Sam King, *Imperialism and the Development Myth: How rich countries dominate in the twenty-first century*, Manchester: Manchester University Press, 2021, p. 238, see also: pp. 219-57.
58 Bieler and Salyga, 'Baltic Labour in the Crucible of Capitalist Exploitation', pp. 196-200.
59 Jenny Chan, Mark Selden and Pun Ngai, *Dying for an iPhone: Apple, Foxconn and the Lives of China's Workers*, London: Pluto Press, 2020.
60 Wargan, 'NATO and the Long War on the Third World'.
61 Forsberg and Patomäki, *Debating the War in Ukraine*, p. 17.
62 Forsberg and Patomäki, *Debating the War in Ukraine*, p. 24; Choonara, 'The Devastation of Ukraine', p. 18.
63 Cafruny and Fouskas, 'Ukraine, Europe, and the re-routing of Globalization', p. 2.
64 Forsberg and Patomäki, *Debating the War in Ukraine*, p. 25.
65 NATO, 2022 Strategic Concept, p. 5, available at: www.nato.int/nato_static_fl2014/assets/pdf/2022/6/pdf/290622-strategic-concept.pdf.
66 Susan Watkins, 'Five Wars in One', *New Left Review*, 137(September-October), 2022, p. 19.
67 Martin Williams, '200 Russian millionaires bought way into UK in seven years since "clampdown"', *openDemocracy*, 2022, available at: www.opendemocracy.net.
68 William I. Robinson, *Can Global Capitalism Endure?* Atlanta, GA: Clarity Press, 2022, pp. 16-17.
69 William I. Robinson, 'Can Global Capitalism Endure?', *Revista de Estudios Globales: Análisis Histórico y Cambio Social*, 1(1), 2021, p. 34.
70 Robinson, *Can Global Capitalism Endure?*, 2022, p. 58.
71 Luuk Schmitz and Timo Seidl, 'As Open as Possible, as Autonomous as Necessary: Understanding the Rise of Open Strategic Autonomy in EU Trade Policy', *Journal of Common Market Studies*, 61(3), 2023, pp. 834-52.
72 Cafruny and Fouskas, 'Ukraine, Europe, and the re-routing of Globalization', p. 7.
73 Food and Water Action Europe, 'European Union Fracking: Coming to your doorstep', March 2023, available at: www.foodandwatereurope.org/wp-content/uploads/2023/03/Fracking_Coming_To_Your_Doorstep2022-1.pdf. See also: Piotr Żuk, 'The War in Ukraine: Consequences for the Economy, Labour Class and Equitable Development in Europe and Beyond', *The Economic and Labour Relations Review*, 34(2), 2023, pp. 346-7.
74 Cafruny and Fouskas, 'Ukraine, Europe, and the re-routing of Globalization', p. 7.
75 Paul Mason, 'As war rages in Ukraine, rearming the UK must be a proud part of Labour's brand', *LabourList*, 27 February 2023, available at www.labourlist.org/.
76 Paul Mason, 'For a New Political Economy of Defence', *Futures of Work*, 10 February 2022, available at: www.futuresofwork.co.uk.
77 Vijay Prashad, 'The War in Ukraine is a War over Europe's Future', *Stop the War Coalition*, 2023, available at: www.stopwar.org.uk.
78 The Editors, 'Notes from the Editors', *Monthly Review*, 74(11), 2023, available at: www.monthlyreview.org.
79 Wargan, 'NATO and the Long War on the Third World'.
80 Robinson, *Can Global Capitalism Endure?*, 2022, p. 73.
81 Yurchenko, *Ukraine and the Empire of Capital*, pp. 3, 45.

82   Yuliya Yurchenko, 'Fighting for Ukrainian Self-determination', interview by Ashley Smith, *Spectre Journal*, 11 April 2022, available at: www.spectrejournal.com.
83   Gilbert Achcar, 'Consistent anti-imperialism and the Ukraine war', *Labour Hub*, 12 March 2023; available at www.labourhub.org.uk. See also: Gilbert Achcar, *The New Cold War: The United States, Russia, and China from Kosovo to Ukraine*, Chicago: Haymarket Books, 2023.
84   Tomáš Tengely-Evans, 'Death Rides Out: NATO, Russia and the War in Ukraine', *International Socialism*, 178, 2023.
85   Tengely-Evans, 'Death Rides Out'.
86   Choonara, 'The Devastation of Ukraine', p. 26.
87   Żuk, 'The War in Ukraine', pp. 345, 348.
88   Nikolai Bukharin, *Imperialism and World Economy* [1917], New York: Monthly Review Press, 1929; and, for how this theory of imperialism is situated within the circuits of value, see: Alex Callinicos, *Imperialism and Global Political Economy*, Cambridge: Polity, 2009; and Morton, 'Mainstreaming Marxism', pp. 1258-61.
89   Choonara, 'The Devastation of Ukraine', p. 9.
90   Bieler and Morton, *Global Capitalism, Global War, Global Crisis*, pp. 117-30.
91   Watkins, 'Five Wars in One'.
92   Volodymyr Ishchenko, 'Ukrainian Voices?', *New Left Review*, 138(November-December), 2022, p. 35; Volodymyr Ishchenko, 'The Minsk Accords and the Political Weakness of the "Other Ukraine"', *Russian Politics*, 8(2), 2023, p. 146.
93   Jonathan Josephs, 'Ukraine war: Push to rebuild economy starts with UK's $3bn'; *BBC News*, 21 June 2023, available at: www.bbc.co.uk.
94   Ishchenko, 'Ukrainian Voices?', p. 30. See also: Żuk, 'The War in Ukraine', pp. 353-4.
95   Bieler and Morton, *Global Capitalism, Global War, Global Crisis*, pp. 206-16.
96   Tengely-Evans, 'Death Rides Out'.
97   G. John Ikenberry, 'The Liberal International Order and Its Discontents', *Millennium: Journal of International Studies*, 38(3), 2010, pp. 512, 514, 521. See also: G. John Ikenberry, *Liberal Leviathan: The Origins, Crisis and Transformation of the American World Order*, Princeton: Princeton University Press, 2011; and G. John Ikenberry, 'The End of Liberal International Order?', *International Affairs*, 94(1), 2018, pp. 7-23.
98   Alex Callinicos, *The New Age of Catastrophe*, Cambridge: Polity Press, 2023, pp. 109, 112.
99   Antonio Gramsci, *Selections from Cultural Writings*, David Forgacs and Geoffrey Nowell-Smith, eds., William Boelhower, trans., London: Lawrence and Wishart, 1985, Q24§3 p. 415.
100 Cafruny and Fouskas, 'Ukraine, Europe, and the re-routing of Globalization', p. 4. See also: Robinson, *Can Global Capitalism Endure?*, 2022, p. 67.
101 Robinson, *Can Global Capitalism Endure?*, 2022, p. 92.
102 Robinson, *Can Global Capitalism Endure?*, 2022, p. 53.
103 Ulrich Brand and Markus Wissen, *The Imperial Mode of Living: Everyday Life and the Ecological Crisis of Capitalism*, London: Verso, 2021, pp. 161-81.
104 Tengely-Evans, 'Death Rides Out'.

THE US AND CHINA'S DIGITAL TECH WAR: A NEW RIVALRY WITHIN AND BEYOND THE US EMPIRE?

TANNER MIRRLEES

From the post-war era to our time, the United States has played a key role in 'the making of global capitalism'.[1] By representing its own national interests as synonymous with the world's interests, the US state has championed the globalization of capitalism, celebrated consumerism as a way of life, and at times both promoted and subverted democracy at home and abroad.[2] Employing a mix of persuasion and repression, the US state and capital have invited and sometimes compelled many states and capitals of Europe, Latin America, the Middle East, and Asia to integrate themselves into the US Empire, winning their consent to the global neoliberal order while organizing their co-administration of it. Unlike the formal European colonial empires that asserted sovereignty over territorial colonies, the informal US Empire has been superintended by the US state, a post-colonial hegemon at the centre of a vast interdependent network of outwardly sovereign nation-states. Its political managers facilitate and legitimize the accumulation interests of multinational corporations, empowering the CEO and shareholder classes to prosper through cross-border investments, mergers and acquisitions, and commodity production, circulation, and sales, all the while disorganizing and degrading working-class life and labour. The US Empire has long secured the global neoliberal order against challenges to its maintenance, and keeping down a new power keen on building and benefiting from an alternative global order seems to be its new bipartisan consensus on China.[3] For the Republican Party's MAGA reactionaries *and* the Democratic Party's technocrats, China is now the foremost rival to the US Empire.[4] Donald J. Trump has described China as 'our [America's] enemy' and Xi Jinping as his enemy;[5] Joe Biden's White House views China as a 'threat' to American sovereignty and global leadership and believes that 'winning the competition with China should unite all of us'.[6]

Today the US and China stand as the contemporary world's foremost economic, military, and media-technological powers, but despite their distinct histories, states, economies, and national cultural identities, these two countries have engaged in decades of collaboration and remain deeply intertwined.[7] For nearly fifty years, China's own development into the 'world's factory' happened within the framework of the US Empire, and so-called 'capitalism with Chinese characteristics' has been heavily reliant on the US's foreign direct investment (FDI), subsidiaries, plant relocations, outsourcing contracts, and vast consumer markets (and debt). More than 70,000 US companies do business in China each year: in 2020, $8.7 billion worth of US FDI flowed into China, and in that same year, China's FDI in the US equaled $7.2 billion.[8] In 2022, bilateral trade between these countries hit a record high of $690.6 billion: US exports to China amounted to $153.8 billion, while imports of Chinese products equaled $536.8 billion.[9] While economic integration persists, what's faded is the optimistic narrative of 'Chimerica', which in the first decade of the 21st century imagined a mutually beneficial *convergence* of the US and China's corporations and government elites managing a peaceful, interdependent world system.[10] Events like the Wall Street-induced global financial crisis of 2007-2009 and the Covid-19 pandemic, alongside the pivot to Asia Pacific strategies pursued by the Obama, Trump, and Biden administrations to contain China's rise and assert more regional control, drove geopolitical *divergence* between the two countries, bringing the ideal of 'Chimerica' to an end.[11]

A new type of asymmetric rivalry between the US and China has emerged that is not identical to the inter-imperial rivalries of the early 20th century but is still marked by a form of national industrial competition and geo-strategic conflict.[12] While China's own status as a lasting periphery of the US Empire and its ascent as a new imperial power are subjects of vigorous debate,[13] it's undeniable that since Xi Jinping declared a new Chinese Dream in 2012, China's party-state has pursued greater independence from the US Empire and sought a more prominent leadership role in the world.[14] The US, the reigning global hegemon, strives to protect and promote the contested foundations of the neoliberal global order; China, an upstart, may seek a new global order. The rivalry between the US and China remains asymmetrical due to the US's superior power resources and capacities. Though not yet on par with the US, China has undeniably stood up to the states and capitals that once subordinated it and may now be subordinating others in the Global South.[15] It is not certain that the decline of the US Empire and the rise of a new Chinese-centred global order is imminent, but the mere possibility of such a paradigm shift has motivated numerous US politicians and CEOs to prioritize confrontation over compromise when dealing with their Chinese peers, and their development of a new 'Washington Consensus' aims to take on and take down the 'Beijing Consensus'.[16] While US and Chinese corporations collaborate and compete, their home states conflict in international politics, unleashing new contradictions. A flashpoint for this contradictory rivalry is the global digital tech sector, which encompasses industries and firms ranging from computer hardware, software, and chips, to telecommunications and smartphones, to internet services and social media platforms.[17]

In this new and developing 'digital tech war' between the US and China, the corporations headquartered in both countries find themselves in a contradictory situation vis-à-vis each other and each super-state. On one side, they continue to collaborate and compete driven by shared and separate profit motives, while on the flip side, there are emerging signs of divergence and discontent stemming from state-directed nationalist industrial innovation campaigns and mounting geopolitical conflicts. The battle between the US and China in and across the global digital tech sector, the most advanced sector of global capitalism, is the frontline of a new asymmetric rivalry between the two countries that is shaping the world system's future, within and potentially beyond the US Empire. How did the US-China digital tech relationship develop? Why has the US state and its allies recently shifted from advocating international free trade, open market competition, and joint corporate ventures with China and its digital tech sector to enforcing national protectionism, subsidized enclosures, and sanctions? What are the economic and geopolitical conditions undergirding the US and China's digital tech war for the world system's future, and what are the implications of this conflagration for countries on its peripheries?

This essay examines the historical and developing contexts of the digital tech war between the US and China. In the post-Cold War era, the US sought to open up China to free trade with Silicon Valley but encountered numerous challenges, primarily stemming from China's 'cyber sovereignty', or, the party-state's exercise of control over the internet infrastructure, data, content flows, and activities of digital tech firms, within its territorial borders. In the 21st century, China's party-state has skillfully managed the presence and expansion of major US-based tech giants, including Apple, Alphabet-Google, Meta Platforms, Amazon, and Microsoft (referred to as 'AAMAM') within its borders, dashing their dreams of maximal profit. At present, US and Chinese state agencies and globalizing corporations intersect and drive the digital tech sectors of the US and China into world markets, and these new US and Chinese digital imperialisms contend for prominence, particularly in the Global South. To ensure that Silicon Valley maintains its leadership position in global digital capitalism, the US state has recently combined sanctions and subsidies to try to restrict the expansion of China's digital tech sector, but the efficacy of this massive containment and control strategy is uncertain.

NAILING INTERNET JELL-O TO A 'GREAT FIREWALL': 'AAMAM' MEETS THE CCP

In every stage of modern history, empires have relied on communications technologies and media industries to expand, and from 1945 to the present day, the US has grown its empire with these industries at its helm.[18] During the globalizing heyday of the 1990s, the US Empire embraced a cyber-libertarian dream of a US-centred capitalist internet that would unite the world through the spread of laissez-faire markets, the free flow of digitized information, and the universalization of freedom and democracy. This dream captivated a wide range of individuals, from tech entrepreneurs to social movement activists. The neoliberal Washington Consensus of privatization, deregulation, and trade liberalization would rely upon the US-centric global internet to imagine a fundamentally new and different world system: all the old imperial conflicts and wars would vanish, states would relinquish their sovereignty, corporations would transcend national boundaries, and nationalism would melt into a global digital village characterized by cosmopolitan peace, cultural hybridity and difference plastered with Walt Disney and Apple logos.

US President Bill Clinton had high hopes that the US Empire's cyber-libertarian dream would gradually permeate China. To achieve this, he advocated for China's accession to the World Trade Organization (WTO). On 8 March 2000, Clinton delivered a speech aimed at winning support for China's WTO membership from US foreign policy elites, Congress, and CEOs.[19] In his speech, Clinton acknowledged that China's joining the WTO would not guarantee its adoption of the Washington Consensus or instantaneously create a 'free' and 'democratic' society. However, Clinton saw WTO rules as guiding China's reform and benefiting US corporations, especially those in Silicon Valley looking to access the world's fastest-growing market. Clinton regarded the American internet as a catalyst for profound change in China, stating, 'We know how much the internet has transformed America, and we are already an open society. Imagine the transformative power it could have in China – liberty will spread through cell phones and cable modems.' He playfully dismissed concerns about China's state control over the internet, quipping, 'Good luck! It's like trying to nail Jell-O to the wall'. The audience responded with laughter.

Over the past 23 years, China's party-state has rejected the US Empire's cyber-libertarian dream, resisting efforts to fully integrate its digital tech sector into a neoliberal global capitalist framework.[20] In 2000, China's Ministry of Public Security authorized Fang Binxing's Golden Shield Project, which effectively nailed internet jell-O into the 'Great Firewall' to territorialize and assert its control over a national version of the internet.[21] This move countered Clinton's vision of a globally borderless and stateless internet. Fast-forward to present-day 'digital China', where major US social networking sites (such as Facebook and Twitter), apps (including WhatsApp and Messenger), search engines (like Google and Yahoo), video sharing services (such as YouTube and TikTok), streaming platforms (Netflix and Amazon Prime), email services (Gmail and Yahoo!), and news media websites (*The New York Times* and *The Wall Street Journal*) are blocked and mostly inaccessible without a VPN. China's state agencies, particularly the Central Cyberspace Affairs Commission and police-linked Security Bureaus, actively monitor, filter, and censor websites and information deemed politically incorrect. This includes voices of Chinese dissidents, videos of street protests, calls for independent unions, as well as American news and democratic socialist websites such as *Jacobin*. Meanwhile, the Propaganda Department pays social media influencer accounts, known as the '50-cent party', to flood the Chinese internet with politically correct posts, shaping the opinions of China's one billion internet users, promoting official nationalism, and maintaining social order.[22] The Chinese state's internet control apparatus is estimated to employ over 2 million people and cost \$6.6 billion.[23] By restricting Silicon Valley's firms from access to China's digital market and banning numerous US-owned social media platforms, China's 'Great Firewall' ensures that Chinese tech corporations take priority in selling to, monitoring, and monetizing the data of China's ever-growing population of internet users. Consequently, Chinese corporations like Alibaba, Baidu, and Tencent, rather than Google or Meta Platforms, profit immensely within this protected enclave.[24]

In the early 21st century, Silicon Valley integrated many countries into its platforms and networks, effectively transforming them into digital peripheries, whose 'national' digital environments largely adhered to the digital models, economic imperatives, and legal and policy frameworks initially established by the US-based internet companies and state agencies involved in their expansion.[25] However, China's party-state stood as an outlier when asserting its concept of 'cyber-sovereignty'.[26] As Chinese President Hu Jintao said: 'Whether we can cope with the internet is a matter that affects the development of socialist culture, the security of information, and the stability of the state.'[27] During Jintao's presidency, China's party-state exercised control over the internet while also enforcing company 'self-regulation'. In 2002, the state introduced the 'Public Pledge on Self-Discipline for China's Internet Industry'.[28] This 31-article framework, administered by the Internet Society of China, required all digital tech companies operating in China to pledge their commitment to 'patriotic observance of law, equitableness, trustworthiness, and honesty' (Article 3). They were also expected to 'create a favorable environment for the development of internet businesses consistent with the fundamental interests of the nation' (Article 4) and refrain from spreading harmful information that could jeopardize state security or disrupt social stability, in violation of laws and regulations (Article 9). Furthermore, they were obligated to respect intellectual property rights (Article 12), support the development of internet businesses (Article 14), and undergird the further advancement of China's internet industry (Article 16). The Information Office of the State Council's 2010 'White Paper on the Internet in China' solidified the concept of cyber-sovereignty under Jintao's leadership. It clarified that the party would 'build, utilize, and administer the internet' to 'safeguard national economic prosperity, state security, social harmony, state sovereignty, dignity, and the basic interests of the people'.[29] The paper explained that 'within Chinese territory, the internet is under the sovereignty of China'.[30]

During Xi Jinping's presidency, the party-state augmented its cyber-sovereignty and advanced the corporatization of China's digital tech industries with a strict protectionist industrial-cultural policy framework that has been a boon to the power of the state and to China's capitalist class.[31] In 2015, Xi Jinping declared: 'We should respect the right of individual countries to independently choose their own path of cyber-development', warning against US interference 'in other countries' internal affairs'. In the same year, Xi Jinping and Premier Li Keqiang issued the 'Made in China 2025' policy through the party's 13th and 14th five-year plans, channeling more than $300 billion into the transformation of China from factory for the world to a nascent leader in advanced digital technologies.[32] In the 12th, 13th and 14th Five-Year plans, the digital tech sector is expected to 'underpin China's rise as a global power and its internal transformation'[33] and 'catalyze domestic reforms and power the country's ambitions to lead global digital capitalism'.[34] For China's tech companies, 'Made in China 2025' increased research and development (R&D) expenditures, delivered subsidies, and incentivized their 'going out' and takeover of foreign companies, all the while protecting them from head-on competition with the Silicon Valley giants wanting to expand into China. Baidu, Alibaba, Tencent, Huawei, and SMIC have been among the beneficiaries of this largesse. Following

'Made in China 2025', the party-state issued the 13th 'Five-Year Plan on National Informatization' (2016-2020) to put even 'more resources into the development of cutting-edge information technology' so China could become fully independent of foreign supply chains and lead to the globe in the 'Fourth Industrial Revolution'.[35] In 2021, the party-state announced its 14th 'Five-Year Plan on National Informatization' which explained how 'accelerating digitized development and building a digital China are inherent requirements for meeting the changed circumstances of a new development phase, grasping the opportunities of the information revolution, building new advantages for national competition'.[36]

Under Xi's leadership, the party-state also passed in 2016 and 2021 cyber security and data security laws to strengthen its grip on the flow of internet information and user data.[37] The 2016 law compels all companies operating in critical digital tech sectors – telecommunications, information services, social media – to verify the identity of their users, and, when required, share this information with state security agencies, expanding the party's power to surveil and target dissent. The law's 'data localization' provision makes digital tech companies operating within China store Chinese user data on servers based in mainland China; to comply with this, foreign companies must either invest in new server infrastructure or partner with and pay to use the servers of Chinese companies such as Huawei, Tencent, or Alibaba. In any case, this is a boon to China's data infrastructure. The law in China also mandates that all companies operating within the country must, upon request, submit their purchases of digital products from foreign corporations (such as US firms) to state cybersecurity agencies for review. This requirement raises concerns as it could provide China's state agencies with access to the software 'blackbox' of US digital tech firms, potentially exposing them to vulnerabilities or even intellectual property theft. Additionally, the 2021 data security law grants the state the authority to shut down or impose fines on companies that refuse to comply with data requests or mishandle the use of security-significant data.[38]

Within the party-state's regime of 'cyber-sovereignty' and 'cyber-security' established, and bolstered by its five-year national plans, a Chinese capitalist class and an oligopoly of digital tech corporations have emerged, and these have in some respects been brought to fruition with support from financial investments and strategic partnerships with Silicon Valley firms, which have conducted business in China while adhering to the country's laws, policies, and regulations. The Chinese party-state has encouraged collaboration between Chinese and US tech companies as long as this would serve China's national plans. To build the 'Great Firewall' of China, Chinese companies bought and utilized hardware and software sold by US firms such as Cisco,

IBM, Microsoft, Intel, and Oracle.[39] By 2006, companies such as Yahoo, Microsoft, and Google had pledged self-discipline and were collaborating with China's state to censor online dissent, contradicting their corporate policies on freedom of expression.[40] For nearly two decades, the AAMAM companies have pursued their bottom line in China, frequently prioritizing profit over the liberal democratic idealism associated with their brands and the 'Californian ideology' of US-centred digital capitalism.

Alphabet-Google entered China in 2006 with its censored search engine, Google.cn, but ceased its censorship in 2010, redirecting Chinese users to its uncensored Hong Kong-based Google search engine. China's state swiftly blocked Google's search, Gmail, and Google Maps services, making them inaccessible within mainland China. Currently, Google's business in China is mostly limited to outsourcing smartphone manufacturing to Foxconn. Apple began outsourcing iPhone assembly to China in the early 2000s and continues to do so with each new iteration of planned obsolescence.[41] Although the US stands as the single largest market for the sale of iPhones, China is the second-largest. Meta Platforms' Facebook has made multiple attempts to enter the Chinese market since 2007, including creating a platform called 'Facebook China'. Despite these efforts, Facebook's main societal networking and Instagram sites remain blocked in China. Even though Meta's platforms are banned in China, Chinese corporations use them to purchase access to the algorithmically targeted attention of billions of users outside of China; demand for Facebook's ad services from internationalizing Chinese corporations continues to increase. Also, Meta manufactures its hardware products such as Oculus VR headsets by contracting with Foxconn. Amazon entered the Chinese market in 2004 through the acquisition of Joyo.com, an online retailer, and competed and collaborated with Chinese internet giants Alibaba and JD.com. However, by 2019, Amazon had shifted its focus to international e-commerce and Amazon Web Services (AWS): Chinese consumers purchase products from non-Chinese firms from Amazon's online marketplace, and Chinese firms advertise their goods to consumers around the world on this platform by paying to use AWS. Microsoft, a player in China since 1992, contracts Foxconn to assemble its surface devices and Xbox gaming consoles, sells its software products and services in the Chinese market, and runs R&D centres in partnership with Chinese tech firms.

Overall, AAMAM operate in China, but mostly when contracting out the manufacture of their hardware; their internet and social media platform services have limited to no presence in China. While mighty around the world, AAMAM's influence within and over China's digital economy is minor as compared to China's own state-owned enterprises (SOEs) and Big Tech firms. China's party-state has constrained or eliminated the activities of many US-based digital tech companies in China's territorial cyber-market, and American internet fortunes have remained small there as compared to the wealth accumulated by China's own homegrown class of tech billionaires and millionaires. Instead of acting as emissaries of the US Empire in China, AAMAM bowed to the Chinese party-state. Far from generating US soft power in China, AAMAM partnered with China's national tech capitalists. Instead of spearheading the Americanization of China, they've 'glocalized' while flexibly adjusting and aligning their globalizing business models, products, and services with local and national political and economic conditions in China. They largely obey the reigning state's cyber-sovereignty and cyber-security prerogatives, partner with China's national digital capitalists, and prop up China's internet surveillance, censorship and propaganda regime. In sum, China's state effectively managed the country's integration into global digital capitalism by fostering partnerships between Silicon Valley and Chinese tech firms to serve its idea of China's national interest, all the while enabling the super-exploitation of the Chinese proletariat for the benefit of the American and Chinese bourgeoisie alike. In effect, China has demonstrated to the world how a state may assert its sovereignty to buffer the full force of US platform imperialism and become a new cyber-power in its own right.

DIGITAL IMPERIALISMS:
STATE, CAPITAL, WAR, SURVEILLANCE, PROPAGANDA

The US and China are not equal global powers, but they are unquestionably engaged in intense competition across economic, military, and media-technological domains. They have the world's largest economies, accounting for 24.7 per cent and 17.5 per cent of global GDP respectively, but China's nominal GDP is projected to surpass the US's in the future. The dollar, not the renminbi, is the world's primary reserve currency, but next to the US, China is the second greatest destination for global financial investments. The US is home to 124 of the world's highest revenue-generating corporations, whereas China is the headquarters for 136. Additionally, the US serves as the headquarters for 590 of the top 2000 largest publicly traded companies globally, while China hosts 351 of them.[42] Also, the US and China have the world's biggest militaries: China has a larger force, with 2 million active personnel compared to the US's 1.35 million and 800,000 in its reserve. However, in 2022, the US's annual defence expenditure of $877 billion far exceeded China's $292 billion, and hundreds of US bases span the globe in support of US conflicts and wars, but China has no comparable modern history of military belligerence. While both countries house major media-tech corporations, the US is home to most of the world's largest, including Apple and Google. Even still, China is a growing player in this domain, with companies like Huawei and Tencent also going global.[43] The US enjoys an outsized global governance role (in the UN, NATO, G7, G20, IMF, World Bank, and WTO), but China is building a 'post-American' global governance regime via the Asian Infrastructure Investment Bank, the BRICS Forum, the Shanghai Cooperation Organization, the Belt and Road Initiative (BRI) and Digital Silk Road.[44]

Significantly, the US and China host the world's largest digital tech sectors, which while being intertwined due to cross-border financial investments, R&D partnerships, manufacturing agreements, and complex supply chains, are not the same.[45] Despite the entanglements of the digital tech sectors in the US and China, a consistent reality persists: the combined power and influence of the state and corporate entities in each country have molded national digital tech models and governance systems for home industries and companies with the greatest stake in global digital capitalism.[46] There is no unified transnational 'Chimerica' class consisting of American and Chinese CEOs, and although wealthy tech elites and their corporations in the US and China engage in cross-border business relations with one another, they are not backed by a truly global or supra-national government. Instead, they remain closely connected to their respective states and may align with the national security interests and geopolitical ambitions of those states.[47]

Predictably, the leaders of each country boast of the digital tech sector's centrality to their national and global power. Chinese President Xi Jinping says 'cyber-power' is key to the 'Great Rejuvenation of the Chinese Nation' and emphasizes how 'the countries that take command of the internet will win the world'.[48] US President Joe Biden affirms a US strategy to 'develop and dominate the products and technologies of the future' in order to 'win the 21st century'.[49] The US and China's digital tech sectors overlap and stretch around the world, and simultaneously, both the US and Chinese states actively promote corporate tech giants internationally and engage in cyber warfare, surveillance, and propaganda *through* digital hardware, software, and services.[50] Pithy phrases such as the US-China 'chip war,' 'gray war,' and 'digital Cold War' reflect these two states' leveraging of digital tech to expand their capitalist base, bolster their military strength, and project nationalist narratives to win hearts and minds. They bolster their sector's trade interests, safeguard it from takeovers, allocate billions in subsidies to national champions, and impose trade barriers and sanctions on international competitors. A brief overview of the relationship between each country's state and digital tech companies illuminates this dynamic.

The US digital tech sector is predominantly owned by corporations, with AAMAM being the most significant. China's sector is ruled by a combination of corporations and SOEs managed by the State-Owned Assets Supervision and Administration Commission of the State Council. American or Chinese, these corporations' internal policy arms and external lobbies represent their political interests to states so as to ensure the meaning of the 'national interest' reflects their own. The Internet Association, the Computer & Communications Industry Association, the Information Technology Industry Council , and the Consumer Technology Association are Silicon Valley's voice in Washington, and AAMAM mobilize advocates, lobbyists, think tanks, political action committees, legislators, policymakers, regulators, political parties, and even presidents to try to articulate their profit interests to the state's 'national interest'.[51] AAMAM possess significant resources that enable them to effectively influence state decision-making, either by indirectly providing financial support or by exerting direct pressure on political officials to translate their private interests into public legislative, policy, and regulatory outcomes. Frequently, the US state props up the interests of AAMAM, and sometimes mobilizes them to serve its own geopolitical goals. Though less established, the China Association for Science and Technology, the China Information Industry Trade Association, the China Software Industry Association, and the Internet Society of China work to raise the political voice of China's big tech companies. In the US and China, state agencies frequently collaborate, coordinate, and often consult with one another and key bourgeoisie in the digital tech sectors to develop and uphold a governance framework that by and large supports the growth of their industries and the profits of key firms. To help them do that, they frequently dole out vast subsidies.

The US and Chinese militaries have also played a role in underwriting the growth of the digital tech sectors in each country.[52] The global internet's American military history is significant: the US Department of Defense (DOD) established DARPA to give the US a cutting edge in military technology. One outcome of this subvention was ARPANET, the world's first advanced computer network. Another was the core hardware and software of today's digital infrastructure: packet-switching, a digital computer, orbiting satellites, and GPS. Even the key components of the earliest iPhones resulted from DARPA subvention. While the internet has since been privatized, and some bemoan a divide between Silicon Valley and the military, the DOD supports the digital tech sector with financing, R&D partnerships, and procurement contracts worth billions.[53] Alphabet-Google collaborated with the DOD on Project Maven, an initiative to enhance AI capabilities for analyzing military drone footage.[54] Apple has worked on optimizing iOS devices and for DOD use, and recently acquired Mira, an augmented reality startup that makes headsets for cyborg soldiers.[55] Meta Platforms is making the metaverse, sometimes with DOD-linked start-ups.[56] Since 2016, Amazon has landed more than 350 contracts with the DOD, as well as other repressive state apparatuses, such as the Department of Homeland Security and the FBI.[57] Microsoft cashes in on many DOD contracts, such as the Army's Integrated Visual Augmentation System utilizing the HoloLens.[58] Recently, Amazon, Google, Microsoft and Oracle started splitting the spoils of a $9 billion cloud computing contract, compliments of the DOD's new Joint Warfighting Cloud Capability program.[59] Given China's legal principle of 'civil-military fusion' (Article 7 of China's National Intelligence Law), the Chinese military and digital tech sector also intertwine:[60] China's military contracts out to firms such as Huawei and ZTE[61] and 'the infrastructure and equipment that Chinese firms build around the world is, by design and definition, a de facto extension of the Chinese government'.[62]

The US and Chinese digital tech giants enjoy an oligopoly in their home markets and are also 'going global' and localizing in many other national country markets through investments in subsidiaries, ownership takeovers, infrastructural development projects, training programs, manufacturing and service outsourcing, commodity circulation, and data extraction. They have expanded internationally with support from the foreign policies of their respective nation-states, and through their cross-border chains of accumulation with other companies in other nation-states. These new US and Chinese digital imperialisms entail the intermingling of the economic interests of these countries' leading digital tech corporations (as they pursue profit by financing, producing, and circulating goods and services) with the geopolitical interests of each territorial state (as it pursues foreign policy, military, and diplomatic goals). In effect, they are establishing and integrating new 'digital spheres of influence'. 'If you were to draw a map,' says Kai-Fu Lee, 'you would see China's tech zone ... stretching across Southeast Asia, Indonesia, Africa and to some extent South America' and 'the US zone would entail North America, Australasia and Europe'.[63] The Global South has become a key sphere of US and Chinese digital imperialisms. Motivated by profits, their corporations are scrambling to exploit labour, develop digital infrastructures, sell digital goods and services to markets, and aggregate, analyze, and monetize user data.[64] These US and Chinese tech companies travel the world, promising to 'develop' and 'advance' others.

In this digital imperialism, nominal benefits are bestowed upon the local countries and their contractors while US and Chinese giants vie for market influence and extract profit along the way.

AAMAM are at the forefront of US-centred digital imperialism, with vast operations in the Global South. These corporations outsource various digital tasks to subcontractors in the region. For example, Google outsources manufacturing of Pixel smartphones and Nest smart home devices to manufacturers in Taiwan, Vietnam, and India, and customer service tasks to call centres in India, the Philippines, and Costa Rica. Apple outsources manufacturing and customer service for iPhones, iPads, and MacBooks to contractors in Taiwan, India, and the Philippines. Meta Platforms globally outsources content moderation, creation, IT support, and data entry. AAMAM are involved in other ventures: Google announced a $10 billion investment plan called the 'Google for India Digitization Fund' in 2021 to build digital infrastructure, and partnered with Telecom Egypt to develop the subsea cable 'Equiano' connecting Portugal and South Africa. Apple established the App Development Center in Bangalore, India, in 2017, launched the Apple Developer Academy in Jakarta, Indonesia, in 2020, and opened its first retail store in Johannesburg, South Africa, in 2021. Meta launched Internet.org (later rebranded as Free Basics) in 2013, providing access to online services in India through a Facebook-controlled portal. Facebook also launched the 'Express Wi-Fi' initiative in Nigeria, Kenya, and Tanzania, and invested in Jio Platforms in India and Nigeria's tech ecosystem. Amazon acquired Souq.com, expanded its Web Services infrastructure in the Global South, and launched a data centre in Cape Town, South Africa, in 2020. Microsoft's 'Airband Initiative' aims to provide affordable broadband access globally, undertake digital infrastructure projects in Kenya, South Africa, and Colombia, and operates the 'Africa Development Center' to foster talent and innovation.

Chinese companies are also expanding in the Global South and 'digitally developing' numerous countries with a made-in-China digital tech 'stack' comprised of network infrastructure, devices, applications, content, and governance models.[65] Across Africa, Alibaba has established the Africa eWTP (Electronic World Trade Platform) Hub, a cross-border trade platform that aims to facilitate e-commerce and digital trade.[66] Alibaba has invested in e-commerce platform Lazada, which operates in Indonesia, Thailand and Vietnam, as well as Pakistan's e-commerce platform Daraz. It has launched the e-commerce platform Jumia, which operates in multiple countries across Africa, providing them with an online marketplace for various products. In Latin America, Alibaba has invested in Brazilian e-commerce giant MercadoLibre.[67] Tencent has made strategic investments in multiple global startups. In India, Tencent has invested in Flipkart, Ola, Swiggy, and Byju. They also hold a significant stake in Sea Limited, the Singaporean company behind platforms like Shopee and Garena. In Africa, Tencent has supported Flutterwave, a fintech company, and invested in Letgo Africa, Rappi, and Ualá, prominent platforms in Nigeria, Colombia, and Argentina, respectively. Additionally, Tencent partnered with South Africa's Naspers to merge their video-on-demand services, gaining access to the South African market. Tencent's investments span diverse regions and sectors, demonstrating their global reach and strategic positioning. ByteDance has experienced significant international growth through its video-sharing platform, TikTok. Baidu has invested in African tech startups and the Brazilian transportation platform, 99. JD.Com has expanded its presence in the South African and Nigerian e-commerce markets and established partnerships across Latin America with companies like Mexico's largest e-commerce platform, MercadoLibre. Huawei has been profiting on telecommunications infrastructure developments encompassing broadband, 5G networks, and mobile systems in Kenya, Nigeria, and Algeria. Huawei has partnered with the Nigerian government to establish the Nigerian Huawei Training Centre and made significant investments in Brazil, including the establishment of a smartphone manufacturing plant in São Paulo. Huawei has also partnered with Mexican telecommunications companies to design and deploy 4G and 5G networks in the country and collaborated with Indonesian and Malaysian telecommunications operators and provided training for workers.

These and other forms of international expansion by the US and China's digital tech companies are backed by the geopolitical strategies of their respective states. US and Chinese foreign policy help corporations export their digital products and services by brokering bilateral and multilateral digital trade deals.[68] For example, China initiated the Regional Comprehensive Economic Partnership (RCEP), a digital trade agreement that prioritizes state cyber sovereignty and promotes a national approach to the internet. Following this, the US initiated the Indo-Pacific Economic Framework for Prosperity, emphasizing digital free trade and the unrestricted flow of digital information and services across borders. Currently, RCEP holds greater appeal and is a larger digital trade bloc in developing countries. It has been signed by all ten Association of Southeast Asian Nations countries and has even attracted participation from US allies such as Australia, Japan, South Korea, and New Zealand. Both the US and Chinese embassies advocate for market access for their digital tech corporations, and diplomats from the US and China consistently engage with foreign governments and businesses, aiming to minimize or eliminate barriers to the trade interests of their home corporations. Additionally, both countries' states strive to institutionalize their own digital tech models in other countries through technology transfers, R&D projects, and training programs. Furthermore, the US and Chinese states actively try to influence global laws, policies, and regulations for the internet and digital tech through international organizations such as the UN, the International Telecommunication Union, the United Nations Conference on Trade and Development, the WTO, the G20, the Organization for Economic Cooperation and Development, and the Internet Corporation for Assigned Names and Numbers.[69] Regional organizations such as the Asia-Pacific Economic Cooperation and the European Union (EU) also play a role in digital tech governance. Both the US and Chinese states support their respective corporations (and to some extent, those of their key yet subordinate allies as well). Locally and globally, nationally and internationally, these states are supporting corporations as they integrate other countries into their digital infrastructures and superstructures, secure their domains, and accumulate profit.

Both the US and Chinese states extensively utilize digital products and services in order to exert influence within other countries, and their 'foreign interference' campaigns are vast and often unseen. The global internet is a new 'domain' of 21st-century warfare, alongside land, sea, air, and space, and US and Chinese military cyber-warfare units disrupt, infiltrate, or attack each other's computer networks and systems.[70] Also, both the US and Chinese states extensively surveil populations through the internet and social media platforms at home and abroad. In the US, state agencies such as the National Security Agency, Federal Bureau of Investigation, Department of Homeland Security, and Central Intelligence Agency conduct internet surveillance, sometimes in partnership with Silicon Valley, as revealed by Edward Snowden's disclosure of the PRISM program. China employs a total system of internet surveillance through the Cyberspace Administration of China, the Ministry of Public Security, and the Ministry of State Security.[71] Additionally, both the US and Chinese states utilize internet interfaces, websites, and content to conduct propaganda and public diplomacy campaigns in other countries.[72] Their state media agencies leverage the services of internet corporations to project and elicit consent to narratives about their national identities, values, and foreign policies. The Department of State's US Agency for Global Media imparts its preferred story about the 'American Way of Life' (and way of war) through social media platforms. China employs the United Front Work Department, State Council Information Office, and the Propaganda Department to shape online narratives about China and manage the country's global image. Furthermore, these countries' 'digital diplomats' utilize social media sites to try to influence global public opinion, portraying their states in a positive light while deflecting criticisms.

Evidently, the international expansion of US and Chinese digital corporations in world markets intersects in significant ways with the geopolitical strategies of their respective territorial nation-states in world affairs. Despite the capitalist interdependence between the US and China's digital tech sectors, the national security interests of their territorial states persist and continue to undergird significant geopolitical tensions and conflicts in world affairs through these sectors. The competition between US and Chinese corporations, both seeking power and influence over different aspects of the world's digital infrastructure and superstructure, is intertwined with the escalating geopolitical conflict between their states. The US state is motivated to maintain Silicon Valley's global digital dominance and perceives China as a significant rival, so leading US security personnel and certain bourgeoisie have devised a new strategy for containing China's digital tech sector.

THE US EMPIRE'S STRATEGY TO CONTAIN CHINA'S DIGITAL TECH RISE

As the economic and geopolitical fault lines between Washington and Beijing deepen, this competition and conflict further divide the American and Chinese corporations presiding over the global digital tech sector. Citing national security concerns about espionage, intellectual property theft, and trade practices, as well as human and privacy rights, the US state has deployed sanctions to close the markets of the US to China's tech expansion and marshalled subsidies to bolster its own tech companies' enlargement. From the Trump presidency to the Biden presidency, the Department of the Treasury (DOT), the Department of Commerce (DOC), the United States Trade Representative (USTR), the Federal Communications Commission (FCC), and the DOD have imposed sanctions on China's key digital technology corporations in an attempt to hinder their growth and undercut their prosperity. Matthew Pottinger, a former Trump administration security adviser, has cheered the Biden administration's continuation of Trump's 'broad assault' on China's digital tech sector: 'The Biden administration understands now that it isn't enough for America to run faster — we also need to actively hamper the P.R.C'.s ambitions for tech dominance.'[73] What follows is a broad five-year overview of the US state's multi-faceted sanctioning of China's digital tech sector.

In 2018, the DOT's Committee on Foreign Investment in the

United States (CFIUS) introduced the Foreign Investment Risk Review Modernization Act to allow it to assess the national security risks associated with Chinese investments in US critical infrastructure, including US digital tech companies. The DOC's Bureau of Industry and Security expanded its 'Entity List' (a trade restriction list consisting of entities such as foreign state agencies, companies, universities, and foreign persons), to cover forty-four Chinese corporations involved in 5G networks, AI, and other advanced technologies deemed to be of use to China's military and contrary to US security (by 2022, this list had grown to include 600 Chinese entities).[74] The DOD reinforced this position by publishing a blacklist of Chinese corporations allegedly interlinked with China's People's Liberation Army. Between 2018 and 2021, USTR levied a 15 per cent tariff on approximately $145 billion worth of Chinese imports from firms involved in China's 'Made in China 2025' plan, covering everything from computers to electronic hardware.[75]

The imperial presidency has likewise used its emergency powers to solidify the US blockade of China's digital tech companies. In November 2020, Donald Trump signed Executive Order 13959 ('Addressing the Threat From Securities Investments That Finance Communist Chinese Military Companies'). In June 2021, this was expanded by Joe Biden's Executive Order 14032 ('Addressing the Threat From Securities Investments That Finance Certain Companies of the People's Republic of China').[76] In August 2023, Joe Biden signed an additional Executive Order that authorized the US Treasury to prohibit or restrict US private equity, venture capital, joint ventures, and greenfield investments in China's tech sector, 'in sensitive technologies and products critical to the military, intelligence, surveillance or cyber-enabled capabilities' such as semiconductors, microelectronics, quantum IT, and A.I. systems.[77] Together, these executive orders prohibit US companies and citizens from investing in, buying, or selling shares of companies identified by the DOD as 'Communist Chinese military companies'. Nearly all of China's major tech corporations have been impacted,[78] and the New York Stock Exchange delisted some of these firms.[79]

The imperial presidency has furthermore used its emergency powers to restrict China's investment in the US digital tech sector. In September 2022, the Biden administration issued a unique executive order (dubbed the 'First-Ever Presidential Directive Defining Additional National Security Factors for CFIUS to Consider in Evaluating Transactions') to stave off Chinese investments that might challenge the maintenance of 'US economic and technological leadership, specifically with respect to protecting national security'.⁸⁰ The directive aims to do this by greatly expanding the investigative scope of CFIUS to include investments 'outside of the defense industrial base' in sectors that may have an effect on 'US technological leadership'.⁸¹ This directive empowers CFIUS to examine investments and transactions by foreign entities that may 'facilitate sensitive technology transfer', exhibit the 'capability and intent to conduct cyber intrusions or other malicious cyber-enabled activity', and support 'the surveillance, tracing, tracking, and targeting of individuals or groups of individuals' data sets. Together, the presidency's executive orders and directives represent a massive restraint on Chinese capital's freedom to invest in the US and transact digital goods and services sales within the US market.

With its massive sanction framework, the US state aims to degrade the profit-maximization powers of China's biggest tech companies, disrupt their supply chains, and hinder the sales of their digital tech goods and services in the US market and elsewhere, all the while shoring up the US's global corporate dominance over key industries in the sector. At the level of media and cultural politics, the US state's sanction campaign is a communicative act that has generated fear of Chinese tech corporations, thereby depleting the currency of their brand images and potentially diminishing their ability to prosper around the world. To illustrate concretely the US sanction regime's effort to contain China's digital tech sector, three cases of coordinated US state repression toward China's leading 5G + smartphones, semiconductor, and social media firms are pertinent.

Huawei Technologies⁸² is a global leader in 5G wireless networking and smartphones, and for a time, it had gained a foothold in the US market and those of its allies, posing a challenge to US digital dominance.⁸³ In 2019, Huawei surpassed Apple to become the second largest smartphone manufacturer in the world, next to Samsung.⁸⁴ In 2021, the Council on Foreign Relations complained that Huawei was winning the 5G network development race against the US in Africa.⁸⁵ Recognizing Huawei's competitive power, the US state worked to roll back its rise.⁸⁶ The Congressionally-approved National Defense Authorization Act for Fiscal Year 2019 prohibited the US federal government's use of Huawei's goods and services. The DOD complied with these measures by forbidding the sale of Huawei hardware and software in retail outlets across its military bases. In the same year, the Department of Justice filed criminal charges against Huawei, including allegations of intellectual property theft and violations of US sanctions against Iran. In 2020, the DOC added Huawei and its affiliates to the Entity List to restrict Huawei's ability to do business with US companies, cutting off Huawei's access to Google's Android operating system and essential components like semiconductors. In 2022, the FCC revoked Huawei's authorization to sell its products and services in the US market and multiple state agencies did the same.[87] In addition to excluding Huawei, the US state motivated the states of Australia, Canada, Japan, New Zealand, and the UK to dutifully restrict the use of Huawei products for 5G development, and other countries in the EU and elsewhere seem to be phasing Huawei out, making markets safe for Apple.[88] US sanctions pummeled Huawei, disrupting its supply chains, closing markets to its products, and tarnishing its brand, resulting in a drop in Huawei's annual profit of nearly 70 per cent.[89]

Expectedly, the US has also targeted China's semiconductor industry, recognizing the crucial role of chips in every digital device. The US is home to significant semiconductor companies such as Intel, Nvidia, and Micron, but US-ally Taiwan's company Taiwan Semiconductor Manufacturing Corporation (TSMC) produces 60 per cent of the world's semiconductors and over 90 per cent of the most advanced ones.[90] There are thousands of semiconductor companies in China, with Semiconductor Manufacturing International Corporation (SMIC) among the strongest,[91] with revenues of $3.9 billion in 2020. However, in December 2020, the US state added SMIC to its US Entity List, prohibiting US companies from selling to SMIC. In October 2022, The White House implemented sweeping export restrictions on the sale of semiconductors and chip-making equipment to China,[92] aiming to choke off SMIC's access to advanced chips and chip production tools sold by US companies. These sanctions aim to severely limit SMIC's access to parts from US suppliers and US trade partners, thereby undermining its ability to manufacture advanced semiconductors. US allies such as Japan, Taiwan, and the Netherlands followed suit, imposing restrictions on the sale of chips to SMIC and other Chinese chip firms. In May 2023, SMIC posted its first quarterly revenue fall in 3 years.[93] The US state's sanctions apply to all Chinese chip firms and aims to 'choke' China's semiconductor industry and hinder China's tech development.[94]

The US state furthermore has taken decisive measures to curb the global growth of Chinese social media companies, including ByteDance's TikTok, a platform for creating and sharing short-form videos currently used by 100 million Americans and 1.53 billion people worldwide.[95] TikTok helped its owner ByteDance generate $80 billion in revenue in 2022.[96] As it has come to be a significant force in the US market, it has faced criticism from both Republican and Democratic Party politicians. Concerns raised by the Democratic National Committee about TikTok's data aggregation practices and former Secretary of State Mike Pompeo's claim that the platform places personal information at the disposal of the CCP have added to the scrutiny.

In August 2020, Trump issued an Executive Order to address the alleged national security threat posed by TikTok, aiming to banish it from the US unless ByteDance, its Chinese parent company, sold TikTok to Walmart and Oracle. The CFIUS further threatened a complete ban on TikTok if ByteDance did not divest its US stake in the app. Subsequently, in December 2022, the Biden Administration enacted the 'No TikTok on Government Devices Act', which prohibits US government workers from downloading TikTok on official government-issued devices. The Biden administration has likewise demanded that Chinese owners of TikTok sell their share to an American company or face a ban from the US digital market.[97] In 2023, Montana legislators passed a bill (SB0419) to banish TikTok from the state and require Google and Apple's online app stores to remove TikTok. CEO Shou Zi Chew has also been grilled for five hours by a Congressional committee in Washington comprised of lawmakers convinced the Chinese-made social media app is a national security threat.[98] The US state's repression of TikTok has been driven by national security concerns, often citing user rights to data privacy. But the state's focus on data privacy is merely a smokescreen for its broader goal of restricting the global expansion of a popular Chinese social media platform and further enabling the US platform oligopoly in the digital data and advertising market. American sub-states like Canada, as well as Italy, Norway and Netherlands, have recently followed suit, banning the TikTok app on government phones, citing security threats.

Following its sanctions, the US state unleashed a massive stimulus program to further strengthen the US digital tech sector vis-à-vis China. In 2023, National Security Agency advisor Jake Sullivan announced a new 'Washington Consensus', a 'modern industrial and innovation strategy—both at home and with partners around the world', that 'invests in the sources of our own economic and technological strength', 'promotes diversified and resilient global supply chains', and 'sets high standards for everything from labour and the environment to trusted technology and good governance'.[99] In his speech, Sullivan lambasted China for being 'integrated' into global capitalism, 'but not responsible or cooperative', and chided it for 'subsidizing at a massive scale' key 'industries of the future', including 'digital infrastructure'. Sullivan also lamented a US loss of 'competitiveness in critical technologies that would define the future'. Sullivan's new Washington Consensus has marshalled $4 trillion in new programs (e.g., the American Rescue Plan, the Bipartisan Infrastructure Law and the CHIPS and Science Act alongside the Inflation Reduction Act) and made 'targeted investments' in sectors that 'are foundational to economic growth, strategic from a national security perspective' and key to building a 'strong, resilient, and leading-edge techno-industrial base' for the US and its 'like-minded partners'. This aims to 'usher in a new wave of the digital revolution—one that ensures that next-generation technologies work for, not against, our democracies and our security'. At present, the US state's Indo-Pacific Economic Framework, the Partnership for Global Infrastructure and Investment, the new Americas Partnership for Economic Prosperity, the US-EU Trade and Technology Council, and trilateral coordination with Japan and Korea are building the consent of the US's 'partners' to this consensus, which is a boon to US tech companies. The CHIPS Act injects $52 billion into semiconductor chip manufacturing and R&D and benefits US companies such as TSMC, Samsung, Micron, and Intel, and those of its partners and allies.[100]

Evidently, the US state has acted swiftly and decisively to sanction China's major tech corporations[101] with the goal of restricting their activities in the US and across its partners' markets, all the while subsidizing US tech corporations and supporting their expansion in world markets. With respect to the US's long history of pushing neoliberalism, the hypocrisy is staggering. Silicon Valley desires an open relationship with China to use its manufacturing base and sell digital goods and services to consumers in the world's largest market. Simultaneously, the US state is trying to weaken China's tech corporations with sanctions and strengthen Silicon Valley with subsidies. The US state has long promoted digital free trade, but its new strategy toward China represents its shift away from trying to open China to Silicon Valley, and toward more repressive and national industrial-protectionist tactics to contain and out-compete China. In that regard, the US state's commitment to global digital free trade seems malleable: it opens the world for Silicon Valley when it stands to benefit most, but closes borders to companies that may loosen Silicon Valley's global grip.

What are the outcomes of the US Empire's strategy to curb China's tech rise? First, the US and China's two-way investments in one another's digital tech sectors have begun to shrink.[102] Between 1990 and 2020, US corporations invested billions in China's digital tech sector and Chinese corporations invested billions in the US sector.[103] Nonetheless, US venture capital investment in China's digital tech sector diminished from $32.9 billion in 2021 to $9.7 billion in 2022, and by mid-2023, US investors had only put $1.2 billion into Chinese tech startups. This divestment could underpin greater divergence between the two countries' digital tech sectors.

Second, Silicon Valley still manufactures much of its hardware in China, but key firms are trying to diversify their supply chains.[104] Google's newest Pixel phone is being partially manufactured in Vietnam; Apple is shifting some iPhone and iPad manufacture to India and Vietnam; Meta Platforms is reportedly searching out alternative production zones; Amazon's Fire TV devices are being made in India; Microsoft's Xbox game consoles are being made in Vietnam.[105] Even still, the super-profits of AAMAM rely on China staying open to their production contracts and sales of their goods and services. For this reason, Apple CEO Tim Cook, Microsoft co-founder Bill Gates, and Tesla and SpaceX CEO Elon Musk visited China in late 2023 to reassure Xi Jinping of their continued intention to produce everything from devices to Tesla's Model Y electric cars with China.[106] Jeff Bezos likewise has an interest in keeping China open because China-based online sellers represent about 75 per cent of new business on Amazon's e-marketplace.[107]

Third, some US digital tech companies support the US state's sanctions on China and others do not. Nvidia, Intel, and Qualcomm are lobbying hard to protect their right to sell semiconductor chips to China, which accounts for more than $50 billion of their combined annual revenue. These companies say that cutting their chip sales to China is gutting their profits and derailing their capacity to support the White House's plan to build up US-based semiconductor factories.[108] Relatedly, US state subsidies have not resulted in fully American chip production. Taiwan's TSMC, the world's most advanced chip fabricator, accepted $15 billion in subsidies from the US state to build a fabrication plant in Arizona, but labour shortages have resulted in construction delays.

Fourth, the US's entire digital infrastructure is in many respects still heavily reliant on products from China, from rare earth minerals to electronic parts to printed circuit boards. This dependence is not limited to the tech sector. A defence company like Raytheon manufactures weaponry, including Tomahawk and Maverick missiles, and sells these to the DOD, but these 'American' weapons systems depend on parts made in China.[109] The DOD has been warning of China's challenge to US hegemony for nearly two decades, but some of the components necessary for the weapons its contractors sell to it, potentially for use in a future war with China, are sourced from Chinese firms.

Fifth, on the international diplomacy front, the US state has encountered challenges in gaining unanimous consent from its allies to sever technological ties with China. Some of these US-allied states host companies similar to Silicon Valley's, which have manufacturing facilities in China or depend on Chinese factories for critical components in their national digital infrastructures. Also, companies based in US-allied states see China as a vast and expanding market for their products and are aware that a complete disconnection from China could negatively impact their profits. For example, prominent Korean semiconductor chipmakers such as Samsung Electronics and SK Hynix have invested over $52 billion in chip plants in China, and want to expand their chip sales within China.[110] They have even lobbied the Korean and US states to seek exceptions to the US sanctions on China, and have been granted them in some instances. Additionally, Taiwan's TSMC, a supplier to Apple, still sources its China factory with US chipmaking tools.

Sixth, the effectiveness of US state efforts to achieve total 'chokepoint control' to contain China's tech rise by restricting access to vital semiconductor components appears limited due to many market leaks and loopholes. The US state's strategy to deter US corporations from selling semiconductor technology to Chinese companies has not prevented these Chinese entities' subsidiaries from procuring the same semiconductor components through international markets, often from companies operating outside the US. These components reportedly find their way into China and are readily available for sale at popular electronics hubs like Shenzhen's Huaqiangbei area, and elsewhere.[111]

Seventh, the US state sanctions designed to contain China have evoked a retaliatory response. China has enforced export restrictions on essential materials like gallium and germanium, which are critical in Silicon Valley's production of computer chips and various digital devices. China's Cyberspace Administration has also banned Chinese companies from conducting business with some US firms, including Micron, citing 'national security risks',[112] while Chinese government officials are reportedly considering a ban on the use of Apple iPhones in state agencies. Furthermore, as early as May 2022, Chinese state agencies and SOEs began phasing out PCs produced by American corporations, opting for PCs from Chinese manufacturers, a shift that increased the demand for products from China's own digital tech sector. At the same time, the Chinese state has expanded its restrictions on US apps and services. And in response to US state subventions, China's state has funneled billions into the coffers of its own digital tech giants, particularly those involved in chip production, hoping to achieve semi-conductor self-sufficiency.

Eighth, the US state sanctions on China have spurred a greater determination by its party-state and corporate class to attain digital independence from the US Empire. Deprived of access to critical products, Chinese companies have achieved technological advancements. Huawei, a company hit hard by the sanctions, has developed its own operating system, HarmonyOS, and integrated it into devices that compete with the Apple iPhone. Huawei has also made substantial investments in R&D, supporting 80 Chinese companies with a semiconductor investment fund, resulting in a 7-nanometer chip, comparable to Nvidia's and Qualcomm's leading

AI processors.¹¹³ Chinese tech giant Baidu has even launched a generative AI system called Ernie, which has gained prominence and is said to have surpassed OpenAI's ChatGPT.¹¹⁴

Overall, despite the US Empire's strategy of containment, the digital tech sectors of the US and China remain significantly integrated, though some key industries and firms are being disintegrated. While the US state strives to separate certain components of the US digital tech sector from China, China's state is pursuing a clear long-term national objective: to 'de-Americanize' segments of its own digital tech sector and potentially attain digital independence from the US Empire.¹¹⁵

TECH WAR / CLASS WAR: ASYMMETRICAL RIVALRY AND (INTER)DEPENDENCE

The digital tech sectors serve as pillars of the US and China's expansive military, geopolitical, and cultural-ideological power and influence. From 1945 forward, the US Empire integrated numerous nation states and capitals under American hegemony, and over the past quarter century, it may have wished to integrate China as a subordinate partner and digital dependency. Today, China deviates from the US Empire's plans by maintaining a level of cyber-sovereignty unlike any other country. Despite ongoing US-China integration in finance, manufacturing and trade, China's state management of its digital tech sector stands as a testament to its national cyber-sovereignty and shows what it takes for a structurally weaker state to develop a national digital tech sector and capitalist class within the US Empire that perhaps points beyond it. The capitalist interpenetration of the US and China's digital tech sectors is still significant, but this will not necessarily persist forever. In the coming years, we can expect greater capitalist competition and geopolitical conflict between the US and China, which may further disintegrate the two countries' digital tech sectors, and lead to intensifying global division and discord.¹¹⁶

The US and Chinese states and corporations are pushing strategic global competition with each other, universalizing their particular visions of global order, touting alternate political superstructures, steering industrial policy, and battling to be the world innovator of the most advanced technologies. If the US and China's national state elites and bourgeoisie refuse to find some compromise, their new asymmetrical digital imperialist rivalry may lead to a war. While the Cold War was a battle between two different systems, today's conflict is between an old enduring imperialist and a rising imperial power within the framework of one interdependent world capitalist system. The US is unlikely to relinquish its global imperial privilege without starting and trying to win another war; China is unwilling to subordinate its national plans to the will of US-NATO. In the midst of this new US-China digital imperial rivalry, which may be a canary in the coal mine of what's to come in other sectors, national elites and working people from both the Global North and South will be pressured and cajoled to align themselves with either the US or China.

Over time, the status of these countries' alignment will manifest in all kinds of asymmetrical and unequal interdependencies and perhaps even new forms of digital technological subordination and dependency. Backed by their home states, the US and Chinese digital tech sectors will exert an influence over the digital economies, polities, and cultures of their peripheral counterparts, with limited reciprocation by those affected. There may be non-reciprocal financial and digital trade relationships between the US, China, and all the countries on the receiving end of their digital imperialisms. The US and China will launch more propaganda and public diplomacy campaigns that try to win the consent of non-US and non-Chinese elites and working classes to diverging digital governance models, products and services. At the cultural level, we may see forms of 'unequal digital mixing' between the US, China, and all the countries they target rather than complete dominance of one country's national digital culture over another (i.e., less digital 'Americanization' and 'Sinicization' and more digital cultural hybridities).

The new digital imperial rivalry between the US and China is not a battle for a post-capitalist future but rather a competition between different states and national digital tech corporations for global dominance. The rivalry is about which states and corporations will have the upper hand in controlling the global digital tech sector, which is the axis of economic, military and cultural power today. While some perceive China as carrying forward the radical anti-colonialism of the Bandung era and leading the way toward a global socialist future, this is idealistic. China's model represents an alternative approach to capitalist development rather than a complete departure from capitalist development. It may attract countries disillusioned with the US's neoliberal capitalist model, but it does not promise a break from global digital capitalism. As the US and Chinese states advance their nationalist tech innovation policies, facilitate and legitimize the accumulation interests of their digital tech oligopolies, and weaponize digital goods and services for cyber-warfare, surveillance and propaganda against each other and everyone else, the bourgeoisie in both countries prosper at the expense of the workers they exploit.

This rivalry between US and China poses a threat to the recognition of shared class interests among American and Chinese workers and undermines the possibility of international class solidarity. Perhaps the new US-China 'digital tech war' should be reconceptualized as a 'class war' that aligns the American and Chinese working classes with their nation-state leaders and bourgeoisie, all the while transferring billions in public wealth upward to those atop the commanding heights of global digital capitalism. Universal freedom from the realm of necessity is nowhere on this innovation agenda. Whenever US and Chinese elites conflate their national interests with those of workers, democratic socialists can consistently critique these ruling designs and support the pro-worker movements and organizations that strive for a truly different world order.

NOTES

1. See: Leo Panitch and Sam Gindin, *The Making of Global Capitalism: The Political Economy of American Empire*, New York: Verso, 2012; Leo Panitch and Greg Albo, eds, *Socialist Register 2019: A World Turned Upside Down?*, London: Merlin Press, 2018; Leo Panitch and Colin Leys, eds, *Socialist Register 2008: Global Flashpoints: Reactions to Imperialism and Neoliberalism*, London: Merlin Press, 2008; Leo Panitch and Colin Leys, eds, *Socialist Register 2005: The Empire Reloaded*, London: Merlin Press, 2005; Leo Panitch and Colin Leys, eds, *Socialist Register 2004: The New Imperial Challenge*, London: Merlin Press, 2004; see also: Stephen Maher, 'A World After Its Own Image, or in Its Own Interest? The Logic of American Empire and the Nature of World Order', *Studies in Political Economy*, 93(1), 2014, pp. 175-92; Stephen Maher, *Corporate Capitalism and the Integral State: General Electric and a Century of American Power*, New York: Springer Publishing International, 2022.
2. See: Spencer Ackerman, *Reign of Terror: How the 9/11 Era Destabilized America and Produced Trump*, New York: Viking, 2021; William Blum, *Killing Hope: US Military and CIA Interventions since World War II*, London: Bloomsbury Academic, 2022; Naomi Klein, *The Shock Doctrine*, Toronto: Knopf, 2007.
3. From the Obama to Trump to Biden presidencies, the US security state has come to view China as the American Empire's greatest threat. The US DOD's 2018 'Summary of the National Defense Strategy of the United States' declared its aim: 'To restore America's competitive edge by blocking global rivals [such as China] from challenging the U.S. and our allies.' In that same year, the US National Security Council published a 'US Strategic Framework for the Indo-Pacific' in which it declared the US's goal in Asia was to 'maintain US primacy in the region'. Noting how China's 'cutting-edge technologies' threaten US national security, the doctrine declares that the US state would need to 'maintain American industry's innovation edge vis-à-vis China' with the support of key allies. Approaching the 2020 election, Joe Biden wrote an article for *Foreign Affairs* titled 'Why America Must Lead Again', emphasizing the need to confront China. The Biden presidency has continued a confrontational approach to China and this has been echoed by the major security agencies and their heads. The US National Security Council's 2021 'US Strategic Framework for the Indo-Pacific' and the White House's 2022 'Indo-Pacific Strategy' both highlight

the goal of securing US global dominance vis-à-vis China. Additionally, the US has sought support from international allies within its Empire to confront China. In 2021, NATO leaders, in a meeting in Brussels, lambasted China's ambitions as a systemic challenge to their idea of a neoliberal rules-based international order. The following year, NATO's 'Strategic Concept' recognized China as a challenge to its interests and committed to addressing this. Furthermore, in 2022, Biden met with the G7 leaders to enhance their competitiveness with China.

4   See: Joan E. Greve and Lauran Gambino, 'Capitol Hill finds rare bipartisan cause in China – but it could pose problems', *The Guardian*, 26 February 2023, available at: www.theguardian.com; Intercept, 'China's Mounting Challenge to U.S. Hegemony', *The Intercept*, 5 April 2023, available at: www.theintercept.com.

5   See: Donald J. Trump, *Crippled America: How to Make America Great Again*, New York: Threshold Editions, 2015; Tucker Higgins, 'In a bad sign for trade talks, Trump deploys a new label for China's Xi – "enemy"', *CNBC*, 23 August 2019, available at: www.cnbc.com; Hal Brands, 'Trump's Campaign Is Already Shaping Global Affairs', *Bloomberg*, 9 July 2023, available at: www.bloomberg.com.

6   James Politi and Lauren Fedor, 'Joe Biden warns China over threats to US sovereignty in State of the Union address', *Financial Times*, 7 February 2023, available at: www.ft.com.

7   See: Sean Kenji Starrs, 'Can China Unmake the American Making of Global Capitalism?', in Leo Panitch and Greg Albo, eds, *Socialist Register 2019: A World Turned Upside Down?*, London: Merlin Press, 2018, pp. 173-200.

8   See: Thilo Hanemann, Daniel H. Rosen, Mark Witzke, Steve Bennion, and Emma Smith, 'Two-Way Street – US-China Investment Trends – 2021 Update', Rhodium Group, 19 May 2021, available at: www.rhg.com; Tianlei Huang and Nicholas R. Lardy, 'Foreign corporates investing in China surged in 2021', Peterson Institute for International Economics, 29 March 2022, available at: www.piie.com.

9   Arendse Huld, 'U.S.-China Trade in Goods Hits New Record in 2022 – What Does it Mean for Bilateral Ties?', *China Briefing*, 15 February 2023, available at: www.china-briefing.com.

10 See: Niall Ferguson, *The Ascent of Money: A Financial History of the World*, New York: Penguin Press, 2007; Yuezhi Zhao, 'The Life and Times of 'Chimerica': Global Press Discourses on U.S.-China Economic Integration, Financial Crisis, and Power Shifts', *International Journal of Communication*, 8(1), 2014, pp. 419-44.

11 See: Niall Ferguson and Moritz Schularick, 'The End of Chimerica', *International Finance*, 14(1), pp. 1-26, 2011; John Lee, 'The End of Chimerica: The Passing of Global Economic Consensus and the Rise of US—China Strategic 136 Technological Competition', Australian Strategic Policy Institute, 2019; Orville Schell, 'The Ugly End of Chimerica', *Foreign Policy*, 3 April 2020, available at: www.foreignpolicy.com.

12 See: Walden Bello, 'At the Summit of Global Capitalism: Accommodation, Rivalry, or Confrontation between the US and China?', in Greg Albo, Leo Panitch & Colin Leys, eds, *Socialist Register 2022: New polarizations, old contradictions*, London: Merlin Press, 2021, pp. 22-52; Rush Doshi, *The Long Game: China's Grand Strategy to Displace American Order*, New York: Oxford University Press, 2021; Ho-Fung Hung, *Clash of Empires: from 'Chimerica' to the 'New Cold War'*, Cambridge: Cambridge University Press, 2022; Clyde Prestowitz, *The World Turned Upside Down: America, China and the Struggle for Global Leadership*, New Haven & London: Yale University Press, 2020;

Volker Perthes, 'Dimensions of rivalry: China, the United States, and Europe', *China International Strategy Review*, 3, pp. 56-65, 2021; Susan Watkins, 'America vs China', *New Left Review*, 115(Jan/Feb), 2019, pp. 5-14.

13   See: Adrian Budd, 'China and imperialism in the 21st century', *International Socialism*, 170, 2021, available at: www.isj.org.uk; John Bellamy Foster, 'The New Cold War on China', *Monthly Review*, 73(3), 2021, available at: www.monthlyreview.org; David Harvey, 'David Harvey's response to John Smith on imperialism', *Radical Political Economy blog*, 3 February 2018, available at: www.urpe.org; Minqi Li, 'China: Imperialism or semi-periphery?', *Monthly Review*, 73(3), 2021, available at: www.monthlyreview.org; Zhongkin Li and David M. Kotz, 'Is China Imperialist? Economy, State, and Insertion in the Global System', *Review of Radical Political Economics*, 53(4), 2021, pp. 600-10; Ashley Smith and Kevin Lin, 'Neither Washington nor Beijing: Socialists, inter-imperial rivalry, and Hong Kong', *Socialist Forum*, Winter 2020, available at: https://socialistforum.dsausa.org.

14   See: Lin Chun, 'China's New Globalism,' in Leo Panitch and Greg Albo, eds, *Socialist Register 2019: The World Turned Upside Down?*, London: Merlin Press, 2018, pp. 150-72; Suisheng Zhao, *The Dragon Roars Back: Transformational Leaders and Dynamics of Chinese Foreign Policy*, Stanford, CA: Stanford University Press, 2023; Yuezhi Zhao and Anis Rahman, 'The Belt and Road Initiative, Communication and Geopolitics', in Lee Artz, ed., *Global Media Dialogues: Industry, Politics, and Culture*, New York: Routledge, pp. 234-59. The Belt and Road Initiative (BRI) and Digital Silk Road exemplify China's global expansion: backed over a trillion dollars in investment, the BRI connects over 100 countries across the Asia Pacific, Latin America, and Africa, interlinking them into an extensive cross-border network of critical infrastructure, production, trade, and digital communications stemming from and centered around China. 'China's private and capitalist ICT manufacturers, telecommunication service providers, and internet companies' take a 'leading role in BRI projects' and 'provide system integration' as the 'digital glue' that binds broader cross border 'infrastructural projects such as railways, airports, and oil pipelines' and undergirds the 'internationalization of the renminbi (RMB)' (Zhao & Rahman, 2023, p. 240).

15   See: Henning Melber, 'China in Africa: A New Partner or Another Imperialist Power?', *Africa Spectrum*, 43(3), 2008, pp. 393-402; Tanner Mirrlees, 'Ten Postulates of a Media Imperialism Framework: For Critical Research on China's Media Power and Influence in the Global South', *Global Media and China*, 2023, available at: https://journals.sagepub.com; Dawn C. Murphy, *China's Rise in the Global South*, Redwood, CA: Stanford University Press, 2022; Jodie Yuzhou Sun, 'China in Africa: between imperialism and partnership in humanitarian development', *International Affairs*, 98(5), 2022, pp. 1826-28.

16   Michael Roberts, 'Modern supply-side economics and the New Washington Consensus', *Michael Roberts Blog*, 8 June 2023, available at: https://thenextrecession.wordpress.com.

17   See: Marco D'Eramo, 'Circuits of War', *New Left Review: Sidecar*, 14 November 2022, available at: www.newleftreview.org/sidecar; Nigel Inkster, *The Great Decoupling: China, America and the Struggle for Technological Supremacy*, New York: Oxford University Press, 2021; Hong Shen and Yujia He, 'The geopolitics of infrastructuralized platforms', *Information, Communication & Society*, 25(16), 2022,

pp. 2363-80; Dal Yong Jin, 'The construction of platform imperialism in the globalization era', *tripleC*, 11(1), 2013, pp. 145-72; Steve Rolf and Seth Schindler, 'The US-China rivalry and the emergence of state platform capitalism', *Environment and Planning A: Economy and Space*, 55(5), 2023, pp. 1255-80; Dwayne Winseck, 'The geopolitical economy of the global internet infrastructure', *Journal of Information Policy*, 7(1), 2017, pp. 228-67; Xiangning Wu, 'Technology, Power, and Uncontrolled Great Power Strategic Competition between China and the United States', *China International Strategy Review*, 2(1), 2020, pp. 99-119.

18 See: Miriyam Aouragh and Paula Chakravartty, 'Infrastructure of empire: Towards a critical geopolitics of media and information studies', *Media, Culture & Society*, 38(4), 2016, pp. 559-75; Lee Artz, ed., *Global Media Dialogues: Industry, Politics, Culture*, New York: Routledge, 2023; Oliver Boyd-Barrett and Tanner Mirrlees, eds, *Media Imperialism: Continuity and Change*, New York: Rowman & Littlefield, 2019; Jill Hills, *The Struggle for Control of Global Communication: The Formative Century*, Urbana and Chicago: University of Illinois Press, 2002; Jill Hills, *Telecommunications and Empire*, Urbana and Chicago: University of Illinois Press, 2007; Harold Adams Innis, *Empire and Communications*, Toronto: University of Toronto Press, 2022; Tanner Mirrlees, *Hearts and Mines: The US Empire's Culture Industry*, Vancouver: University of British Columbia Press, 2016; Herbert I. Schiller, *Mass Communications and American Empire*, Boston: Beacon Press, 1969; Herbert I. Schiller, *Communication and Cultural Domination*, New York: M.E. Sharpe, 1976; Dwayne Winseck and Robert M. Pike, *Communication and Empire: Media, Markets, and Globalization, 1860-1930*, Durham and London: Duke University Press, 2007.

19 Bill Clinton, 'Speech on China Trade Bill', *The New York Times*, 9 March 2000, available at: https://archive.nytimes.com.

20 Yuezhi Zhao and Dan Schiller, 'Dances with wolves?: China's integration into digital capitalism', *Info*, 3(2), 2001, pp. 137-51.

21 See: James Griffiths, *The Great Firewall of China: How to Build and Control an Alternative Version of the Internet*. New York: ZED Books, 2018; Elizabeth C Economy, 'The great firewall of China: Xi Jinping's Internet shutdown', *The Guardian*, 29 June 2018, available at: www.theguardian.com.

22 See: Gary King, Jennifer Pan and Margaret E. Roberts, 'How the Chinese Government Fabricates Social Media Posts for Strategic Distraction, Not Engaged Argument', *American Political Science Review*, 111(3), 2017, pp. 484-501.

23 Ryan Fedasiuk, 'Buying Silence: The Price of Internet Censorship in China', Center for Security and Emerging Technology, 12 January 2021, available at: https://cset.georgetown.edu; Margaret E. Roberts, *Censored: Distraction and Diversion Inside China's Great Firewall,* Princeton and Oxford: Princeton University Press, 2018.

24 Eric Chu, 'China's Digital Economy: Full Steam Ahead', HKTDC Research, 2 February 2023, available at: https://research.hktdc.com.

25 See: Nick Couldry and Ulises A. Mejias, *The Costs of Connection: How Data Is Colonizing Human Life and Appropriating it for Capitalism*, Redwood, CA: Stanford University Press, 2019; David B. Nieborg, Chris J. Young and Daniel Joseph, 'App imperialism: The Political Economy of the Canadian App Store', *Social Media + Society*, 6(2), 2020, pp. 1-11; Dal Yong Jin, *Digital Platforms, Imperialism and Political Culture*, New York: Routledge, 2015; Michael Kwet, 'Digital colonialism: US empire and the new imperialism in the Global South', *Race & Class*, 60(4), 2018,

pp. 3-26; José van Dijck, 'Guarding Public Values in a Connective World: Challenges for Europe,' in Oliver Boyd-Barrett and Tanner Mirrlees, eds, *Media Imperialism: Continuity and Change*, New York: Rowman & Littlefield, 2020, pp. 175-87.

26 Yu Hong and G. Thomas Goodnight, 'How to think about cyber sovereignty: The case of China', *Chinese Journal of Communication*, 13(1), 2019, pp. 8-26.

27 Al Jazeera, 'China seeks to purify' internet', *Al Jazeera*, 25 January 2007, available at: www.aljazeera.com.

28 China Services Info, 'Public Pledge of Self-Regulation and Professional Ethics for China Internet Industry', 26 December 2018, available at: https://govt.chinadaily.com.cn.

29 Information Office of the State Council of the PRC, 'White paper on the Internet in China', Chinadaily.com, 8 June 2010, available at: www.chinadaily.com.cn.

30 Shannon Tiezzi, 'China's 'Sovereign' Internet', *The Diplomat*, 24 June 2014, available at: www.thediplomat.com.

31 Elizabeth C. Economy, *The Third Revolution: Xi Jinping and the New Chinese State*, New York: Oxford University Press, 2018.

32 United States Chamber of Commerce, 'Made in China 2025: Global Ambitions Built on Local Protections', 16 March 2017, available at: www.uschamber.com/assets/archived/images/final_made_in_china_2025_report_full.pdf

33 Yu Hong, 'Reading the 13th Five-Year Plan: Reflections on China's ICT policy', *International Journal of Communication*, 11(1), 2017, pp. 1755-74.

34 Min Tang, 'Not Yet the End of Transnational Digital Capitalism: A Communication Perspective of the U.S.–China Decoupling Rhetoric', *International Journal of Communication*, 16(1), 2022, pp. 1506-31.

35 The State Council of the PRC, 'State Council releases five-year plan on informatization', 27 December 2016, available at: http://english.www.gov.cn.

36 Roger Creemers, Hunter Dorwart, Kevin Neville, Kendra Schaefer, Johanna Costigan, Graham Webster, 'Translation: 14th Five-Year Plan for National Informatization', DigiChina, 24 January 2022, available at: https://digichina.stanford.edu.

37 Jack Wagner, 'China's Cybersecurity Law: What You Need to Know', *The Diplomat*, 1 June 2017, available at: www.thediplomat.com.

38 Xinmei Shen and Coco Feng, 'Data privacy in China: Beijing to define data that will not be allowed to leave the country easily', *South China Morning Post*, 2 August 2021, available at: www.scmp.com.

39 Ryan Gallagher, 'How US Tech Giants are Helping to Build China's Surveillance State', *The Intercept*, 11 July 2019, available at: www.theintercept.com; Robert McMahon and Isabella Bennett, 'US Internet Providers and the "Great Firewall of China"', Council on Foreign Relations, 23 February 2011, available at: www.cfr.org.

40 Amnesty International, 'Undermining freedom of expression in China. The role of Yahoo!, Microsoft and Google', 19 July 2006, available at: www.amnesty.org; James Griffiths, 'Report claims US tech companies continue to power China's surveillance state', *The Globe and Mail*, 3 August 2021, available at: www.theglobeandmail.com; Tina Rosenberg, 'Building the Great Firewall of China, with Foreign Help', *The New York Times*, 18 September 2005, available at: www.nytimes.com.

41 Jenny Chan, Mark Selden, Pun Ngai, *Dying for an iPhone: Apple, Foxconn, and the Lives of China's Workers*, Chicago: Haymarket Books, 2020; Hannah Bryan, 'Where Apple

goes When it Leaves China', *Leaders*, 13 April 2013, available at: https://www.leaders.com.

42 See: Fortune Global 500, available at: www.fortune.com/ranking/global500; Forbes Global 2000, available at: www.forbes.com/lists/global2000.

43 See: Mirrlees, 'Ten Postulates of a Media Imperialism Framework'; Graham Murdock, 'The empire's new clothes: Political priorities and corporate ambitions in China's drive for global ascendency', in Oliver Boyd-Barrett and Tanner Mirrlees, eds, *Media Imperialism: Continuity and Change*, New York: Rowman & Littlefield, 2020, pp. 291-304; Colin Sparks, 'China: An emerging cultural imperialist,' in Oliver Boyd-Barrett and Tanner Mirrlees, eds, *Media Imperialism: Continuity and Change*, New York: Rowman & Littlefield, 2020, pp. 275-90; Daya K. Thussu, Hugo de Burgh, and Anbin Shin, eds, *China's Media Go Global*, New York: Routledge, 2018.

44 Michael Schuman, 'Xi Jinping is Done with the Established World Order', *The Atlantic*, 9 September 2023, available at: www.theatlantic.com.

45 See: Nigel Inkster, *The Great Decoupling: China, America and the Struggle for Technological Supremacy*, New York: Oxford University Press, 2021; Shinjoung Yeo, *Baidu: Geopolitical Dynamics of the Internet in China*, New York: Routledge, 2023; Shinjoung Yeo, *Behind the Search Box: Google and the Global Internet Industry*, Champaign, IL: University of Illinois Press, 2023, p. 172.

46 See: Jacob Helberg, *The Wires of War: Technology and the Global Struggle for Global Power*, New York: Simon & Schuster, 2022; Yu Hong, *Networking China: The Digital Transformation of the Chinese Economy*, Urbana, IL: University of Illinois Press, 2017; Dan Schiller, *Digital Capitalism: Networking the Global Market System*, Cambridge, MA: MIT Press, 1999; Dan Schiller, *Digital Depression: Information Technology and Economic Crisis*, Champaign, IL: University of Illinois Press, 2014; Yuezhi Zhao, *Communication in China: Political economy, power, and conflict*, London and Toronto: Rowman and Littlefield, 2008.

47 For instance, Tencent's management team primarily consists of Chinese citizens, while Alphabet-Google's is predominantly composed of American citizens.

48 Zhou Xin, Coco Feng, and Minghe Hu, 'With rising confidence, Xi Jinping wields the internet as a tool of empowerment and control, speeches reveal', *South China Morning Post*, 18 March 2021, available at: www.scmp.com.

49 Evelyn Cheng, 'Biden calls for the U.S. to become more competitive against a "deadly earnest" China', CNBC, 29 April 2021, available at: www.cnbc.com.

50 See: Nick Dyer-Witheford and Svitlana Matviyenko, *Cyberwar and Revolution*, Minneapolis: University of Minnesota Press, 2019; Shane Harris, *@War: The Rise of the Military-Internet Complex*, New York: Houghton-Mifflin-Harcourt, 2014; Jacob Helberg, *The Wires of War: Technology and the Struggle for Power*, New YCork: Simon & Schuster, 2022; Joshua Kurlantzick, *Beijing's Global Media Offensive: China's Uneven Campaign to Influence Asia and the World*, New York: Oxford University Press, 2022; Yasha Levine, *Surveillance Valley: The Secret Military History of the Internet*, New York: Public Affairs, 2018; Chris Miller, *Chip War: The Fight for the World's Most Critical Technology*, New York: Scribner, 2022; Shawn M. Powers and Michael Jablonski, *The Real Cyberwar: The Political Economy of Internet Freedom*, Urbana and Chicago, IL: University of Illinois Press, 2015; David E. Sanger, *The Perfect Weapon: War, Sabotage and Fear in the Cyber Age*, New York: Crown, 2018; P. W. Singer and Emerson T.

Brooking, *LikeWar: The Weaponization of Social Media*, New York: Houghton-Mifflin-Harcourt, 2018.

51 See: Rob Larson, *Bit Tyrants: The Political Economy of Silicon Valley*, Chicago: Haymarket Books, 2020; Nikos Smyrnaios, *Internet Oligopoly: The Corporate Takeover of Our Digital World*, Bingley: Emerald Group Publishing, 2018; Tanner Mirrlees, 'Getting at GAFAM's "Power" in Society: A Structural-Relational Framework', *Heliotrope*, 2021, available at: www.heliotropejournal.net.

52 See: Dan Schiller, 'The Militarization of U.S. Communications', *Communication, Culture and Critique*, 1(1), 2008, pp. 126-38; Fred L. Block and Matthew R. Keller, *State of Innovation: the U.S. Government's Role in Technological Development*, New York: Routledge, 2011; Mariana Mazzucato, *The Entrepreneurial State: Debunking Public vs Private Sector Myths*, New York: Penguin, 2013.

53 See: Robert J. González, 'Militarising Big Tech: The Rise of Silicon Valley's Digital Defence Industry', The Transnational Institute, 7 February 2023, available at: www.tni.org; Jack Poulson, 'Reports of a Silicon Valley / Military Divided Have Been Greatly Exaggerated', *Tech Inquiry*, 7 July 2020, available at: www.techinquiry.org; Edward Ongweso Jr., 'Big Tech Has Made Billions Off the 20-Year War on Terror', *Vice*, 9 September 2021, available at: www.vice.com; Alex Press, 'Big Tech's Unholy Alliance with the Pentagon', *The New Republic*, 7 February 2019, available at: www.newrepublic.com.

54 Tom Simonite, '3 Years After the Project Maven Uproar, Google Cozies to the Pentagon', *Wired*, 18 November 2021, available at: www.wired.com.

55 Zoe Schiffer and Alex Heath, 'Apple has bought and AR headset startup called Mira', *The Verge*, 6 June 2023, available at: https://www.theverge.com/2023/6/6/23751350/apple-mira-ar-headset-startup

56 Matthew Broersma, 'Facebook Metaverse to Use Tech From Former Military Contractor', *Silicon*, 27 December 2021, available at: www.silicon.co.uk; Mike Killian, 'The US Military Is Building Its Own Metaverse', *Wired*, 17 May 2022, available at: www.wired.com.

57 Karen Hao, 'Amazon is the invisible backbone of ICE's immigration crackdown', *MIT Technology Review*, 22 October 2018, available at: www.technologyreview.com.

58 Jon Harper, 'Army issues task order to Microsoft to develop better version of IVAS headset', *Defensescoop*, 5 January 2023, available at: www.defensescoop.com.

59 Brian Fung, 'Pentagon awards multi-billion-dollar cloud contract to Amazon, Google, Microsoft and Oracle', *CNN Business*, 8 December 2022, available at: www.cnn.com.

60 Amy J. Nelson and Gerald L. Epstein, 'The PLA's Strategic Support Force and AI Innovation', *Tech Stream*, 23 December 2022, available at: www.brookings.edu.

61 Tony Capaccio and Jenny Leonard, 'Huawei on List of 20 Chinese Companies That Pentagon Says Are Controlled by People's Liberation Army', *TIME*, 25 June 2020, available at: www.time.com; Brandi Vincent, 'Pentagon's list of Chinese military-linked companies operating in the U.S. grows', *Defensescoop*, 6 October 2022, available at: www.defensescoop.com

62 Jacob Helberg, *Wires of War*, p. 43.

63 See: Nathan Gardels, 'The Great AI Duopoly', *Noema Magazine*, 24 September 2018, available at: www.noemamag.com; Kai-Fu Lee, *AI Superpowers: China, Silicon Valley and the New World Order*, Houghton-Mifflin-Harcourt, 2018.

64 INSIKT Group. 'China's Digital Colonialism', 1 July 2021, available at: www.recordedfuture.com; Michael Kwet, 'Digital colonialism: The Evolution of US Empire', The Transnational Institute, 4 March 2021, available at: https://longreads.tni.org.

65 Bryce Barrows, Nathan Kohlenberg, and Etienne Soula, 'China and the Digital Information Stack in the Global South', Alliance for Securing Democracy, 15 June 2022, available at: https://securingdemocracy.gmfus.org; Min Tang, 'From "bringing-in" to "going-out": Transnationalizing China's internet capital through state policies', *Chinese Journal of Communication*, 13(1), 2020, pp. 27-46.

66 HKDCT Research, 'RWANDA: Africa's First eWTP Hub Set up with Alibaba', 22 February 2023, available at: https://research.hktdc.com.

67 Adina-Laura Achim, 'How Alibaba Won Latin American e-commerce', *Jing Daily*, 22 July 2021, available at: https://jingdaily.com.

68 Ulfah Aulia and Sheila Alifia, 'US is losing Asia's multilateral trade game', *Asia Times*, 19 June 2023, available at: www.asiatimes.com.

69 See: The Asia Policy Institute, 'Determining the Future of the Internet: The U.S.-China Divergence', 2023, available at: www.asiasociety.org; Shazeda Ahmed, 'Refocusing on the 'world' at the World Internet Conference', *China-U.S. Focus*, 20 December 2017, available at: www.chinausfocus.com; Denis Degterev, Mirzet Ramich, and Danil Piskunov, 'U.S. & China Approaches to Global Internet Governance: "New Bipolarity" in Terms of "The Network Society"', *International Organisations Research Journal*, 16(3), 2021, pp. 7-33; Laura Denardis, *The Global War for Internet Governance*, New Haven and London: Yale University Press, 2014; Rebecca MacKinnon, *Consent of the Networked: The Worldwide Struggle for Internet Freedom*, New York: Basic Books, 2013; Sarah McKune and Shazeda Ahmed, 'The contestation and shaping of cyber norms through China's Internet sovereignty agenda', *International Journal of Communication*, 12(1), 2018, pp. 3835-55; Milton Mueller, *Will the Internet fragment? Sovereignty, globalization and cyberspace*, Cambridge, UK: Polity Press, 2017; Mark Scott and Clothilde Goujard, 'Digital great game: The West's standoff against China and Russia', *Politico*, 8 September 2022, available at: www.politico.eu; Justin Sherman, 'China's War for Control of Global Internet Governance', 27 July 2022, available at: https://ssrn.com/abstract=4174453.

70 Elizabeth Van Wie Davis, *Shadow Warfare: Cyberwar Policy in the United States, Russia and China*, New York: Rowman & Littlefield, 2021.

71 Josh Chin and Liza Lin, *Surveillance State: Inside China's Quest to Launch a New Era of Social Control*, New York: MacMillan Books, 2022.

72 See: Burcu Baykurt and Victoria De Grazia, eds, *Soft-Power internationalism: Competing for Cultural Influence in the 21st-Century Global Order*, New York: Columbia University Press, 2021; Ingrid d'Hooghe, *China's Public Diplomacy*, Leiden: Brill, 2015; Wu Fei and Ji Yao, 'The Development and Game of US Digital Diplomacy under Geopolitics', *International Relations and Diplomacy*, 10(5), 2022, pp. 197-206; Joshua Kurlantzick, *Beijing's Global Media Offensive: China's Uneven Campaign to Influence Asia and the World*, New York: Oxford University Press, 2022; Jan Melissen and Jian Wang, eds, *Debating Public Diplomacy: Now and Next*, Leiden: Brill, 2019; Tanner Mirrlees, *Hearts and Mines: The US Empire's Culture Industry*, Vancouver: UBC Press, 2016; Colin Sparks, 'China's soft power from the BRICS to the BRI', *Global Media and China*, 3(2), 2018, pp. 1-8; Jian Wang, 'Public diplomacy and our digital

future', USC Center on Public Diplomacy, 7 November 2019, available at: https://uscpublicdiplomacy.org; Herman Wasserman, 'China's 'soft power' and its influence on editorial agendas in South Africa', *Chinese Journal of Communication*, 9(1), 2016, pp. 8-20.
73   Ana Swanson and Edward Wong, 'With New Crackdown, Biden Wages Global Campaign on Chinese Technology', *The New York Times*, 13 October 2022, available at: www.nytimes.com.
74   US Department of Commerce, 'Commerce adds seven Chinese entities to entity list for supporting China's military modernization efforts', 23 August 2022, available at: www.bis.doc.gov.
75   David Lawder, 'Importers Paid $32 Billion in US Tariffs on Chinese Tech Imports, Report Shows', *Reuters*, 19 July 2022, available at: www.reuters.com.
76   The White House, 'Executive Order on Addressing the Threat from Securities Investments that Finance Certain Companies of the People's Republic of China', 3 June 2021, available at: www.whitehouse.gov.
77   The White House, 'Executive Order on Addressing United States Investments in Certain National Security Technologies and Products in Countries of Concern', 9 August 2023, available at: www.whitehouse.gov.
78   China Communication Construction Company, China Construction Technology, China Electronics Corporation, China Electronics Technology Group, China Mobile, China Telecom, China Unicom, Global Tone Communication Technology, GOWIN Semiconductor Group, Hikvision, Huawei, Panda Electronics, Semiconductor Manufacturing International (SMIC), and Xiamoi Corporation have been impacted.
79   Reuters, 'Five Chinese companies delisted from NYSE', *Reuters*, 12 July 2022, available at: www.reuters.com.
80   The White House, 'FACT SHEET: President Biden Signs Executive Order to Ensure Robust Reviews of Evolving National Security Risks by the Committee on Foreign Investment in the United States', 15 September 2022, available at: www.whitehouse.gov.
81   Rishi Iyengar and Jack Detsch, 'China's Tech Money is Now Radioactive', *Foreign Policy*, 2 February 2023, available at: www.foreignpolicy.com.
82   Chang Che, 'Huawei, pummeled by U.S. Sanctions, Reports Plunge in Profit', *The New York Times*, 31 March 2023, available at: www.nytimes.com.
83   Min Tang, 'Huawei Versus the United States? The Geopolitics of Exterritorial Internet Infrastructure', *International Journal of Communication* 14(1), 2020, pp. 4556-77.
84   Lisa Eadicicco, 'Huawei just overtook Apple', *Insider*, 3 May 2019, available at: www.businessinsider.com.
85   David Sacks, 'China's Huawei Is Winning the 5G Race. Here's What the United States Should Do To Respond', Council on Foreign Relations, 29 March 2021, available at: www.cfr.org.
86   Scott Brown, 'The HUAWEI ban explained: A complete timeline and everything you need to know', *Android Authority*, 10 April 2023, available at: www.androidauthority.com; Catherine Tunney and Richard Raycraft, 'Canada bans Chinese tech giant Huawei from 5G network Social Sharing', *CBC News*, 19 May 2022, available at: www.cbc.ca/news.
87   CBS News, 'U.S. bans imports of Chinese tech from Huawei, ZTE', *CBS News*, 25 November 22, available at: www.cbsnews.com; Carly Page, 'US government bans

88 Joe Panettieri, 'Huawei: Banned and Permitted in Which Countries?', *ChannelE2E*, 27 April 2023, available at: www.channele2e.com.
89 Che, 'Huawei, Pummeled by US Sanctions'.
90 The Economist, 'Taiwan's dominance of the chip industry makes it more important', *The Economist*, 6 March 2023, available at: www.economist.com.
91 Arran Hope, 'China's top 10 semiconductor firms', *The China Project*, 3 February 2023, available at: www.thechinaproject.com.
92 Ana Swanson, 'Biden Administration Clamps Down on China's Access to Chip Technology', *The New York Times*, 7 October 2022, available at: www.nytimes.com.
93 Arjun Kharpal, 'China's biggest chipmaker posts first quarterly revenue fall in 3 years as semiconductor woes persist', *CNBC*, 12 May 2023, available at: www.cnbc.com.
94 Gregory C. Allen, 'Choking off China's Access to the Future of AI', Center for Strategic and International Studies, 11 October 2022, available at: www.csis.org.
95 Kim Lyons, 'TikTok says it has passed 1 billion users', *The Verge*, 27 September 2021, available at: www.theverge.com.
96 Zheping Huang, 'ByteDance Matches Tencent's $80 Billion Sales After TikTok Boom', *Bloomberg*, 3 April 2023, available at: www.bloomberg.com.
97 David McCabe and Cecilia Kang, 'U.S. Pushes for TikTok Sale to Resolve National Security Concerns', *The New York Times*, 15 March 2023, available at: www.nytimes.com.
98 Kari Paul, 'TikTok CEO grilled for over five hours on China, drugs and teen mental health', *The Guardian*, 23 March 2023, available at: www.theguardian.com.
99 The White House, 'Remarks by National Security Advisor Jake Sullivan on Renewing American Economic Leadership at the Brookings Institution', 27 April 2023, available at: www.whitehouse.gov.
100 Don Clark, 'Silicon Valley, Cradle of Computer Chips, Gains Big New Research Center', *The New York Times*, 22 March 2023, available at: www.nytimes.com; Ana Swanson, 'The CHIPS Act Is About More Than Chips: Here's What's in It', *The New York Times*, 28 February 2023, available at: www.nytimes.com;
101 Tanner Mirrlees, 'Sanctioning China's Tech Industry to "Secure" Silicon Valley's Global Dominance', in Stuart Davis and Immanuel Ness, eds, *Sanctions as War*, Leiden: Brill, 2021, pp. 105-26.
102 Thil Hanemann, Armand Meyer, and Danielle Goh, 'Vanishing Act: The Shrinking Footprint of Chinese Companies in the US', Rhodium Group, 7 September 2023, available at: www.rhg.com.
103 See: www.us-china-investment.org/; Thilo Hanemann, Daniel H. Rosen, Mark Witzke, Steve Bennion, and Emma Smith, 'Two-Way Street – US-China Investment Trends – 2021 Update' Rhodium Group, 19 May 2021, available at: www.rhg.com;Tianlei Huang and Nicholas R. Lardy, 'Foreign corporates investing in China surged in 2021', Peterson Institute for International Economics, 29 March 2022, available at: www.piie.com.
104 Daisuke Wakabayashi and Tripp Mickle, 'Tech Companies Slowly Shift Production Away From China', *The New York Times*, 1 September 2022, available at: https://www.nytimes.com.

105 Michael Caster, 'Tech giants' pivot out of China can usher in a human rights reset', *Al Jazeera*, 19 January 2023, available at: https://www.aljazeera.com.

106 Selina Cheng and Dan Strumpf, 'Beijing Says Musk Opposes Decoupling of U.S., China', *The Wall Street Journal*, 30 May 2023, available at: www.wsj.com; Sheila Chiang, 'China's Xi tells Bill Gates he's the 'first American friend' he met in Beijing this year', *CNBC*, 16 June 2023, available at: www.cnbc.com; Arjun Kharpal, 'Elon Musk wrapped up his first visit to China in years. Here's what the Tesla CEO was up to', *CNBC*, 1 June 2023, available at: www.cnbc.com; Kathleen Magramo and Jake Kwon, 'After TikTok chief's grilling in Washington, Apple's Tim Cook is all smiles in Beijing', *CNN Business*, 25 March 2023, available at: www.cnn.com.

107 Global Online Marketplaces, 'China-based Sellers Increasingly Important on Western Marketplaces', *ECDB*, 28 September 2023, available at: www.ecommercedb.com.

108 Tripp Mickle, David McCabe and Ana Swanson, 'How the Big Chip Makers Are Pushing Back on Biden's China Agenda,' *The New York Times*, 5 October 2023, available at: www.nytimes.com.

109 David P. Goldman, 'US at grave risk of China tech war retaliation', *Asia Times*, 16 September 2023, available at: www.asiatimes.com.

110 John Liu and Jin Yu Young, 'What the U.S. China Chip War Means for a Critical American Ally', *New York Times*, 1 October 2023, available at: www.nytimes.com.

111 Karen Freifeld, Andrea Shalal, and David Shepardson, 'Biden orders ban on certain US tech investments in China', *Reuters*, 10 August 2023, available at: www.reuters.com; Sarah Wu and Ben Blanchard, 'TSMC expects permanent U.S. approval to supply chip tools to its China factory', *Reuters*, 13 October 2023, available at: www.reuters.com; Alexandra Alper and Karen Freifeld, 'Exclusive: Biden eyes adding AI chip curbs to Chinese companies abroad', *Reuters* 13 October 2023, available at: www.reuters.com.

112 Joyce Huang, 'Beijing's Latest Strike in US-China Chip War May Hurt China, Experts Say', *VOA News*, 23 May 2023, available at: www.voanews.com; Paul Mozur and John Liu, 'With Ban on Micron, China Escalates Microchip Clash With U.S.', *The New York Times*, 22 May 2023, available at: www.nytimes.com.

113 Arjun Kharpal, 'Huawei reportedly says it has developed domestic chip design tools despite U.S. sanctions', *CNBC*, 7 March 2023, available at: www.cnbc.com.

114 Jason Cohen, 'China Ramps Up Crackdown on American Tech', *The Daily Caller*, 2 October 2023, available at: www.dailycaller.com.

115 Chang Che and John Liu, '"De-Americanize": How China Is Remaking Its Chip Business', *New York Times*, 11 May 2023, available at: www.nytimes.com.

116 Bloomberg, 'How China Aims to Counter US "Containment" Efforts in Tech', *The Washington Post*, 5 April 2023, available at: www.washingtonpost.com

CONTINUITY AND CHANGE IN INDIA'S FOREIGN POLICY: REALPOLITIK, HINDU NATIONALISM AND MODI

ACHIN VANAIK

The term 'national interest' is particularly handy for foreign policy practitioners. Even as realpolitik considerations constrain choices, the subjective dimension – the ideological beliefs, values, and ambitions of the leadership coterie that decides foreign policy – remains crucial in deciding directions taken. The term then is not so much one of analysis or guidance as of justification. Completely opposite policy paths, e.g., supporting or opposing a particular alliance, can be chosen in its name.

The use of the word 'national' is both misleading and important. It is misleading because even a liberal-democratic state's claim to being representative of its citizen body is fraudulent. States are never socially neutral but are structurally biased in favour of dominant ruling classes and only in rare circumstances, such as a struggle against unjustifiable external military intervention, can they be seen as genuinely representative of the 'national popular will'. It is important because the *nationalist character* of the ruling elite – its motivating set of historical and contemporary beliefs, values, and ambitions – will significantly affect the state's political behaviour domestically and externally.

This must be kept in mind when evaluating foreign policy perspectives and practices under Modi's Hindu Nationalist BJP that won the 2014 general elections, secured a comfortable majority in 2019, and looks likely to secure a third term of office in the forthcoming 2024 elections. Hindu Nationalism (HN) or Hindutva (Hinduness as the national essence) comes in different shades of interpretation, marking both the politics of governments led by the Congress and by non-Congress/non-BJP party coalitions. But its foundational principles have always been most harshly laid down by the now-huge *Sangh Parivar* (Family of Organizations), whose parent body, the

Rashtriya Swayamsevak Sangh (RSS – National Volunteer Corps), was set up in 1925 and whose post-independence political-electoral wing was first the Jan Sangh (JS, formed in 1951) and is now the Bharatiya Janata Party (BJP, formed in 1980).

Between 1947 and 1998, the basic parameters of Indian foreign policy were set by the Congress Party, and were basically unaltered by the three short interludes of non-BJP/non-Congress coalition governments of 1977-80, 1989-91, 1996-98. This included major readjustments carried out by the 1991-96 Congress-led government after the break-up of the USSR and Yugoslavia and China's successful transition to a 'party state capitalism'. The first ever BJP-led government coalitions under Prime Minister Vajpayee emerged thereafter, ruling from 1998 to 1999 and then from 1999 to 2004. Two consecutive five-year terms of a Congress-led government from 2004 to 2014 followed. What, then, were the shared and differing foreign policy perspectives of the Congress party and the HN triumvirate of the RSS/JS/BJP between 1947 and 1998? What breaks took place under the Vajpayee regime? What are the lines of continuity and departure of the Modi regime from that of Vajpayee and the preceding two Congress-led governments?

Here, briefly, are the main characteristics of Indian foreign policy between independence and the first BJP-led governments of 1998-99 and 1999-2004.

The Cold War Period, 1947-1991

First, the religious bitterness of Partition, and more so, the dispute over Kashmir, would crucially shape the foreign policies of India and Pakistan. Despite phases of détente, hostility has lasted to this day.

Second, the US determination to contain Communist USSR and then China led it to seek alliances with many newly emerging countries. Prime Minister Jawaharlal Nehru's India adopted 'nonalignment' to maximize its autonomy by keeping out of East-West bloc rivalry. Nonalignment became the supposed hallmark of India's foreign policy through to the end of the Cold War.

Third, India's external behaviour was actually somewhat different. The US's military alliance with Pakistan and diplomatic support for its stance on Kashmir guaranteed that India would have a strategic tilt toward the USSR for around four decades, reinforced by Moscow's continuous supply of all kinds of military equipment and help in developing a heavy industrial base in support of India's effort at import-substituting industrialization. As the economy expanded and its bigger capitalists grew from the late 1970s onwards, India would strongly reorient economically towards the US, Western Europe, and Japan.

Fourth, immediately after independence, India adopted Britain's 'forward defence policy'. This meant preserving a domineering attitude and policy towards the Himalayan crest nations of Nepal, Bhutan (which basically remains), and Sikkim, whose protectorate status was transferred to India in 1950. But in 1975 Sikkim was simply taken over after a manipulated referendum under military occupation.

Fifth, China's military takeover of Tibet had its counterpart in India's war with Nagaland which unsuccessfully fought for secession over several decades. The failure to resolve the India-China border dispute can in large part be attributed to India's insistence on accepting the boundary lines drawn by British imperialism as essentially inviolable rather than a give-and-take resolution respecting geography and different interests. In the 1962 war China defeated India, unilaterally retreated from its most advanced positions to where it considered its boundary to lie, and over the next few months released all Indian prisoners.

Sixth, there were also three wars with Pakistan in this period. The 1948 war saw the province of Jammu and Kashmir (J&K) bifurcated. The Indian part became the only Muslim-majority state in the Union. The 1965 war was a stalemate. In 1971 India defeated the Pakistani army in its former eastern territory, which became the independent country of Bangladesh.

Seventh, India carried out a 'peaceful' nuclear test in 1974 and entered the club of countries having the nuclear option.

Eighth, in the mid-1950s Sinhala, the language of the Buddhist majority of Sri Lanka, was made the only official one. This led first to discrimination against the minority Tamil population in civil services/public sector employment, later extending to university enrolments and even some takeovers of Tamil peasant lands. Periodic communal riots erupted, and by the 1970s an electoral Tamil opposition party, the Tamil United Liberation Front (TULF), emerged along with more militant groups that then converged to become the Liberation Tigers of Tamil Eelam (LTTE). In July 1983 a government-led pogrom resulted in well over 5,000 Tamil deaths and some 250,000 displaced from majority Sinhala areas, thereby precipitating a civil war-type situation with one Tamil section demanding regional autonomy and the much stronger LTTE pursuing armed struggle for secession of the northeast Jaffna province. New Delhi became a party to the dispute, giving sanctuary and training to Tamil guerrillas as its own southern province of Tamil Nadu, on grounds of ethnic kinship, supported the independence struggle. In 1987 Colombo, in negotiations with New Delhi, offered devolution of power but not independence to the northeast. India agrees and sends an Indian Peace Keeping Force (IPKF) to act as the principal arbiter in Sri Lanka's civil war, going after the very forces to which it had earlier provided succour. This represented the zenith in India's effort at regional pre-eminence, but its failure to subdue the LTTE led to Colombo's demand for IPKF withdrawal, completed in March 1990. This civil war only ended in 2008 after the decisive defeat of the LTTE.

In 1988 a serious coup attempt against the ruling government of President Gayoom in the Maldives was foiled when India, unlike Singapore, Sri Lanka, and Pakistan, accepted Gayoom's request to come to his military rescue. India's efforts to emerge as a significant 'middle power' with its own 'sphere of influence', a euphemism for securing regional dominance, achieved only limited success and were not made any easier by Pakistani contestation in South Asia.

In the Aftermath of the Cold War, 1991-98

In the mid-80s, Gorbachev, the principal leader of the USSR, pursued major de-escalation of tensions with the US and Western Europe but domestically unleashed policies of opening out economically (*perestroika*) and politically (*glasnost*) that uncontrollably led to the unanticipated break-up of the USSR and the Soviet bloc in 1990-91. Unsurprisingly, India (among others) significantly reordered its foreign policy perspectives.

First, India accelerated its late-1980s turn towards neoliberal capitalist globalization, opening out to steadily greater foreign trade, investment, and finance.

Second, given the Soviet collapse, India made a decisive geopolitical shift towards the US, forging a 'strategic friendship' but not yet a 'partnership' since the US was still relying on Pakistani support for its intervention in Afghanistan.

Third, shifting geo-political arrangements between China-US-Russia meant Sino-Indian relations qualitatively improved, with the Border Peace and Tranquillity Agreement (BPTA) of 1993 being followed by mutually agreed Confidence Building Measures (CBMs) in 1996.

Fourth, an intense debate took place in India between 1994 and 1996 on whether it should sign the Comprehensive Test Ban Treaty (CTBT) then being negotiated worldwide. All political parties including those of the Communists (mainstream and Maoist) opposed the Treaty and India remained out.[1]

Fifth, in 1992 the Congress-led government established full diplomatic relations with Israel for technological, military, and political reasons, seeing it as a useful conduit to reinforcing ties with the US.

HINDU NATIONALIST THINKING
BEFORE THE VAJPAYEE REGIMES

From its inception in 1925 the RSS took the view that achieving a Hindu *Rashtra* (nation) required the transformation of society by reawakening Hindu consciousness through glorification of the Hindu-Indian past, recognizing the supposed insidiousness of the long period of 'Muslim' rule along with the conversions to Islam and Christianity. Also rejected was the 'foreign' ideology of Communism and its carriers. Hindu unity would be created by the Sangh Parivar developing dedicated cadres and branches of the RSS to carry out everyday cultural-ideological activities to attract loyalties, beginning with middle and lower middle-class Hindu families in urban and semi-urban north and central India. Once having achieved such a mass base, it would seek to expand its activities and allegiances geographically and across classes and castes. A political-electoral wing, the JS, was set up to contest ruling governments and their policies. This was secondary and complementary to the long-term grassroots struggle. The JS remained electorally marginal from 1951 to the time of Emergency (1975-77), thus reinforcing this orientation. The JS first participated in government enjoying important ministerial postings when it dissolved itself into the Janata Party that ran the post-emergency government (1977-80). After the fall of this government the BJP was formed and, with its appetite for state power now whetted, it would take campaigning much more seriously, emerging as a steadily growing electoral force from the late-1980s to the early-1990s onwards.

Before the advent of the Vajpayee-led government, what were the main foreign policy perspectives of the Sangh? Hostility to Pakistan was central, and from the very beginning it opposed J&K – India's only Muslim majority province – having the special autonomy status sanctioned by Article 370 of the Constitution, hence the demand for its abrogation. Anti-Communism was also basic, but because of Soviet diplomatic support to India on Kashmir, the Sangh would broadly go along with Nehru's nonalignment while insisting it should move closer to the West. The JS supported Tibet's independence, as it did for Taiwan. In 1963 – before China's nuclear test the following year – the JS called for India to go nuclear, and after the 1974 test it was the only party to call for exercising the nuclear option.[2] Even after the 1967 Israel-Arab war, only the JS called for establishing full diplomatic relations with Israel. Not long after Bangladesh became independent, the BJP raised concerns about Muslim migration into India, decrying New Delhi's 'appeasement' in not doing enough to prevent this. On the other hand, Hindu migrants were to be treated as refugees.[3]

Interestingly, in keeping with its hardcore HN, the Sangh promoted an 'economic nationalism' stressing self-reliance, and in 1992 opposed the Congress government's turn to neoliberalism, instead insisting until the mid-1990s, that India continue with 'import-substitution … in every sphere'.[4] However, the Sangh's successful campaign of prolonged mass mobilization (mid-1980s to December 1992) to destroy the Babri Masjid supposedly built on the ruins of a temple dedicated to the mythical God-king Ram at Ayodha, his alleged birthplace, made it for the first time a serious electoral contender for central power. To forge a strong relationship with Indian capital, it had to rethink its earlier economic stance.

The BJP Governments of 1998-99, 1999-2004

In my 1995 book I predicted that should the BJP come to power it would make three major policy shifts.[5] It would take steps to halt Muslim migration from Bangladesh. It would continue ruthless military operations in Kashmir, but also move towards eliminating its autonomous status and change the demography of the province. Thirdly, it would 'very likely go openly nuclear'. The first two predictions were fulfilled after Modi's second term began. Shortly after its election victory in May 1998, the Vajpayee government, to the complete surprise of all other parties including its own partners, carried out five nuclear tests, declaring its membership of the club of nuclear weapons states (NWSs). It was taken aback by Pakistan unexpectedly carrying out its own tests later that month.

A very disturbing nuclear dimension had now been added to the already tension-filled South Asian standoff. But worse from New Delhi's perspective was the anger in Washington which imposed sanctions on both countries as per Congressional law. The initiator of South Asian nuclearization had to calm things down, hence Vajpayee's February 1999 Pakistan trip to allay fears of a future war. However, a few months later war broke out after Pakistani incursions in the Kargil border area, with both sides readying their respective nuclear arsenals. Behind-the-scenes US intervention forced a Pakistan retreat. Concurrent top-level negotiations lasting fourteen months between the US and India resolved matters, with the latter assuring the former of its willingness to be a strategic partner in its wider geopolitical plans and ambitions – an outcome crowned by Clinton's official visit to India in March 2000, the first by a US president since 1978. In due course, Vajpayee declared the two countries to be 'natural allies'. After 9/11, despite the long US war on Al Qaeda and its need for Pakistani support in Afghanistan, the US strategic tilt towards India became progressively stronger, while Pakistan would drift closer to China.

The India-Pakistan situation would get worse before becoming better. In December 2001 a five-man Islamist group with a base in Pakistan attacked India's parliament and before themselves dying killed 14 people. The reaction of the first HN government was extremely disproportionate. The most massive ever troop mobilization on the border was carried out, pushing Pakistan to do the same. This lasted for nine dangerous months before matters were allowed to cool down – the largest-ever peacetime military confrontation since the end of World War II. This is also when India prepared plans for an integrated and rapid offensive strike into Pakistani territory, popularly referred to as the 'Cold Start Doctrine'.[6] Pakistan then formulated in 2002 its own doctrine of using tactical nuclear weapons should India cross any of 'four red lines' i.e., large-scale capture of Pakistani territory; large-scale destruction of its armed forces; economic strangulation; major political destabilization.[7]

The Vajpayee government in the early 2000s made three policy changes. First, it significantly accelerated Indo-Israel relations, hosting the first ever prime ministerial visit of Ariel Sharon in 2003, while military cooperation was greatly deepened – Israeli support, material and informational, helping India during the Kargil war. Second, on the migrant issue, hardly noticed by its coalition partners or the public, two new laws were promulgated. A National Register of Citizens (NRC) and a National Population Register (NPR) were introduced, which could expel or punish illegal migrants – the government had Muslims in mind. However, Hindus with Pakistani citizenship were *never* to be designated as 'illegals'. For the first time, a principle of religious discrimination was introduced into citizen-related laws. Third, the government jettisoned HN's 'economic nationalism' to continue along the neoliberal path set by its predecessors. The BJP, like the Congress Party, understood it must have big capital on its side, and thus generally supported its material interests and acted as an arbiter among factions even while creating favoured cronies. Hence, the general acceptance of greater economic integration with foreign capital, especially from the West and Japan, provided an economic basis for geopolitical realignments.

Congress-led Coalition Governments, 2004-14

The BJP's 1998 nuclear breakthrough was now the new normal accepted, barring the left, by all other parties including the Congress Party. Publicly committing to No First Use, all governments moved towards triadic nuclear deployment, including developing a submarine arm. Less motivated by HN, the Manmohan Singh Congress-led government nevertheless shared the belief that India must 'fulfil its destiny of becoming a great world power'.

The Bush administration's decision to accelerate strategic ties between India and the US opened the way to the 2005 ten-year Defence Framework Agreement for much deeper technology transfer and co-production, information sharing, and joint military cooperation and exercises. Prolonged negotiations beginning in 2005 culminated in 2008 with the signing of the India-US Civil Nuclear Agreement, signalling de facto international acceptance of India's NWS status, and its ability to use its domestic uranium sources for building such weapons. A US-organized waiver from the Nuclear Suppliers Group (NSG) that sets the international trading guidelines so as to prevent nuclear weapons proliferation potentially enables India to develop its civilian nuclear capabilities through foreign deals. Ironically, the NSG was set up in 1975 as a reaction against India's test in 1974, which had been made possible by its illegal violations of civilian energy deals with the US and Canada. Pakistan, however, got no such waiver – further evidence of where US strategic priorities now lay.

The other foreign policy issue of note in these years, apart from consolidating the military relationship with Israel, was India and Pakistan apparently coming closer than ever before to some kind of workable resolution of the Kashmir question.[8] In July 2001, President Pervez Musharraf suggested a four-point formula to the Vajpayee regime that was turned down. The four points were: a) demilitarization through phased troop withdrawal; b) no change of borders, but free movement of Kashmiris across the Line of Control; c) self-government without independence for the whole disputed area; d) joint supervision over J&K through a mechanism involving India, Pakistan, and Kashmiris. After the accession of the Congress-led government in 2004, the details of this basic formula were worked out through constant back-channel dialogue between the two governments throughout the period 2005-08. A domestic conflict in Pakistan pitting a massive lawyers' movement for genuine judicial independence against Musharraf's rule is said to have derailed this back-channel process.[9] Subsequently, Musharraf resigned in 2008 for fear of impeachment and went into exile abroad.

THE MODI ERA

With only a very slim majority in his first term of office (May 2014 to May 2019), Modi had to tread carefully in his foreign policy. However, after securing a comfortable majority in mid-2019, Modi could increase the weight given to Hindutva concerns about Muslims even while further promoting neoliberal globalization and pursuing conventional realpolitik. On the economic front, following the Vajpayee pattern, favoured cronies were to provide loyalty and regular funds in return for getting contracts, directly from or supported by the state. Modi had already been engaged in such activities as Chief Minister (2001-14) through his 'Gujarat model of development', and as PM especially favoured Gujarati TNCs.[10] Modi has also promoted joint ventures between foreign investors and private Indian companies to create a deeper military-industrial complex. India is now the world's largest importer of military equipment and Israel's top customer, reinforcing bilateral relations.[11]

Indeed, Modi in 2017 became the first Premier to officially visit Israel and the first high political Indian dignitary not to then immediately visit the Palestinian leadership, making clear who has the higher priority. To Palestinian consternation, Modi has welcomed the Abraham Accords wherein so far Bahrain, UAE, Morocco, and Sudan have normalized relations with Israel. Modi has also joined the new security grouping I2U2 comprising India, Israel, the UAE, and the US. The Sangh has always had an ideologically driven admiration for Zionism, embodying as it does a racially exclusivist nationalism, even as Indian governments continue to pay lip service to the Palestinian cause and give money to the Fatah-run Palestine Authority. But even at the formal diplomatic level there is a change. In 2018, after a three-hour Ramallah meeting between Modi and Mahmoud Abbas, the usual official Indian declaration endorsed the creation of a 'sovereign' and 'independent' Palestinian state. But for the first time two words 'united' and 'viable' were missing, as was any reference to East Jerusalem as its capital. This means India will go along with any Israeli Bantustan-type 'solution' were it offered. Indian abstentions from UN resolutions condemning Israel are now more frequent, and in November 2019 India's Consul-General in New York, Sandeep Chakravorty, publicly suggested that Israel's settlement policy holds lessons for how to help the Hindu Pandit community of Kashmir retain their land and culture. Since 2014-15, senior Indian police officers have regularly travelled to Israel to be trained in counter-insurgency, crowd control, 'border management', and 'counter-terrorism'.[12] In the October 2023 Israel-Hamas conflict and the following assault on Gaza, Prime Minister Modi immediately expressed 'full solidarity' with Israel only. The Genocidal onslaught, soon to enter its fifth month, has never been forthrightly condemned; nor at any point has New Delhi called for an *immediate* ceasefire. Worse is the Modi government's complicity on two fronts. Instead of protecting Indians from going into a dangerous battle zone area, there is a fast-tracking of the process whereby Indian workers are being recruited to replace outlawed Palestinian labour in Israel. Furthermore, as widely reported at home and abroad – amid the ongoing war 20 Hermes 900 military drones, produced jointly by Adani-

Elbit Advanced systems India Ltd, have been sent for possible deployment in Gaza.

South Asian Concerns

Despite Pakistani contestation, Modi has been determined to expand India's regional authority. His preferred label for pursuing an Indian 'sphere of influence' is 'Neighbourhood First'. On coming to power in 2014, he visited Afghanistan, Myanmar, and the Maldives, paying particular attention to Hindu Nepal, which he visited four times. Besides the handshakes, the fist was shown. In June 2015, the Indian army – without seeking Yangon's permission – crossed deep into Myanmar territory to chase down Naga insurgents. Residing in the plains of Nepal are 'Madhesis', or Hindus retaining ancestral links in India, whose mother tongue is not Nepali and who in 2015 were opposing the provincial boundaries being prepared in the Nepal Constitution that would reduce their political influence. They carried out a blockade (with New Delhi's complicity) of essential goods from India into Nepal. In February 2016 the blockade ended through a constitutional amendment that satisfied India but not the Madhesis, whose protests nevertheless eventually petered out. However, the downside for Modi is that Chinese investments and aid to Nepal, Bangladesh, Sri Lanka, and Myanmar are way beyond anything India can offer, and all four have joined the Belt Road Initiative. China helps them balance against their closest big neighbour.

The most obviously Hindutva-motivated policy change was the parliamentary passage of the Citizenship Amendment Act (CAA) in December 2019. Under the act, non-Muslim religious minorities in India's three overwhelmingly Muslim neighbours, Afghanistan, Pakistan, and Bangladesh, are automatically deemed to be persecuted and therefore can avail of *fast-track naturalization* as Indian citizens if they claim to have come before 31 December 2014 and stayed for five years (until the end of December 2019), when the new law came into existence. Those coming after 2014 can always claim that they came before but, being persecuted, have no documentary proof to show of this! This law is something like the promulgation of a selective and easy to qualify 'neighbourhood right of return' for the 'true' citizens of India, who are Hindus, Sikhs, Buddhists, and Jains – all considered by the Sangh to be indigenous to India.[13] Really persecuted communities, like Rohingyas from Myanmar, who are Muslim, are therefore excluded. The Hindu Jaffna Tamils from Sri Lanka cannot be fast-tracked because that would mean that Buddhist majority countries (Myanmar, Sri Lanka) are guilty of religious persecution – logically implying that a Hindu majority country like India could also be persecuting its religious minorities such as Muslims and Christians.

Pakistan: the Indus Water Treaty and Kashmir

The one hitherto consistent bright spot in the turbulent Indo-Pakistan relationship has been the 1960 Indus Water Treaty arranged and negotiated by the World Bank. Of the six rivers covered, India is the upper riparian in three whose use (hydel projects) is restricted to roughly one-third or 62.2 cubic km, compared to 170.3 cubic km allowed for Pakistan. Complaining about excessive Indian water use, Pakistan in August 2016 called for court arbitration under the aegis of the World Bank, bypassing the first step of referral to a Neutral Expert and thereby incurring Indian procedural objections. On 18 September 2016 there was an armed cross-border attack by Islamist militants on an Indian army camp in the Jammu region, killing 18 soldiers. Eleven days later Modi publicly declared 'blood and water could not flow together', meaning the IWT would now be held hostage as part of India's severe pressure tactics. In the years that followed, Modi inaugurated the completed 330MW Kishanganga hydel project and authorized more hydel projects totalling 4000MW when completed, which will certainly jeopardize the flow of water to Pakistan. However, to Indian discomfort, the WB court of arbitration said it has the 'competence' to consider this matter and has subsequently initiated parallel action at both procedural levels. The only way the treaty can be modified or ended is by common bilateral agreement. On 25 January 2023, India sent through its Commissioner to the IWT a 90-day notice to Pakistan to enter into negotiations, effectively rejecting the arbitration process with the implied threat of India possibly walking out of the treaty. That period has now passed, with Pakistan so far not meeting its Indian counterpart. New Delhi's unilateral rejection of the Treaty would definitely create a warlike situation. Hopefully this will not happen, but Modi has already shown his willingness to politically up the ante to very dangerous levels, and at the very least will appropriate more water.[14]

Indeed, the single most dramatic change took place in August 2019, when his government unconstitutionally annulled Article 370 that legally guaranteed an asymmetrical autonomy to J&K as compared to most other states in the Indian Union.[15] J&K province was then bifurcated into two Union Territories of J&K and Ladakh, which borders China. Consciously sending messages to Pakistan and China, India's home minister and Modi's old Gujarati sidekick Amit Shah announced that this muscular new India would not only retrieve the territories of J&K lost to Pakistan (which has leased a part to China), but also the Aksai Chin region lost to China in the

1962 war.[16] What this annulment means is that there can no longer be any compromise formula for resolving the Kashmir issue and ending the bitter decades-long hostility. Pakistan, currently facing its most severe economic crisis ever, is effectively being told it must now accept peace on Indian terms. If not, then this will further fuel the Sangh view that Muslim Pakistan must be seen as India's permanent enemy from when it 'raped Mother India', i.e., Partition.

In February 2019 a suicide bomb attack at Pulwama in Jammu by a local Kashmiri youth (trained by the Jaish-e-Mohammed in Pakistan) killed forty soldiers. The Indian response was again out of all proportion. Modi ordered an air bombing deep into Pakistani territory on the group's suspected base. For the *first time ever* one nuclear power had carried out a conventional bomb attack deep in the territory of another nuclear power, reinforcing the view that South Asia remains the world's most dangerous nuclear flashpoint. We now know, as revealed by Trump's former Secretary of State, Mike Pompeo, that once again both sides prepared their nuclear arsenals and that the US stepped in to de-escalate matters.[17]

THE QUADRANGLE: INDIA, CHINA, US, RUSSIA

Not expected by the Modi government was China deciding to 'teach India a lesson'. Beginning in May 2020 China crossed the Line of Actual Control in Ladakh to take over more territory, with periodic armed clashes over the next few months causing mutual casualties for the first time since 1975. Three years later, China retains control of its territorial advances and there is an uneasy standstill. Why this Chinese action? In mid-2017 India intervened in a border dispute between Bhutan and China to oppose Chinese infrastructural construction near a narrow 'chicken neck' strip of land joining mainland India to its north-eastern states. After 74 days some kind of settlement was reached. But the point to note is that although Bhutan is an independent country, Indian troops patrol its border with China. Although China has offered generous terms for a final border settlement that many in Bhutan would favour, it is India that so far has been calling the final shot. China has also been worried by Modi's fast-tracking of military-related infrastructural developments that give it direct access to a section of the Tibet-Xinjiang highway, as well as enabling it to oversee the Gilgit-Baltistan region (which India still claims) through which the China Pakistan Economic Corridor (CPEC) passes. Such preparations have been going on for some time, so this alone would not have ignited the border clash. Indian Home Minister Amit Shah's political pronouncement that accompanied the annulment of Article 370 may have been the trigger for China's border action, but the key cause has much more to do with Modi's forging of a progressively deeper military relationship with the US.[18]

This has been formalized in various agreements: i) the extension of the Ten Year Defence Framework Agreement; ii) the 2016 Logistics Exchange and Memorandum of Agreement (LEMOA), enabling port calls, joint exercises, logistical support, and training; iii) the signing of the Communications Compatibility and Security Agreement (COMCASA) in September 2018, allowing deeper information sharing and transfer of advanced communications technology; (iv) the signing of the Basic Exchange and Cooperation Agreement (BECA) in October 2020 to advance geo-spatial cooperation; and let us not forget the consolidation of the US-led Quadrilateral Security Dialogue (QUAD), whose other three nodes are Australia, Japan, and India, and which is clearly directed to contain China by focusing on the Indo-Pacific region and waters. This involves information exchanges, joint naval exercises, and military drills aiming to patrol key sea routes for strategic and trading purposes. This clearly hardens the India-China relationship. In June 2020, Modi signed an Acquisitions and Cross-Servicing Agreement (ACSA) with Australia opening up bases for each other's army, navy, and air forces. A similar deal was signed on 10 September 2020 with Japan, with which there are already such joint military exercises. India is now planning to construct full-fledged fighter bases in its island territories of Andaman & Nicobar and Lakshadweep to strengthen its role as 'net security provider' in the Indian Ocean.[19] Over the last two decades, China has transited in Washington's eyes from strategically being something of a 'partner' to 'competitor' to 'rival' and now to 'opponent' – and (in some US circles) even 'enemy'. After the US withdrawal from Afghanistan and the collapse of its puppet regime there, Iran, Pakistan, Russia, and China have their own economic, social, and political reasons to cooperate, both to influence the Taliban regime and to come closer against the common US threat. The Russia-China axis has been strongly reinforced after Russia's invasion of Ukraine.

The successor Russian state to the USSR has become progressively less important for New Delhi. Over time, with whatever reservations, Russia drew closer to China as Beijing's political relations with the US worsened. As India sees China as its main strategic problem and draws ever closer to the US, Russia is no longer seen as a serious counterweight to a rising China. Economically, Indian trade and investment patterns are now overwhelmingly with the West and Japan, while its trade balance with China is very much in the latter's favour. Russia's main contribution lies in its steady concessionary oil supplies (currently in Rupees), and in maintaining and upgrading India's heavy-duty military equipment. India has been steadily diversifying arms purchases, particularly from Israel, France, and the US, but much of its military budget is still devoted to Russia because an ever more belligerent India is not satisfied with simply defending its borders but desires to expand its military power projection. Russia is still the single largest supplier of arms to India, but its share of total arms purchases between 2017 and 2022 has fallen from 62 per cent to around 45 per cent. Behind this Indian hubris lies an elite frustration that while China is widely seen as a great and growing power, India still has a long way to go in its own and the world's eyes. Personnel-wise, India has the second largest armed forces in the world after China. Its defence budget ranks third after the US (way ahead of all others) and China. India is also the world's largest importer of arms and related equipment. When it comes to its health budget as a percentage of its GDP, it ranks fourth lowest from the bottom among nations. Yet because of the geographical proximity of its two opponents, China and Pakistan, whose own relationship is become stronger after the US withdrawal from Afghanistan, India cannot dominate, as it certainly wishes, South Asia.

Given this current military dependence, and long history of steadily weaker but on the whole equable relations between the USSR and then post-Soviet Russia, India saw no reason to unnecessarily embitter diplomatic relations through a formal condemnation of Russia's brutal and unjustified invasion of Ukraine. It also rightly calculated that given the predominant trend of an ever-closer Indo-US nexus, this stance of 'neutrality' would not damage ties between the two. It is therefore hardly surprising that Russia's invasion has evoked no Indian condemnation, only platitudes about respecting the principle of national sovereignty. None of the parliamentary opposition parties, including the CPM and CPI, have demurred from this official stance of 'strategic neutrality'. The latter two, and most of the non-party affiliated Indian left, condemn US/NATO expansionist plans as the *primary* culprit in causing Putin's 'reaction'. Generally ignored or relegated as motivations are dreams of a 'Great Russia' articulated by Putin, and Russia's own imperialist ambitions as expressed in its actions in Georgia, Moldova, Belarus, its previous collaborations with the US/NATO, or its own military alliance structure, the Collective Security Treaty Organization (CSTO) under which Putin rushed troops to stabilize the authoritarian Kazakhstan regime about a month before its Ukrainian Invasion. Even Putin's nuclear blackmail attempts have not led to unequivocal condemnation by the Indian government, or left parties which have otherwise opposed the Indian bomb.[20] Of course the US has the most pernicious historical record of nuclear irresponsibility and blackmail, as well as being the only nuclear power to station NWs elsewhere in NATO countries. Now Russia has for the first time stationed tactical NWs outside its own territory in Belarus. The refusal by the left and other opposition forces to indict the Modi government has only boosted Modi's hypocritical efforts to pose as something of a global peacemaker when his is a far-right regime out to establish an ever stronger electoral autocracy.

The Indian PM's state visit to the US on 21-24 June 2023 marked a significant step forward in their strategic relationship. Apart from Modi's ego being deliberately massaged as a result of his being invited for the second time to address a joint session of Congress (a rare honour), the key material pay-offs are twofold. First is the new and promising access to US expertise in certain hi-tech fields under the Initiative on Critical and Emerging Technologies (ICET). For some time now, Indian governments have been keen to develop a military-industrial complex involving private Indian capital that would be greatly involved in production, fabrication and modernization. This is where the second pay-off comes in. Now the way has been cleared for much greater collaboration with the US military-industrial complex to move in just this direction. In due course, Indian dependence on Russia on this front will progressively lessen. Geopolitically this makes sense for India since growing closeness between Russia and China means the former less than ever can be a restraining factor on the latter vis-a-vis India.[21]

MULTILATERAL ENGAGEMENTS

India is a member of numerous multilateral groupings. Those like the WB and IMF are part of the global neoliberal economic system, whose decisions are disproportionately shaped by the interactions of the truly major players such as the US, EU, China, and Japan, with India of little consequence. India shows hardly any interest in a range of specific-issue groupings, like the IAEA and ILO. What can we say about its participation in the annual Conference of the Parties (CoP) to the UNFCCC regarding global warming and environmental protection? What also of Indian involvement in the BRICS, and regional forums such as Shanghai Cooperation Organization (SCO), South Asian Association for Regional Cooperation (SAARC), and the G-20, of which India is the current year's president?

The new millennium Congress-led governments were bad enough in prioritizing the pursuit of high growth rates above all else, though they did claim to be 'balancing' this with environmental protection measures. On coming to power the Modi government made sweeping attacks to environmental restrictions on forests, coasts, wildlife, and waste management to satisfy the land acquisitions and investment proclivities of Indian capitalists big and medium. In 2014 India's rank in the world's Environmental

Performance Index was 155 out of 178 countries. By 2020 India had fallen to 168 from 180.[22] At CoP26 in 2021, countries were allowed to give their own timelines for Nationally Determined Contributions (NDCs) to carbon reduction, reporting over every five-year cycle. India has pledged to reach net zero carbon emissions only by 2070, although it is the world's third largest emitter of GHG, but 'hides behind the poor' by emphasizing that its per capita emissions are so much lower than most others – as if the environment is not affected by total emissions! The Indian 'middle class', conservatively estimated at 15 per cent or over 200 million people, has a carbon footprint approximating that of their developed country counterparts. Most electricity is generated via coal-based thermal power plants amounting to about 75 per cent of total power generation. At CoP27 Indian pressure resulted in the final text replacing the call for a coal 'phase-out' to 'phase-down'. India is hardly alone in this unfortunate prioritization of supposedly national concerns over global necessities, but given its long peninsular coastline it will suffer greatly from the future inevitable rise in sea levels – 1.5 degrees will be crossed. When this happens it will cause massive internal displacement, with huge numbers looking for shelter and livelihoods in the better-off areas. If today's right-wing or far-right politics continues to hold sway based on a 'fortress mentality' among the rich, the powerful and the better-off will be inclined to justify a strongly repressive response to such migration.

It is security-related political groupings with the US like the Quad that India considers most important, even as, unlike Australia and Japan, it does not have a formal alliance treaty with the US but what many Indian commentators consider a cautious approximation that also protects the Indian image as a major independent power not subservient to anyone. SAARC is basically a dead letter given enduring India-Pakistan hostility. Even economically there is little to commend. Apart from India being Nepal's largest trade and investment partner all others have stronger links externally than within South Asia. Pakistan never extended MFN trade status to India, and following the 2019 Pulwama attack, India withdrew its MFN status to Pakistan. The SCO, like so many other such smaller or larger multilateral groups, continues because cross-country bureaucracies have a vested interest (if only for self-importance) in ensuring this. Also, heads of states can burnish their extra-national credentials, and there can be limited mutual economic payoffs. The most important such group is supposed to be the BRICS, in which China is most active and influential. But given internal political differences, as a collective geopolitical actor it is greatly limited. Mutual economic benefits exist but have not reached the levels expected. The 2008-12 'Great Recession' didn't cause a serious break from the earlier pattern of neoliberal globalization even as this now operates within a longer-term cycle of lower growth and more frequent downturns in capital accumulation. Nor have the BRICS seriously countered the financial power of the IMF and WB or their imposed austerity policies for debt-relief to recipient governments in the South. It will likely be diluted politically by newer entrants.

Similar limitations apply more strongly to the G-20 (19 countries plus the EU) whose formation downgraded the G-77 by weaning away the relatively bigger, more developed countries to join up with the major powers, making them less accountable to the poorer countries. Basic political tensions in the G-20 mean economic and financial issues represent the only common ground. It was in any case the 2008 global recession that raised G-20 to the status of having an annual summit meeting of heads of states with a rotating presidency. Not only does politics translate into economic and financial policy disputes, but here too it will be the big three – the EU, China, and the US – that have the strongest say. The point here is simple. The most important aspect for India as host of the G-20 in 2023, with its multiple meetings at different inter-governmental levels, was the opportunity it gave Modi to magnify his image and that of India under his helmsmanship.[23]

The India-Canada Imbroglio

The extra-judicial killing of a domestic citizen in their home country, if organized by the agencies of a foreign government, does constitute a grave and unjustified violation of that country's sovereignty. It is this concern that finally led Canadian Prime Minister Justin Trudeau on 18 September 2023 to publicly call out the Indian government for its failure to seriously cooperate in the investigation into the assassination in British Columbia on 18 June 2023 of Hardeep Singh Nijjar, a Canadian citizen of Indian origin. This was shortly after the G-20 summit which Trudeau and Biden had attended. In both August and September, Jody Thomas, Canada's National Security Advisor, spent some days in India sharing information with her Indian counterpart, Ajit Doval, that indicated a 'potential link' to Indian agents. Since the revelations may not have pinpointed the culprits, help was being requested. This information had been garnered from the Five Eyes Intelligence Alliance of which Canada and the US are members and both Trudeau and Biden at the Summit had personally met Modi and urged him to take up the issue.

Apparently frustrated by the private responses from the Indian government, Trudeau's resort to a public declaration was also accompanied by the expulsion of an Indian intelligence officer diplomat in Ottawa. The

Indian response was equally sharp. The Modi government declared that no 'credible evidence' had been provided to justify the request for more cooperation and that Nijjar was a known Khalistani activist and terrorist. It further castigated Canada for providing a 'safe haven' for such elements and in a retaliatory manner expelled a similar serving diplomat from the Canadian High Commission in New Delhi. This was later followed by the demand that Canada must withdraw 40 of its officials from its Indian consulates/High Commission so that there is full parity with the total number of Indian personnel serving in Canada.

Why the Indian hard-line response? Is it justified? It is not. The Khalistan demand for the Sikh majority province of Punjab to secede from India has no meaningful resonance in the province itself. Although there are more supporters of this demand among the Sikh diaspora in the US, Canada, and UK than in India, even there the great majority of Sikhs are not supportive of this demand. As for those who are supportive, their right to free speech and legal activity for their cause remains. Even if individuals or groups are suspected of illegal acts and wrongdoing, extra-judicial assassinations by a foreign government are unacceptable. And there is good reason to doubt the bona fides of India in this case.

Early in the BJP government's first term, the Modi-Doval duo adopted a 'defensive-offence' doctrine whereby one is prepared to intrude covertly or even overtly where the offence is coming from. Hence, the 2015 'hot pursuit' of Naga rebels in Myanmar in 2015 and in response to group attacks on Indian soil, the 2016 cross-border and 2019 airstrike (no less) into Pakistan. More to the point, in July 2020 Nijjar was officially designated by the Home Ministry as a terrorist and in July 2022 its National Investigative Agency posted a reward of one million Rupees on him. This could well have served as an incentive for locals, including rival Khalistan groups in Canada, to collaborate in some way with the Indian government. Since 2019 and particularly in the last two years a dozen or so decreed enemies of India have been killed overseas, mainly in Pakistan but also in Nepal, Afghanistan and Italy.[24]

It remains to be seen whether, when and how, Indo-Canadian relations might recover from this never before reached nadir.

Soft Power and Self-Obsession

As Chief Minister of Gujarat, Modi had command responsibility for not preventing – civil society groups claim he encouraged – the 2002 pogrom in which around 2000 Muslims were killed and some 150,000 displaced. This made him something of an international pariah banned from travelling to the US, UK, and some European countries. From 2014 to 2020, when the Covid pandemic arrived, no Indian PM had been as peripatetic as he in visiting some 60 countries. Most such trips were unnecessary for achieving various bilateral agreements routinely handled at diplomatically lower levels. This had everything to do with overcoming his earlier pariah status and wanting to project himself as a person of global stature representing a 'new and self-confident' India. Any casual visitor to India will be astonished at the Goebbelsian-like inundation of public spaces and electronic and print media with Modi's image, even taking pictorial credit for government schemes that had nothing to do with his policies. A ridiculous extreme was reached when every Covid vaccination certificate issued to citizens had his image embossed on them. Modi is the only Indian PM never to have held a public press conference, has only the rare interview with favoured journalists, and leaves his ministers to answer questions during parliament's Question Hour, preferring monologues – speeches on the campaign trail and a monthly radio broadcast.[25]

In an era when much greater levels of mediatization and personalization of political messaging have gone hand-in-hand, Modi's obsessive self-promotion has paid dividends. All poll surveys show him to be much more popular than his party, and even among non-BJP voters his national stature is higher than that of any other political figure. It is in two respects that he has added if not newer, certainly much stronger, emphases to Indian foreign policy. First, putative successes on the external front are regularly attributed more to his personal dynamism than to his party or government. Second, there is a more systematic effort to promote 'soft power', understood as the projection internationally of India as a longstanding Hindu civilization with its distinctive virtues available for admiration and emulation.[26]

This is a 'cultural messianism' grounded on the Hindutva belief that India is the oldest of world civilizations imbued with a unique capacity for global spiritual guidance because of its ancient Hindu beliefs and practices. A host of 'think tanks' run by acolytes of HN have sprung up since 2008, holding international conferences/seminars where senior government functionaries (including Foreign Minister Jaishanker) and select Hindutva intellectuals go on about India's 'civilizational power' whose glorious democratic, pluralist, and tolerant past holds profound lessons for the construction of a humane world order.[27] Modi has adopted what the Hindu sage Vivekananda first declared at the turn of the twentieth century – that India should be a *Vishwaguru* or 'World Teacher'. Isn't the fact that the UN inaugurated an International Yoga Day a tribute to Modi's successful enhancement of 'Hindu Pride'? Modi now repeats ad nauseam that India is the 'mother of democracies'. Of course. this is a ridiculous claim, since the modern conception of democracy does not just demand universal adult suffrage but replaces 'subject-hood' by the principle of a territorially-bounded 'citizenry' having legal civic and political rights (individual and group) of a kind that never existed in the past. An International Buddhist Confederation has been set up, and the first Global Buddhist Summit took place in April 2023. While there is much ado about India being the birthplace of Buddhism, there is silence about how Buddhism was thereafter completely marginalized.

Modi has also consolidated the earlier Vajpayee outreach to the Indian Diaspora, especially those sections supportive of the BJP and its cultural body the World Council of Hindus (VHP) in the Anglophone world and Western Europe. In 2003, Vajpayee initiated the annual meet in India of the *Pravasi Bharatiya Divas*, or Indian Diaspora Conclave, to woo the primarily middle-class and upper-caste Hindu Non-Resident Indians (NRIs) abroad. Those long settled in Africa or the Caribbean are not considered important. In the US, there is the Overseas Friends of the BJP that has good relations with, and tries to emulate, the American Israeli Political Action Committee (AIPAC). At mass cultural events among NRIs it often invites pro-Hindutva speakers and artistes. In the UK and Australia, there are Hindu cultural bodies like the Hindu Swayamsevak Sangh and the Hindu Council close to the VHP. All these bodies have a three-fold task: they serve as the international choir praising Indian policies at home and abroad, collect funds for the BJP, and act as a political lobbying group in their countries of residence. NRI groups in the West active against these pro-Hindutva organizations lack support from New Delhi.

INDIA, MODI AND WORLD ORDER

The key contending capitalist and imperialist powers today and tomorrow are the US, Russia, and China. The UK and France also qualify as smaller imperialist powers, while in Japan there are growing voices calling on it to globally flex its military and political muscles more seriously. But unlike the post-1945 evolution in UK, France, Germany, and Japan, the historical development and behaviour of the ruling classes of Russia and China in both their Communist and post-Communist phases has always been much more independent and politically conflictual (not subordinate) towards the US. This remains the case even today. Russia is a military superpower but little else, and will remain a regional force uneasily tied to a China otherwise outpacing it even in Central Asia. The comparison between an unevenly rising China and a US undergoing a relative erosion economically in the world market faced with the rising share of especially China, but also others like India, will continue to favour the latter.[28] The US is the only truly global power, and it will retain its relative supremacy. Most of the smaller, weaker, or poorer countries have ruling classes preoccupied with maintaining their domestic dominance and increasing their wealth with their foreign policy geared accordingly. Even with some having grown economic ties with China they remain geopolitically inconsequential. The so-called emerging powers like India, Turkey, South Africa, Saudi Arabia, Brazil, Pakistan, Iran, Argentina, and Mexico are not the constituents of a new genuinely multi-polar order. They strive for respective 'spheres of influence', but even where they partially succeed they cannot stabilize them, and are merely junior partners/associates aligned with one or the other among the big three. This behaviour is better characterized as the pursuit not of 'strategic autonomy' but of a degree of foreign policy flexibility afforded by the shifting balances between the big three who really set the overall strategic parameters. Russia gets a place in this triad primarily because of its military power. So it heads the military pact, the Collective Security Treaty Organization (CSTO) oriented towards maintaining influence over the Central Asian Republics as well as its determination to control its 'near abroad' states. But given its economic weakness – in GDP terms it ranks eighth, even behind Italy – its position among the big three is precarious.

Where does Modi's India stand among all this? His Hindutva-based transformative project has much more going for it domestically than externally. At the same time, opposition to his domestic actions and policies is much greater than to his foreign policies. During the Cold War period of bloc rivalry, India, unlike many other countries roughly comparable in potential, never faced strategic hostility from either the USSR or the US. That era is over. Kashmir's changed status is now a fait accompli no future opposition party coalition in power will alter, thus ensuring that a deeper hostility to Pakistan will endure. India's partnership with the US will deepen, which means a once-resolvable border dispute with China has become more intractable, and a reason for treating each other as strategic opponents. India will become an 'emergent power', but one whose global ambitions and pretensions will remain well ahead of its actual capacities and influence.

The future trajectory globally is not either the US or China becoming victor or loser, but that both are incapable of adequately addressing an increasingly unmanageable, turbulent, and chaotic world order caused by i) persistent mass poverty amidst obscenely accelerating inequalities of income and wealth; ii) ecological devastation – major biodiversity loss and accelerated global warming; iii) steady democratic erosion everywhere; and iv) the ever present possibility of a nuclear breakout. Among the countries most strongly marked by all these four features is Modi's India, especially the last. For the radical left in India and internationally, this is all the more reason for fighting against Modi and the forces of Hindutva in the name of a progressive socialist internationalism.

NOTES

1. The two parliamentary parties are the Communist Party of India (Marxist) (CPM) and the older Communist Party of India (CPI). Both come from the Stalinist tradition. The two main parties from the Maoist tradition are the legal, above ground Communist Party of India (Marxist Leninist) Liberation and the underground Communist Party of India (Maoist).
2. 'Effective and Massive Deterrence', 6 April 1963, Delhi Central Working Committee, pp. 95-6, in Bharatiya Jana Sangh, *Party Documents 1951-72, Volume 3: 'Resolutions on Defence and External Affairs,* New Delhi: Bharatiya Jana Sangh, 1973. Referenced by Rahul Sagar, 'Hindu Nationalists and the Cold War', in Manu Bhagavan, ed., *India and the Cold War*, Chapel Hill: University of North Carolina Press, 2019, p. 241.
3. Two general surveys are provided. One by Balraj Madhok, early President of the JS: Balraj Madhok, 'Indian Foreign Policy – The Jan Sangh View', *India Quarterly: A Journal of International Affairs,* 23(1), 1967, pp. 3-7; and one by S.K. Arora, Chief of BJP's Foreign Affairs Cell: S.K. Arora, 'BJP's Foreign Policy – An Overview', in *Bharatiya Janata Party, 1980-2005: Achievements and Looking Ahead*, BJP publication, 1 January 2005.
4. Sagar, 'Hindu Nationalists and the Cold War', p. 246.
5. Achin Vanaik, *India in a Changing World: Problems, Limits and Successes of its Foreign Policy*, New Delhi: Orient Longman, 1995, p. 123.
6. Ajay Shukla, 'Why General Bipin Rawat Acknowledged the Cold Start Doctrine', *The Wire*, 20 January 2017, available at: www.thewire.in.
7. D.P. Srivastava, *Nuclear Deterrence and Ideology*, New Delhi: Vivekananda International Foundation, 2020, p. 9. Former Head of the Strategic Plans Division, Lt. Gen. Khalid Kidwai formulated these 'red lines'. See 'A Conversation with Gen. Khalid Kidwai', Carnegie International Nuclear Policy Conference 2015, Washington DC: Carnegie Endowment for International Peace, 23 March 2015, transcript available at: https://carnegieendowment.org/files/03-230315carnegieKIDWAI.pdf.
8. In July 2007, a $2.47 billion deal was signed for the joint production of a missile system, at the time the biggest deal of its type between the two states. See: 'Report: India, Israel to Jointly Develop $2.47b. Missile System', *Haaretz*, 13 July 2007, available at: www.haaretz.com.
9. Mani Shankar Aiyar, 'A path between distant neighbours', *Indian Express*, 15 March 2023, available at: www.indianexpress.com. See also: Khushid Kasuri, *Neither a Hawk nor a Dove*, Karachi: Oxford University Press, 2015. Kasuri was a former Pakistan foreign minister; and Satinder Kumar Lambah, *In Pursuit of Peace: India-Pakistan Relations Under Six Prime Ministers*, London: Penguin Random House, 2023. Lambah was a special envoy to Pakistan between 2005 and 2014.
10. The Ambani brothers and the Adani Group benefited immensely. Anil Ambani, having no experience in the field of aircraft production, was the beneficiary of the

highly controversial Indo-France deal for the purchase of 36 Rafale fighters. This included massive French investment in his company to build aero, electronic and engine components. Mukesh Ambani was the world's 40th richest person on the 2014 Bloomberg list of dollar billionaires. Adani, whose plane Modi used repeatedly during his electoral campaign, had an even more remarkable rise. In 2014, he was the 608th richest person but by August 2022 had become the world's 3rd richest. He dropped to 24th in Spring 2023 because a short-selling company, Hindenburg Research, reported on his presumably illegal financial manipulations – which had been ignored, if not aided, by the government. This created a major domestic ruckus, with the opposition demanding a Joint Parliamentary Committee (still not appointed) to investigate possible government corruption.

11 India has the second largest army in the world and the third largest military budget. Its healthcare expenditure as a proportion of GDP is the fourth lowest in the world and it has the largest absolute number of malnourished and undernourished people in the world.

12 The best, most up-to-date study of the depth and scale of Indo-Israel collaboration is by Azad Essa, *Hostile Homelands: The New Alliance Between India and Israel*, London: Pluto Press, 2023.

13 Parsis and Christians are also included, in a crude attempt to cover up the Hindutva bias.

14 See Harikishan Sharma and Amitabh Sinha, 'Indus Treaty notice to Pak', *Indian Express*, 25 January 2023, available at: www.indianexpress.com; Sanjay Dutta, 'Blood & Water Can't flow together: PM signalled hard line after Uri Attack', *Times of India*, 28 January 2023, available at: timesofindia.indiatimes.com; Rezaul H Laskar, 'Won't join proceedings at Hague tribunal: India on Indus water dispute with Pak', *Hindustan Times*, 6 July 2023, available at: www.hindustantimes.com.

15 The Supreme Court, through its failure so far to rule on its unconstitutionality, has implicitly endorsed this action. Despite murmurings, the Congress and other bourgeois parties in parliament have basically accepted this annulment. While the CPM and the CPI do call for restoration of the article, they have never called for respecting the full 'right to self-determination' for Kashmiris, despite the longstanding brutal occupation and repression by India's army.

16 'When Shah thundered on Aksai Chin', 18 June 2020, available at https://www.telegraphindia.com.

17 Mike Pompeo, *Never Give an Inch: Fighting for the America I Love*, New York: Harper Collins, 2023.

18 See Achin Vanaik, 'The Escalating Crisis on the India-China Border,' *Jacobin*, 23 June 2020, available at: www.jacobin.com.

19 'India to Upgrade Airstrips in Andaman and Nicobar Islands into Full-Fledged Fighter Bases to Counter China', *Swarajya*, 25 August 2020, available at: swarajyamag.com.

20 For a survey of the divisions among the left internationally and in India, see: Achin Vanaik, 'Russia's War on Ukraine and Divisions within the Left', *South Asia Citizens Web*, 8 November 2022, available at: www.sacw.net/. My position is in line with those sections of the revolutionary socialist left within Ukraine that have always been hostile to US imperialism and NATO, are anti-Stalinist, support armed resistance against Russian aggression and call for international solidarity while being opposed to

policies from Ukrainian and foreign sources that promote neoliberalism, right-wing authoritarianism and all kinds of socio-cultural-political discriminations.

21 Incidentally, the rupee trade payments for discounted oil imports from Russia are running into trouble. Moscow has huge stacks of rupees that it does not know what to do with and is asking for part payments in other internationally tradable hard currencies, as well as lowering the discount rate to India. See: Diksha Munjal, 'Why are India-Russia trade payments in crisis?', *The Hindu*, 9 July 2023, available at: www.thehindu.com.

22 Rohan D'Souza, 'Environmental History of South Asia in the Time of Hindutva', *Environmental History*, 27(4), 2022. Also, between 2015 and 2020 the scale of Indian deforestation was second only to Brazil. See: Mimansa Verma, 'India has lost the second-largest forest area among all countries in five years', *Quartz*, 17 April 2023, available at: www.qz.com.

23 To present a prettified image of the cities that G20 dignitaries would be visiting, there was a ruthless eviction drive against beggars, the homeless and roadside shanties, accompanied by cultural-political tourism and showboating for visiting delegates.

24 Abhijit Majumder, 'Is R&AW the new Mossad? India's image turns from "soft State" to hard under Modi and Doval', *Firstpost*, 20 September 2023, https://www.firstpost.com/opinion/is-raw-the-new-mossad-indias-image-turns-from-soft-state-to-hard-under-modi-and-doval-13144392.html.

25 Not since Nehru has foreign policymaking been so centralized in the PM's Office. Modi's key consultants are his National Security Adviser, A. Doval, followed by his foreign minister S. Jaishankar.

26 One person paying serious attention to this is Ian Hall. See: Ian Hall, *Modi and the Reinvention of Indian Foreign Policy*, Bristol: Bristol University Press, 2019.

27 Srirupa Roy, 'Hindutva Establishments: Right-Wing Think Tanks and the Mainstreaming of Governmental Hindutva', in Thomas Blom Hansen and Srirupa Roy, eds, *Saffron Republic: Hindu Nationalism and State power in India*, Cambridge University Press, 2022.

28 On the process of de-dollarization, I remain cautious. See: Patrick Bond, 'The G7 Provides a Divide-and-Conquer Trap, as BRICS Countries try to Reconstitute', *Counterpunch*, 24 June 2022, available at: https://www.counterpunch.org.

JAPAN'S 'NEW PRE-WAR': FIVE DISLOCATIONS OF ITS HISTORICAL DEVELOPMENT

KEN C. KAWASHIMA

Marx, in discussing the capitalist mode of production in *Capital,* calls the type of *intertwining of the different times* (and here he only mentions the economic level), i.e., the type of 'dislocation' (*décalage)* and torsion of the different temporalities produced by the different levels of the structure, the complex combination of which constitutes the peculiar time of the process's development. – Louis Althusser[1]

As any middle-school child in the Japanese educational system is instructed to believe, Japan's long 'post-war' period (*sengo,* 戦後) begins with the end of World War II, the war that is said to have ended Japan's 'pre-war' period (*senzen,* 戦前). Since 1945, it has been official common-sense to believe that the 'pre-war' period naturally comes before the 'post-war' period, and that the 'post-war' naturally comes after the 'pre-war'. Today, after forty years of neoliberal deregulation, industrial hollowing-out and social precarity, this common-sense belief in historical periodization has collapsed, leading to a peculiar inversion that has dislocated the usual periodization of history. Now, the 'post-war' paradoxically comes *before* the 'pre-war', and the 'pre-war' comes *after* the 'post-war'. As Shakespeare would say, 'time is out of joint!' This inversion was recently declared in Japan, not by a veteran of war, parliamentary politician, or empiricist scholar, but rather by Tamori (Kazuyoshi Morita), a well-known television comedian, who always wears sunglasses. When asked in early 2023, 'What comes after the "post-war"?' Tamori unflinchingly declared, 'It's the new pre-war!'– a dialectically impeccable statement that caused laughter and horror in the Japanese media.[2]

Why the laughter? Surely because a 'new pre-war' can only be a joke, given Japan's earlier pre-war fiascos: its violent colonial history in Hokkaido, Okinawa, Taiwan, Korea, and Manchuria from the 1870s to 1945; its ultranationalist, fascist policing tactics after 1925; its military coup d'état in 1936; and its punctual, apocalyptic and atomic ending in Hiroshima and Nagasaki on 6 and 9 August 1945. Why the horror? Surely because the new pre-war is less a joke than an accomplished fact as seen, for instance, in the Japanese Ministry of Defence's recent military deals and contracts, dutifully overseen by Fumio Kishida, the present Prime Minister of Japan, leader of the Liberal Democratic Party (LDP), the quiet sycophant of the recently assassinated Abe Shinzō, and current president of the G7 and host of their annual gathering in May 2023 in Hiroshima. Continuing the hawkish militarism of the late Abe Shinzō, Fumio Kishida has concluded huge contracts – to the tune of 380 billion yen (US $2.8 billion) – between the Japanese Ministry of Defense and Mitsubishi Heavy Industries, the premier pre-war *zaibatsu* (conglomerates of Japanese finance capital) that led the pre-war economy out of chronic depression in the late 1930s by boosting armament production.

The new defence budget will by 2027 make Japan the third largest military spender in the world, behind the US and China. The shopping spree involves the purchase of 400 Tomahawk inter-continental ballistic missiles from the US, as well as a battery of Type-12 surface-to-ship missiles from Mitsubishi. The Ministry of Defence is additionally recruiting pre-war firms that led the post-war electronics boom, like Hitachi, established in 1910 for its electronics, and Fujitsu, established in 1935 for its information technologies (IT).[3]

A recent cover of *TIME* magazine, published in advance of the G7 summit in Hiroshima, features Fumio Kishida's image and reads: 'Japan's Choice: Prime Minister Fumio Kishida wants to abandon decades of pacifism—and make his country a true military power', a by-line that provoked guffaws and embarrassment among established LDP leaders, perhaps for calling a spade a spade all too bluntly.[4] In short, while the Shōwa state in Japan (1926-1989) once declared and professed, after 1945, that the pre-war always comes before the post-war, the present Reiwa state (2019-present) is, without professing it, behaving as if the opposite is the truth, that the pre-war always comes *after* the post-war.

Given this unsettling and unconscious dislocation, how are we to grasp the pre-history of the so-called new pre-war? Certainly, it would have to correspond to the historical limits of Japan's long-standing, post-war client-state status with the US, which continues to demand from Japan the use of Okinawa as a key American military base in the Pacific, especially in the event of a proxy war between the US and China over Taiwan.[5] The new pre-war in Japan is certainly a result of Japan's precarious place in the world market after servicing a now declining Pax Americana in dutiful, transpacific complicity for over seventy years, and after forty neoliberal years of industrial hollowing-out and foreign direct investment in China's special economic zones. It is certainly a sign of the new alliance between the LDP and South Korea's new right-wing president, Yoon Suk-Yeol, who is rushing South Korea headlong into America's new Cold War against China and North Korea.[6] It is certainly a sign of the contradictions of the post-war Japanese constitution, co-authored by the US Occupation (1945-52), which 'forever renounced' war and stripped Japan's sovereignty of the 'right to belligerence' in Article 9.[7] The new pre-war is certainly a pious wish of the LDP and the Self-Defence Forces (SDF) to extricate the national economy from out of 'zero-growth' capitalism since the 1990s by way of state-led investments in military industries and high-tech technologies. And it is certainly a repetition compulsion of specific roles from Japan's pre-war dramaturgy of the 1930s, such as the role of Mitsubishi Heavy Industries in the production of armaments, and the survival of the Japanese emperor at the heart of the ideological state apparatus. The 'new pre-war' certainly can be observed from all of these perspectives.

The problem is that these observable aspects of the 'new pre-war' cannot explain how, when or why its multiple histories have, by various contingencies, necessarily constituted the peculiar time of the new pre-war, and in a combined, compulsively repeated and complex articulation in the present. To grasp the peculiar time of the new pre-war, our conception of historical time must account for this repetition compulsion, and for the mixed times that are implied by the articulation of these many elements, which has created a disturbing sense that 'time is out of joint'. In this time of time out of joint, historical time does not exist chronologically or linearly, like the times of departure and arrival posted on an airport screen, which dictates our sense of what is 'late' and what is 'ahead of schedule'. In the mixed-up temporality of the new pre-war, what is late can suddenly become ahead of schedule, and what is 'backward' can be 'recorded' and then 'fast-forwarded' to the present, as in a tape-loop. Put differently, while the pre-war was originally grasped through the historical retrospection of Japan's experience of World War II, the problem now is that, in the present conjuncture of zero-growth capitalism in Japan after forty years of neoliberal state policies, the retrospection (and even interpretation itself) of Japan's past wars has been disavowed by a defensive projection of imminent war and by an aggressive repetition of a pre-war era, only now it is outfitted in business suits for the G7 and uniforms for the Self-Defence Forces (SDF), NATO, and the QUAD (Quadrilateral Security Dialogue between Japan, the US,

India, and Australia).

The new pre-war is not something that can be grasped by merely taking stock of a single historical timeline in which all of these empirical facts pile-up in the present. The new pre-war should not only be grasped empirically but also abstractly, as a historical *form* of capitalist development itself – a form endemic to the origins of the capitalist state in Japan, a form that is repeated in reaction to periodic and inevitable capitalist crises that have punctuated Japan's 155 year history of capitalist development, and a form that continues to have troubling and dislocating effects upon the fundamental contradictions of the 'capitalist mode of production, its relations of production and forms of intercourse corresponding to it'.[8]

Approaching the new pre-war as a repeated form of capitalist development demands that we emphasize the dislocating effects of the superstructural elements of the present conjuncture, i.e., the dislocating effects of the state-form, state power and the state apparatuses in respect to the historical development of the capitalist mode of production. This does not mean, however, restricting our analysis to that of the most contemporary form of the capitalist state in Japan, which I will call the 'Reiwa state', or the state named after the current emperor of Japan. Rather, in order to grasp the mixed-up time of the new pre-war conjuncture led by the Reiwa state, we will have to go back to the transition to capitalism and to the Meiji state, named after emperor Meiji, who reigned from 1868 to 1912.

The significance of the Meiji state is that it was born into a form of the pre-war in the transition to capitalism, a transition that took place, moreover, in an era that was quickly becoming dominated by finance capital. Due to the violent, monopolistic and financially oligarchical and imperialist milieu in which Japan's first capitalist state emerged in the world market after 1868, the fate of the Meiji state is that the transition to capitalism, which the Meiji state strained to actualize in a hurry as a so-called late-developing country, took place within the crucible of the world-historical stage of imperialism. In the transition to capitalism, Japan was 'stamped' with defensive pre-war 'birthmarks' from the outset, so to speak.[9]

Broadly speaking, these pre-war birthmarks of the Meiji state were over-determined by two broad transitions that still haunt Japan in the world today. The first is represented by capitalism's transition from a liberal or laissez-faire stage of development (1820s-1866), dominated by Britain and industrial capital, to an imperialist stage of development after the 1870s, dominated by finance and monopoly capital in countries such as Germany and the US. The Meiji state's first economic policies of mercantilism were born amidst the world historical transition from liberalism to imperialism, and from the outset, the Meiji state had to (but also did *not* have to, yet *did* nonetheless) militarize itself to defend the infant capitalist nation-state against imperialist forms of colonial domination. The Reiwa state has inherited these militarist 'birthmarks' of the Meiji state.

The second transition is the geopolitical and hegemonic transition implied by the end of Pax Brittanica after the world crisis of 1873. This transition parallels the first transition from industrial capital to finance capital, and it emboldened the US and Japan to compete with and against Britain in a race to conquer China for its vast markets – a competition that turned deadly for Japan in World War II. Today, the sense of the end of Pax Americana, which is triggering the defence mechanisms of the Reiwa state, harks back to the end of Pax Brittanica, which arguably triggered the 'originary' pre-war form in the Meiji state. The fate of the contemporary Reiwa state is that it cannot escape the birthmarks of Japan's first capitalist state, the Meiji state, which can be said to have been born into the form of the 'pre-war' from the outset.

Keeping these transitions and 'birthmarks' in mind, we can schematically reconstruct the 'new pre-war' from the perspective of what we will call 'five dislocations of its historical development'.

FIRST DISLOCATION: MERCHANT CAPITAL, FORCE (*GEWALT*) AND PRIMITIVE ACCUMULATION

In the transition period, the forms of law and of state policy are not, as hitherto, adapted to the economic structure (articulated with the peculiar limits of the structure of production) but *dislocated* with respect to it: as well as showing force as an economic agent, the analyses of primitive accumulation also reveal the *precedence of law* and of the forms of the state with respect to the forms of the capitalist economic structure. This dislocation can be translated by saying that the correspondence appears here, too, in the form of a *non-correspondence* between the different levels.
– Etienne Balibar[10]

A first articulation of the pre-war can be said to have emerged in the transition to capitalism and in the Meiji state's process of primitive accumulation, and in a period dominated by merchant capital. Drained financially from the social revolution that toppled the feudal Tokugawa government in 1868, the new Meiji state first established economic policies of mercantilism.[11] At the centre of the new mercantile policies was the 1873 land tax system, which expropriated thousands of peasants from the land by the force of law.

The land tax system of 1873 killed two birds with one stone. On the one hand, by taxing the peasants at 3 per cent per year and demanding cash payments, the Meiji state was able to fill its bank coffers. With the primitive accumulation of capital, the Meiji state purchased heavy industrial factories, technologies and 'know-how' from the US and Britain, especially those related to the state's 'key industries' for military and naval development: iron and steel manufacturing and shipbuilding.[12] The Meiji state then leased these factories to private entrepreneurs at low interest rates, a practice known as *harai sageru,* and eventually sold them off entirely to the private sector. Exemplary here is the history of Mitsubishi Heavy Industries, founded by Iwasaki Yataro, who leased the Nagasaki Iron Foundry (*seitetsusho*) from the Meiji state in 1884, renamed it Nagasaki Shipyard and Machinery Works in 1887, and then entered the shipbuilding business on a large scale. Iwasaki purchased the shipyards outright in 1887 and established Mitsubishi Heavy Industries in 1891. Based on the Meiji state's expropriation of peasant land and a new land tax system after 1873, the new nation-state was militarized by actively working with Mitsubishi to develop a modern navy, and by 'fast-forwarding' heavy-industrial production for military development, even before the generalisation of industrial capital nationwide.

On the other hand, the land tax system had the effect not only of expropriating peasants from the land, but also of creating a social basis for the military conscription of peasants as soldiers into a standing army (between 1872 and 1880), as well as into the new state police system (1874), which would continue unchanged until the mid-1920s. With these forces already established by 1880, the Meiji state began its colonial conquests – first, of the northern island of Ezo (contemporary Hokkaido), which led to the genocide of Ainu communities, and second, of the southern Ryūkyū islands, which became Okinawa prefecture in 1879.[13] The first dislocation of the form of the pre-war in Japan has origins in the violent birthmarks of the Meiji state that continue to stamp the contemporary Reiwa state.

This first dislocation recalls Marx's insights on the role of the force and violence of the state in the transition to capitalism and in the process of primitive accumulation. In the case of Meiji Japan, this transition occurred within the compressed and traumatic geopolitical transition from liberalism to imperialism, and within the hegemonic shift away from Pax Brittanica. It identifies how the Meiji state had to catch up to the dominant form of capital from a position of relative backwardness, and to ferment the conditions of capitalist development from above, as in a 'hothouse'. As Marx wrote:

> These methods [of primitive accumulation, introduced by the capitalist

epoch] depend in part on brute force, for instance the colonial system. But they all employ the power of the state, the concentrated and organized force of society, to hasten, as in a hothouse, the process of the transformation of the feudal mode of production into the capitalist mode, and to shorten the transition phase. Force is the midwife of every old society which is pregnant with a new one. It is itself an economic agent.[14]

SECOND DISLOCATION: INDUSTRIAL CAPITAL, FINANCE CAPITAL AND 'TOTAL WAR'

The pre-war form can be further dislocated in relation to the historical development of liberal economic policies dominated by industrial capital, and imperialist policies dominated by finance capital and 'total war'. Unlike laissez-faire in Britain between the 1820s and the 1860s, Japan's stage of liberalism, based on its industrial revolution in the cotton industries after the capitalist crisis of 1890, only lasted two decades, from 1890 to 1910.[15] With the addition of the newly established Bank of Japan and the stabilized currency of the yen, this stage of capitalist development witnessed a gradual absorption of surplus populations from the countryside into centres of industrial production in Tokyo, Osaka, Yokohama, Nagoya, Kyoto, and Kobe, thereby establishing the commodification of labour-power as a culminating point of so-called primitive accumulation. However, it was also during this stage of liberal economic policies that the Meiji state carried out two geopolitically transformative wars: the Sino-Japanese war of 1894-95, which resulted in Japan's colonisation of Taiwan, and the Russo-Japanese war of 1904-05, which resulted in Japan's colonization of Korea in 1910. In Japan's liberal stage of capitalist development, the Meiji state's pre-war machine went on a rampage, backed by free trade economic policies and the dominance of industrial capital.

Japan's pre-war form further developed in respect to the emergence of finance and monopoly capital in the capitalist stage of imperialism in Japan after 1910. Following the colonization of Korea in 1910, the capitalist mode of production in Japan was dominated by finance capital and *zaibatsu* conglomerates, such as Mitsubishi Heavy Industries, Mitsui, and Sumitomo, which invested huge sums into larger and larger forms of fixed capital to service large-scale industrial production. While Japan profited greatly from World War I by exporting manufactured goods to countries in Europe and Asia, the end of the war in Europe caused a tremendous constriction of industrial capital, leading to the reactionary crisis of 1920, which plunged Japanese society into a chronic depression that would be exacerbated by the great crisis of 1929.[16] The overall result of these crises was the chronic existence of a vast capitalist contradiction between 'excess capital' and 'surplus populations'. It is within this contradiction that the Showa state – which increasingly promoted ultranationalist, fascist thought and a 'second restoration' of the Emperor – called upon Mitsubishi Heavy Industries once again. But now it was to develop Japan's 'total war', to expand its colonial empire into Manchuria in 1932, to give settler-colonial reason to export Japan's unemployed surplus populations to Manchuria, and to contribute towards the extrication of the national economy from chronic depression with a massive turn towards, and investments in, armaments production.[17] As Uno Kōzō writes, it was in this stage of capitalist development in Japan that 'excess facilities of fixed capital and a chronic surplus of labour-power appeared at the same time, revealing the peculiar meaning of the unproductive military industry'.[18]

In short, the Shōwa state reacted to the great crisis of 1929 with policies to absorb surplus populations into a new state-capitalism and statist war machine, by means of an extraordinary expansion of the repressive state apparatus. In 1937, the Shōwa state invaded mainland China and a year later issued the 'state general mobilization law' (*kokka sōdōinhō*), which led to the forced labour of Korean and Chinese workers in Mitsubishi and Mitsui-owned coal mines, as well as to the sex slavery of Korean and Chinese women. By the outbreak of World War II, Mitsubishi was also the leading manufacturer of Japan's heavy bombers and long-range fighter aircraft, exemplified by the famous Zero planes (*reisen*) that attacked Pearl Harbor on 7 December 1941, and that carried out suicide missions at the end of the 'total war'.

THIRD DISLOCATION: 'SURVIVALS', THE EMPEROR, AND THE IDEOLOGICAL STATE APPARATUS

Marxist political practice is constantly coming up against that reality known as *'survivals'*. There can be no doubt that these survivals exist – they cling tenaciously to life …. What is its theoretical status? Is it essentially social or 'psychological'? … Or does it refer as much to *other structures,* political, ideological structures, etc.: *customs, habits,* even 'traditions' such as the *'national tradition'* with its specific traits? The term *'survival'* is constantly invoked, but it is still virtually uninvestigated, not in *its name* (it has one!), but *in its concept.* – Louis Althusser[19]

One of the clearest examples of the problem of 'survivals' in Japan's new pre-war is that of the emperor system. Originally invented discursively in the seventh century, the Emperor system was restored in the Meiji Restoration of 1868, resurrected in a 'second restoration' after the crisis of 1929, and rejuvenated by the US Occupation of Japan between 1945-52. I will briefly mention the emperor system's peculiar survival from three perspectives: the emperor's 'body', the emperor's 'voice', and the Japanese emperor as a 'puppet' of American empire after 1945.

The emperor's body. As historian Harry Harootunian has shown, the Meiji Restoration of 1868, which overthrew the feudal government of the Tokugawa state, was a 'restoration' of the emperor system, which was marginalized politically by the Tokugawa *bakufu* during the feudal era (1603-1868).[20] The Meiji emperor in Japan had, in fact, two bodies: the empirically visible and biological one, and a metaphysical one bound to an eternal and timeless lineage of national mythemes. The Meiji state restored the archaic meaning of the Emperor to the ideological centre of the modern state apparatus as a unifying symbol of a still undefined nation that was torn asunder by a class revolution that toppled the feudal Tokugawa regime. Moreover, as historian Tak Fujitani has shown, the dissemination of the image of the emperor's body, depicted in paintings and photographs of Emperor Meiji, circulated the emperor's patriarchal and policing gaze upon individuals and masses who were thrust into the social chaos of the class revolution that defined the Meiji Restoration.[21]

The emperor's voice. The emperor's voice survives as a site of state ideological interpellation, or the process of 'hailing' individuals as subjects, which represents an 'imaginary relationship of individuals to their real conditions of existence'[22] (Althusser, 1971: 162). We can identify three 'moments' of the emperor's voice of interpellation after 1868. In a first moment, it is heard in two imperial 'rescripts': the 1882 Imperial Rescript to Soldiers and Sailors (*Gunjin Chokuyu*), which was issued by Emperor Meiji to all of the new soldiers and sailors to be memorized,[23] and the 1890 Imperial Rescript on Education.[24] A second moment of the emperor's voice can be heard with the Emperor's 'Jewel Voice Broadcast' (*gyokuon hōsō*), which was recorded on 14 August 1945 and replayed on national radio on 15 August.[25] In the wake of the atomic bombings of Hiroshima and Nagasaki on 6 and 9 August 1945, and to break the deadlock between the Japanese army, which wished to continue the war in China, and the Japanese navy, which was losing in the Pacific theatre against the US, Emperor Hirohito recorded his voice to be heard by the public for the first time and to declare the end of the war. As I have discussed elsewhere, the emperor's analogue recording of the 'Jewel Voice Broadcast' was not only his 'greatest hit'. It also 'humanized' the emperor, 'eternalized' his voice as the 'voice of the nation', and created a vocal tie with the beleaguered masses amidst a historical conjuncture in which the very difference between the crisis of the sovereign state and the crisis of capitalism was virtually indistinguishable.[26] A third moment of deploying the emperor's voice, once again in reaction to the outbreak of crisis, can be heard in the aftermath of the Fukushima earthquake and nuclear disaster of 11 March 2011, when Emperor Akihito addressed the now wireless, imagined community of the nation.[27] In all of these moments, the emperor's voice is a 'survival' at the heart of the ideological state apparatus.

The e*mperor as puppet.* The survival of the emperor system in the present conjuncture also has to be considered a result of how the Japanese emperor was used as a puppet by the US after 1945. The US Occupation actively spared the life of Emperor Hirohito, and in doing so it ensured the 'survival' of the emperor system in the post-war era. It was a US strategy of policing Japan within the new geopolitical order in the Pacific after the war. Already in 1942, three full years before the Allied Occupation, Edwin Reischauer – future ambassador to Japan under the Kennedy administration in the 1960s – had written the 'Memorandum on Policy Towards Japan'. In his pre-war, Orientalist representation of what he called the 'Japanese mentality', Reischauer wrote:

> The possible role of the Japanese Emperor in the post-war rehabilitation of the Japanese mentality has definite bearing upon the present situation. To keep the Emperor available as a valuable ally or puppet in the post-war ideological battle we must keep him unsullied by the present war. In other words, we cannot allow him to be portrayed to the American people as the counterpart of Hitler and Mussolini in Asia or as the personification of the Japanese brand of totalitarianism. General reviling of the Emperor by our press or radio can easily ruin his utility to us in the post-war world.[28]

As Naoki Sakai has discussed in *The End of Pax Americana*, the American Occupation of Japan essentially copied Japan's pre-war colonial occupation of Manchu-kuo (Manchuria), which made a puppet out of emperor Pu Yi, and which discursively utilized his nationality as a means to govern Manchu-kuo as colony within Japan's multi-ethnic empire. Japan's pre-war colonial strategy was duly noted by Reischauer, and when Japan lost its empire in 1945 he recommended that the Allied Occupation of Japan effectively do the same thing that Japan did in Manchu-kuo. The US would sub-contract Japan's former empire as part of a post-war American multi-ethnic empire across the Pacific, one that would use Emperor Hirohito as a national puppet to be kept alive and never tried for war crimes. With the death of Hirohito in 1989, Emperors Akihito, who reigned as emperor from 1989-2019, and Naruhito, who has reigned since 2019, represent the survival of the imperialist puppetry of the post-war emperor system within the contemporary pre-war conjuncture.

FOURTH DISLOCATION: CONSTITUTIONAL LAW AND THE REPRESSIVE STATE APPARATUS

> If the ruling class has lost its consensus, i.e. is no longer 'leading' but only 'dominant', exercising coercive force alone, this means precisely that the great masses have become detached from their traditional ideologies, and no longer believe what they used to believe previously.
> – Antonio Gramsci[29]

The new pre-war of Japan cannot be understood without grasping how the US Occupation of Japan from 1945-52 dictated the limits of the post-war Japanese constitution and the repressive state apparatuses. Between 1945 and 1948, the US Occupation championed the idea of 'demilitarizing and democratizing' Japan, and of dismantling Japan's war-time military dictatorship, its pre-war police apparatus, and its monopolistic landholdings and powerful *zaibatsu* conglomerates, such as Mitsubishi. After the communist revolution in China, however, the US Occupation in Japan famously reversed course and began the opposite process of re-militarizing Japan and re-monopolizing finance and industrial capital in Japan as a bulwark against communist China and the Soviet Union.

Importantly, the US Occupation restricted Japan's state sovereignty in Article 9 of the post-war Japanese constitution. Article 9 stipulates that Japan 'forever renounce war as a sovereign right', and that its 'right to belligerence' will not be recognized.[30] With Article 9, the post-war Japanese constitution that was co-authored by the US Occupation and Japan (and what would become the LDP) restricted the Japanese state to having only a Self-Defence Force, which is still considered, legally speaking, to be an extension of the national police force. In short, in contemporary Japan, the repressive state apparatus (RSA) is over-determined by the US Occupation's co-authorship of Japan's post-war constitution. As a result, the RSA in Japan does not have the same clear juridical boundaries between the military and the police as states whose sovereignty has been allowed to maintain 'the right to belligerence'. The RSA in Japan is forced to be defensive only. The defensive injunction upon Japan's military by the US, which stripped Japan of its 'right to belligerence' (as a condition of 'unconditional surrender' in 1945), has not, however, eliminated Japan's state belligerence. Rather, it has been dislocated and displaced from its military roots and arguably projected into an expanding police function of the RSA.

In the new pre-war conjuncture of contemporary Japan, Shinzō Abe acolytes, such as Fumio Kishida, legalistically dislocate the contradictions of capitalist society in Japan into interminable interpretations of paragraph (2) of Article 9, i.e., into endless legal exercises of stretching the interpretation of the 'right to belligerence' in relation to the national security of Japan and its allies (i.e., the US). The US state – a primary co-author of Japan's 'pacifist' post-war constitution – does not see any contradiction whatsoever in re-arming Japan's Self-Defence Forces (SDF), or in supporting the LDP's interminable re-interpretations of Article 9.

The tragi-comedy, however, is that the Ministry of Defence's military spending is outpacing the expansion of the Self Defence Force itself. Now, the SDF is experiencing its own kind of labour shortage. For the past two years, the SDF has been finding it difficult to win over new recruits.[31] To make matters worse for the SDF, in June 2023, an eighteen-year old SDF trainee shot and killed two SDF members in a live ammunition firing exercise, additionally tarnishing the SDF's public image.[32] A *Nikkei Asia* article writes, 'The SDF has struggled to secure enough personnel as the eligible population shrinks, especially now with the government pushing to bolster the country's defense capabilities'.[33] The article notes that the SDF was only able to recruit 4,300 members in 2022, less than half of its planned total, and despite a raise in the upper age limit of members from 26 to 32. The war in Ukraine and tensions over Taiwan are also said to have influenced the decisions of many in Japan not to enlist in the SDF. Simply put, the SDF is no longer popular in Japan.

FIFTH DISLOCATION: THE MULTIPLE CRISES OF NEOLIBERALISM AND THE RETURN OF THE PRE-WAR FORM

What has been called the pre-war period was 'discovered' within the post-war conjuncture, but it was largely repressed during Japan's period of high growth between 1955 and 1973. The high growth period was based on the electronics industry and led by corporations such as Hitachi (for electronics) and Fujitsu (for information technology and computers), two pre-war corporations with post-war successes that are presently being recruited by the new pre-war, specifically for the development of microchips and superconductors.[34]

The crisis of 1973, however, marks the end Japan's post-war high growth. It inaugurated what the late Professor Itoh Makoto called 'the long downturn in the Japanese economy' and a 'spiral reversal of capitalist development'. As Itoh writes, 'In the course of the restructuring of capitalist firms during the great depression since 1973, the precedent trends in capitalist development for about a century were largely reversed among advanced countries, including Japan.'[35] Following Itoh's analysis, we can note five characteristics of the 'long downturn' after 1973, which also distinguish capitalist development under neoliberal policies in Japan.

(1) The long downturn and phases of economic instability after the crisis of 1973, characterized by an inflationary crisis, 1973-75; recovery through exports and state expenditure, 1976-79; a long downswing, 1979-83; recovery with Reaganomics, 1983-1985; depression due to the soaring yen, 1985-86; and recovery by a real estate bubble, 1987-1990.
(2) The competitive restructuring of capitalist firms with the introduction of information technology, factory automation, office automation, and robots controlled by computers.
(3) Changes in industrial structure, stemming from industrial hollowing-out; the shift towards a tertiary sector and microchip electronic technology.
(4) Chronic depression and 'zero-growth capitalism' after the bursting of the real estate and trading bubble of the late 1980s, triggered by fiscal and monetary policy to expand domestic demand, and exacerbated by the Kobe earthquake of 1995.
(5) Changes in company restructuring and a sharp increase of irregular and part-time female workers after the 1990s, leading to reduced birth rates and a demographic crisis.

As Itoh writes, 'With such a reduced birth rate, the long-run trend of Japanese economic growth will be constrained by a tendency towards a falling population. The Achilles heel of a capitalist economy is the commodity labour-power, especially the difficulty of regulating the balance between its supply and demand.'[36]

The historical failures of neoliberalism in Japan since the 2008 financial crisis, the 2011 Fukushima nuclear crisis, and the Covid-19 pandemic of 2020-22 have all exacerbated and dislocated the contradictions that labour-power represents to capital as a commodity. These crises and contradictions have led to the return of the repressed pre-war form in the present, led by a holy trifecta of finance and monopoly capital (Mitsubishi, Hitachi, Fujitsu, and so forth), the repressive state apparatus (the SDF, the Ministry of Defence, the Police), and the ideological state apparatus (e.g., the emperor system, the imagined and wireless community of the nation, soft-power cultural policies of 'Cool Japan', anime, manga, etc.).

Japan's new pre-war, which can be said to have begun with the rise of so-called Abe-economics immediately following the Fukushima earthquake-tsunami-nuclear crisis of 2011, is a state reaction to repeated, cyclical and ever-worsening manifestations of capitalist crisis, which can be defined as a vast contradiction between excess capital and surplus populations based on the commodification of labour-power.[37] The state of the new pre-war, like the state of the original pre-war, cannot fix this contradiction. It can only disavow, deny and repress it into an unconscious realm, where it can be replaced by fantasies and fetishes of non-contradiction.

The dominant political superstructure in Japan, led by the Liberal Democratic Party (post-war Japan's 'one trick pony/party'), envisions Japan-in-the-world today, as well as society-in-Japan today, in non-class, non-antagonistic and non-dialectical terms, namely those of a tiny handful of the super-rich financial oligarchs and tech-wizards. It disavows the reality and truths of the struggles of bearers of labour-power with interminable state discourses of a golden-like return to a new period of re-militarized 'high growth'. Not to a new golden age of growth (e.g., Japan's high growth period of the 1960s) but rather to an economic fairy tale of Goldilocks. 'We have a chance for the economy to move to a new Goldilocks phase for the first time in 30 years', Kishida said. 'We must not miss this opportunity.'[38]

In contemporary bourgeois economics, a 'Goldilocks phase' is considered to be ideal for investments in an imagined economic community in which steady growth is 'not too hot, not too cold, just right'. It is an ideal model of capitalist investment and accumulation that purports to be capable of avoiding the contradiction of extreme economic prosperity (too hot) and extreme economic crisis and depression (too cold). Kishida's Goldilocks fairy-tale is at the heart of his 'grand design and action plan for a new form of capitalism', one that invests in 'people, technology, and startups'.[39] This 'grand design' seeks to double income for a new middle class by 'reskilling' the existing precarious labour force, by developing new technical innovations such as artificial intelligence, and by investing in so-called human capital. The 'Goldilocks' strategy also seeks to attract more foreign direct investment to Japan's technology sectors (e.g., Samsung from South Korea and BlackRock from the US), a precondition of the proposed 'reskilling' of various strata of an industrial reserve army that has all but disappeared since the 1990s, the result of foreign direct investment in, and the export of manufacturing to, China, Japan's largest trading partner. The grand design of this new form of capitalism finally involves the manufacture of phallogo-ballistic means of destruction (i.e., hypersonic missiles), whose surplus-values hold the promise of becoming realized as profit in the grand sales event of a proxy war between the US and China over Taiwan.

The US, China and Taiwan: could these be the geopolitical 'three bears' of the Goldilocks fairy-tale, whose 'porridge, chairs and beds' will have been discovered, tried, tested and ultimately abandoned by lucky Goldilocks, who hopes to return home safely and under a rising – and not setting – sun? How can Goldilocks in Japan escape doom quickly and unscathed, just before the bears come home to eat? Indeed, the re-militarizing character of Japan's new pre-war reveals a hypersonic character, a sound frequency that is five times the speed of sound. To wit: if Trump's plea to 'Make America Great Again' revealed an American ideology, the Japanese ideology of Kishida and the LDP is a plea to 'Make Japan Speedy Again', a pious wish given the fact that living labour in Japan is ageing and demographically slowing down faster than any tendential fall in corporate rates of profit, and more rapidly than the LDP can conjure up fascist fantasies of national eternity and techno-financial sovereignty.

'JAPAN AS A LINK IN THE WORLD'

Japan's new pre-war is a post-colonial and imperialist symptom of Japan's precarious place within the geopolitical conjuncture and inter-state system today. Going against ultra-nationalist and fascist ideology, the pre-war Marxist philosopher, Tosaka Jun, once described Japan as 'a link in the world'.[40] Today, Japan as a link in the world is experiencing the full weight of the historical contradictions of having lost its former colonial empire in Asia to the US, and of having become the premier imperialist sub-contractor and client-state for American monopoly capital in the region. At the same time, it is experiencing the long term consequences of having exported capital to China since the 1990s in order to cut manufacturing labour costs and decimate trade union organising in Japan. Japan has contributed to a decline in Pax Americana by investing capital in 'rising' China – Japan's largest trading partner now – but on the political and military level of the state, Japan is still compelled to support the reproduction of Pax Americana. Caught between a declining US empire and an ascending Chinese hegemon in Asia and the world-market, Japan is torn between its economic investments in China and its political and military investments with the US.

This overarching geopolitical contradiction has directly impacted the national capitalist commodity-economy of Japan, which is at a historical crossroads. Flummoxed and chagrined by forty years of no growth capitalism under neoliberal policies of the state, sycophants of capital in Japan are reaching the limits of prognosticating future capitalist development there. The LDP and Kishida have had to rely on economists who resort to fairy tale logic (the 'Goldilocks' phase of economy) to save capitalism, which, for the past forty years, has only produced indications of how capitalism in Japan – once a late-developing country but now an advanced capitalist one – has not been able to avoid going into a prolonged and morbid decline. This decline finds form in declining capitalist accumulation, declining manufacturing, declining wages, a declining population, declining birth rates, a declining labour force, a declining military force, and, most recently, the declining value of the national currency of the yen.

As a means by which to ideologically compensate for these indicators of decline, the LPD and Kishida are engineering and promoting a 'new form of capitalism' in Japan, one that prays for Japan to become a global high-tech manufacturing hub for superconducting microchip R&D, as well as for the production of hypersonic missiles, AI and robots. Japan can only do so, however, by combining national and tech-savvy corporations like Mitsubishi Heavy Industries, Hitachi and Fujitsu with global monopoly and finance capital corporations such as Samsung from South Korea and Blackrock from the US.[41] In the Asia-Pacific context, this combination has led to new forms of imperialist opportunism and diplomacy between Japan and South Korea. It is a new opportunism encouraged by the US, which wants its most important Asian allies to 'get along' in a new pre-war bulwark against China, North Korea and Russia. Monopoly capital in Japan and Korea is driving both states to agree to forget about the nineteenth and twentieth century history of Japanese colonialism and imperialism in East Asia for the sake of shared profit-making and national security under Pax Americana. It is hedging its economic bets in China by simultaneously supporting US military influence against China (and North Korea) in the Asia-Pacific region, but this is a contradiction that can no longer be squared.

The new pre-war opportunism has led to new contradictions and problems, especially in East and Northeast Asia. In South Korea, the migration of Samsung capital and manufacturing plants to Japan (and to the US) has led its workers in South Korea to go on strike against the export of jobs abroad. The new opportunism between the LDP's Kishida in Japan and conservative South Korean president Yoon Suk-Yeol also tacitly agrees to toss into the dustbin of history ongoing South Korean political demands for the corporate and state payment of reparation money to workers who were unremunerated and super-exploited in coal mines owned by Mitsubishi Heavy Industries during 'total mobilisation' and the wartime economy. The new pre-war opportunism, as an attribute of the new re-militarisation in Japan, stokes North Korean and Chinese fears of a NATO-esque military encirclement of the Asia-Pacific, and stokes North Korean plans to further develop its production of intercontinental ballistic means of destruction, which are by now routinely tested and lobbed over the northern island of Hokkaido.

Japan is also standing at a contradictory crossroads vis-à-vis Taiwan, Japan's former colony from 1895 to 1945. Japan fought China between 1894-95 during the Japanese state's period of laissez-faire economic policies (1890-1910), and colonized Taiwan as a result of that war until 1945, when Japan lost its empire to the US. The present and future sovereignty of postcolonial Taiwan is now at stake in the current trade wars between the US and China, as well as in the endless military exercises and war games between the two superpowers in the South Seas. Japan's new pre-war, which could be easily interpreted as a pro-American preparation for a potentially explosive and dangerous proxy war in Taiwan against China, is bound to logistically support the current war games of the US, but it is also bound to economically try and tip the existing trade war against China and in favour of the US, especially in terms of the production of the now globally dominant commodity of the twenty-first century, the superconducting microchip, which Taiwanese manufacturing has amply proven to have already mastered. Taiwan's manufacture of superconducting microchips is considered one of the best, if not the best, in the world, but it may fall under Chinese control in the ongoing geopolitical re-orderings of the Asia-Pacific region. To pre-emptively counter this possibility, Japan (and the US) wants to attract superconducting microchip manufacturing to Japan with American support, outside the orbit of Chinese market influence and one step removed from a direct dependence on Taiwanese manufacturing. The hypersonically tense military situation in and around the straits of Taiwan is thus over-determined not only geopolitically, between the contradiction of the US and China, but also in terms of the contradictions that surround the superconducting microchip and its attendant supply chains.[42]

In sum, the new pre-war in Japan reveals how the political superstructure (the law and the ideological and repressive state apparatuses), in combination with monopoly capital and *zaibatsu* firms like Mitsubishi, does not exist or develop historically in a direct and one-to-one correspondence with the historical development of the fundamental contradictions of the capitalist mode of production and the economic base. It is a twisted and cyclical combination of multiple histories that dislocates fundamentally economic contradictions. The state-led dislocations reveal a fundamental gap between the political and the economic, a dislocation (*décalage*) and torsion of the economic by the political superstructure, a twisting political action around the fundamental contradiction of the capitalist mode of production, its relations of production, and the forms of exchange corresponding to it, namely the contradictory movement of the commodification of labour-power.

All of the dislocations recounted here ultimately come together to dislocate the memory and consciousness of the contradiction and conundrum that labour-power represents to capital as a commodity. The axiomatic contradiction or conundrum goes like this: On the one hand, capital must consume labour-power as a commodity in order for capital to 'be itself' and to produce new values and surplus-value. On the other hand, capital cannot produce labour-power as a commodity directly, because labour-power only exists in the mortal, finite body and mind of living people, which capital cannot produce directly as a commodity. Capital cannot escape the ontological fact that it is ultimately dependent on commodifying (and now 'financializing') labour-power, and this is capitalism's basic weakness, its fatal addiction. It is a weakness that discloses the fundamental question of whether it is world-historically necessary for labour-power to be, or not to be, a commodity.[43]

This fundamental weakness of capital around our labour-power, however, has been erased in the state amnesia of the new pre-war ideology. It is thus necessary to dialectically counter the amnesia of Japan's new pre-war with a dialectical, materialist and rigorously anti-Orientalist *anamnesia*.[44] The ideological dislocations of the new pre-war in Japan should themselves be dislocated beyond the fascist fantasies of bourgeois ideology. They should be re-located and replaced, in thought and in practice, by an internationalist recognition of the power and capacity of bearers (*Träger*) of labour-power to push forward towards the construction of socialism and a communist society in Japan, as a link in the world.

The author thanks Harry Harootunian, Gavin Walker, Asad Haider and Kuni Kamizaki for their helpful suggestions and comments.

NOTES

1 Louis Althusser, *Reading Capital: The Complete Edition,* London: Verso, 2015, p. 252, original emphasis.
2 On Tamori's statement, see: Naoto Maeda, 'タモリさんが言った「新しい戦前」どう回避　本音を言えなかった日本', *Asahi Shinbun,* 18 February 2023, available at: https://www.asahi.com/articles/ASR2K3V66R2KUPQJ005.html.
3 See: Ryosuke Hanada, 'Fighting to fund Japan's historic defence budget increase', *East Asia Forum,* 17 May 2023. On Mitsubishi Heavy Industry's historic contract with the Japanese Ministry of Defense, see also: Reuters, 'Mitsubishi Heavy expects record defence orders as Japan pours money into military', *Reuters (Japan),* 10 May 2023.

4   *TIME*, 22/29 May 2023. See also: Kana Inagaki, 'Japan scraps pacificist defence strategy to counter China threat', *Financial Times*, 16 December 2022.

5   See: Gavin McCormack, 'Japan's Client State (Zokkoku) Problem', *The Asia-Pacific Journal: Japan Focus*, 11(25), no. 2, 23 June 2013. See also by same author: 'Japan: Prime Minister Abe Shinzo's Agenda', *The Asia-Pacific Journal: Japan Focus*, 14(24), no. 1, 15 December 2016; and 'Japan, Australia, and the Rejigging of Asia-Pacific Alliances', *The Asia-Pacific Journal: Japan Focus*, 18(22), no. 1, 15 November 2020. See also: Wada Haruki, 'Japan, Korea, and Northeast Asia – the Abe Shinzo Legacy', *The Asia-Pacific Journal: Japan Focus*, 20(3), no. 2, 1 February 2022.

6   See: Dae-Han Song and Alice S. Kim, 'South Korea pivots to conflict', *The Bullet*, 11 May 2023, available at: www.socialistproject.ca; Simone Chun, 'US is maintaining tensions with North Korea to draw its allies against China', *Truthout*, March 3, 2023.

7   See: Klaus Schilichtmann, 'Article Nine in Context: Limitations of National Sovereignty and the Abolition of War in Constitutional Law', *The Asia-Pacific Journal: Japan Focus*, 7(23), no. 6, 6 June 2009.

8   Karl Marx, *Capital, Volume 1*, London: Penguin, 1990, p. 90.

9   As Marx wrote, 'What we have to deal with here is a communist society, not as it has *developed* on its own foundations, but, on the contrary, as it *emerges* from capitalist society; which is thus in every respect, economically, morally and intellectually, still *stamped* with the *birthmarks* of the old society from whose womb it emerges.' Karl Marx, *Critique of the Gotha Programme*, New York: International Publishers, 1938, p. 8, emphases added.

10 Etienne Balibar, 'Elements for a Theory of Transition', in Louis Althusser, *Reading Capital: The Complete Edition*, Verso, 2015, p. 478, original emphasis. See also: Etienne Balibar, 'Reflections on *Gewalt*', *Historical Materialism*, 17, 2009, pp. 99-125; and Etienne Balibar, 'Marxism and War', *Radical Philosophy*, 160(March/April), 2010.

11 See: Tsutomu Ouchi, *Ouchi Tsutomu Keizaigaku Taikei*, Vol. 7, *Nihon Keizairon*, Tokyo: Tokyo University Press, 2000, chap. 2.

12 See: Moritaro Yamada, *Nihon Shihonshugi Bunseki* (1934); and E.H. Norman, 'The Agrarian Settlement and its Social Consequences', chap. 5, in *Origins of the Modern Japanese State*, New York: Pantheon Books, 1975.

13 On the Ainu genocide, see: Katsuya Hirano, 'Thanotopolitics in the Making of Japan's Hokkaido: Settler Colonialism and Primitive Accumulation', *Critical Historical Studies*, 2(2), 2015. On Okinawa, see: Wendy Matsumura, *The Limits of Okinawa: Japanese Capitalism, Living Labour, and Theorizations of Community*, Durham, NC: Duke University Press, 2015.

14 Karl Marx, *Capital, Vol. 1*, pp. 995-6.

15 See: Tsutomu Ouchi, *Ouchi Tsutomu Keizaigaku Taikei*, chap. 3.

16 See: Kiyoshi Oshima, *Nihon Kyōkōshiron*, chap. 5, 'The Shōwa Crisis', Tokyo: Tokyo University Press, 1955, pp. 315-66.

17 See: Yasushi Yamanouchi, J. Victor Koschmann, and Ryūichi Narita, *Total War and 'Modernization'*, Cornell University Press, 1998.

18 Kōzō Uno, *Theory of Crisis*, Leiden: Brill, 2021, p. 26.

19 Louis Althusser, *For Marx*, London: Verso, 1990, pp. 114-15.

20 Harry Harootunian. *Towards Restoration*, University of California Press, 1991.

21 Takashi Fujitani, *Splendid Monarchy: Power and Pageantry in Modern Japan*, University of California Press, 1998.

22   Louis Althusser, *Lenin and Philosophy and Other Essays*, London: NLB, 1971, p. 162.

23   The Imperial Rescript to soldiers and sailors thus interpellated: 'Soldiers and Sailors, We are your supreme Commander-in-Chief. Our relations with your will be most intimate when We rely upon you as Our limbs and you look up to Us as your head. Whether We are able to guard the Empire, and so prove Ourself worthy of Heaven's blessings and repay the benevolence of Our Ancestors, depends upon the faithful discharge of your duties as soldiers and sailors.' See: Wm. Theodore de Bary, Carol Gluck, Donald Keene, eds, *Sources of Japanese Tradition, vol. 2*, New York: Columbia University Press, 1958, pp. 198-200.

24   The Imperial Rescript on Education begins with the following interpellation: 'Know ye, Our subjects: Our Imperial Ancestors have founded Our Empire on a basis broad and everlasting and have deeply and firmly implanted virtue; Our subjects ever united in loyalty and filial piety have from generation to generation illustrated the beauty thereof. This is the glory of the fundamental character of Our Empire, and herein lies the source of Our education.' See https://www.japanpitt.pitt.edu/glossary/imperial-rescript-education.

25   The 'Jewel Voice Broadcast' stated, for example: 'How are We to save the millions of Our subjects, or to atone Ourselves before the hallowed spirits of Our Imperial Ancestors? This is the reason why We have ordered the acceptance of the provision of the Joint Declaration of the Powers…Let the entire nation continue as one family from generation to generation, ever firm in its faith in the imperishability of its sacred land and mindful of its heavy burden of responsibility, and of the long road before it.' For the Japanese recording, see: www.kunaicho.go.jp/kunaicho/koho/taisenkankei/syusen/syusen.html. For the English transcription, see: en.wikipedia.org/wiki/Hirohito_surrender_broadcast.

26   Ken Kawashima, 'The Voice of Interpellation and Capitalist Crisis: Notes towards an investigation of post-war Japanese ideology', *Boundary 2*, 42(3), 2015, pp. 63-77.

27   Akihito said: 'I am deeply saddened by the devastating situation in the areas hit by the Tohoku-Pacific Ocean Earthquake, an unprecedented 9.0-magnitude earthquake, which struck Japan on March 11th … Relief operations are now under way with the government mobilizing all its capabilities, but, in the bitter cold, many people who were forced to evacuate are facing extremely difficult living conditions due to shortages of food, drinking water and fuel … I wish to express my appreciation to the members of the Self-Defense Forces, the police, the fire department, the Japan Coast Guard and other central and local governments and related institutions.' Imperial Household Agency (宮内庁),16 March 2011, available at: www.kunaicho.go.jp/e-okotoba/01/address/tohokujishin-h230316-mov.html

28   Quoted in: Naoki Sakai, *The End of Pax Americana: The Loss of Empire and Hikikomori Nationalism*, Durham, NC: Duke University Press, 2022, Appendix 1, p. 288.

29   Antonio Gramsci, *Selections from the Prison Notebooks*, New York: International Publishers, 1989, p. 276.

30   The constitution reads as follows: 'ARTICLE 9. (1) Aspiring sincerely to an international peace based on justice and order, the Japanese people forever renounce war as a sovereign right of the nation and the threat or use of force as means of settling international disputes. (2) In order to accomplish the aim of the preceding paragraph, land, sea, and air forces, as well as other war potential, will never be sustained. The right of belligerency of the state will not be recognized.' See Klaus Schilichtmann,

'Article Nine in Context: Limitations of National Sovereignty and the Abolition of War in Constitutional Law', *The Asia-Pacific Journal: Japan Focus,* 7(23), no. 6, 6 June 2009.

31 Kana Inagaki and Leo Lewis, 'Is Japan's military fit for purpose?', *Financial Times*, 4 May 2023; and Leo Lewis, 'Japan's biggest defence fair raises questions about military expansion', *Financial Times*, 19 March 2023.

32 Masaki Horikoshi, 'Japan SDF shooting underscores challenges in recruiting, training', *Nikkei Asia*, 15 June 2023.

33 Yusuke Takeuchi, 'Japan's Self-Defense Forces miss recruiting target by more than half', *Nikkei Asia,* 19 April 2023.

34 On Hitachi and Fujitsu's role in the new pre-war, see the Cabinet Secretariat dossier on 'The Realization of the New Capitalism' and 'The Subcommittee on the Trinity of Labour Market reforms' (三位一体労働市場改革分科会), presentations 6 and 7, 26 April 2023, available at: www.cas.go.jp/jp/seisaku/atarashii_sihonsyugi/bunkakai/roudousijou_dai1/index.html.

35 Makoto Itoh, *The Japanese Economy Reconsidered,* London: Palgrave, 2000, p. 44.

36 Itoh, *The Japanese Economy Reconsidered*, pp. 1-29, 87-105.

37 Uno, *Theory of Crisis*; Kawashima and Walker, "Supplementary Essay: Uno Kōzō's *Theory of Crisis* Today", in *Theory of Crisis,* 2022.

38 Kana Inagaki and Leo Lewis, 'Fumio Kishida calls on Blackrock and other funds to "invest" in Japan's future', *Financial Times,* 6 October 2023.

39 Cabinet Secretariat, 'Grand Design and Action Plan for a New Form of Capitalism: Investing in People, Technology, and Startups', 7 June 2022, available at: www.cas.go.jp/jp/seisaku/atarashii_sihonsyugi/pdf/ap2022en.pdf.

40 Tosaka Jun, *Tosaka Jun: A Critical Reader,* Ken Kawashima, Fabian Schaeffer and Robert Stolz, eds, Ithaca: Cornell University Press, 2014.

41 See: Inagaki and Lewis, 'Fumio Kishida calls on BlackRock and other funds to 'invest' in Japan's future'. See also: Leo Lewis, 'How Japan got its swagger back', *Financial Times,* 19 May 2023.

42 See: Leo Lewis and Kana Inagaki, 'Global chipmakers to expand in Japan as tech decoupling accelerates', *Financial Times*, 17 May 2023.

43 On the concept of labour-power, see: Ken Kawashima, 'Labor-Power (*Arbeitskraft*, 労働力)', chap. 28, in *Contemporaneia: A Glossary for the 21st Century,* Michael Marder and Giovanni Tusa, eds, Cambridge: MIT Press, 2024 (forthcoming).

44 On anamnesia, see: Ranjit Hoskote, 'Anamnesia', chap. 2, in *Contemporaneia: A Glossary for the 21st Century,* Marder and Tusa, eds.

GERMANY IN THE NEW CAPITALIST GEOMETRY

THOMAS SABLOWSKI

Germany has been in recession since the third quarter of 2022. This is not due to one of the cyclical crises in world markets; rather, there is much to suggest a structural crisis in Germany's export-oriented mode of development. The International Monetary Fund (IMF) has predicted comparatively low growth rates for Germany in the coming years.[1] First and foremost, the current economic situation is a result of the distortions caused by the Covid-19 pandemic, the war in Ukraine, and the associated high rate of inflation. In addition, increasing tensions between the US and China, changes in US foreign economic policy, and economic problems in China are having a negative impact on growth in Germany. On top of these unfavourable changes in international relations, however, a role is also played by internal contradictions in the mode of development.

In the first part of this essay, I will outline the German economy's fragile foundations and internal transformations. I will then look at Germany's relations with the US, Russia, China, the EU and the rest of the world, and highlight the reactions of the German power bloc to the changing capitalist geometry. Finally, the challenges of the new situation for a socialist strategy will be addressed.

THE CONTRADICTIONS OF THE EXPORT-ORIENTED MODE OF DEVELOPMENT

The German economy is highly dependent on the world market. For a relatively large industrial country with a developed domestic market, Germany has exceptionally high ratios of exports to GDP and imports to GDP. These have risen sharply in recent decades; in 2022, exports of goods and services exceeded 50 per cent of GDP for the first time.[2] Moreover, Germany has also had consistently high current account surpluses over the past twenty years, reaching a height of 8.6 per cent of GDP in 2015-16 and a still high 4.2 per cent of GDP in 2022, despite the dramatic increase in the cost of fossil fuel imports. Current account surpluses of more than 6 per cent of GDP are again forecast for the coming years.³

The high level of exports is predominantly seen by the German public as a strength. In fact, there is something to be said for this view. Germany has long occupied one of the top positions in the hierarchy of the international division of labour, after the US and alongside Japan. The strength of German capital is based first of all on the country's broadly diversified production apparatus, characterized by a notable sectoral coherence, i.e., the interlocking of the country's various industries. Despite a trend toward tertiarization, industry's share of GDP has remained above the international average for comparably advanced economies. One specific strength is in the area of machinery and equipment manufacture, which has always been dominated by a relatively small group of capitalist centres. Those who control the production of means of production for the production of means of production are also pacemakers in increasing labour productivity, on which, in turn, their position in the hierarchical international division of labour largely depends. The proverbial German engineering skills, the tradition of dual vocational training, and the negotiated involvement of workers are the basis of high product quality and incremental innovation that contribute to the high competitiveness of capital (beyond pure price competitiveness). In addition to mechanical and plant engineering, Germany's export strength is concentrated above all in the chemical, electrical and automotive industries. German automotive manufacturers have gained global weight in recent decades; they also have above-average strength in the particularly profitable premium class of vehicles. The number of employees in the production of motor vehicles and parts in Germany rose from 726,415 in 2007 to 833,937 in 2018.

However, the fundamentals of export-oriented development have also changed considerably in recent decades. Of note here is the fact that not only goods exports but also capital exports have increased sharply. Germany's stock of outward foreign direct investment (FDI) rose from 17.4 per cent of GDP in 1990 to 47.3 per cent of GDP in 2022.⁴ After the US, the Netherlands, the UK, China, Hong Kong, Canada and Japan, Germany had the highest share of the total stock of outward FDI worldwide that same year.⁵ This direct investment serves not only to open up markets and circumvent trade barriers, but also reduces costs and increases the rate of profit. Due to their geographical proximity to eastern Europe, German companies have benefited most from the integration of eastern Europe into the world market after the fall of the 'Iron Curtain'. China has also become an increasingly important production location for German companies. The number of employees in foreign subsidiaries of German corporations has grown significantly, both in absolute terms and relative to the number of wage-earning employees in Germany. In 1995, about 2.8 million workers were employed in the foreign subsidiaries of German companies; in 2021, the figure was more than 7.9 million. This represents an increase from 8.3 per cent to 19.3 per cent of the number of wage earners employed in Germany.[6] Thus, although it is still possible to speak of a strong export-orientation in German development, this fails to capture the strategic direction being pursued by the leading corporations because their foreign production has grown faster than their exports. The importance of Germany as a production location has become much lower for these companies. Some examples: at BASF, the world's largest chemical group, the share of total group sales accounted for by foreign subsidiaries rose from 58 per cent in 2007 to 82.6 per cent in 2022.[7] At Siemens, one of the world's leading companies in areas such as production automation, building technology, rail technology and medical technology, the share of consolidated sales generated by foreign subsidiaries rose from 71.2 per cent to 81.2 per cent over the same period.[8] Automobile manufacturers produced 3.5 million passenger cars in Germany in 2022, of which 2.6 million were exported. But foreign production by member companies of the German Association of the Automotive Industry (VDA) amounted to 9.6 million passenger cars.[9]

The internationalization of production also induces an increase in foreign trade, as elements of the production of complex goods are shifted abroad while the German market is also supplied from abroad by German corporations or other companies integrated into their production networks. A large part of the country's growing foreign trade is intra-industry trade, or intra-group trade. The relationship between the production locations of German companies at home and abroad is contradictory. On the one hand, the relocation of labour-intensive parts of complex value chains and the exploitation of labour at lower wages abroad certainly serve to secure jobs at home, insofar as they increase the profitability of the overall production of complex goods and the competitiveness of companies. On the other hand, production abroad also directly competes with production at home. Ultimately, the internationalization of production has meant that many products that were previously produced in Germany are now imported. This became painfully clear, for example, during the Covid-19 pandemic, as important and urgently needed medical products such as protective masks or certain active pharmaceutical ingredients were no longer produced in Germany and instead only produced in a handful of foreign locations, primarily in Asia.

The internationalization of production and the intensification of international competition have put considerable pressure on wages and working conditions in Germany. The classic 'normal employment relationship' – permanent full-time employment subject to social insurance – has been replaced in many cases by 'atypical' employment relationships such as part-time work, temporary employment, fixed-term employment and 'mini-jobs'. The 'core workforces', which are to some extent unionized and protected by collective agreements, have shrunk, while the unprotected 'fringe workforces' have grown. The institutions of co-determination at the plant and company level continue to exist, as does collective bargaining at the industry level. However, the unions have suffered significant membership losses and many companies have left the employers' associations. Collective bargaining coverage of employment relationships has declined significantly. In many cases, industry-level collective bargaining has been replaced, or at least eclipsed, by company-level negotiation processes. Trade unions have accepted modifications to collective bargaining agreements, allowing the lowering of standards in some cases, resulting in lower wages and worsening working conditions. Although the institutional framework of industrial relations has largely remained in place in formal terms, its content has changed considerably. 'Social partnership' has paid off less and less for wage earners; it is no longer possible to speak of a 'Model Germany' in the sense that the Social Democratic Party of Germany (SPD) did in its 1976 election program. The 'Model Germany' project sought the modernization of domestic production for world markets and social progress for workers.[10] In Marxist discussions, the project was criticized at the time as a form of class domination, of subordination of the trade unions to the hegemony of the capitalist class, and its social selectivity was emphasized.[11] In the Fordist era, however, wages still grew more or less in line with labour productivity; the same applies to the growth of the domestic market in relation to exports. This is no longer the case.[12] Fordist mercantilism has been replaced by competitive mercantilism, in which potentials for growth stemming from wage increases are largely suppressed.[13]

From this perspective, Germany's high ratios of exports to GDP and imports to GDP as well as high current account surpluses also appear in a different light. There are increasing tensions between the internationalization and restructuring strategies of the leading corporations and the development of the German economy. The German production apparatus already has considerable gaps. In certain key high-tech industries, Germany has already lost its former strong position. This applies, for example, to the manufacture of telecommunications networks and even, to some extent, to the pharmaceutical industry.

High current account surpluses mean that Germany is constantly producing more than it consumes and saving more than it invests. This is problematic from various points of view.[14] To sell the surplus goods, German companies depend on solvent demand abroad. Ultimately, Germany must create this demand itself through capital exports, through international lending. For the owners of capital, the interest income from international debt service is an additional source of income, but the mass of workers in Germany gains nothing from it. For them, Germany's export surpluses mean nothing other than the renunciation of part of the wealth they have generated. From this point of view, the current account surpluses can be interpreted as the result of too low wage increases.[15]

The current account surpluses also point to insufficient domestic investment. This applies to both private and public investment. Gross fixed capital formation as a share of GDP has been trending downward; it was 24.9 per cent of GDP in 1991 and 22.5 per cent of GDP in 2022. The share of investment in machinery and equipment fell from 7.7 per cent of GDP in 1991 to 4.6 per cent of GDP in 2022, which also goes some way to explaining the sluggish development of labour productivity in Germany, notwithstanding discussions about digitization or a fourth industrial revolution. The falling domestic investment ratio also reflects the relocation of production to low-wage locations for the purpose of increasing profitability. Government investment is also at a low level, thanks to neoliberal fiscal policy. It declined from 3.1 per cent of GDP in 1991 to 2.7 per cent of GDP in 2022. The deficiencies in public and social infrastructure are thus the flip side of high export ratios and surpluses.

The export-oriented mode of development is undermining its own foundations. Infrastructure deficiencies have now reached a level that calls into question the competitiveness of domestic production. For example, the increasing number of closures of roads, bridges, and rail lines for repair due to long term neglect adds considerable costs in the area of logistics, even for private companies, due to necessary detours and longer transport times, and slows down the turnover of capital. The current shortage of skilled workers is also partly the result of deficiencies in the education system, restrictive migration policies and racist and sexist discrimination, and to that extent is self-inflicted. At the same time, the high export to GDP ratio means a high vulnerability to crises, international upheavals and unfavourable policy changes on the part of important trading partners. For example, German GDP slumped by 4.7 per cent as a result of the global financial crisis in 2009, while the average for advanced countries was 3.2 per cent.[16] In 2020, during the Covid-19 pandemic, exports of advanced countries declined by 8.8 per cent, while German exports declined by 10 per cent.[17]

However, despite the depth of these crises, they were still overcome relatively quickly. In the past, German companies have been surprisingly successful in compensating for deteriorations in their situation in individual countries or regions by relocating exports or production capacities to other countries and regions. For example, German companies coped in part with the eurozone crisis that began in 2009 by exporting more to, or investing in, regions outside Europe, especially China. That is not to say, however, that this will always be possible. Since the global financial crisis, international relations have in many respects developed to the detriment of Germany's export-oriented mode of development.

THE RELATIONSHIP WITH THE US

There is an asymmetrical relationship between the US and Germany, with Germany being dependent on the US in many respects.[18] The asymmetry is expressed, for example, in the currency hierarchy. The introduction of the euro has done little to change the dominant role of the US dollar as the world's money; as was the case with the deutschmark, the euro is of secondary importance. The US has remained the most important export market outside the EU for German companies – despite rapidly growing trade with China. Even more important, however, may be the asymmetrical capital linkages in which the dominance of US capital over German capital manifests itself. For example, US-based asset managers and investment companies are the largest shareholders in many of the most important large German companies. The specific dependence on the US also exists at the political-military level and tends to lead to Germany's subordination despite partly different interests, as has been shown, for example, in the resumption of US sanctions against Iran, in the Ukraine war and in the changed relationship with China.

In its trade with the US, Germany has for a long time run large export surpluses; as with other countries, especially in East Asia, the US has acted as a consumer of last resort. For a long time, US governments accepted Germany's mercantilist 'beggar-my-neighbour' policy, but the Trump administration avowedly pursued the goal of reducing US current account deficits not only with China but also with Germany. The Trump administration's imposition or threat of punitive tariffs directly hurt the interests of German capital. It raised the question of whether the US is still available as a growing export market or whether much greater localization of production in the US will be necessary for German companies. Under the Trump administration, Germany's relationship with the US deteriorated also for reasons beyond trade policy; the US withdrawal from the WHO, the cancellation of the nuclear agreement with Iran, the cancellation of arms control agreements with Russia and Trump's disparaging remarks about NATO all met with massive criticism. Fears were voiced that the US could no longer be relied upon as an ally and protective power.

The Federation of German Industries (BDI), arguably Germany's most important business association, responded with a dual strategy. On the one hand, it pleaded for a strengthening of the EU in order to be able to bring greater weight to bear in international negotiations. They argued that the EU should not allow itself to be blackmailed by the US government and that it should appeal to the WTO over US violations of trade policy rules. On the other hand, however, the BDI and other business associations advocated defusing the conflicts with the US government wherever possible and striving for a new start in transatlantic relations. In this context, the BDI also took a rather critical view of trade policy retaliation by the EU in response to punitive tariffs levied by the US. The German government and the European Commission also more or less followed this dual strategy. On the one hand, US punitive tariffs indeed prompted retaliation via corresponding countermeasures, but on the other hand the EU Trade Commissioner Phil Hogan proposed to the Trump administration in June 2020 the establishment of a joint council for trade and technology policy issues in order to resolve transatlantic conflicts. The Trump administration, however, did not take up this offer.

Regarding the termination of the nuclear agreement with Iran and the imposition of renewed sanctions on the country by the US, the BDI refused to suspend German foreign trade with Iran as demanded by the US government. The European Commission instead sought to develop alternative payment arrangements with Iran to escape from US control of the international payments system and US sanctions. However, it turned out that most internationally active banks and industrial companies did not want to risk being excluded from the US market and would prefer to grudgingly sacrifice business with Iran. In this respect, a gap opened up between the officially expressed German and EU positions on the one hand and the practice of companies on the other.

The election victory of Joe Biden and the Democrats was widely welcomed in Germany. The German government and business associations now hoped for a new start in transatlantic relations – not without reason, as it turned out. The new US president coordinated his policies more closely with Western allies on several issues. On 15 June 2021, Joe Biden and European Commission President Ursula von der Leyen announced the establishment of the joint Trade and Technology Council, in which they would seek agreement on trade and technology policy issues. While the Europeans primarily wanted to settle trade policy conflicts with the US and reduce tariffs and non-tariff trade barriers, the US government sought above all to persuade the Europeans to take a tougher line on China. However, despite the renewed unity that had been invoked, it soon became apparent that differences remained between the German government and the EU on the one hand and the US government on the other. In addition to long-standing conflicts over subsidies for Boeing and Airbus, and US tariffs on steel and aluminium imports, other government measures are also controversial between the parties. The US government sees the EU's planned CO_2 border adjustment mechanism as a protectionist measure, while German trade associations and the German government view the local content provisions in the Inflation Reduction Act as an obstacle to trade. In addition, there are differences over the relationship with China. It is true that US and German capital share an interest in preventing the development of additional competitors in China, and China's further rise to a position of technological leadership. However, the strategies for achieving this differ. While in the US an openly confrontational policy toward China has prevailed, in Germany and the EU ambivalence tends to dominate, reflected in the formula of China as 'partner, competitor and systemic rival'.

The war in Ukraine has drastically demonstrated Germany's subordination to the US despite partially diverging interests. The US has been the winner so far, while Germany is one of the losers. The US government has not only achieved the goal of increasing US oil and gas exports to Germany and the EU. By undermining German-Russian relations, the war has also tied Germany and the EU even more closely to the United States. Nevertheless, the agenda of greater independence from the US has not been entirely marginalized, even for the German power bloc; efforts to this end could see renewed impetus if the right wing of the Republicans in the US returns to power.

THE RELATIONSHIP WITH RUSSIA
AND THE WAR IN UKRAINE

Until recently, German-Russian relations were characterized by both common and conflicting interests. The common capital interests included, above all, the supply of fossil fuels on a growing scale. While the Russian accumulation regime was heavily dependent on energy and raw material exports after the collapse of the Soviet Union, the German economy benefited considerably from favourable supply contracts for oil and gas. German-Russian energy relations had been established at the time of the Cold

War and were successively expanded.[19] Conflicts of interest arose, however, between Germany and Russia with regard to Ukraine and other post-Soviet states. While Russia wanted to continue to bind these states to itself, German capital saw new opportunities for expansion in this region. The tug of war between Russia and the 'West' over Ukraine finally tore apart the country, which had over the centuries shifted between different domains and had only achieved national independence at a late stage. Due to its history and economic structure, western Ukraine was oriented more toward the West and eastern Ukraine more toward Russia. While the German government long opposed the US bid to integrate Ukraine into NATO, it supported Ukraine's linkage to the EU through an association agreement that ruled out Ukraine's incorporation into the Eurasian Economic Union, which Russia had sought. In doing so, the German government underestimated or ignored the economic, political and ideological importance of Ukraine to Russia and the potential consequences of a break with Russia for the German economy. In any case, the asymmetric war that had developed in Ukraine since 2014 as a result of the 'Euromaidan' overthrow of the Yanukovych presidency and, finally, Russia's large-scale attack in February 2022, changed everything.

The EU sanctions and Russian counter-sanctions as a result of the escalation of the war, and, finally, the destruction of the Nord Stream pipelines have now brought most bilateral trade and, above all, Russian oil and gas supplies to Germany to a standstill.[20] It speaks volumes that the question of who blew up the Nord Stream pipelines has been little discussed in Germany, even though the attack was clearly also directed against German capital interests. Criticism of the current US administration and other NATO partners who are possible perpetrators does not seem opportune. Germany's exports to Russia, which accounted for 1.9 per cent of total exports in 2021, almost halved in 2022. In the first seven months of 2023, exports to Russia fell by another 40 per cent. Imports from Russia fell nearly 90 per cent during the same period. The cost of mineral fuel imports has increased tremendously – by 62 per cent in 2021 and 81 per cent in 2022 when compared to the previous year.

German companies, which in the past had been notable beneficiaries of relatively cheap oil and gas imports from Russia, are now also particularly affected by their disappearance. It is not easy for Germany to compensate for this, because other suppliers which used to be of greater importance can no longer step in. The Netherlands, for example, recently shut down its natural gas production in what was once Western Europe's largest gas field due to resulting earthquakes, building damage and protests. The UK has also lost importance as a supplier due to the depletion of its oil and gas reserves in the North Sea. In the short term, imports from Norway in particular have increased. Oil and liquefied natural gas imports from more distant countries incur higher transport costs and, in cases such as fracking and other unconventional extraction methods, entail higher production costs. The fact that the production of renewable energy has not been expanded more in recent decades is now also becoming a direct economic problem. Rising energy costs lead to lower profit rates and thus slower capital accumulation. They are also, alongside the disruption of global supply chains due to the Covid-19 pandemic, a key driver of the inflation rates that have risen so sharply since 2021.

Inflation rates have not risen equally in all countries, and their development is uneven. In the US, the rise in the inflation rate began somewhat earlier than in the EU, but the rate has also fallen again earlier. In August 2023, the year-on-year inflation rate in the US was only 2.5 per cent, while in Germany it remained higher at 6.4 per cent. The inflation rate in Germany was 3.2 per cent in 2021 and 8.7 per cent in 2022, while in France it was only 2.1 per cent in 2021 and 5.9 per cent in 2022.[21] Germany's higher inflation rates mean that the competitiveness of domestic producers is deteriorating relative to competitors in countries with lower inflation rates. While producers in Germany have benefited particularly from cheap supplies from eastern Europe in recent decades, they are now also affected by above-average inflation rates in eastern Europe. In Poland, the inflation rate in 2022 was 13.2 per cent, in the Czech Republic 14.8 per cent, in Slovakia 12.2 per cent and in Hungary 15.3 per cent.[22] These are countries of high importance for German production networks. It remains to be said that by destroying its relations with Russia for the sake of linking Ukraine to the EU, the ruling class in Germany has not only lost an important market but has accepted that its competitiveness on the world market will be undermined – certainly an unintended consequence of German imperialist policy.

Domestically, the escalation of the war in Ukraine enabled Chancellor Scholz to push through an extensive rearmament program, even against his own party, the SPD. In his government statement on the war against Ukraine in the session of the German parliament on 27 February 2022, the chancellor spoke of a '*Zeitenwende*', or 'epochal shift', and announced the establishment of a 'special fund', the borrowing of 100 billion euros officially outside of the national budget to rearm the German military. In addition, Germany would invest more than 2 per cent of its gross domestic product in defence every year from now on. The 2 per cent target had been under discussion in Germany for some time, but until then it had been highly controversial among the SPD and the Greens and tended to be rejected.[23]

The German government also made a policy change with its arms deliveries to Ukraine. In the past, arms exports to conflict areas had been officially taboo, although there had been repeated domestic political disputes in this regard because despite this taboo weapons had been supplied to numerous countries that were involved in armed conflicts. Overall, the escalation of the war in Ukraine and the 'epochal shift' proclaimed by the German government have contributed significantly to the normalization of the military and militarism in German society.

To the extent that security discourse was brought to the fore by the war in Ukraine, the hegemonic project of a 'green' capitalism was weakened. Instead of an 'energy turnaround', the accelerated production of renewable energy, the focus was now on securing the supply of natural gas. The decommissioning of the last German nuclear power plants was postponed for several months; in opinion polls, the majority for a nuclear phase-out became visibly thinner. The decommissioning of coal-fired power plants was also postponed in light of the war in Ukraine and the loss of Russian energy imports. The government's draft for the 2024 federal budget envisages a further increase in defence spending, while areas such as development cooperation, climate protection and health are to see cuts, some of them drastic, and the financing of some projects agreed by the governing coalition, such as the introduction of basic child benefits, is in question.

THE RELATIONSHIP WITH CHINA

With the increasing industrialization of China, the interests of German capital in relation to the country have shifted in a similar way to those of US capital. For several decades, China was primarily a reservoir of cheap labour for German companies as well as an important investment destination with an eye on the huge domestic market that was emerging there. The development of the production apparatus and state infrastructure in China meant extraordinarily high growth rates for German companies in machinery, plant engineering and other sectors. However, the development of the production apparatus and infrastructure in China is coming to a turning point, with the investment boom of the past decades reaching its limits. In fact, overcapacity has already been created in many areas, and its partial destruction is foreseeable. In the future, it will be less a matter of investing in expansion projects than of reproducing and rationalizing the existing production apparatus. The accumulation regime in China is thus likely to shift from predominantly extensive accumulation to predominantly intensive accumulation. However, this transition is proving to be crisis-ridden. The creeping real estate crisis and the high indebtedness of many market actors point to the over-accumulation of capital, and China is currently in a situation of deflation. The crisis can perhaps be overcome if the living standards of the great mass of workers and peasants are raised further and rising wages make new growth possible. But the party and state leadership are reluctant to liberalize labour relations and allow the right to strike, with free trade unions and collective bargaining, because it fears a loss of control and because the immediate economic interests of the individual capitals, which together carry a great deal of weight in the Chinese power bloc, also stand in the way. The decline in growth rates in China is also becoming a problem for German companies, which have profited enormously from the boom there.

In addition, the relationship between Western companies and China has deteriorated as the Chinese government has restricted market access in certain strategic areas and as Chinese companies have increasingly become significant competitors in the global market. The Chinese government supports the development of domestic enterprises, urges Western enterprises to transfer technology, and has long aimed to reduce dependence on the West through import substitution and keeping foreign investment in China under control. Last but not least, the government maintains state-owned enterprises in a number of key sectors. This is the background against which conflicts over the protection of intellectual property rights and market access have intensified significantly. One way in which Chinese capital expands and organizes technology transfer is through taking over foreign companies, not least in the EU and Germany. Flows of outward direct investment by Chinese companies have grown sharply since the 2007-08 global financial crisis. The Belt and Road Initiative, the 'new Silk Road' project announced by the Chinese government in 2013, also aims at increasing Chinese capital exports. The project is, on the one hand, a reaction to the over-accumulation tendencies in China and, on the other hand, a response to US attempts to isolate China internationally. In Germany, the takeover of robot manufacturer Kuka by the Chinese Midea Group in 2016 marked a turning point, as since then the German government has pursued a more restrictive policy toward Chinese direct investment in Germany.

The rhetoric of business associations and state apparatuses in Germany and the EU has changed significantly with regard to China. China is increasingly described as a 'systemic rival', while the description of China as a 'partner, competitor and systemic rival' has now become a quasi-official language in German and EU state discourse. Political differences between the ruling parties now only relate to which of the three characterizations is emphasized. Behind this discursive shift is growing uncertainty regarding China's future policies and the prospects for exports to and investments in China that will result from them. The ruling forces in Germany and the EU have registered that China does not submit entirely to the neoliberal rules of the game, even if capitalist production relations prevail in the country, and even more that since Xi Jinping took office in 2012, the Chinese government has tried to strengthen state control in many areas at the expense of companies' freedom of action.

The US government's attempt to prevent China's further rise by imposing export restrictions on semiconductors and other strategic goods is also having a negative impact on German exports, as the US claims extraterritorial validity for its sanctions and as such aims to bring its allies into line politically. The German government is increasingly aligning itself with the US government's aggressive course toward China, even though China remains of paramount importance to German companies as a market and investment location. Foreign and security policy considerations are increasingly gaining weight over purely economic ones. While the ruling class is not pursuing a 'decoupling' from China, it would like to reduce the risks associated with a possible political or even military confrontation. Chinese investments in strategically relevant areas of the German economy are being blocked; the sources of supply for important raw materials and intermediate products are to be diversified in order to reduce dependence on Chinese imports; certain key products such as semiconductors or batteries are to be produced domestically wherever possible. The changed government policy towards China is already noticeable in the structure of foreign trade. Although both exports to, and imports from, China grew in absolute terms over recent years, China's share of German exports is declining since 2020. While China's share of German exports was 7.9 per cent in 2020, it was 6.6 per cent in July 2023. By contrast, the US share of German exports rose from 8.6 per cent in 2020 to 10.8 per cent in July 2023.[24]

THE RELATIONSHIP WITH THE EUROPEAN UNION

Even after Brexit, more than half of Germany's exports still flow elsewhere within the EU. However, the upheavals resulting from the global financial and euro crises, austerity policies in response to them, the Covid-19 pandemic and the war in Ukraine have meant that trade relations with countries outside the EU have gained in weight compared to those with other EU states. The share of total German exports going to the twenty-seven post-Brexit EU states has fallen from 61.6 per cent in 2008 to 52 per cent in 2022. The share of imports from the EU-27 in total German imports has declined from 57.6 per cent to 51.1 per cent over the same period.[25]

However, although intra-European trade linkages have lost relative weight, the political importance of the EU for the capitalist class in Germany has, if anything, increased since the eurozone crisis. This is because the ruling class assumes that only through the EU can it assert its interests in the intensifying global political conflicts. For this reason, Germany's European policy has also changed considerably since the eurozone crisis.

During the eurozone crisis, Germany was one of the countries in the EU that pushed for tough austerity policies in the member states most affected by the global financial crisis.[26] However, the hegemonic faction in the German power bloc then drew the conclusion from Brexit, the spreading calls for an exit from the European Monetary Union in Italy, and the trade war unleashed by Trump, that it was necessary, at all costs, to ensure the cohesion of the EU. The German government's response to the crisis associated with the Covid-19 pandemic was thus different to its response to the eurozone crisis. With the 'NextGenerationEU' program, it accepted that the European Commission should for the first time borrow on a large scale to finance counter-cyclical crisis management measures. The fact that, since Brexit, Germany and its remaining allies no longer have a majority in the Council of the EU may also have played a part. To a greater extent than in the past, Germany is forced to compromise with Italy and other southern European member states. A change in policy has also been evident in other areas in recent years. For example, the German government accepted a softening of the EU's strict neoliberal state aid law to allow industrial policy measures, primarily a reaction to China's technological rise and intensified world market competition.

While the German government used to reject the concept of promoting 'European champions', which has long been advocated by the French government, it is now also inclined to do so. Industrial policy has played a stronger role since the then Federal Minister of Economics Peter Altmaier published the 'Industrial Strategy 2030' in 2019.[27] The German EU Commission President Ursula von der Leyen, elected in 2019, made the direction clear with her talk of a 'geopolitical' EU and a 'European Green Deal', with a focus on 'de-carbonization' and 'digitization'. Geopolitical objectives are also the reason behind the EU's 'Global Gateway Initiative', which aims to mobilize investments of up to 300 billion euros from 2021 to 2027. The project seeks to expand transport and communications networks between the EU and Asia and Africa, binding emerging and developing countries more closely to the EU through infrastructure investments. These initiatives are competing with the Chinese government's Belt and Road Initiative. One catch to the Global Gateway Initiative is that some of the budgeted EU funds come from existing programs, so this money is merely being rebranded. Another catch is that public funds are to be used primarily to mobilize private investment. To what extent the expected leverage effects will materialize, however, is completely unclear.

In addition to the softening of neoliberal competition policy, and a greater emphasis on industrial policy, there have also been substantial changes in a number of other policy areas. The result of the 2016 referendum on EU membership in the United Kingdom led directly to a revival of plans for military cooperation within the EU. Brexit enabled the German government to take a stronger approach on this alongside the French government, which had long argued for an expansion of EU military policy, because the United Kingdom now ceased to be a major veto power against such plans. In 2017, twenty-five EU member states agreed to 'Permanent Structured Cooperation' in the area of military policy, which could lead to a 'European Defence Union', or EU army, in the longer term. Despite numerous new EU projects in the area of armaments and military policy, however, the EU is far from being able to replace NATO's role in its security strategy, as became clear with the escalation of the war in Ukraine.

IN SEARCH OF NEW MARKETS AND INVESTMENT TARGETS

The German government and business associations are striving to square the circle: on the one hand, they are trying to deepen relations with the US, and on the other, they are trying to increase the EU's 'strategic autonomy' and maintain market access in China. At the same time, they are increasingly trying to expand into other countries and regions to find substitutes for deteriorating relations with Russia and China. The German government supports the EU's efforts to reach trade and investment protection agreements with Australia, MERCOSUR, Mexico, Chile, Kenya, New Zealand, India, Indonesia and Thailand, as well as the resumption of corresponding negotiations with Malaysia and the Philippines. States in the post-Soviet region that are not EU members would like the German government to forge closer ties with them, within the framework of the EU's 'Eastern Partnership'.

The German government is also continuing its efforts to conclude EU Economic Partnership Agreements with the states of the Organization of African, Caribbean and Pacific States. Africa is important to Germany and the EU for many reasons. First, they rely on the cooperation of African states in their migration control efforts. Second, a number of African states have great importance as suppliers of raw materials to the EU. Third, African states are a destination for surplus capital from Germany. In this context, German 'development cooperation' has played an important role, for example, in establishing local bond markets in African states.[28] In addition, the hoped-for 'energy turnaround' and 'decarbonization' of the German economy has led to speculation that African states could produce 'green' hydrogen on a large scale for Germany and the EU in the future. Last but not least, the ruling actors in Germany and the EU are eyeing China's and Russia's activities in Africa with anxiety. Russian mercenary forces are involved in various African armed conflicts, and China's influence is growing, especially on the economic and political level. But Western interests in the region are not uniform either; for example, there have always been tensions between the US and France over West Africa. Overall, the struggle among imperialist powers for influence in Africa is intensifying. During its G20 presidency in 2017, the German government had already set an Africa policy focus and initiated the 'Compact with Africa' and the 'Marshall Plan for Africa'.[29] Twelve African states receive money under the Compact with Africa and in return must commit to various reform measures, such as the facilitation of foreign investment. In 2019, the 'AfricaConnect' and 'AfricaGrow' development investment funds were launched to encourage private investment in Africa. The intensification of armed conflicts and the proliferation of military coups in parts of the continent, particularly in the Sahel, indicate that living conditions have deteriorated and internal contradictions in affected societies have intensified. At the same time, criticism of the neocolonial behaviour of the imperialist powers is growing. Despite their efforts, Germany and the other imperialist states of the West are threatened with losing ground in many African countries.

Most of the countries targeted by the German power bloc as destinations for the export of goods and capital cannot take on the role that China has played in recent decades for Germany's economic development, if only on account of their smaller size, even when taken together. Even a state like India does not have the same state capacity as China for the initiation of a comparable accumulation process. For all these reasons, it is rather unlikely that Germany will again experience an export boom like that of the last decade.

CHALLENGES FOR A SOCIALIST STRATEGY

The immanent contradictions and crisis tendencies of Germany's export-oriented model of development point to the need to fundamentally change it.[30] However, the German power bloc adheres to competitive mercantilism. Even initiatives to decarbonize the economy are driven primarily by a desire to create technological superiority and new export opportunities in the changed geopolitical environment, increasing energy security, reducing energy costs, ergo increasing the rate of profit. But the project of 'green' capitalism is not progressing well, not only because of the continuing reliance on fossil fuels, increased military spending and neoliberal fiscal policy, but also because the forces within German society that are opposed to it are enormous.

The Alternative for Germany (AfD) party, which unites nationalist conservatives, authoritarian populists and neo-fascists, has made climate change denial part of its core brand and is currently gaining popular approval. In opposing substantial climate policy measures, it joins with both the conservative Christian Democrats (CDU/CSU) and the neoliberal Free Democratic Party (FDP), the latter being a member of the current governing coalition. Although the CDU/CSU and FDP do not deny climate change, there is no cross-party consensus on how to achieve the necessary reduction in greenhouse gas emissions. This points to contradictions between different capital fractions. For example, state subsidies for large companies are highly controversial, regardless of whether the aim is to decarbonize the steel industry and other energy-intensive sectors or to attract the chip industry and reduce geopolitical risks. Approaches to a new industrial policy that is as much geopolitically as ecologically motivated still stand in contrast to very strong neoliberal fiscal policy orientations. For its part, the government has not even been able to agree on a general speed limit for road traffic – a measure that has long been implemented in most European countries that would not only directly reduce CO_2 emissions, but also reduce the number of traffic fatalities while costing practically nothing and potentially even saving money.

Even a more substantial project of 'green' capitalism could, as things stand, only be advanced by a government of social democrats, greens and leftists, but there is currently no social majority for this – let alone for an ecosocialist project. Social democracy has lost a large part of its electorate; the same is true on a smaller scale for the left party (Die Linke). The latter has the problem that the anti-neoliberal consensus on which it was founded is no longer sufficient. In recent years there have been no common positions in the left on many issues, including European policy, migration policy, climate policy, attitudes toward the Covid-19 pandemic and the war in Ukraine. In addition, minorities within the left party do not want to comply with majority decisions; leading party representatives repeatedly express opinions in public that run counter to what the majority has decided. As a result, it becomes unclear what their party stands for. Die Linke has difficulties dealing productively with the objective contradictions and differing positions within its own ranks; contradictions have become entrenched and led to the loss of many members and a split in the party. With the formation of a new party around former parliamentary group leader Sahra Wagenknecht, Die Linke is in danger of losing further significance. Sahra Wagenknecht has taken a rather conservative stance on many political issues – for instance in relation to migration, ecology and gender relations. She refers positively to the ordoliberal concept of the 'social market economy' and deliberately avoids references to the socialist tradition. Whether this will succeed in winning a relevant number of voters away from the AfD or the liberal-conservative parties remains to be seen.

At the same time, the working class, without which an ecosocialist transformation is not possible, is in danger of losing further power due to the looming structural crisis of the export-oriented mode of development in Germany. The trade union IG Metall, for example, has already lost more than 100,000 members since 2019. The combination of further profit-oriented relocations of production abroad, declining labour volumes due to the shift from the internal combustion engine to the electric engine in the automotive industry and the impending loss of market share to new competitors, could, for example, lead to a sharp decline in employment in the German automotive industry.[31] Although a reduction in the weight of the automotive industry is actually necessary for socio-ecological reasons, under the given conditions this could have the undesirable side effect of further undermining the decisive power base of IG Metall. A loss of power by IG Metall and other trade unions would have far-reaching negative effects on industrial relations and the entire development of society in Germany. All progress in social, democratic and ecological terms had to be wrested from capital by organized labour and other social movements. This will also be true of any forthcoming ecosocialist transformation, which is necessary to avert the collapse of civilization on this planet. A convergence between the labour movement and the climate justice movement is therefore critically important. It is necessary to oppose both the fetishization of exports and 'competitiveness', and to socialize the production apparatus while transforming it based on social and ecological principles.

In the short term, however, the unions and the left will probably also have to prove themselves capable of fending off new attacks on workers. In view of the continuing shortage of skilled workers in many sectors and the current recession, parts of the ruling class are already calling for an extension of working life, pension cuts and a reduction in social welfare. At the same time, there are also positive developments. For example, at present IG Metall and the German Train Drivers' Union (GDL) are fighting for a reduction in the working week to 32 hours. This is a courageous step in these gloomy times. The simultaneous recession and shortage of skilled workers shows how contradictory the situation is. As the export-oriented mode of development reaches its limits and the scope for reformist politics shrinks, the danger of authoritarian temptations grows, as does the need for radical socialist politics beyond social democracy and 'left' conservatism.

NOTES

1   See IMF, World Economic Outlook, Washington, DC, October 2023, Washington, DC, p. 121.
2   Unless otherwise stated, figures in this text are based on data from the Genesis online database of the Federal Statistical Office of Germany and the author's own calculations.
3   See IMF, l.c., p. 136.
4   According to UNCTAD, data centre, foreign direct investment: Inward and outward flows and stock, annual, see: https://unctadstat.unctad.org/datacentre/dataviewer/US.FdiFlowsStock.
5   According to UNCTAD, data centre, foreign direct investment: Inward and outward flows and stock, annual, see: https://unctadstat.unctad.org/datacentre/dataviewer/US.FdiFlowsStock.
6   The author's calculations based on data from the German central bank and the German Federal Statistical Office.
7   Figures according to BASF's Annual Reports for 2007 and 2022.
8   Figures according to Siemens AG Annual Reports for 2007 and 2022.
9   According to VDA, see: https://www.vda.de/de/aktuelles/zahlen-und-daten/jahreszahlen/automobilproduktion.
10 Cf. the program pamphlet produced by two social democratic pioneers: Volker Hauff, Fritz W. Scharpff, *Modernisierung der Volkswirtschaft*, Frankfurt am Main: Europäische Verlagsanstalt, 1975.
11 See, for example, Josef Esser et al., 'Grenzprobleme des "Modells Deutschland"', *Prokla. Zeitschrift für kritische Sozialwissenschaft*, 10(40), 1980, pp. 40-63.
12 See Bernd Röttger, 'Noch immer "Modell Deutschland"? Mythen und Realitäten politökonomischer Kontinuität einer Gesellschaftsformation', *Prokla. Zeitschrift für Kritische Sozialwissenschaft*, 42(166), 2012, pp. 29-48.
13 See Stefan Beck, *Vom Fordistischen zum Kompetitiven Merkantilismus. Die Exportorientierung der Bundesrepublik Deutschland zwischen Wirtschaftswunder und Europäischer Krise*, Marburg: Metropolis Verlag, 2014.
14 For a critique of German 'exportism', see: Heribert Dieter, *Deutschland in der Weltwirtschaft. Ein Modell mit Zukunft?*, Bonn: Bundeszentrale für politische Bildung, 2016; Andreas Nölke, *Exportismus. Die deutsche Droge*, Frankfurt am Main: Westend Verlag, 2021.
15 In fact, the wage share has been trending downward; it was still above 71 per cent of GDP in the 1990s and is currently below 70 per cent of GDP. In 2022, wage earners as a whole suffered a real wage loss of 4 per cent, i.e. nominal wage increases were

far from able to compensate for the high inflation rates. The loss of purchasing power affects the lower strata of the working class with low wages disproportionately, as they are forced to spend it primarily on rents, energy and food - and it is precisely the prices of the latter that have risen particularly sharply.

16   See IMF, *World Economic Outlook*, Washington, DC, October 2010, p. 178.
17   According to IMF, World Economic Outlook database, October 2023.
18   See: Nicos Poulantzas, *Classes in Contemporary Capitalism*, London: Verso, 1978, p. 37ff; Leo Panitch and Sam Gindin, *The Making of Global Capitalism*, London: Verso, 2012.
19   See: Franziska Lindner, *Die deutsch-russischen Energiebeziehungen. Kontinuitäten und Brüche im geopolitischen Feld,* Köln: Papyrossa Verlag, 2018.
20   The sanctions are circumvented; Russian oil or its derivatives reach the EU in a roundabout way via other countries – but at higher costs.
21   According to Eurostat data, harmonized index of consumer prices (prc_hicp).
22   According to Eurostat data, harmonized index of consumer prices (prc_hicp).
23   In the 1990s and 2000s, the German armed forces were significantly downsized. Heavy investment in classic territorial defense was considered unnecessary after the end of the Cold War. The German armed forces were to be retooled for out-of-area missions in the Global South. The share of defence in total government spending fell from 3.9 per cent in 1991 to less than 2 per cent in 2010. Since the Russian occupation of Crimea and the start of the war in eastern Ukraine, territorial defense has regained more weight and overall security policy discourse has gained in importance. However, domestic resistance to renewed rearmament and greater militarization of German foreign policy remained considerable until the escalation of the war in Ukraine in 2022.
24   According to the Federal Statistical Office of Germany, Genesis online database, code 51000, 'foreign trade', the author's calculations.
25   Author's calculations based on Eurostat data, national accounts (ESA 2010), dataset: Exports and imports by member states of the EU/third countries, online data code: nama_10_exi.
26   See: Frederic Heine and Thomas Sablowski, *Die Europapolitik des deutschen Machtblocks und ihre Widersprüche. Eine Untersuchung der Positionen deutscher Wirtschaftsverbände zur Eurokrise,* Berlin: Rosa-Luxemburg-Stiftung, 2013, available at: https://www.rosalux.de/fileadmin/rls_uploads/pdfs/Studien/RLS_Studien_Europapolitik.pdf.
27   See Etienne Schneider, 'Germany's Industrial strategy 2030, EU competition policy and the Crisis of New Constitutionalism. (Geo-)political economy of a contested paradigm shift', *New Political Economy*, 28(2), 2023, pp. 241-58.
28   See Frauke Banse, 'Der "globale Pool privaten Geldes" in Afrika. Anleihemärkte in lokaler Währung und die deutsche Entwicklungszusammenarbeit', *Peripherie*, 41(162-163), 2021, pp. 251-74.
29   See: www.compactwithafrica.org/content/compactwithafrica/home.html.
30   See also: Mario Candeias, *Wirtschaftswende jetzt. Die Erosion des deutschen Exportmodells erfordert Elemente einer neuen Ökonomie,* Berlin: Rosa-Luxemburg-Stiftung, 2023.
31   Domestic production has already fallen from more than 5.7 million passenger cars in 2016 to less than 3.5 million in 2022, according to data from the Automotive Industry Association. See: www.vda.de/en/news/facts-and-figures/annual-figures/automobile-production.

EUROPE, THE WORLD ECONOMY AND NEW IMPERIAL GROSSRAUMS

ALAN CAFRUNY AND VASSILIS K. FOUSKAS

Neoliberal globalization, a policy and a process led by the United States and unevenly spread across the world since the stagflation of the 1970s, has witnessed setbacks since the global financial crisis in 2007-08 and the ensuing eurozone crisis. Central banks committed trillions of their taxpayers' money to save capitalism, a state policy that produced untold levels of austerity, which in the great majority of cases pushed Western electorates to support extreme right-wing and xenophobic parties in absence of any meaningful socialist alternative. In fact, socialism, as a reformist and/ or radical project of the working class and its subaltern allies was greatly weakened by the very processes of neoliberal globalization and European 'integration'. The former entailed outsourcing of major corporations and industrial enterprises to the Global South, especially China and South Asia, rendering the working class invisible and 'identity politics' fashionable; the latter gradually deprived the members of the European Union (EU) and, later, the eurozone, of the Keynesian policy tools capable of re-formulating a pro-socialist welfare policy at the national level.

However, neoliberal globalization and European 'integration' have never been one and the same thing. European, especially German, big capital and industries continue to compete fiercely with their US rivals on the global market. A characteristic case is that of the aviation industry – Europe's Airbus versus America's Boeing. Indeed, this dynamic within neoliberalism has been mirrored at the global level as well, with Japanese car manufacturing companies and advanced semi-conductor industrial sectors seriously challenging the primacy of the United States in those markets during the 1980s.[1] Yet, these conflicts were contained through the various channels of multilateral economic diplomacy and discipline, or through protectionist measures imposed by the US. None of these conflicts and 'trade wars' could lead to a real war within the western core (Europe, US, Japan) because the

US controlled the security and the geopolitical environment of its allies via its hub and spoke system of governance set up in the late 1940s and which remained unaltered after the end of the Cold War.[2] In fact, the US expanded this system via the eastern enlargement of NATO and associated policy initiatives. The Ukraine crisis is the latest in a series of US advances deeper into Eurasia using NATO as a vehicle and thereby challenging the security of Moscow. For the economic and highly institutionalized conflicts that take place within the global capitalist core controlled by the United States, we utilize the term 'intra-imperialist antagonisms'. From this perspective, Europe's imperialism is encased with America's *grossraum*, or wider area.[3]

Neoliberal globalization has also transformed the Global South, with the results uneven. Countries of the South saw no substantial benefits by giving up their old import-substitution strategies and opening up their markets to Western corporations operating in the hybrid manner of global production networks and financialization. Real economic development in most was very limited and poverty alleviation elusive.[4] But in some other cases, outsourcing by Western corporations in the pursuit of cheap labour and the recycling of profits back to the Western fold created centres of local capital accumulation that were hard to ignore. Asian enterprises, especially Chinese state-owned ones, that could develop economies of scale nationally as well as regionally have entered the global competition and, in some sectors such as semi-conductors, are competing on equal footing with American and other Western corporations. China, whether at home, in Africa or elsewhere, controls most of the world's rare earth elements and minerals, which are of paramount importance for the transition to 'green energy' – the West's official policy response to climate change and global heating.[5] Chinese corporations, moreover, have followed the Western path: for some time now, they been outsourcing in pursuit of cheap labour in Africa, Latin America, Southeast Asia, and the former Soviet space (East-Central Europe, the Balkans and the MENA region). China's leadership of the BRICS (the semi-formal alignment of Brazil, Russia, India, China, and South Africa, now expanded to include Saudi Arabia, Egypt, UAE, Iran, and Ethiopia), the Shanghai Cooperation Organization and the Belt and Road Initiative is indicative of its global economic power projection and reach. Central to our argument is the following: it seems to us that China is developing a global imperialist posture that competes head-on with the West, although in the field of military capabilities the United States still reigns supreme.

However, unlike the conflicts that take place within the core and are contained and controlled by the institutionalized framework established and still led by the US, China's political process and geopolitics remain uncontrolled by the US. China, Russia and other states of the Global South, such as Iran, are not part of the hub and spoke system of US imperial primacy. Thus, for the economic and highly politicized conflicts that take place mainly between China and Russia on the one hand, and the United States and its – at times uncooperative – allies on the other, we utilize the term 'inter-imperialist contradictions'. From this perspective, China's *grossraum* is politically independent.

Explaining the interpenetrations and expansionist dynamics of these two blocs of capital and their possible outcomes, or the role of intermediating 'sub-imperialisms' in specific geographical sites, such as that of Brazil or Turkey, are very demanding tasks that deserve their own dedicated space. This essay deals with the following specific matters. We argue that Russia's invasion of Ukraine added a formidable interlocking spin to this complex set of intra-imperialist and inter-imperialist dynamics, mobilizing pre-existing subterranean trends and forces in the global system. It amalgamated, albeit provisionally, US primacy in the core by way of subordinating the EU, especially Germany, and cutting off any meaningful ties between western Europe and Russia. At the same time, it strengthened intra-South economic and geopolitical cooperation. This is something which transpires not just in the voting pattern of the UN General Assembly after Russia's invasion, but also in the BRICS' meetings and China's determination to assist its corporations in expanding globally, including their penetration of the markets of the core, something which the West, under pressure from the US, resists.

However, a detailed political economy analysis of the processes and consequences of the conflict in Ukraine indicates that both neoliberal globalization and European 'integration' are experiencing transformative crises. Policy processes and structural forces are rerouting global dynamics, shifting the centres of global capital accumulation away from Europe – at least for the time being. The war in Ukraine and the policies employed primarily by the United States tend to recompose and reorganize global capital in the geography of North American and Chinese orbits. Many of these policies and trends, such as the neo-mercantilist policies of the US (and of Germany within the EU bloc), were visible long before the war. The war in Ukraine, however, coming on the heels of the global pandemic, was the straw that broke the camel's back: the Ukraine crisis, with no end in sight at the time of writing, may well have a lasting transformative impact on world politics and lead to the implosion of inter-imperialist contradictions.

CUTTING-OFF THE RUSSIAN LINK: ENERGY AND INFLATION

Reacting to US policy, and in the midst of an international legal regime imposing sanctions against Russia, Europe is seeking to reroute its oil and gas supply network. The new policy framework imposed on the EU dictates that hydrocarbons should be delivered to the EU not via oil and gas pipelines connected to Russia and Russian state companies, but via specially built tankers and new port terminals that must be constructed in order to receive liquefied natural gas (LNG) and other products from the US. During this transition period and after prolonged elite discussions (and disagreements) among Western executives, a decision was made by the EU, the G7 and Australia to cap the price of purchases of Russian seaborne oil at $60 per barrel. The ostensible aim was to curtail Russia's ability to finance its conflict in Ukraine, given more than 45 per cent of the Russian state's revenue comes from the sale of hydrocarbons. Skeptics, however, pointed out that this reduction was not good enough, especially since the Brent crude oil price in January 2023 was at just over $76 per barrel, below the price of $86 recorded before the start of the war in January 2022, and by September 2023, had risen to over $92 per barrel. This provides an indication that the war in Ukraine is by no means entirely responsible for Europe's spike in inflation. Ukraine itself – as well as Poland – argued that the West should stop purchasing hydrocarbons from Russia altogether, further privileging the sale of expensive American LNG to Europe.

This nature of this discussion between the Western allies is, however, in many respects incomplete and misleading. American LNG alone is not enough to fuel Europe's economic and social infrastructure. Furthermore, LNG imports require the construction of special tankers and terminals, which Europe has only just started building, although Germany has been especially quick to build the infrastructure needed.[6] In the meantime, Russia has already begun diversifying its crude oil and gas exports to Asian markets, especially in China and India, making new agreements and building new pipelines, although it is forced to sell to Asian powers below market price, thus reducing the revenues accrued. Furthermore, there is an important aspect of the contractual situation between Russian export consortia and Western states in particular that undermines the Western strategy in this realm. More than 77 per cent of total Russian gas exports are under contracts stipulating that importers must continue to pay up to 85 per cent of the contracted price of the gas even if they do not receive it. These long-term contracts that work in favour of Russia, and European importers can do nothing about them.[7] Germany, whose dependence on Russian gas stands at 41 per cent of national requirements, has had to swallow a very bitter pill by accepting the sacrifice of Nord Stream pipelines at the altar of US policy, thereby cutting off direct geostrategic links to Russia. Further undermining Europe's role in this strategy is the fact that India is re-exporting Russian oil back to the EU.

European inflation is not simply reducible to the above processes. US import costs could also be argued to be contributing to European inflation (although this is very difficult to measure empirically). Moreover, approaches that attribute the inflationary trends in Europe to the war fail to account for inflation in the UK, at the highest rate of any country in the Western core, yet in a state with minimal connection to Russian hydrocarbons. Technically, inflationary trends in both the US and Europe were triggered by the pandemic and have soared to multi-decade highs, dramatically raising production costs and spurring interest rate increases throughout Europe, the US, and the UK. This has been accompanied by decreased purchasing power at the same time as total debt as a share of GDP across the G7 economies exceeds 100 per cent. Standing at $33 trillion, US national debt is 22 per cent higher than the country's GDP of $27 trillion.[8] Forced to raise interest rates, central banks, including the European Central Bank, are unable to reprise quantitative easing strategies as they did in 2008-09 in the wake of the collapse of Lehman Brothers and again in 2020-21 in response to the Covid-19 pandemic.

But if the pandemic triggered the inflationary trend, its structural causes are more deeply rooted in the regime of financialized globalization and the erosion of the productive material base of Western economies. For decades now, Western economies have recorded a low rate of investment, especially for public investment, alongside low labour productivity and low real wage growth. This is particularly the case for Germany.[9] Aggregate supply could not support a sustainable rate of growth that generated high rates of profit (measured as the percentage increase on capital invested) for enterprises. The way out for businesses was to push for inflation in order to compensate for the pressures on the rate of profit in conditions of low labour productivity and the increasing domination of a financialized service economy.[10] As perceptive analyses of financialization have shown, a big chunk of the profits repatriated by western enterprises operating in the Global South were financialized instead of being reinvested in the real economic sector and thus contributing to growth, including wage growth. The financialization of non-financial enterprises has been a major characteristic of neoliberal globalization.[11] Thus, in aggregate, real wage growth in the West – with the partial exception of the US – fell behind the rate of inflation.

This, however, has not been the case with most economies in the Asia-

Pacific region, another angle from which one can see the relative economic rise of Asia compared to Europe as a whole.[12] As we shall see below, the worries of the US lie precisely in the technological advantage China may acquire in the following years.[13]

PROTECTIONISM IN THE INTRA-IMPERIALIST BLOC

If the rerouting of European energy supplies and the headache of inflation are major challenges to the EU's economic and geopolitical security, the US strategy for the technological containment of China represents yet another significant challenge to European industry, and especially to Germany. Starting with the Trump administration, the United States deployed the threat of extraterritorial sanctions in a range of European industries, blocking attempts to develop alternative sources of oil and natural gas in Iran and cooperation with Huawei in the development of 5G networks. Many of these actions directly benefited US corporations and provoked widespread resentment in Europe.[14] As well as blocking Chinese acquisition of assets, something that has also taken place in Europe and Australia,[15] more recent steps have been taken by the US to impede European cooperation with Chinese semi-conductor companies, notably the introduction of the Chips and Science Act (CSA) with its provisions of over $280 billion to support the US digital and semi-conductor industries. Washington appears to be seeking, through a combination of sanctions and subsidies, to partially 'de-couple' from China the semi-conductor companies of both itself and its allies, further polarizing and politicizing the global economic environment. This imposes heavy costs on Europe, which is heavily dependent on Chinese telecommunications infrastructure. Huawei, for example, has a larger market share in Berlin than in Beijing, but the Federal Republic is now caught in the crosshairs of Washington's anti-Huawei campaign, increasingly embraced also by the European Commission.[16] Meanwhile, the US company Intel has secured a 10 billion euro subsidy for a 30 billion euro investment in Magdeburg. The same trend applies to trade, although now EU officials, such as European Commission President Ursula von der Leyen, call it 'de-risking' rather than 'de-coupling' from China.[17] Moreover, the war in Ukraine disrupts trade in terms of freight, which is an important part of China's Belt and Road global infrastructure development strategy.[18]

The Biden administration's recently passed Inflation Reduction Act (IRA), which includes $369 billion in subsidies to American energy, manufacturing, and transport, represents a further significant protectionist initiative. Arguably violating the rules of the moribund World Trade Organization (WTO),[19] the IRA seeks to decrease greenhouse gas emissions by providing tax cuts and subsidies for electric cars and wind farms. But the sourcing requirements are effectively protectionist and incentivize European and even Asian firms to shift operations and factories to the United States. The combination of US subsidies, inflation, and the costs involved in the rerouting of energy supplies threatens the competitiveness of European corporations and risks further significant deindustrialization.

The US approach in this regard has potentially contradictory outcomes for US interests. On the one hand, US policies are attempting to protect American companies while trying to attract high tech investment in the US proper. On the other hand, the regime of sanctions against Russia, combined with this US protectionism and the securitization of the whole of Europe, pushes European enterprises to look to China and other regions of Asia as well as the US. This trend could even be characterized as a 're-globalization' rather than 'de-globalization,' as Asian infrastructure and hybrid production networks will be used as new launching pads toward global expansion and the US also becomes a more attractive investment opportunity.[20] In this context, global supply chains and networks are restructured and industrial relations regimes reformed under different jurisdictions and normative regional frameworks.

Many European companies, including those in the sectors related to oil, gas, fertilizers, chemicals and, importantly, rare earth elements (including lithium battery factories), as well as high-tech companies, are contemplating exit. Russia and China are major world exporters and refiners of rare earth elements upon which the high tech and microchip industries depend, including in those involved in electric cars and defence. Europe's car industry, especially in terms of electric cars, appears antiquated when compared to the productive capacities in China or the US. Given the dependence of European economies upon imported manufactures and complex supply chain networks, the mayhem that has been inflicted on them through both the fallout of sanctions on Russia and the US domestic subsidy regime is likely to have lasting consequences. Re-globalization would mean a new wave of the relocation of key industries and services that pursue the openings afforded through globalization and the shifting of global production networks away from Europe to either China, other parts of Asia or the US as their operational base. This would undoubtedly strengthen the stakes in capitalist globalization for both the US and China, whereas the EU would confront permanent austerity and continuous competitive pressures toward de-industrialization. In other words, the policy developments triggered by the war in Ukraine have sharpened the conflict between the US and China, making the overall framework of inter-imperialist contradictions more acute as they turn Europe into a dependent – even a vassal – area whose key policy options are increasingly determined by the US.

Maintaining wage restraint, cutting pensions, and privatizing welfare state institutions remain, to be sure, common interests of the transatlantic ruling bloc. Keeping the rate of interest below the rate of inflation, and the rate of inflation above real wage growth, means that real interest rates, despite their rise, are still in fact negative for capital while it hopes to increase the rate of return (the profitability of enterprises). But profitability cannot increase as long as labour productivity and investment are low, with the result being downward pressure on wages and the erosion of household savings. However, enduring austerity regimes and the breakdown of welfare institutions does not deter the migration of European business and logistics operators to Asia, especially China, or even to the US. A dangerous aspect of these competitive trends in relation to world peace is the conflict between a globalizing Asia under Chinese primacy and a securitized, protectionist transatlantic bloc that aims at the subordination of its economic rivals via both administrative coercion and military means. From this perspective, it is worth remembering that it was not Nazi Germany that closed itself off from the outside world, but the liberal and 'open door' US, especially with the introduction of Smoot-Hawley tariffs promulgated in 1930. By raising tariffs, the US effectively blocked European exports to American markets, making the repayment of European war debts untenable, further accentuating the contradictions of the Versailles settlements and thus paving the way to the Second World War.

ZEITENWENDE – FOR GERMANY AND EUROPE

The combined impact of the IRA and CSA, the loss of Russia's cheap energy supplies, and the imposition of business restrictions with China calls into question Germany's distinctive export-led and neo-mercantilist developmental model. This represents a major turning point for the Federal Republic, now widely referred to as the 'sick man of Europe'. The so-called 'German model', which allowed the country to reconfigure the European economy via the European Community treaties, was predicated on a supply-side constitution separating what were deemed strictly political struggles from central banking, while leaving intact the anti-inflationary principle. Austro-German 'ordoliberalism' was premised on an apolitical, individualistic and disciplinarian regulation of markets and social relations – what Michel Foucault called 'biopolitics'.[21] This model can be traced back to the negotiations for the Treaty of Rome in the 1950s, through to the Maastricht Treaty in the 1990s and the Stability and Growth Pact of 1999.

Aspects of it recently displayed include not just a succession of disciplinary labour policies, embodied in Germany's 'Agenda 2010' reforms, but the restructuring of German business through a strategy of selective outsourcing and export mercantilism, underwritten by a devalued (for Germany) euro that for years enabled substantial trade surpluses with both the US and the periphery of the EU. As an example, Germany's trade surplus in 2017 was 234 billion euros (compared to 390 billion and 140 billion euros for China and Japan respectively).

Whereas the US, UK, and French manufacturing sectors fell below 10 per cent of GDP in 2022, the German manufacturing sector represented 19 per cent in the same year.[22] This was a factor limiting the extent of Germany's domestic austerity while accounting for Germany's relative political stability for decades, which included only modest flirtations with extreme right-wing movements – something which is no longer the case. The collapse of the Soviet Union and the East Bloc incentivized German manufacturing and commodity supply chains – primarily geared toward the assembly stage – to relocate throughout central and eastern Europe, thereby enabling Germany's neo-mercantilist model to increase its international competitiveness both inside and outside of the EU.[23] The asymmetries of the European Monetary Union (EMU) and these supply chains constitute an 'astonishing continuity in the basic structure of German capitalism',[24] enabling it to generate permanent surpluses at the expense of an increasingly indebted periphery, especially EU/eurozone periphery. They demonstrate the vast scope of German leadership over the European economy. In 2021, exports accounted for 39 per cent of Germany's GDP, while Germany accounts for approximately 25 per cent of EU exports and 30 per cent of European GDP. However, if supply chains and added values are taken into account, the figures are considerably higher. These trade surpluses served to export ordoliberal deflation, producing debt and unemployment in not just in Europe's periphery but also the United States, sparking resentment and serving as the key rationale for Trump's tariffs on Europe, which have been maintained by Biden. Furthermore, in 2016 the US Treasury added Germany to its list of countries engaging in 'unfair currency practices' even though, technically, Germany does not have its own currency.[25]

The bases of the German model thus portend acute long-term vulnerability, which has now been thrown into sharp relief by the energy crisis, US protectionism, and growing pressure on German industry and trade to 'decouple' from China. Furthermore, the general trend to interest rate hikes is not conducive to trade, because they increase the cost of import-export creating hard currencies – not to speak of the borrowing requirements and debt for the global periphery – for all parties concerned. It is not unrelated that the EU's trade deficit with China has roughly tripled over the last five years (2019-23), shooting up to 400 billion euros.[26] Germany has been the hardest hit of all EU and G7 countries, experiencing a period of protracted stagflation in which, ironically, only weak industrial demand – 14 months of consecutive contraction – has served in part to balance gas demand by 2023.[27]

German primacy in the EU was reinforced not only by its control of the ECB but also by its position as the central hub linking Russian natural gas to Europe, a position it had maintained despite resistance from many EU member states, the Commission, and furious opposition from both US LNG companies and the Pentagon. But the pandemic turned the ordoliberal discipline of the EU's Stability and Growth Pact into a broken reed. Under intense international and competitive pressure, the anti-inflation criterion of the central banking mechanism could no longer hold, and inflation spread regardless of EU and German ordoliberal policy. Accordingly, German industry faced massive new costs and Berlin faced extensive new claims on its budget. For Germany as of 2022, energy accounts for 26 per cent of metallurgy industry production costs; 19 per cent for basic chemical production; 18 per cent for glass manufacture; 17 per cent for paper; and 15 per cent for construction materials.[28] At the same time, over the period 2021-2026 the EU is delivering 750 billion euros to its member states through its Next Generation EU program, partly in the form of aid and partly through loans, in order to assist them in dealing with the impact of the pandemic. The EMU's ordoliberal 'stability' and discipline are dead. Had the Greek debt crisis broken out today, it is doubtful that Wolfgang Schäuble would have got his way. As a result of these changes and processes leading to austerity and unemployment, the neo-Nazi Alternative for Germany (Alternative für Deutschland – AfD) party shot up in terms of electoral and popular support. The inflow of migrants from Central Asia and the MENA region via Turkey, the Balkans, and Italy adds to the mix of reasons turning the electorate to the far right. Polls in early fall 2023 show the party as the second strongest, behind the Christian Democratic Union (Christlich Demokratische Union Deutschlands – CDU) at 27 per cent and ahead of Chancellor Olaf Scholz's Social Democratic Party (Sozialdemokratische Partei Deutschlands – SPD) at 19 per cent. The AfD was in fact the strongest party in Saxony, Thuringia, and Brandenburg, polling at between 32-35 per cent.

With Russia's invasion of Ukraine looming in February 2022, the German leadership initially sought to maintain its longstanding linkages to Russia, symbolically and materially represented by the Nord Stream 1 and

2 pipelines. President Frank-Walter Steinmeier and Chancellor Scholz sent just 5,000 helmets to Kyiv and refused to allow the Baltic states to provide Soviet-era artillery that had been manufactured in the GDR. After the invasion, Ukraine declared Steinmeier *persona non grata* and refused to allow him to visit Kyiv, while Ukraine's ambassador to Germany, Andriy Melnyk, publicly praised Nazi collaborator Stepan Bandera and called Scholz an 'offended liver sausage'.[29] During his visit to Washington on 7 February 2022, Scholz continued to equivocate following Biden's warning that the US would 'bring an end' to Nord Steam 2 if Russia invades and that 'I promise you we will be able to do it'.[30]

Pushed by both Washington and hawkish Green Party and FDP (Freie Demokratische Partei) coalition members, the German political leadership capitulated to these deliberate humiliations – apparently unconditionally. Scholz and Steinmeier abjectly proclaimed their fealty to Washington.[31] Facing a chorus of criticism, the previous Chancellor, Angela Merkel, confessed that she was in fact never committed to Minsk II and supported it only to buy time for Ukrainian rearmament.[32] Scholz announced an immediate increase of 100 billion euros for the German military budget. German air force chief, Ingo Gerhartz, declared that 'for credible deterrence, we need both the means and the political will to implement nuclear deterrence if necessary'.[33] The dramatic political and ideological transformation was expressed most clearly within the German media which, downplayed the economic costs for Germany and, with the exception of *Der Spiegel*, 'served as cheerleaders for re-armament and war'.[34]

Responsibility for the sabotage of the Nord Stream pipelines has not been officially determined or publicly disclosed, although US intelligence officials eventually acknowledged the lack of evidence in initial reports that blamed Russia.[35] There can be no doubt that the destruction represents not simply a severance of German-Russian energy ties but a fundamental and likely permanent transformation of US-German and transatlantic power relations. Ironically, throughout the war Russia has continued to export natural gas through Ukraine according to an agreement reached in 2019 that provides Kyiv with $7 billion in revenue through 2024. The other operational pipeline that has continued to supply Russian gas to the EU is via Turkey. However, as a result of what the *Financial Times* has described as 'the investment exodus across the Atlantic driven by US incentives and cheaper gas prices' in August 2023, 32 per cent of German companies favoured foreign investment over domestic, twice that of August 2022.[36]

This is exemplified by the actions of BASF, the largest integrated chemical firm in the world, and Volkswagen. BASF's Ludwigshafen site has been severely downsized and the company is now building a $10 billion plant in China, representing the largest investment in its history. Faced with a 2.2 billion euro increase in energy costs in the first nine months of 2022 when compared to 2021, BASF's chief executive announced plans to downsize in Europe 'as quickly as possible and also permanently'.[37] At the same time, BASF has become increasingly intertwined with China, which accounts for 12 billion euros of its annual revenues. Meanwhile in the case of Volkswagen, it is making massive investments in North America, thereby greatly consolidating its foothold in the North American free trade area while also expanding its activities in China.[38]

As a result of these trends, Germany is compelled to navigate increasing pressure from the United States and numerous EU member states to 'de-couple' or 'de-risk' and address its economic reliance on China, which still constitutes Germany's largest export market. In October 2022, Berlin succumbed to US pressure to prevent China's Cosco purchasing a majority stake in the Port of Hamburg. In November 2022, Scholz's visit to Beijing, accompanied by numerous CEOs, triggered deep divisions within Germany and Europe, and elicited harsh criticism from the United States and NATO. Germany's first ever national security strategy, released in June 2023, reflected this contradictory imperative: 'Today's Russia is for now the most significant threat to peace and security in the Euro-Atlantic area … China is a partner, competitor, and systemic rival … the elements of rivalry and competition have increased in recent years.'[39]

THE LENGTHENING SHADOW OF US HEGEMONY

Following his visit to Washington at the end of November 2022, Emmanuel Macron not only called for a negotiated peace in Ukraine but also publicly attacked the IRA, the Biden Administration's centre-piece policy, warning that by excluding European products from US markets it could 'fragment the West'.[40] German officials and industrialists have been even more blunt, openly accusing US firms of profiting from the war. Noting the 'flight of capital and production facilities out of Europe and into the dollar', Siemens CEO Joe Kaeser has asserted that Europe is now 'in systematic competition not only with China but also to some extent with America'.[41] As a result of sanctions, German automobile companies have been driven out of Russia, the world's fifth largest economy on a purchasing power parity basis and Europe's largest consumer market, while Chinese companies are purchasing their European plants at knock-down prices.[42] The Bundestag's Vice-President, Wolfgang Kubicki, protested that Germany risks bankruptcy and is 'on the way to becoming a dysfunctional state', where 'infrastructure, energy prices, and the inability of the Bundeswehr to protect' the country are all urgent challenges requiring immediate action.[43]

Yet, a concerted European response to US neo-mercantilist policies would engender massive transatlantic conflicts and potentially endanger the single market. Notwithstanding China's rise the transatlantic space continues to represent the most important 'region' of global capital accumulation. Europe remains critically dependent on the US not only for more than 50 per cent of natural gas imports but also with respect to trade and investment. In 2022 US-Europe trade in goods ($1.2 trillion) exceeded EU-China goods trade ($897 billion). However, foreign direct investment flows across the Atlantic exceed those to China by a factor of 10.[44] Fearful of challenging Washington at the WTO, the European Commission has appealed – so far unsuccessfully – to the Biden administration to incorporate Europe within its regime of subsidies. The Commission is also seeking to develop its own riposte to the IRA. However, the EU is deeply divided. Germany, Sweden, and Denmark have so far opposed Commission proposals for a 'sovereignty fund' that would provide common European funding in response to the IRA and other American protectionist policies. Germany, instead, has allocated 200 billion euros in subsidies to its own industries alongside a 15 billion euro payout to its energy companies, challenging basic precepts of the EU's single market and its associated treaties, while antagonizing France and other EU member states.

At this point, both France and Germany are riding along on America's military-security bandwagon, as expressed through NATO, having jointly reneged on previous commitments towards the Minsk agreements while increasingly adopting its security strategy for Eurasia.[45] German rearmament is taking place in conjunction with the US military-industrial complex, as illustrated by its decision to purchase Lockheed Martin F-35 fighter jets that are capable of carrying US nuclear weapons, a purchase that seemingly jeopardizes the development of Franco-German cooperation on a joint fighter jet and, more generally, serves further to integrate European military production capacities with the US. The Brussels grandees codify their loyalty to the US by pledging to 'shed EU bureaucratic torpor, defend Ukraine, embrace enlargement and move closer to fulfilling Ursula von der Leyen's ambition for the EU to become a "geopolitical force"'.[46] At EU Council meetings there is less talk about trade regulations and debt financing and more regarding weapons systems and ammunition supply chains. The EU's financing of military equipment for Ukraine comes from the newly founded European Peace Facility, with Brussels aiming to place the European defence industry on a war footing. Under pressure from the US, these efforts have also been matched by a rise in the defence spending of European states. This is ultimately of direct benefit to the US, given it is the main supplier for the nearly 80 per cent of European military purchases that are sourced from outside the EU. The EU is facing all of these challenges, including that of admitting Ukraine as a member, at the same moment as the bloc's trade deficit with China has, as noted above, widened to 400 billion euros.

EUROPE BETWEEN THE AMERICAN AND THE CHINESE GROSSRAUMS

While the nations of the Global South have experienced the most protracted and deadly impacts of the war outside of Ukraine and Russia, due chiefly to the contraction of the global trade and the scarcity of grain and cereals, the consequences for Europe have been far more severe than for the US or China. US oil and gas companies have benefited substantially from the sanctions on Russian energy, while its defence contractors gained enormously by securitizing Europe's eastern orbit. We have shown that protectionist measures taken by the US, in combination with the regime of sanctions on Russia, have wreaked havoc on key European industries as well as global supply chains, leading to pressures for a re-routing of globalization along the lines of an incipient US–China economic-technological bi-polarity. Thus, the re-routing of globalization is taking shape via the consolidation of US primacy in Europe in an increasingly polarized geo-political environment between the US and China.

All future scenarios for the war in Ukraine would reinforce these present tendencies. Germany would be hard pressed to compensate for a reduction in US support for Ukraine – a distinct possibility should the Republican party emerge victorious in the 2024 elections. A Republican president, moreover, would likely pursue more aggressive policies against China, further damaging Germany's relationship with its key trade partner. A negotiated settlement of the Ukraine conflict would also entail dramatic reconstruction costs on Germany, a state already compelled to hold the EU together through more expansive budgetary policies, even as it faces severe budgetary constraints amid pressure from deindustrialization, high energy prices, and demands from Washington for further German rearmament. The possible future entry of Ukraine to the EU would require a major readjustment of EU policy and treaties, alongside even greater new expenditures.

The war has thus deepened Europe's economic and geopolitical dependence on the US while exacerbating intra-imperialist divisions, drawing a sharp demarcation line on the map between the West and the East. It has led to the exclusion of Russia from European affairs and the breaking of its link with Germany for the foreseeable future. Intra-imperialist divisions and antagonisms have been provisionally settled at the highest political level within the American-led *grossraum*. Europe's leaders have decided to hitch themselves to the US bandwagon, participate in an escalating conflict with Russia and, potentially, benefit from the division of spoils arising from the future reconstruction of Ukraine. But the US has no seat on China or Russia's security and war councils. China's *grossraum* is wholly independent of Western influence, as opposed to the EU's *grossraum*, which is encased in the US geopolitical and security matrix. Thus, the inter-imperialist contradiction is the one that matters the most: as acute as never before since the fall of the Berlin Wall, it is menacing world peace at an exceptionally fast pace.

NOTES

1   Work by Robert Brenner in the anglophone literature (see his *The Economics of Global Turbulence*, London: Verso, 2006), that of Michel Aglietta and the 'regulation school' in France, and the pioneering work of Klaus Busch in (West) Germany in the late 1970s (see his *Die Krise der Europäischen Gemeinschaft*, Cologne: EVA, 1978) provide a compass for a solid understanding of economic conflict within the core triad of the US, Germany and Japan during the so-called 'Golden Age of Capitalism' and beyond.
2   On this, see the contributions by Peter Gowan, *The Global Gamble*, London: Verso, 1999; and Leo Panitch and Sam Gindin, *The Making of Global Capitalism,* London: Verso, 2013.
3   The concept of *grossraum* (open spaces) was developed by Carl Schmitt on the eve of World War II to describe Nazi Germany's hegemonic ambitions, which he believed were patterned on the Monroe Doctrine: 'The core, the idea of a Völkerrechtliche Grossraumsordnung, can be transferred to other spaces [Räume], other historical situations, and other friend-foe groupings.' The *grossraum* 'shapes the borders, sovereignty, and identity of a territory or region.' Quoted in Matthew Specter, 'Grossraum and Geopoliltics', *History and Theory*, 56(3), 2017, pp. 398-406
4   See, among others: Francis Boateng Frimpong, *Financialization and Poverty Alleviation in Ghana. Myths and Realities,* Leiden: Brill, 2022. This exceptional work of comparative scholarship shows how neoliberal globalization-cum-financialization has impoverished Ghana and most Sub-Saharan economies.
5   Jared Cohen, et al., 'Resource Realism: The Geopolitics of Critical Mineral Supply Chains', Goldman Sachs, 13 September 2023.
6   The EU is struggling to find alternative sources of cheap energy. In late 2022 it concluded an agreement with Azerbaijan to import gas, made possible only by Baku's significant gas imports from Russia (see: David O'Byrne, 'Azerbaijan's Russian Gas Deal Raises Uncomfortable Questions for Europe', *Eurasianet*, 22 November 2022). The EU also approved the construction of the East Med pipeline, which involves Israel, the Republic of Cyprus and Greece, a costly project which may never come to fruition. It also faces objections from Turkey due to its exclusion from the project. More encouraging are recent indications of large deposits of hydrocarbons south

of Crete, within Greece's Exclusive Economic Zone (EEZ). The scramble for hydrocarbons in the eastern Mediterranean has increased tensions between Greece and Turkey over maritime rights and delimitation of the EEZ. See: Vassilis K. Fouskas, 'Economic drivers of Turkey's foreign policy and the issue of "strategic autonomy" (sub-imperialism)', Policy Paper III, Centre for Advanced Turkish Studies and Yasar University Centre for Mediterranean Studies, January 2023.

7   See: Vassilis K. Fouskas, 'The Russian predicament', Valdai Discussion Club, 27 January 2023.

8   At the moment, this does not mean much. The US borrows its own currency from international markets and its privileges stemming from the dollar serving as world money means it does not have to pay its debt back in its entirety. It can issue bonds to pay principals on old bonds, or even borrow to pay interest as long as overall debt does not rise too much above revenue, or as long as the lenders, such as China, Japan or Saudi Arabia, do not withdraw their dollar holdings and start investing in alternative currencies.

9   See, especially: Marcel Fratzscher, *The Germany Illusion: Between Economic Euphoria and Despair*, Oxford: Oxford University Press, 2018, ch. 6.

10 It follows that curing inflation in the West requires a high rate of investment in the productive sectors of the economy, high labour productivity and higher real wages. See: Vassilis K. Fouskas, 'Curing the UK inflation rate: investment, high labour productivity, high wages', *Open Access Government*, 25 January 2023, available at: www.openaccessgovernment.org.

11 The key account here is Costas Lapavitsas, *Profiting Without Producing*, London: Verso, 2013. For a review of this work, Vassilis K. Fouskas, 'Socialism in one country?', *The Political Quarterly*, 90(3), 2015, pp. 596-8.

12 For comparative data on inflation and wages, see: Alan Cafruny and Vassilis K. Fouskas, 'Ukraine, Europe and the re-routing of globalization,' *Journal of Balkan and Near Eastern Studies*, v.26, n.1, 2024, pp. 1-22..

13 For a comparison on the global political economies of the U.S and China, see: Vassilis K. Fouskas, Shampa Roy-Mukherjee, Qingan Huang and Ejike Udeogu, *China and the USA. Globalisation and the Decline of America's Supremacy*, London & New York: Palgrave, 2021.

14 Alan Cafruny and Ksenia Kirkham, 'EU "sovereignty" in global governance: the case of sanctions', in Leonid Grigoriev and Adrian Pabst (eds), *Global Governance in Transition: Challenges for International Cooperation*, New York: Springer, 2019.

15 See: Vassilis K. Fouskas and Bülent Gökay, *The Disintegration of Euro-Atlanticism and New Authoritarianism. Global Power-Shift*, New York: Palgrave, 2019, ch. 6.

16 Rhyannon Bartlett-Imadegawa, Mailys Pene-Lassus and Catherine De Beaurepaire, 'EU Struggles to Limit China's Involvement in Sensitive Tech Areas', *Nikkei Asia*, 11 October 2023; Mathew Pollet and John Hendel, 'The West is on a world tour Against Huawei', *Politico*, 28 November 2023, available at: www.politico.

17 However, lacking policy instruments other than its normative framework of regulations, the EU acts also at the level of nation state, such as in the semi-secret agreement between US-Netherlands-Japan further restricting the sales of chips and chipmaking to China; see: Alan Beattie, 'The EU will struggle to de-risk its trade with China', *Financial Times*, 2 February 2023.

18 Jens Kastner, 'China Belt and Road dreams fade in Germany's industrial heartland', *Financial Times*, 2 February 2023.
19 Euractiv, 'German Top Adviser Cautious About Possible WTO Case Against US', 3 October 2023, available at: www.euractiv.com
20 Adam Tooze seems to be close to this position in his 'Three ways to read the "deglobalization" debate', *Financial Times*, 30 January 2023.
21 See: Vassilis K. Fouskas and Shampa Roy-Mukherjee, 'Neoliberalism and ordoliberalism: One or two critiques?', *Critical Sociology*, 45(7-8), 2019, pp. 953-65. This is the introduction to a special issue of *Critical Sociology* on Germany's ordoliberal model.
22 World Bank, 'National Accounts Data On-line, 1960-2022', available at https://data.worldbank.org/indicator/NV.IND.MANF.ZS?locations=DE-FR.
23 'German-Central Europe supply chain – cluster report', IMF Country Report, No. 13/263, Washington: International Monetary Fund, 2013.
24 Julian Germain, 'Beyond 'geo-economics': advanced unevenness and the anatomy of German austerity', *European Journal of International Relations,* 24(3), 2017, pp.590-613.
25 See: US Treasury, 'Foreign exchange policies of major trading partners of the United States', Report to Congress, Washington DC: Office of International Affairs, 2016.
26 Martin Sandbu, 'Europe should worry but not panic over China', *Financial Times,* 30 September 2023.
27 Javier Blas, 'What Gas Crisis: Europe's Best Friend is also its Worst Enemy', *Bloomberg,* 29 August 2023.
28 Ben Aris, 'Energy crisis: Europe's industry shutting down', *BNE Intellinews,* 20 September 2022.
29 Amanda Rivkin, 'Controversial Ukrainian envoy leaves Berlin for Kyiv', *Deutsche-Welle,* 15 October 2022.
30 Myah Ward, 'Biden vows to shut down Nord Stream 2 if Russia invades', *Politico,* 7 February 2022.
31 Olaf Scholz, 'The global *zeitenwende*. How to avoid a new Cold War in a multi-polar era', *Foreign Affairs,* January-February 2023.
32 Gabriel Rinaldi, 'Merkel admits failures in defense policy', *Politico,* 7 December 2022. In her 7 December 2022 interview with *Die Zeit,* Merkel stated that 'The 2014 Minsk Agreement was an attempt to buy time for Ukraine. Ukraine used this time to become stronger, as you can see today … it was exactly what gave Ukraine the priceless time'. This perspective was then corroborated by Francois Hollande, as well as by Petro Poroshenko. Unless Merkel's 'confession' was an attempt to rehabilitate her reputation in the context of virulent pro-war sentiment and recriminations against all proponents of *Ostpolitik,* it effectively provides further dispositive evidence of the NATO's bad faith in dealing with Moscow.
33 J.A. Allen, 'NATO generals pledge troops to war against Russia, with nuclear weapons', *Then24,* 20 June 2022, available at: www.then24.com/.
34 'The quality of media reporting on the Ukraine war', Otto Brenner Stiftung, University of Mainz, 15 December 2022, available at: www.otto-brenner-stiftung.de.
35 Shane Harris, John Hudson, Missy Ryan and Michael Birnbaum, 'No conclusive evidence Russia is behind Nord Stream attack', *Washington Post,* 21 December 2022. Noting that the US 'is now the leading supplier of LNG to Europe, US Secretary of State Antony Blinken characterized the sabotage as 'a tremendous opportunity to once

and for all remove the dependence on Russian energy … and offers a tremendous strategic opportunity for years to come'.

36 'European industry pivots to US as Biden subsidy sends dangerous signal', *Financial Times*, 20 November 2022.

37 Guy Chazan and Patricia Nilsson, 'Germany confronts broken business model', *Financial Times,* 5 January 2022.

38 Melissa Eddy, 'VW Will Invest $193 Billion in Electric Cars and Software' *New York Times*, 15 March 2023.

39 Federal Republic of Germany, *Integrated Security for Germany: National Security Strategy*, Berlin: Federal Foreign Office, 14 June 2023.

40 Leila Abboud, 'Macron Says Climate Law Risks Fragmenting the West', *Financial Times*, 1 December 2022.

41 'In "systemic competition" with the USA', German Foreign Policy, 22 November 2022, available at: www.german-foreign-policy.com.

42 'China's auto positioning in the 2023 Russian market', *Silk Road Briefing*, Dezan Shira and Associates, 6 January 2023.

43 'Germany becoming a dysfunctional state', *Bild Am Sonntag*, 18 December 2022.

44 Daniel Hamilton and Joseph Quinlan, *The Transatlantic Economy 2023*, Washington: U.S. Chamber of Commerce, 2023, available at: https://transatlanticrelations.org/wp-content/uploads/2023/03/Transatlantic-Economy-Report-2023-Summary.pdf.

45 Guy Chazan, 'US and Germany to send armored fighting vehicles to Ukraine', *Financial Times,* 5 January 2023.

46 Patrick Wintour, 'No turning back: how the Ukraine war has profoundly changed the EU', *The Guardian,* 30 September 2023.

CLASS, STATE AND GEOPOLITICS: EXPLAINING ERDOĞAN'S TURKEY

EREN DUZGUN AND CAN CEMGIL

Perhaps no question concerning the Middle East and Europe today has been more loudly voiced than 'What is Turkey doing (yet again)?' And rightfully so. Once hailed by the liberal international community as a role model in its region, Turkey has become an increasingly 'unpredictable' and 'unintelligible' actor in the last ten years of the AKP's (Adalet ve Kalkınma Partisi, or Justice and Development Party) rule. For example, Turkey has been fighting against US-backed Kurdish forces in Syria and keeping Sweden at the gates of NATO while actively participating in several NATO missions and selling armed drones to Ukraine for use against the Russian invasion. It has been keeping the Turkish Straits shut to Russian military vessels as it also objects to US and NATO presence in the Black Sea, and at the same time procuring S-400 missile systems from Russia, all the while intending to act as a peace broker in the Ukrainian conflict. Besides pushing for regime change in Syria, it has been actively involved in the civil war in Libya and openly extended military support to Azerbaijan against Armenia while adopting – until very recently – an increasingly militaristic posture in the Eastern Mediterranean. If you ask President Recep Tayyip Erdoğan and his entourage, there is nothing surprising about any of this, for it is precisely what the 'new Turkey', as they like to call it, is about. Geopolitically speaking, they say the new Turkey is both a staunch NATO ally and an independent regional player struggling against Western imperialism. Economically, it is a fully functional market economy but one that thinks outside the box, implementing policies against western economic dogmas. Politically, it is an electoral democracy, if one with Turkish characteristics. For several critical commentators, however, whatever Erdoğan himself chooses to believe, Turkey now seems to be a textbook case for nationalist authoritarianism, economic irrationality, and geopolitical aggression.

In this essay, we will attempt to make sense of Erdoğan's new Turkey. We will argue that the new Turkey has been a product of a complex interplay of external and internal struggles; and indeed, what appear to be 'irrational' and 'incoherent' state policies have been vital to the reproduction of Erdoğan's rule at home and sway abroad. Classes and power-blocs, organized in and around the Turkish state, have developed historically specific strategies of reproduction and spatialization as a response to a set of internal and external challenges and opportunities, which have ultimately led to the seemingly contradictory bundle of policies associated with the new Turkey.

Undoubtedly, the most important external catalyst of Turkey's new round of activism in world politics has been the relative retreat of the US from the active hegemonic management of regional geopolitics. The repositioning of the US has created a power vacuum, leading to the rise of rival spatialization strategies in the region. Yet, the logic of new Turkey cannot be understood simply as an automated response to the pressures of an 'international system' (as often conceptualized from a structuralist-functionalist perspectives).[1] Instead, the new Turkey has been fuelled, at least in part, by the increasing intensity of the domestic crisis of governability. For one, on the political economy front, what has become crystal clear in the last decade is that with the downturn in the global economy and the draining of available credit channels, the AKP has found it increasingly difficult to muster electoral support and solve the heightening social contradictions at home through the financialized and rules-based forms of economic management, an inability that has loudly manifested itself since the Gezi Park uprising of 2013. Consequently, economic management has become more and more short-termist, arbitrary, and unaccountable – all in order to meet the government's immediate debt recycling requirements, the needs of an expansionary monetary policy, and electoral concerns. In addition, when economic incentives and imperatives have not been enough to mute social dissent and demands, the AKP has resorted not only to increasingly authoritarian measures to undermine existing constitutional political and civil rights but also to the excessive instrumentalization of foreign policy for domestic purposes. Most notably, the AKP saw the Arab Spring as an opportunity to redesign the region and bolster ailing popular support for the government at home. Turkey has pushed for regime change, armed insurgent groups, and become militarily involved in various conflict zones in its (extended) neighbourhood, most notably in Syria and Libya, in a desperate move to fill the power vacuum and hold up its domestic image as a regional superpower. While scoring easy geopolitical points seemed to have paid off for a time in terms of mustering domestic popular support, this activity has led to Turkey's increased diplomatic isolation within the Western alliance and the region, further undermining the already ailing economy. In short, the militarization of foreign policy and the 'randomization' of economic management have gone hand in hand as mutually reinforcing strategies of reproduction, contributing to AKP's survival in the past ten years.

This essay will proceed in three steps. We will first address the social and institutional transformations that marked Erdoğan's Turkey since the new millennium. In particular, we will contend that this period witnessed the consolidation of capitalist property relations in Turkey, resulting in the formulation of new methods of domestic governance and regional spatialization, that is, a bundle of domestic and external policies fashionably labelled as 'neo-Ottomanism'. Next, we will analyze the rise of authoritarian politics in the domestic sphere and then the progressive militarization of Turkish foreign policy by looking into the challenges to Erdoğan's rule at home and abroad. We will conclude by providing a summary as well as commenting on the future trajectory of Turkish foreign policy.

CONSOLIDATION OF CAPITALIST MODERNITY IN TURKEY

Erdoğan's AKP came to power in the aftermath of the 2001 economic crisis. The crisis was so severe that the political parties of the 1990s were completely crushed in the 2002 elections, pushing big business to the margins of future power arrangements as well as threatening the dominant role of the Kemalist military and judicial elites in statecraft. In this sense, the election of the AKP with a strong parliamentary majority signalled the breaking down of the power bloc that had ruled Turkey since the 1960s. The constitutive actor in the old power-bloc was a class of big industrial capitalists. Between 1960 and 1980, they made easy profits behind high tariff walls under the conditions of import substitution. Following the military coup of 1980, the junta and the successive political parties that came to power initiated a process of neoliberal restructuring, aiming to promote export-competitiveness; yet this process remained incomplete, partly because the big capitalists undermined it. Throughout the 1980s and 1990s, the social reproduction of the big capitalists, in spite of their rhetorical support for structural reforms, remained largely dependent on the state's systematic transfer of monopoly and financial rents. Most of their profits were obtained through the financial activities associated with the holding of government securities.[2] Likewise, due to their immense resources and political links to the Kemalist bureaucracy, the bulk of export subsidies were still received by large holding companies with almost no export potential and who did not have to compete to survive.[3] Furthermore, the pace of the privatization of state-owned enterprises (SOEs) was very slow until the 2000s, in part due to the unwillingness of large businesses to buy into the privatization process, and their opposition to the sale of SOEs to foreign competitors. In short, industrialists represented an 'infant' capitalist class whose very presence became an impediment to the further development of capitalism in Turkey. In this context, Kemalist secularism and nationalism were deployed to provide a sense of unity and an ethos of conduct among the business and bureaucratic elite, while being used to keep the gates of the state and economy closed to potential contenders. Given the continuing centrality of the state in the social reproduction of the dominant power bloc, any attempt at widening the 'nation' and 'religion' beyond its previously designated boundaries would endanger the foundations of capitalist modernity in Turkey.[4]

There were, of course, contenders to the Kemalist regime of reproduction. While all working-class organizations were brutally suppressed by the 1980 junta, Islamists, who were initially promoted by Kemalist elites as a bulwark against communism, turned into the most formidable actors against the prevailing forms of property and political subjectivity in the 1990s. Islamists were supported by a class of underprivileged capitalists in Anatolian towns. This was a new capitalist class excluded from the official credit channels and business privileges enjoyed by the old elite. Its exclusion from state-generated rents forced it to envision a type of society in which economic competitiveness, underlined by a specific politico-religious subjectivity, would be the ultimate basis for societal reproduction. In their vision, overcoming 'injustice' and 'poverty' was intrinsically linked to the deepening of market competition and 'moral mobilization' against the relations of an 'oligarchic' and 'anarchic' capitalism. In this respect, they considered a transformation away from Kemalist secularism vital to the restructuring of both the state and economy. 'Production mobilization' was possible only if a spiritual transformation could be achieved and the old transnational Muslim community (umma), 'uncorrupted' by Western influences, could be recovered. The umma would replace 'Western-imposed' rights and duties in society with religiously sanctioned networks of trust and solidarity. This new sociality and morality would not only ensure free competition, productivity, and loyalty, but also provide a space wherein Western-imposed social differences such as nation and race are transcended. Transforming the Kemalist understanding of secularism therefore was not about asserting a new interpretation of religion only, but reconstructing the regime of property and ethnicity based on socio-intellectual resources untroubled by the legacy of Kemalism.[5]

Against this new vision of capitalism from 'below', the Kemalist political and economic elites increasingly securitized the principle of secularism to safeguard their economic and political privileges. Understandably so, for Islamists excelled at mobilizing the urban poor as well as the class of underprivileged capitalists to muster electoral support, ultimately becoming the first-placed party in 1995 elections. In a context where winning votes through union-based working-class populism was no longer feasible, and redistributive policies were associated with inflation and unemployment, the left was increasingly crippled in its ability to deliver anything substantial to the urban poor, whose numbers had grown tremendously since the 1980s. By contrast, the Islamists, organized in the Welfare Party (Refah Partisi, RP) of the 1990s, offered a way out of the existing system by invoking a world wherein the secular privileges that sustain the Kemalist political economy are destroyed. In its quest for power against the Kemalist political and economic elite, the Welfare Party derived from Islam the structure of a fully capitalist society, that is, one that recognizes no secular privilege for property and links economic development and the welfare of the poor to the 'improvement' of property. That said, in 1997 against what they called 'rising Islamic fundamentalism', the Kemalist military elite intervened once again, removing Islamists from government through a 'soft coup'.

Yet, the Islamists, forced out of the government in 1997, reseized it in 2002 with a brand-new party, the AKP, established only 19 months before the elections and with a new leader, Recep Tayyip Erdoğan. Initially, Erdoğan faced the same hurdles encountered by his Islamist predecessors. He had no support from the military and civil bureaucracy, nor did he enjoy strong backing from relatively well-established fractions of the capitalist class. In this context, Erdoğan adopted policies to widen his domestic and international support. Unlike earlier Islamists, the AKP leadership represented themselves as Western-friendly modernizers and reformers, not least to ward off any intervention from the Kemalist military-bureaucratic-judicial elite. Treading warily, it sought to secure American and European support as a counterweight to the challenge from the institutional establishment. The AKP adopted European Union membership as a strategic objective, improved relations with the US and Israel, continued economic growth enabled by a global expansion of credit, employed a relatively more liberal discourse in relation to minorities and dissenting voices (more on this below), and curbed the influence of the military on government. Although publicized widely at the time as 'Europeanization', this was more a survival and consolidation strategy in the face of the challenge the AKP felt and feared from the extant military-bureaucratic-judicial state elite and the more established sections of the big capitalists.[6]

Meanwhile, the AKP also took several measures to create a broad social base that would support the expansion and deepening of capitalist social relations. The Islamic capitalist class became the supporter of structural reforms implemented by the AKP, helping to consolidate the reform process and ensure its irreversibility. In turn, the AKP provided various incentives to the Islamic capitalists, reversing their unfavourable treatment in public contracts and privatization bids, leading to their further enrichment and internationalization. With the AKP and Islamic capitalists converging on an anti-monopolist agenda, the more established fraction of big capitalists were to make strategic compromises to the Islamic capitalists concerning the political and institutional structure of the economy. Forced by the new configuration of political power, and encouraged by the prospects for economic expansion under a single-party government and European Union membership, the large conglomerates ceded their resistance to structural reform, which has enabled them to become the main beneficiaries of state investment incentives and privatization processes since 2002.[7]

Relatedly, the period under AKP rule has witnessed massive privatizations and the implementation of measures designed to shield economic decision-making from popular measures and party politics, such as the creation of 'independent' economic institutions like the Central Bank, the Competition Board, and the Privatization Administration. Furthermore, the introduction of banking reforms and the deregulation of the energy and telecommunication sectors has reinforced the tendency toward subjecting the private sector to the rules of competition in an increasingly internationalizing market. Until the early 2010s, the 'independence' of economic decision-making was propped up by favourable credit conditions worldwide. Global liquidity eased the socio-economic costs of restructuring at home and helped finance the chronic capital account deficit, the credit requirements of the private sector and households without having to interfere with the autonomy of 'independent' institutions. While this eventually caused the national debt to skyrocket, it also ensured the acceptability and 'neutrality' of market outcomes. This global liquidity helped, at least for a while, to reproduce the impersonal, depoliticized and rule-based appearance of the markets, hence signalling the qualitative transformation of state–business relations under AKP rule.

On the whole, such a sociopolitical restructuring marked the radical reorganization of the private sector; that is, a departure from the previous pattern of accumulation based on the redistribution of profits through the state toward a mode of accumulation based on expanding production through increasing international competitiveness.[8] A historically specific political economy was emerging which, despite the continuity of corruption and extensive use of political power for personal economic advantage, is ultimately premised on the ability of public and private powers to achieve material reproduction through the world market and on the capacity to reproduce the fiction of self-regulating markets. Equally important, despite the growing insecurity and flexibility of labour, considerable increases in welfare spending weakened opposition to neoliberal policies, hence facilitating the deepening of capitalist social relations. For example, according to the World Bank, the number of citizens living at or under the poverty threshold in Turkey (US$5.50 a day) has decreased from 31.8 per cent of the population in 2002 to 9.9 per cent in 2016.[9] Therefore, while welfare and cheap sources of finance lifted the poor out of the worst forms of poverty, this success was made possible only by linking the welfare of the poor to their acceptance of the logic of workfare, charity, credit-dependence, and the discipline of capitalist accumulation.

The overall result is a consolidation of capitalist social relations, one that is unprecedented in Turkish history. In this context, given that economic competition and compulsion has become the main determinant for the social reproduction of all echelons of society (the capitalist class included), one may expect, following the conventional liberal creed, that cultural, religious and political hierarchies of the previous period would lose their centrality in the production and distribution of socioeconomic power and, concomitantly, a separate political arena in which subjects enjoy wider democratic rights would emerge and expand. The point here is, clearly, not that the more there is capitalism the more there is democracy; or even that capitalism is necessarily less authoritarian than other modes of socio-economic organization. Capitalism can and has been historically compatible with different forms of political rule and labour control, such as fascism and coerced wage labour, as well as limited forms of democracy such as liberal democracy. Yet, the opposite is also very much true: as capitalism effectively denies any rights of participation in decisions related to the organization of production, thereby shielding itself from any kind of democratic accountability in the workplace as well as in the institutionally and formally separated 'economic sphere', it may also create a wider space of citizen involvement in which political and cultural rights can be exercised without overstepping the productive use of property. Hence capitalism's possible, yet not necessary, contingent, and tangled congruity with the requirements of a liberal form of democracy.[10]

Indeed, the very trajectory of the AKP rule since 2002 has confirmed how quickly the prospect of capitalist democracy can vanish, to be replaced by capitalist authoritarianism. The 2000s have witnessed perhaps the most revolutionary political and cultural changes ever made in the history of the

Turkish Republic. The dominance of the Kemalist bureaucracy in key state institutions has been eliminated, as have the economic privileges enjoyed by army-run corporations. Most military spending has been made subject to review by civil auditors. Constitutional amendments have been passed to increase parliamentary control over the system of appointments to the high courts. The decisions taken by the Supreme Military Council, the body with authority over promotions and dismissals in the army, have been opened to judicial and parliamentary review, which had not been possible previously.

It is important to point out that none of this would have been possible without the assistance of an Islamist network known as the Gülenists. Although active since the 1970s, this Islamic cult, led by a US-based preacher, Fettullah Gülen, has had a formidable presence in the police, judiciary, education, military, and media since the 2000s. Between 2007 and 2011, the Gülenists entrenched in the police and judiciary system initiated a series of anti-coup investigations against (mostly) Kemalist-minded high-ranking military staff, politicians, civil society actors and journalists, which not only led to their detention for years on fake charges, but also enabled the AKP government to consolidate fully its power within the state and civil society.

Considering the 'success' of the AKP–Gülen alliance in transforming the state and civil society, it is no wonder that the main parameters of Kemalist modernity have been opened to public debate. Secularism has been largely overhauled, as the AKP cadres and Islamic intellectuals have reinterpreted secularism away from the French-inspired Kemalist laïcité toward the Anglo-Saxon model, where secularism is understood not as 'freedom from religion' but 'freedom of religion'. Headscarf bans in universities and the civil service have been lifted. Discrimination against religious school students in the university entrance exam, in effect since 1997, has ended. Additional religion-based courses have been added to secular public school curricula. In a similar fashion, the dominant conception of nation seems to have gone through a drastic change, as the AKP initiated a 'peace process' with the aim of resolving the longstanding 'Kurdish question'. Indeed, in April 2013, negotiations with the PKK (Partiya Karkerên Kurdistanê, Kurdistan Workers' Party) came to the brink of a historic peace deal aiming to secure the disarmament of the PKK in exchange for the wider recognition of Kurds' political and collective rights. Certainly, this is not meant to disregard the authoritarian tendencies already apparent in the first decade of the AKP's rule. These were evident, most notably in the police brutality deployed against workers who opposed privatizations and in the use of judicial measures to eliminate bureaucrats with Kemalist inclinations. Still, the so-called 'democratic openings' initiated by the AKP during this period created expectations amongst the liberal intelligentsia, the Kurdish minority, and even some segments of the left that it would radically redefine the main parameters of the past, nurturing a new subjectivity and a more inclusive collectivity as the foundation of a new political economy.

The initial expectation from such a restructuring of state–society relations was a form of Islamic multiculturalism, inspired by a romanticized Ottoman imperial pluralism and encouraged by the accession process to the European Union. Islamic values and old imperial forms of rule were reformulated to prepare the ground for a form of liberalism, which sought to promote new forms of political community and subjectivity. This involved the creation of a new citizenship ethic largely derived from narratives based on the prophet Muhammad's life, especially with regard to his 'tolerance' for minorities and the fact that he was a merchant. Koranic verses were transformed into slogans that provide the moral basis for 'economic competition' and fairness of market outcomes. 'Tolerance', 'fairness', and 'economic competition' were all related to a community where subjects internalize a capitalist competition ethic and some liberal democratic values based on a narrative of peaceful social coexistence derived from an imagined Ottoman-Islamic past.[11] It is this discursive ground on which a shift occurred, at least for a while, from the monolithically understood political space toward a new collective subjectivity based on the peaceful coexistence of different ethno-religious and cultural groups, which some commentators called a new 'Ottoman commonwealth'.

The Ottoman commonwealth was not only a domestic reproduction strategy, but also part of an attempt at regional re-spatialization with the blessing of the US, which generated serious implications on Turkey's foreign policy orientation. That involved the emergence of a 'trading state', which sought to unburden itself from the costs of the most chronic issues in Turkey's international affairs by promoting economic and cultural integration in the old Ottoman geography while respecting the existing political boundaries, a policy fashionably labeled as 'neo-Ottomanism'. This was made possible by Turkey's positioning in the Middle East as a US partner, continuing economic growth, and the search for new markets, as well as the reluctance of the US to engage itself with the Middle East militarily. Until the early 2010s, therefore, Turkey pursued a 'zero problems with neighbours' policy, and in doing so, it amplified its soft power in the Balkans, the Middle East, Central Asia, and Africa by increasing its economic engagement, providing developmental assistance, and acting as an impartial broker for such thorny regional disputes as Iranian nuclear proliferation and the Israel–Palestine conflict. The AKP's foreign policy activism by and large conformed to the expectations of the Western alliance, playing the role of 'a benign regional power' and 'a good citizen of the liberal order'.[12]

The AKP's initial approach to governance, both at home and abroad, was predicated on the development and reproduction of a historically specific political economy and subjectivity. Domestically, rights were tolerated only insofar as they did not disrupt the reproduction of this new mode of life, which was itself conditioned on the availability of global liquidity and successful competition in the global marketplace. Modes of life, inspired by past or alternative experiences, can be tolerated only if they are assimilated into capitalist values and subordinated to the requirements of capitalist competition. Needless to say, behaviours, thoughts and habits rooted elsewhere, say in the early Kemalist project, in the institutions and constitution of 1961, or in the dream of an 'eco-socialist' Kurdistan, sit uneasily with the idea of Islamic multiculturalism. And, considering that capitalist social relations are being consolidated in such a globally competitive and geo-politically fragile context, perhaps there has been only a little room for even temporary toleration of these radically different forms of sociality. From this angle, it is hardly surprising that over the last decade, the AKP's initial approach to governance, both at home and abroad, has undergone a significant shift. Neo-Ottoman commonwealth has lost much of its earlier connotations, turning into an increasingly authoritarian and militarized strategy of reproduction. This is the subject of the remainder of this essay.

FROM NEO-OTTOMAN COMMONWEALTH TO CAPITALIST AUTHORITARIANISM

By 2013, Erdoğan's AKP continued to command extensive popular support, already having secured half of all votes in the 2011 general elections. Besides, it also enjoyed broad support from big capital including its nascent capitalist base in the construction and energy sectors, popularity in the proverbial 'Arab street', tolerance and active backing in Western capitals, and the appreciation of global finance capital, culminating in the upgrading of Turkey's sovereign credit rating to investment grade and pushing interest rates as low as 4.5 per cent in May 2013, a record low in Turkey's recent history.

It became clear less than a month later, however, that all of this was nothing but a house of cards when the mass protests around Istanbul's Gezi Park shook the country. Erdoğan's redevelopment plans in Gezi Park, involving the rebuilding of an Ottoman era military barracks as part of a residential and commercial complex, and the response of security forces to a handful of protestors, instigated one of the largest protest movements in the history of the Republic. The outbreak of the Gezi protests, when

Erdoğan's rule was in its prime, demonstrated the fragility of the AKP's purported democratization, prosperity, and peace project. The authoritarian undercurrent, which time and again had surfaced in suppressing dissent, disciplining labour and attempting to engineer the sociocultural life of the country in the first ten years of the AKP's rule, popped up strikingly in the context of the Gezi protests. Perceiving the Gezi protests as a coup attempt, along the same lines as those that brought down Mohammad Morsi's Muslim Brotherhood in Egypt, the AKP violently repressed the demonstrations, foreshadowing the later shows of state brutality and authoritarianism that were to characterize the upcoming years.[13]

Putting events in a chronological order, 2013 also saw the tightening by the US Federal Reserve of the global supply of credit, on which Turkish growth, particularly in the construction sector, was dependent. Simultaneously, the alliance between the AKP and the Gülenists ended in 2013. Having disagreed over issues related to the control of the state, education and foreign policy, both parties increasingly drifted apart, culminating in the 17-25 December 2013 corruption investigations against members of the cabinet and Erdoğan's family. In June 2015, Erdoğan's AKP failed for the first time in 13 years to secure a parliamentary majority to form the government. Meanwhile, Turkey's involvement in the Syrian Civil War deepened, costing the country its fragile peace process with the PKK and its allies in Syria. The PKK's Syrian affiliate, the PYD (Partiya Yekîtiya Demokrat, Democratic Union Party), rejected Turkey's proposal that it join ranks with the so-called Free Syrian Army (FSA) against Assad, citing the FSA's ethnic identification of the movement as an Arab one. The consequent split resulted in the collapse of the Kurdish peace process in the summer of 2015, followed by six months of urban warfare in southeastern towns in Turkey. In June 2016, the continuing conflict with the Gülenists culminated in a military coup attempt that marked the beginning of a new phase of authoritarianism. Describing the coup attempt as a 'gift from God', Erdoğan suppressed the putsch attempt and declared a two-year-long countrywide state of emergency, which he used not only to cleanse the state of the Gülenists, but also as an excuse to stifle all opposition to his increasingly authoritarian rule. In this context, Erdoğan turned to nationalist extremists for support both in party politics and, significantly, within the institutional complex of the state. This contributed to the formation of a power bloc that has a staunch anti-Kurdish and anti-democratic orientation at home and abroad.[14]

Testament to this are not only the thousands of political activists, dissident students, investigative journalists and radical academics who have faced police violence, imprisonment and losing their jobs since 2013. Erdoğan has also, on a daily basis, been intimidating the supporters of even the most 'ordinary' centre and centre-left political parties by accusing them of treason, terrorism, cooperation with imperialism and the like. Furthermore, the electoral rights of a significant portion of the Kurdish population have been tacitly yet effectively cancelled, as the government removed from power almost all of the democratically elected mayors of the Peoples' Democratic Party (Halkların Demokratik Partisi, HDP), whose electoral base is largely Kurdish, on terrorism charges. Through systematic prosecutions and harassment campaigns against dissenting voices, the AKP has considerably limited civil liberties and freedom of expression while invoking monolithic conceptions of the nation.

On the economic front, especially after 2010, the AKP has increasingly perceived the 'independence' of 'independent' economic and juridical institutions such as the Central Bank and the Constitutional Court more as a problem than a solution to its domestic and international woes, regularly intervening in the election of their board members.[15] With the downturn in the global economy and the concomitant draining of available credit channels, the AKP is no longer able to solve the heightening social contradictions through financialized, impersonal and rule-based forms of economic management. The shift in power, from the longstanding parliamentary system to a centralized Russian-style presidential one in 2018, has helped to consolidate this new trend, further centralizing and personalizing the processes of economic decision-making.[16] With the removal of checks and balances on the president's power, economic management has become more and more short-termist, arbitrary and unaccountable, all to meet the needs of an expansionary monetary policy and electoral concerns. The lack of a clear and consistent economic strategy has made economic management look increasingly random, leading to currency crisis, inflation and widespread poverty. As a result, 'official' annual inflation increased from 8.6 per cent in 2004 to over 60 per cent in October 2023, while a group of independent economists declared the annual inflation rate to have reached over 126 per cent as of end of October 2023. The Turkish lira has been almost in freefall since 2018. The US dollar–Turkish lira exchange rate was roughly 3.5 liras per dollar in 2017, but it increased to almost 29 in July 2023, despite the desperate measures of the Erdoğan administration to hold it steady through foreign exchange protected deposits and direct and back-channel interventions into foreign exchange markets. GDP per capita decreased from US$12,600 in 2013 to $8,500 in 2020, with a slight bounce back in 2021 and 2022 to $9,661 and $10,616 at the expense of massive levels of inequality and poverty.[17] All this is not to say, however, that the Erdoğan administration was unaware of what they were doing.

GEOPOLITICAL ADVENTURISM AS A REPRODUCTIVE STRATEGY AT HOME AND ABROAD

In fact, the randomization of AKP's economic policy has also been fuelled by the militarization of its foreign policy and vice versa. Over the last decade, as 'soft power' has lost most of its relevance, neo-Ottomanism has turned to an increasingly assertive foreign policy strategy. Empowered by a rapidly growing indigenous arms industry, the AKP cadres saw the Arab Spring as an opportunity to improve Turkey's geopolitical standing and prop up the ailing popular support to the government at home. Yet, the drive to surf the Arab Spring on its own particularly in Syria, without the blessing of the US, resulted in the isolation of the country.

Syria has been the most important theatre of Turkey's geopolitical adventurism. Here, the bone of contention has been the US-backed Kurdish YPG (Yekîneyên Parastina Gel, People's Defence Units), an organization that has deep connections to the Turkey-based PKK. The PKK has been waging a guerrilla war against Turkey since the 1980s, and while it is considered a terrorist organization by the US and the EU, the YPG is not. The US has partnered with and provided financial and military support to the YPG in an effort to fight ISIS (Islamic State of Iraq and the Levant) and limit Russian and Iranian influence in the region. Turkey has been adamantly opposed to the US backing of the YPG, raising 'existential' security concerns. It has pressed for the formation of a 30 km deep 'buffer' zone along its 800 km border with Syria to protect its borders from the claimed risk of YPG attacks and to resettle Syrians who have been displaced by the conflict.

Whether or not one agrees with the AKP's security concerns, it is far from clear how the proposed solution, of establishing an 800 km long and 30 km deep 'buffer zone', can improve Turkey's security, let alone the near impossibility of effectively securing such a long corridor. Also, there are huge question marks concerning the logistics of how to resettle and provide millions of displaced Syrians their most basic needs (food, water, and jobs) in an economically sustainable way. Moreover, the buffer zone de facto shifts the Turkish border into Syrian territory, hence not necessarily protecting the lives of Turkish soldiers. From this angle, the proposed buffer zone looks to be much less about Turkey's security per se and much more about undermining any political status for Kurds, scoring geopolitical points for domestic consumption, as well as obtaining geopolitical bargaining chips that can be used in future rounds of international negotiations for Syria.

Regardless of these logical objections, Turkey has carried out four major cross-border operations into Syria since 2016. The first incursion was ostensibly to uproot ISIS from its border regions around Jarablus and Al Bab, while simultaneously preventing the YPG-led Syrian Democratic Forces (SDF) from extending the reach of its territorial control with US support. Greenlit by the US, the operation gave Turkey a foothold in Syria, while simultaneously cutting off the expanding SDF-controlled areas in the northeast from the westernmost Afrin canton. Due to the disillusionment with the US and making use of the opportunity arising from a lack of US involvement in the Middle East that had continued well into the Trump administration, Turkey has been engaging with Russia and Iran in what is called the Astana Process since 2017, setting up military posts in Idlib to oversee the demilitarization of the region and the de-escalation of the civil war.

With its newfound confidence, the Erdoğan administration launched another incursion into Kurdish controlled Afrin in the northwest of Syria, taking control of this town as well. This operation did not provoke a strong reaction from either the US and its European allies or from Russia and Iran. Yet, US officials, and not least President Trump himself, made it clear to Turkey that a similar operation in Manbij would not be acceptable. Gauging the likely ire of the US in particular, the Erdoğan administration made the assessment that it could not at that stage further flex its military muscles. In 2019, however, as Trump ordered the withdrawal of US troops from Syria except for a small presence in a handful of bases, Turkey launched a new operation, this time taking control of border regions extending from Tall Abyad to Ras al-Ayn, while both the US and Russia sought to contain the scope of the operation. Turkey's broader longstanding strategy of reproduction has involved a form of 'geopolitical rentierism',[18] that is, attempts to play major powers off against one another by making use of its geostrategic position. But this new military activism had a novel dimension. It was much more daring for Turkey compared to its historical predecessors in that direct military confrontation with both Russia and the US was an immediate possibility.

While such unilateral geopolitical manoeuvres seemed to have paid off for some time in terms of amplifying Erdoğan's political grandeur at home and mustering domestic popular support, they also led to Turkey's increased diplomatic isolation within the Western alliance and the region, instigating the emergence of rival regional strategies. Most notably, Greece, frightened and emboldened by the increasingly assertive and unilateral moves of its eastern neighbour, has successfully internationalized the long-standing bilateral issues over the Eastern Mediterranean, including the exclusive economic zones (EEZs), gas extraction rights, territorial waters as well as control of corresponding air spaces, and the future of the divided island of Cyprus, culminating in the formation of international alliances in the region against Turkey.

There have been long-standing disputes concerning sea and air space borders between Turkey and Greece. Due to the unsettled nature of these borders, both sides have traditionally accused each other of violating their sovereignty, which has brought them to the brink of war at least four times since the 1970s. On the one hand, Greece has traditionally had maximalist claims in terms of territorial waters and airspace in the Aegean Sea and the delimitation of exclusive economic zones (EEZs) in the Eastern Mediterranean, which together raises the fear on the Turkish side that Turkey's access to international seas will be blocked. On the other hand, Turkey's intervention in the Libyan civil war in 2019 and the subsequent announcement of an equally maximalist maritime delimitation agreement between Turkey and Libya has escalated geopolitical tensions in the Eastern Mediterranean to a completely different level.

Turkish-Greek relations deteriorated over the mid-2010s as Greece and Cyprus bilaterally concluded EEZ delimitation agreements with states with which Turkey's relations had soured since the Arab Spring, most notably Egypt and Israel. These agreements led them to sign a multi-billion pipeline project that was meant to ship gas from Israel and Egypt to Europe through a pipeline running via Cyprus and Greece, a project that bypassed the Turkish mainland, the shortest and cheapest route to European markets. Turkey's increasing sense of isolation led the country to use military deterrence in enforcing control of its self-declared EEZ, including one for the so-called 'Turkish Republic of Northern Cyprus'.

In response to its isolation in the Eastern Mediterranean, in early 2020, Turkey threw its weight behind the internationally recognized interim government of Libya (Government of National Accord, or GNA) against the forces of Khalifa Haftar (Libyan National Army, or LNA). While the GNA was established and recognized through a UN initiative and nominally supported by the US, UK, Italy and other Western powers against the French, Russian, Greek, Egyptian and UAE (United Arab Emirates) backed LNA, no concrete support was extended to the GNA by these Western allies. It was through strongly backing the GNA that Turkey changed the fate of the war, particularly by delivering the control of Libya's airspace to the GNA and actively transporting and coordinating a supply of battle-hardened Syrian rebel militants to the GNA forces on the ground.[19] The change of tides in the Libyan civil war in favour of the GNA allowed Turkey to conclude an EEZ agreement with Libya that effectively cut off the planned Eastern Mediterranean pipeline that was set to bypass the Turkish mainland, much to the chagrin of France and Greece.[20] Turkey has consequently claimed a huge chunk of the Eastern Mediterranean as its new 'Blue Homeland', an officially proclaimed and legally dubious doctrine that gives Turkey energy exploration rights in very close proximity to even large Greek islands such as Crete. In return, against what it sees as Turkish encroachments on its sovereignty, Greece has signed bilateral defence agreements with France and the United States.

France has long been disturbed by the rise of Turkey as a contending economic and military player in Libya and sub-Saharan Africa. As a result of the Franco-Greek defence deal (2021), France has promised to come to the aid of Greece in the event of an 'external' threat (even if the 'aggressor' is a NATO member), and Greece is in the process of obtaining highly advanced Rafale fighter jets and battleships from France, which the Turkish air force and navy can barely match.

What is more, the Turkish-US stalemate in Syria raises the suspicion that the US has become reluctant to maintain the balance of power, which it has traditionally upheld between Turkey and Greece since the beginning of the Cold War. For one, while opening new US bases in Greece and upgrading Greek F-16 fighter jets, the US has been holding off on providing support to Turkey in modernizing its air force. This poses a major problem for the Turkish ruling elites, given that a substantial portion of the Turkish F-16 fleet is nearing the end of its operational lifespan, and Turkey's quest for an alternative jet fighter has yet to yield any results. Turkey is actively engaged in the development of a domestic jet fighter, but even under the most optimistic scenarios, this new aircraft is not expected to achieve full operational capability until the mid-2030s. Likewise, unable to modernize its F-16s, Turkey has recently shifted its focus to Europe for the acquisition of Eurofighter jets. However, this move is highly unlikely to materialize due to Germany's serious reservations concerning Turkey's democratic and geopolitical credentials.

Furthermore, following the Greek prime minister's visit to Washington in May 2022, the US seems very likely to greenlight the sale of F-35 stealth fighter jets to Greece, whereas it removed Turkey from the F-35 co-production program after Turkey purchased Russian S-400 missile systems. Should Greece obtain F-35s, it will acquire critical abilities to strike deep into Anatolia without the chance of detection by Turkish radar systems, a massive game-changer that would tip the balance of airpower between the two NATO rivals across the Aegean Sea. Because the nations share only a relatively short and mountainous land border, the Turkish military's numerical superiority in land forces is much less important than air and naval capabilities. Furthermore, another growing fear in the Turkish ruling class circles is that the US-Greek rapprochement could undermine Turkey's strategic importance, and that new US bases in Greece can serve as an alternative to the Incirlik airbase in Turkey, which has been critical for NATO operations in the Middle East (and which Erdoğan mused about shutting down). Of course, the possibility of war between two NATO members has been historically slim. Yet, at least until very recently, Athens's successful diplomatic alliances gave it less motive to seek a compromise with Turkey, and amidst a plethora of pressing issues with Ankara, it has not been clear to what extent the US has been willing to continue to act as the peacekeeper in the region.

Of course, none of this is to suggest that Turkey has experienced a complete shift in its geopolitical orientation. While growing critical of the West, it is important to remember that Turkey also shot down a Russian jet fighter in 2015 for violating its airspace, and although Turkey and Russia have since repaired their strained relations, they have been supporting opposing sides in Syria and Libya, engaging in a regional rivalry, as well as cooperating to undermine the existing liberal international order. Furthermore, Turkey has upset the power balance in the South Caucasus – an area which Russia likes to see as its own geopolitical backyard – through its unconditional support for Azerbaijan in its conflict against Armenia over Nagorno-Karabakh. Besides ethnic ties, Turkey has shown geopolitical interests in Azerbaijan since the end of the Cold War. Although Turkey's direct involvement in the 2020 Azerbaijani-Armenian war was limited, its help in terms of military planning and tactics as well as the supply of armed drones led Azerbaijan to emerge victorious from the war. Russia, in return stopped backing Armenia, and allowed Azerbaijan to fully take over Nagorno-Karabakh in 2023 due to a perceived Armenian 'flirtation' with NATO.[21] In this sense, Turkey's support for Azerbaijan had as much to do with balancing Russia and Iran in the region as it was economic interests, and its position was broadly shared, if not openly espoused, by Israel and the United States.

In summary, Turkey's recent military activism is as much due to the erosion of the hegemonic US-led liberal international order as it is due to the faltering popular support for the Erdoğan administration. In the absence of a set of common norms enforced by a hegemonic bloc, Turkey has asserted itself militarily within its region. At the same time, Turkey's military assertiveness, alongside the randomization of its economic policy, has contributed to the hold of the Erdoğan administration over a core electorate as a counter to the weakening of the AKP's wider popular support. Militarization of Turkish foreign policy and the randomization and short-termism of its economic policy have gone hand in hand, forming the basis of the reproductive strategies that have kept Erdoğan in power in the past ten years.[22]

POST-ELECTION TURKEY: TURNING THE PAGE?

Overall, then, since the last decade the classes organized in and around the AKP have carried out a form of geopolitical and economic brinkmanship to reproduce themselves politically. Erdoğan did everything at his disposal economically to remain in power. These included years of unorthodox policies, which, beneficial as they may have been in the short run, brought the country to the brink of economic crisis by the time of the presidential and parliamentary elections in May 2023. Despite causing record-breaking inflation, however, these unorthodox policies also helped Erdoğan beat the odds and win the elections once again, much to the dismay of his opponents. Yet now that the elections are over, the end of Erdoğan's economic brinkmanship has been signalled. Less than a week after his re-election, Erdoğan appointed orthodox technocrats trusted by international investors to the top management positions of the Turkish economy, including the ministers for Finance and the Treasury and the Governor of the Central Bank. While these moves hint at a degree of change in the direction of economic policy-making, they reflect more the chokehold facing Turkey's current growth strategy than the mere 'rationalization' or 'normalization' cherished by financial markets.[23] These changes in economic management and policies are yet to produce a major U-turn, as the economic strategy is still based on an inflationary model that delivers growth and boosts profit at the expense of workers and in the context of still record levels of negative real interest rate despite hikes in policy rates.[24]

Geopolitically, for the past decade the Erdoğan administration has been able to overplay its hand relatively successfully, as the US in Syria and the Eastern Mediterranean, and Russia in Syria, Azerbaijan and Libya, have not been willing to confront Turkey head on. This has enabled the Erdoğan administration to punch, at times, above its weight. Erdoğan has known when to stop or step back in the face of a more determined stance from these rival partners, such as in Syria or in Eastern Mediterranean, or in the face of a failure of deterrence as observed very recently in Turkey's attempts at resetting relations with Israel and Greece. Likewise, as soon as the Erdoğan administration declared electoral victory, it took steps to break

Turkey's international isolation through a re-pivot toward the West and formerly alienated Middle Eastern states such as Saudi Arabia, UAE, Egypt and Israel. Partly rooted in the urgent need to finance its record-breaking current account deficit, the Erdoğan administration has declared a renewed interest in the revival of Turkey's EU accession process, the revision of the Customs Union agreement and visa-free travel for Turkish citizens in the Schengen Area. As well, Turkey has publicly supported Ukraine's membership of NATO, released Ukrainian Azov commanders (to the ire of Russia), greenlit Sweden's NATO membership, and initiated the restoration of relations with Egypt.

Erdoğan seems well aware that the actual and potential costs of Turkey's geopolitical adventurism begin to massively outweigh its political and economic benefits. Yet, it is not clear to what extent Erdoğan and his entourage are ready to go through with a complete overhaul of their foreign policy options. Undoubtedly, the litmus test in this regard will be the AKP's stance on the Kurdish question. On the one hand, the AKP cadres can perpetuate their self-deceiving and self-defeating nationalism by continuing the never-ending war against the PKK and YPG. While this may bring some easy territorial gains in Syria as well as help the AKP remain in power by consolidating nationalist voters, it will also put extra strain on Turkish-US relations, further undermining Turkey's economic and security interests. Moreover, although the war in Ukraine seems to have reminded the West of the geopolitical significance of Turkey, and while Turkey has been trying to mend ties with regional rivals such as Israel, Egypt and Greece, two things should not be forgotten. First, Turkey's charm offensive in the Middle East and Europe has yet to produce any tangible outcome. And second, the persistence of overconfident and short-term foreign policy decisions will sooner or later lead to Turkey's further diplomatic isolation while further weakening an already ailing economy, thereby aggravating the authoritarianism and randomization of Erdoğan's regime at home.

On the other hand, Turkish policy makers could choose to take a radically different path: they could end the 40-year-long war with the Kurds. They could recognize the new international realities on the ground and initiate another peace process to solve the 'Kurdish question' – something tried between 2013 and 2015, but which collapsed as a result of a series of road bumps encountered in the process.[25] If Turkey manages to demilitarize its own Kurdish issue, this will help moderate the PYD's view of Turkey, as well as normalize Turkey's relations with the US and the West in general. Normalizing relations with the US would help in the restoration of power balances in the Aegean and Eastern Mediterranean, a reversion to the status quo ante that is the only basis from which one can hope to reach a diplomatic solution to the most persistent geopolitical problems in Turkey's neighbourhood in the present context.

Admittedly, Turkey taking this latter path is a highly unlikely scenario. In his over two decades of ruling the country, Erdoğan successfully tilted the institutional balance of power to his side, pacified popular reaction to his economic failures through credit, charity and social assistance programmes, secured the support of, or even engendered a loyal and dependent big capitalist class fraction particularly in energy, construction, tourism, and defence sectors, fortified his sway over shopkeepers, minimum wage workers, and rural industrialists as well as large chunks of population in the Anatolian heartland, gained the passive compliance of the formerly dominant urban capitalist class composed of financial capital as well as large industrial conglomerates who had previously constituted the backbone of the *ancien régime*, silenced critics through judicial means, and eliminated political competition by jailing potential rivals with concocted charges. Having lost the support of Kurds and others starting from 2015, he enlisted the backing of ultranationalists to make up for these electoral losses, giving rise to even more extreme forms of authoritarianism as well as criminality in politics and business.

What is worse, it is not solely Erdoğan but also the opposition that is to blame for this failure. What has enabled the Erdoğan administration to oscillate between seemingly contradictory strategies of reproduction both domestically and internationally has been – at least partly – its ability to successfully determine the limits of the opposition's political repertoire of action. Particularly since the 2016 coup attempt, Erdoğan has managed to keep the opposition in line by effectively imposing on them a framework as to what is and what is not acceptable opposition and declaring whoever dared to step outside these limits to be terrorists or terror affiliates, especially in relation to the Kurdish question. In turn, most of the opposition parties succumbed to the pressure and accepted these political boundaries of acceptable discourse, action, and geo-political positioning. In the misguided over-confidence in the Erdoğan administration eventually losing an election due to the severity of the economic crisis, most of the opposition parties ignored other possible forms of resistance to the government including working-class action, youth protests, and direct supports for the environmental and women's movement.[26] Thereby a lifeline to the Erdoğan administration was effectively extended whenever it was in trouble by absorbing the potential for direct action on the streets into conventional parliamentary opposition. Read together, Erdoğan has been able to incorporate the policies and programmes of the opposition whenever they fit the broader strategy of his administration, and hence has been able to undercut the opposition's *raison d'être* or render it questionable at best.

Geopolitically, too, the Erdoğan administration was appeased and tolerated, if not directly encouraged and supported. In the absence of strong external constraints, the Erdoğan administration demonstrated a readiness to flex muscles, especially in response to perceived imminent threats, such as the establishment of a political entity for Kurds in Syria. The relative US withdrawal from the active management of world order first under the Obama administration, then under the Trump administration has not been fully reversed till this day. Seeing this opening as the leader of an ultranationalist coalition, Erdoğan made full use of geopolitical rentierism. He also ensured the complicity of European states by cornering them through the strategic use of migrants in Turkey. The Erdoğan administration was able to overplay its hand relatively successfully as the US in Syria and Eastern Mediterranean and Russia in Syria, Azerbaijan and Libya were not willing to confront Turkey head on. This hesitation is closely tied to the observed and experienced changes in the international order. As a result, the Erdoğan administration was able to exert influence beyond its conventional capabilities. Furthermore, these dynamics cannot be solely explained by any erraticism or instability in the Erdoğan administration's foreign policy. This is evident in its strategic acumen, knowing when to halt or step back in response to a more determined stance from rivals, as seen in Syria and the Eastern Mediterranean.

All these factors, including the complacency of the opposition and Western powers, allowed Erdoğan to follow seemingly contradictory, random, incoherent and irrational policies. For example, administration officials, including Erdoğan himself, could call the UAE leadership the financiers of the 2016 coup attempt and then seek to establish good relations; call Bashar Assad of Syria a murderer and then try to re-establish a top level dialogue with him; call Sisi of Egypt a murderer and then reappoint ambassadors; vocally criticize Saudi Arabia for the murder of Jamal Khashoggi and then transfer the case to Saudi Arabia; condemn Israel for atrocities in Gaza, all the while continuing to do business with Israel as usual.

In short, Turkey needs a different kind of opposition to democratize its internal politics and transform its foreign policy. The extent to which this can be achieved will determine the political and international horizons and future of Turkey. While one may harbour hope for potential openings for democratic and socialist struggles amidst the circumstances created by new geopolitical alignments, and inconsistencies and blunders at home, social actors seeking to exploit this vacuum are of limited capacities or constrained by electoral politics. Whether new actors and movements, alongside existing working-class, women's, and student movements, will emerge and overcome these limits will depend on their ability to respond to the multiple crisis of the country not least the crisis of the political system and its geo-political setting, and the post-election 'rationalization' of the social contradictions of the economy.

NOTES

1   H. Tarık Oğuzlu, 'Turkish foreign policy in a changing world order', *All Azimuth: A Journal of Foreign Policy and Peace*, 9(1), 2020, pp. 127-39; Evren Balta and Soli Özel, 'Turkey's Foreign Policy: Opportunities and Constraints in a New Era', *Social Research: An International Quarterly*, 88(2), 2021, pp. 539-60.
2   Ali Burak Güven, *Peasants, Bankers and the State: Forging Institutions in Neo-liberal Turkey*. PhD thesis. Toronto: University of Toronto, 2009, pp. 238-9.
3   Vedat Milor and Jesse Biddle, 'Institutional Influences on Economic Policy in Turkey: A Three-Industry Comparison', World Bank PSD Occasional Paper No. 3, 1995, p. 57.
4   For the origins and ideology of this new capitalist class see: Eren Duzgun, *Capitalism, Jacobinism and International Relations: Revisiting Turkish Modernity*. Cambridge: Cambridge University Press, 2022, Ch. 6.
5   Duzgun, *Capitalism, Jacobinism*, pp. 222-31.
6   Clemens Hoffmann and Can Cemgil, 'The (un) making of the Pax Turca in the Middle East: understanding the social-historical roots of foreign policy', *Cambridge Review of International Affairs*, 29(4), 2016.
7   İsmail Doğan Karatepe, 'Türkiye'de Devlet, Burjuvazi ve Yatırım Teşvikleri', in Hakan Mıhçı, ed., *Finansallaşma, Devlet ve Politik İktisat*, İstanbul: Nota Bene, 2015, pp. 244-45.
8   Şebnem Oğuz, *Globalization and the Contradictions of State Restructuring in Turkey*, PhD thesis, Toronto: York University, 2008, p. 118; Zülküf Aydın, 'Global Crisis, Turkey and the Regulation of Economic Crisis', *Capital & Class*, 37(1), 2013, p. 100.
9   Yonca Özdemir, 'AKP's Neoliberal Populism and Contradictions of New Social Policies in Turkey', *Contemporary Politics*, 26(3), 2020, p. 16.
10 Ellen Meiksins Wood, *Democracy against Capitalism*, Cambridge: Cambridge University Press, 1995, p. 237.
11 Nikos Moudouros, 'The "Harmonization" of Islam with the Neoliberal Transformation: The Case of Turkey', *Globalizations*, 11(6), 2014.
12 Mustafa Kutlay and Ziya Öniş, 'Understanding Oscillations in Turkish foreign Policy: Pathways to Unusual Middle Power Activism', *Third World Quarterly*, 42(12), 2021.
13 Can Cemgil, 'Militarisation of Turkey's Foreign policy and the Crisis of the Capitalist International Order', in Görkem Altınörs, Mehmet Erman Erol, and Gönenç Uysal, eds, *Turkey and the Global Political Economy: Geographies, Regions, and Actors in a Changing World Order*, London: Bloomsbury, 2024.
14 Cemgil, 'Militarisation of Turkey's foreign policy'.

15 Işık Özel, 'Reverting Structural Reforms in Turkey: Towards an Illiberal Economic Governance?', *Global Turkey in Europe Policy Brief*, May 2015, p. 5.
16 Pınar Bedirhanoglu, 'Economic Management under the Presidential System of Government in Turkey: Beyond the Depoliticization versus Repoliticisation Dichotomy', *Journal of Balkan and Near Eastern Studies*, 24(1), 2022, p. 98.
17 Duzgun, *Capitalism, Jacobinism*, p. 254.
18 Hoffmann and Cemgil, 'The (un)making of the Pax Turca'.
19 United Nations Panel of Experts on Libya, 'Final report of the Panel of Experts on Libya addressed to the President of the Security Council', 24 May 2022, available at https://digitallibrary.un.org/record/3976750.
20 Cemgil, 'Militarisation of Turkey's foreign policy'.
21 'Nagorno-Karabakh crisis lays bare Armenia's deteriorating relations with Russia', *CNN* 20 September 2023, available at https://edition.cnn.com/2023/09/20/asia/nagorno-karabakh-russia-reaction-intl/index.html.
22 Duzgun, *Capitalism, Jacobinism*, pp. 253-6.
23 The Turkish franchise of Bloomberg Businessweek featured on its cover page 'The rise of Turkish lira from the ashes', *Bloomberg Businessweek*, 7(1), December 2023. S&P Global changed Turkey's rating from stable to positive outside of its rating calendar. See: 'Turkish Bank Stocks Rally as S&P Global Raises Rating Outlook', *Bloomberg*, 1 December 2023, available at https://www.bloomberg.com/news/.
24 Despite a 5 percentage point rate hike to 40 per cent on 22 November 2023 (from a low of 8.5 per cent in June) by the Central Bank of the Republic of Türkiye, official inflation rate remains over 60 per cent, marking real interest rates as still negative. See: 'Turkey's central bank hikes interest rates again as it tries to tame eye-watering inflation' *APNews*, available at https://apnews.com/.
25 On the one hand, the Erdoğan administration failed to come to terms with the left-wing, pro-Kurdish HDP's electoral gains, which came at the expense of the AKP. The HDP's campaign aimed at obstructing Erdoğan's strengthened executive presidency. The AKP has also been reluctant to recognize the autonomous stance, territorial gains, and status advancements of the PYD during the Syrian civil war (presumably at the expense of Turkey-backed Islamist rebels). The peace process has therefore stumbled. The Turkish state insisted that the PYD partner with the Islamist rebels, a proposal that the PYD rejected. On the other hand, emboldened by the PYD's gains in Syria, the PKK-affiliated youth in Turkey declared autonomy in a series of Kurdish majority towns, underestimating the wrath of the Turkish state. This miscalculation resulted in the complete abandonment of the peace process, widespread destruction of these towns, and ultimately, a spiral of militarization both domestically and internationally. Authoritarian tendencies were further fuelled in Turkey. See: Can Cemgil, 'The geopolitics of the Kurdish question', in Nikos Christofis, ed., *The Kurds in Erdoğan's 'New' Turkey: Domestic and International Implications*, Abingdon: Routledge, 2021, pp. 183-198; Can Cemgil, 'The Geopolitics of Democratic Confederalism in Syria: Geopolitics as the Interplay of Multiple Strategies of Spatialisation', *Geopolitics*, 26(4), 2021, pp. 1046-1074.
26 Şebnem Oğuz, 'New Fascism and the Question of Socialist Strategy: Reflections on the Turkish Case', *The Bullet*, 19 November 2023, available at www.socialistproject.ca.

THE NEW GEOPOLITICAL SCENE IN LATIN AMERICA

CLAUDIO KATZ

Latin America is the scene of an important battle in the new Cold War – a battle the United States is waging globally in its bid to regain primacy.* Its international relevance restored, Latin America has become a major prize contested by the great powers. They all seek its immense natural resources.

With just 7 per cent of the world's population, Latin America has 42-45 per cent of the world's freshwater, half of its biodiversity, and immeasurable reserves of oil, gas, and minerals. It is also home to a large part of the most coveted raw materials on the world market (lithium, fluorite, silver, rhenium, tin). These materials are in great demand by global value chains, and few regions can provide them in the quantity that Latin America can. Managing this bounty is thus a priority for Washington.

US designs to reassert control are consistent with the domination it has historically exercised over Latin America, unparalleled in its involvement in other parts of the world. Since its very formation as a nation, the Northern giant has treated the neighbourhood to the south as its own backyard. It used the Monroe Doctrine to ensure its continued primacy, displacing European competitors. The Doctrine even defined the United States' own borders: it encouraged westward expansion, land seizures, the plunder of Mexico, and the occupation of the Caribbean. During the 20th century it also ensured the dominance of US firms south of the Rio Grande.

The Monroe Doctrine identified the term 'America' with the United States, excluding the rest of the continent and associating the term with Anglo-Saxon prosperity, in contrast to the underdevelopment prevailing in Latin America. US domination of the region was further consolidated through countless incursions by the US Marine Corps. But this long

---

* This article summarizes concepts presented in my book *Las encrucijadas de América Latina. Derecha, progresismo e izquierda en el siglo XXI* [The Crossroads of Latin America: The Right, Progressivism, and the Left in the 21st Century], Battle of Ideas, forthcoming. All references are included there.

historical trajectory began to falter in the second decade of the 21st century. The leading power is rapidly losing ground to an unexpected rival, resulting in an erosion of all the pillars of the regional order.

DISORIENTATION IN THE FACE OF THE NEW RIVAL

China has driven an unprecedented wedge into the old fiefdom of the United States. Its landing in Latin America was impressive. Following a strategic plan (detailed in the 2008 and 2016 white papers), its commercial penetration of the region began, with operations that grew at a rate of 26 per cent per year. The volume of trade jumped from 18 billion dollars in 2002 to 450 billion dollars in 2021, and China became the main trading partner of Argentina, Brazil, Chile, Peru, and Uruguay and the second trading partner of Mexico and Colombia. Its prominence was also established through the signing of free trade agreements with Latin American countries on the Pacific Ocean, which were later brought together into the Pacific Alliance regional bloc.

Initially, Beijing's interest was focused on raw materials, and to secure them, it pursued a strategy very similar to its forays into other parts of the world. In so doing, China began to displace the United States in its own backyard. Its commercial advance was followed by a wave of financing, which in the last decade reached 130 billion dollars in bank loans and 72 billion dollars in corporate acquisitions. This credit lending was in turn strengthened by a series of direct investments in infrastructure projects to improve supply for the new major power.

Chinese corporate acquisitions are concentrated in the strategic sectors of gas, oil, mining, and metals. Beijing coordinates the actions of all its firms under a meticulously designed plan. The financial entity in this effort, the Asian Infrastructure Investment Bank, provides the funds necessary for all projects. Recently, China has begun to consummate this expansion with the deployment of more sophisticated technological products.

In just 20 years, the Eastern giant has managed to achieve an economic presence similar to that of its main rival. It has captured the markets of the region with a subtle combination of economic audacity and geopolitical ingenuity. Instead of confronting its adversary openly, it does so indirectly, demanding that its clients break off diplomatic relations with Taiwan. Recognition of the 'One China' principle is a condition for any agreement with the new power. Beijing thereby consolidates its global importance and erodes the traditional submission of Latin American governments to Washington's dictates.

China managed to bring this change about with unusual speed. The influence that Taiwan had managed to maintain until 2007 in Central

America and the Caribbean quickly evaporated, through diplomatic initiatives that would later spread to South America. Currently, Beijing is negotiating the severing of ties with Paraguay, one of the few countries still closely connected to Taiwan. During the recent pandemic, China added another feature to its menu of attractions for Latin American governments: deploying a clever 'mask diplomacy', it provided vaccines and medical supplies to the United States's traditional allies in the hemisphere, while the Trump administration withheld them.

China concentrates all its efforts in the economic sphere and avoids frictions in the geopolitical and military arenas. It has chosen the most favourable battleground for its current international profile. It is aware of Washington's sensitivity to any foreign presence in a territory it considers its own, so it exhibits special caution in this region. The uniqueness of this policy is evident when compared to the strategy deployed by Moscow. With economic interests in the region infinitely smaller than China's, Russia conducted several joint military exercises with Venezuela, testing a logic of geopolitical reciprocity to deter aggressions from Washington on its own Eurasian borders. This type of military presence is inconceivable for China. Unlike Russia, it restricts its military action to its own domain and avoids military displays outside of that orbit.

THE BELT AND ROAD INITIATIVE VERSUS AMERICA CRECE

The US State Department has been stunned by China's overwhelming entry into the Americas. Despite countless attempts, the foreign policy establishment has been unable to develop an effective strategy in the face of such a challenge.

Trump tried an aggressive trade reaction to increase the placement of American products in the region, but it did not improve the US surplus with Latin American countries. Nor did it halt the avalanche of agreements between these countries and China. It managed only a respite with the renewal of its treaty with Mexico and Canada (USMCA), which extended the duration of benefits to US firms in the maquiladoras and imposed some restrictions on China's agreements with Mexico. The United States was not, however, able to expand this model to the rest of Central America and the Caribbean, and the reprieve it achieved with Mexico did not compensate for its loss of influence in the rest of the Americas.

The failure of Trump's protectionism led Biden to turn to Keynesian instruments for an answer to the China problem. He appealed to New Deal rhetoric to gather support for increased public spending, with the aim of rebuilding revenues and boosting infrastructure investment. The obstacles blocking many of these initiatives, however, have only seemed to confirm the logjam in the United States. The international primacy of the dollar, the country's high-tech advantages, and the sway of the Pentagon have not been sufficient to outcompete China on the global stage. As a result, Biden has been unable to thwart China's continued advance in Latin America.

This adversity is particularly evident in the competition for international megaprojects. China has embarked upon the creation of a gigantic belt of infrastructure, ports, and through the Belt and Road Initiative, a project that surpasses even Europe's post-World War II reconstruction plans. Beijing has expanded this initiative to Latin America after having initially prioritized Africa. In just four years, it added 20 countries in the region to the project. Argentina was the most recent addition, and Argentina's involvement facilitates the participation of the three other major players yet to join (Brazil, Mexico, and Colombia).

China negotiates with its partners without imposing the commitments typically required by the United States, and it does not share the US tradition of being an oppressive creditor to insolvent debtors. Time will tell how Beijing ultimately behaves in the face of potential defaults by borrowers. For now, it boasts a 'friendlier' profile than its rival and advances at a pace that is unsettling for the US.

To deal with this onslaught, Trump proposed a project in 2019 to block China's advance – a project called America Crece ('America Rising'). He announced some vague objectives and obtained the endorsement of 14 governments in the region for the initiative. The plan promotes privileged agreements with US firms, especially in the promising energy sectors and in different areas of infrastructure (telecommunications, ports, roads). But the proposal never went beyond generic recommendations, and it lost momentum before it achieved any significant concrete results. The uncertainties also revived tensions between protectionist and globalist factions within the United States, which further obstructed America Crece – an initiative already lacking state financial support. America Crece was conceived as a plan to create business opportunities for the private sector, in contrast to China's offer of direct state support. This is the main difference with the Belt and Road Initiative and the major problem with the US proposal. Without direct Treasury support, Washington cannot compete with its Asian rival.

Biden inherited these difficulties with no solutions on offer. He adopted the same approach as his predecessor, yet with a more pompous name (Americas Partnership for Economic Prosperity), and sponsored incentives to encourage US firms established in Asia to return to the United States. Negotiations to drive this new package forward with 11 Latin American countries are progressing slowly and have not sparked as much interest as hoped.

SETBACKS AND FAILURES

US struggles to contain China reflect the setbacks the United States has faced in Latin America since the failure of the Free Trade Area of the Americas (FTAA). That project collapsed during the Bush presidency and was not replaced by any other plan of comparable scale. The limited bilateral agreements that took its place did not yield the expected results, and the old US aspirations for Pan-American supremacy have been shelved. The United States abandoned its free trade offers after seeing that it could not compete with China in this sense. Hence Biden avoids Obama's multilateralism as well as the globalist initiatives of his predecessors. He seeks instead to fuel a US resurgence with only peripheral approaches along these lines.

Free trade has always been the banner of the most competitive economies. It became the great emblem of London in the 19th century, of Washington in the 20th century, and it is now the hallmark of Beijing today. China's competitiveness explains its fervent defence of trade liberalization at Davos summits. The lip service paid to the ideal of free trade in much of the West contrasts with its real promotion by the new epicentre in the East.

The United States also has a huge fiscal deficit that hampers its competition with China, rendering it unable to revive its ambitious economic projects of decades past. A simple comparison with the White House's actions in the 1960s, taken in response to the Cuban Revolution, throws this difference into stark relief. At that time, Washington turned to the Alliance for Progress with an abundance of loans and investments, and it did not have to contend with the economic threat of another global power in the region. Now it lacks those resources and is faced with a Chinese competitor with a presence in its own hemisphere.

These adversities have extended to the geopolitical and military realms. The erosion of US leadership in the last two decades could not be countered by a greater deployment of the Southern Command, the Fourth Fleet, military bases in Colombia, or the presence of the DEA, the CIA, or the FBI. The White House has not attempted to repeat the occupations of Grenada (1983) or Panama (1989). It has certainly reinforced the blockade against Cuba and tried to conspire against Venezuela, but it has not been able to rebuild the Organization of American States or organize the continental counter-coup envisioned by the Lima Group.

To deal with this series of failures, the neoconservative camp exerts great pressure on Capitol Hill to reinstate the Monroe Doctrine and implement drastic actions against China. Its liberal opponents – who at the beginning of the new millennium suggested burying the Doctrine – now advocate for its resurrection, though more subtly and with some strategic discursive reframing. Both groups acknowledge the difficulties of their proposals. For the first time in two centuries, a rival is simply ignoring the Monroe Doctrine, undermining the long-standing supremacy of the US in the region. No US president has found the formula for overcoming this challenge.

We need only look at what has happened in Panama to appreciate the magnitude of China's arrival in Latin America. The traditional stronghold that the United States erected around the Panama Canal has been eroded by the privileged financial and commercial relationship Beijing has forged with Panama's rulers. After inducing Panama to distance itself from Taipei with promises of investment, China pressured its new partners with the threat of building an alternative canal in Nicaragua. This intimidation bore fruit, and the presence of Chinese investors has grown at an exponential rate. Chinese capital has managed to secure numerous contracts to modernize the country's infrastructure. They have built bridges and are currently constructing a high-speed rail line. They also reached a preliminary agreement for three flagship companies (Huawei, Alibaba, and Tencent) to lead the installation of high-tech 5G telecommunications equipment. With these initiatives, Panama has become the Central American country that attracts the most investment from China (in proportion to the country's size). Without sending a single soldier, Beijing has come to threaten Washington's historic control over a key crossroads for control of the seas.

THE RELUCTANCE OF OLD PARTNERS

Washington – through its embassies – continues to intervene on a daily basis in the internal affairs of Latin America. Republicans and Democrats promote this interference through their shared state policy toward the region, which they implement with a carrot-and-stick approach. However, the new regional scenario has upended relations between the dominant power and the region's ruling classes. The total subordination of local elites that prevailed during the 20th century no longer exists; the submission of these sectors to the dictates of the State Department has been eroded. In practice, no Latin American government (of any political stripe) is turning down the opportunity to increase its exports to, or to receive investments from, China. They all know that the United States demands their geopolitical subordination without offering any significant economic benefits in return.

The White House has made numerous attempts, with meagre results, to reverse the situation. Trump openly demanded alignment against Beijing, and his two allies in the region – Macri and Bolsonaro – did threaten to distance themselves somewhat. But these measures were abandoned when exporters from both countries fought to protect their huge sales of agricultural and mining products to China. Biden is following suit, yet without achieving any ruptures between regional elites and China. This relationship represents the Latin American ruling classes' pragmatic response to the lack of any offers of compensation from the United States.

Biden's difficulties at the Summit of the Americas (Los Angeles, 2022) illustrate this quagmire. This event is the main political forum of the Americas, and all the summits in recent decades have reflected the *degree of harmony* between the White House and Latin American governments. In the first three summits (Miami, 1994; Santiago, 1998; Quebec, 2001), during the rise of neoliberalism and the collapse of the USSR, Washington's total pre-eminence was clear. This dominance was abruptly curtailed at the fourth summit (Mar del Plata, 2005) with the defeat of the FTAA, in a context of crumbling unipolarity.

Obama managed a stalemate in the three summits that followed (Puerto España, 2009; Cartagena, 2012; Panama, 2015). He was unable to finalize any bilateral treaties to replace the FTAA and had to accept the presence of Cuba. He adopted a conciliatory discourse of equality among the countries of the Americas and distanced himself from Pan-Americanism. In contrast, Trump returned to a belligerent approach with displays of force and insolence toward the summit itself (Lima, 2018).

Biden sought a fresh approach to heal wounds in the region, promoting an agenda with all the topics currently in vogue (clean energy, digital infrastructure, green economy, democratic governance). But he also used the platform of the summit (Los Angeles, 2022) to reassert US primacy, excluding Nicaragua, Cuba, and Venezuela from the event. Aiming to reclaim US leadership as the host and chair of the summit, he instead caused the summit to break down. Mexico led a widespread repudiation of the exclusions, and Biden was snubbed by a number of governments that opted not to attend. The diplomatic fiasco symbolized the changing balance of power in the region.

TESTING A NEW STRATEGY

Biden has attempted to use the war in Ukraine to restore the subordination of Latin American foreign ministries. He sought to involve them in campaigns condemning Putin and demanding punishment for Russia's incursion, with no mention of NATO's role in the conflict. The apparent purpose of this demand was to constrain the region's autonomy.

This pressure was, obviously, ignored by leaders who oppose the White House (Venezuela, Bolivia, Cuba, and Nicaragua). But it also had little effect on the administrations with more ambiguous stances toward Washington (Argentina, Chile). The State Department was also challenged by Mexico's proposal for a ceasefire in Ukraine, which Brazil supported following Lula's inauguration. These positions contrast sharply with Latin America's traditional deference to US leadership throughout the past century, especially during times of global conflict (World Wars I and II) and the peak of the anti-communist crusade.

Most of the region currently rejects the US ultimatum, in contrast with the obedient alignment that Washington has successfully imposed on Europe. The difference, of course, is due to the Ukrainian conflict's location in the Old Continent. However, Europe's submission predates the war and reflects the total dominance of NATO in the transatlantic region. As a result of its traumatic past with the United States, Latin America has developed greater resistance to US demands than Europe has. The White House makes no secret of its campaign's economic objectives. It is extorting Latin America to cancel its paltry business arrangements with Russia, with the aim of harming Moscow's Chinese ally.

Militarism is the primary tool the United States wields to contain Beijing's presence and diminish the autonomy of Latin America's local capitalist classes. Neither Republican nor Democratic leaders entertain the possibility of retreating from their 'backyard'; all are in favour of strengthening the monumental military structure that the United States has established in the region, of a scale comparable to the Pentagon's presence in the Persian Gulf and the Mediterranean.

Latin America has been the historical target of US interventionism. From 1948 to 1990, the State Department was involved in overthrowing 24 governments: 4 cases involved the Marines, 3 involved CIA-orchestrated assassinations, and 17 involved Washington-orchestrated coups d'état. Many of these assaults were perpetrated by the seventy thousand gendarmes the United States trained between 1961 and 1975 to carry out all kinds of massacres. The 'war on drugs' is the most recent form of this escalation and has already resulted in the murder of a dramatically high number of Latin Americans, with no reductions in drug trafficking.

The State Department disguises its aggressions with implausible pretexts. First it was the communists, then the Taliban, later the drug traffickers, and most recently, terrorists. Hollywood actively contributes to this masquerade, perpetuating stereotypes that conform to the prevailing myths. China has now been added to the list of threats drawn up by the State Department, which denounces China's imperialist intentions but omits any evidence of such a threat. It obfuscates the fact that there is a vast difference between China's economic expansion and the militarism of the United States. China is not deploying troops in the region and does not use its embassies to organize conspiracies. The accusers themselves recognize this asymmetry and thus provide only vague warnings instead of direct accusations.

Some US officials believe that Eastern dominance will make inroads through culture, language, or customs, but they do not explain how such an abrupt displacement of Western dominance in Latin American social life might take place. In fact, China simply competes in business sectors unattached to military pressures, against a rival that turns to military deployment to safeguard its declining ventures.

Washington's big problem lies in the fact that – unlike in previous periods – it can no longer dispatch troops to its backyard. It compensates for this shortcoming with covert incursions to overthrow troublesome leaders, but these actions, in turn, generate a growing backlash. There are more embargoes, plots, and covert operations against Cuba, Venezuela, Nicaragua, and Bolivia, but there is also more criticism of this interventionism throughout the region.

COUNTERATTACKS WITH NEOLIBERALS AND THE RIGHT

The United States counts on two political allies in Latin America to try to restore its waning control: old neoliberals and the new ultra-right. The first faction has already been leading an intense ideological campaign to exalt the advantages of subordination to Washington.

Its proponents claim that the dispute with China will bring in Western investors, and they recommend issuing friendly invitations to encourage this engagement. They emphasize that capital inflows will facilitate the development of the region, without explaining why such inflows have not already done so in recent decades. They fail to mention that mining extractivism enriched the companies supported by Washington and that the industrial maquiladora model is the antithesis of inclusive social development, which Latin America needs. Neoliberals sidestep this issue and dismiss the reluctance of US companies to invest. Most of these companies seek quick profits with minimal risk and are not offering the imaginary opportunities promised by their admirers in the South. Their reluctance stems from the significant imbalances present in Latin American economies.

Instead of acknowledging this reality, neoliberals blame their fellow citizens for the region's misfortunes. They claim that the problems 'are ours' and unrelated to the US presence, as if the domination exercised by the leading power for more than a century had no bearing on Latin America's woes. Following the same script, these friends of the White House attack the region's 'populist governments', claiming they are squandering the opportunity to regain the North's benevolence by offering no new displays of docility. They cannot, however, provide a single example of any benefits that might have been derived from such docility in the past.

Neoliberals attribute underdevelopment to the idiosyncrasies, customs, and behaviours of the majority of the population. They fail to acknowledge that for most of the region's history, the course of society was determined not by the majority but by small ruling elites and officials. They look down on their compatriots and admire the powers that have profited from appropriating the region's common goods. First, they praised the European oppressors, and then they embraced their US replacement.

Since the 19th century, regional liberals have shown a clear fascination with the North and a matching contempt for Indigenous peoples of the South. They constructed their own states by exalting US 'civilization' and repudiating the 'barbarism' they saw in the South. This elitist tradition is now reappearing with both traditional spokespeople and new ultra-right proponents.

This latter group has gained influence by disguising its conservatism with messages of rebellion. They often blame vulnerable minorities for the misfortunes caused by capitalism. They oppose social demands and reject all the nationalist and developmentalist traditions of their predecessors. They ardently defend neoliberalism and submit, explicitly, to Washington's dictates. Trump maintains solid connections with this sector, which has established its base of operations in Florida. Biden, on the other hand, prioritizes connections with the traditional right. With the support of both sectors, the State Department prepares its counterattacks to restore US dominance.

The more moderate Latin American partners in this counteroffensive recognize the decline of the United States but still highlight the benefits of privileged ties to a weakened power. They fail to explain why Washington's patronage would be beneficial for Latin America, given China's growing influence. It is widely known that declining empires increase their extraction of resources from peripheries, exacerbating the hardships of their subordinates.

ONGOING DECLINE

Any US attempt to regain influence with the support of neoliberals will have to deal with the disastrous track record of leaders professing this ideology. These presidents' administrations have been disastrous, exacerbating all the hardships of dependent capitalism. The neoliberal zenith at the beginning of the new century (Salinas, Cardoso, Menem, Aylwin) was just as harmful as its recent conservative restoration (Macri, Duque, Peña Nieto, Bolsonaro, Piñera). The economic policies of these governments deepened the region's peripheral and dependent integration into the global economy. They included privatization, financial deregulation, and trade liberalization, reinforcing the regressive specialization of the Latin American economy in the lower levels of global productive activity. This alignment further squandered the region's enormous surplus, which was never used to develop endogenous processes of accumulation or sustained growth. Instead, it has simply flowed abroad, to the detriment of domestic development.

The neoliberal models that govern this outflow prevent the region from benefiting from favourable contexts (high prices of raw materials) and exacerbate the adverse effects during downturns (depreciation of exports). This mismanagement explains the region's recurring financial strangleholds, marked by external constraints, trade imbalances, and capital flight. These tensions often lead to dramatic situations of inflation, devaluation, and declining purchasing power.

The pandemic and the war in Ukraine have only exacerbated these conditions. The war caused a sharp increase in the price of food and fuel, which Latin America tends to supply in large quantities and at reduced costs. The higher prices reinforced the regional focus on exports, without any corresponding domestic benefits in return. The terrible consequences of this model for the bulk of the population are obvious. Since the pandemic, the region has faced a worsening of poverty and indigence. Unemployment has also risen, affecting especially the informal sector, which employs half of the urban workforce.

Latin America has the highest level of social inequality in the world, and both the number of multimillionaires and the size of their fortunes have increased significantly in recent years. To make matters worse, during the pandemic, the collapse of GDP was twice the size of the decline recorded in the rest of the world, and this decade started off already shouldering another 'lost decade'. GDP in 2020 was practically equal to its 2011 equivalent, and its recent recovery has been only tenuous. The struggle between the United States and China for control of the region's resources is thus unfolding in a context of ongoing economic and social decline.

The two powers are vying for control of the valuable minerals needed for the energy transition, much of which is found in the region's subsoil. The United States (along with its Canadian and European partners) has grown accustomed to managing these resources as if they were their own, and they are now taken aback by China's influence. In some countries, such as Peru, Beijing has become a major player, controlling 25 per cent of the copper, 100 per cent of the iron ore, and 30 per cent of the oil. These advances are displacing the United States, which is struggling to find a recipe for containing its rival.

PROGRESSIVES AND RADICALS

Washington faces growing difficulties containing Beijing in the current political situation, with the rise of a new progressive wave throughout the region. This resurgence follows the short-lived conservative restoration over the previous decade and has taken on some features of the progressive cycle that was prevalent at the beginning of the new century.

This new wave is both more widespread and more fragmented than the previous one. It includes governments that maintain high popular expectations (Colombia, Brazil, Mexico) and others that have already led to disillusionment due to unfulfilled electoral promises (Chile, Argentina). Yet they all face a very aggressive far-right, which has consolidated its influence in certain countries (Chile) and brought back coups d'état in others (Peru). These reactionary sectors have also recently been dealt resounding defeats in several nations (Brazil, Bolivia, and Venezuela).

The extreme right and its traditional partners are fighting hard to modify the regional map. They provoke confrontations that evolve quickly, with highly uncertain outcomes. These outcomes are affected by the dynamics of popular uprisings, which, over the past five years, contributed to the current progressive scenario. In several countries, these uprisings had immediate electoral effects and led to the hasty departure of right-wing presidents (Bolivia, Chile, Peru, Honduras, and Colombia). In other nations, social discontent did not lead to such protests but did result in similar victories at the polls (Mexico, Argentina, and Brazil). In some places, significant victories were achieved in the streets, yet with political effects that are still vague (Ecuador and Panama). There are also unresolved situations of sustained resistance from below in a context of governmental indeterminacy (Haiti).

These battles are decisive for the development of a popular project – one that can allow Latin America to overcome its passive role in the current geopolitical dispute. In building this alternative, the region's real options are at stake. Will the region maintain its traditional peripheral, dependent position in the world economy, or will it pursue a process of sovereign regional integration to eradicate underdevelopment?

This dilemma remains unanswered. There is a new global scenario that opens up possibilities for a historic change in Latin America. If the region can seize the opportunity presented by the US decline and China's rise, it may forge its own project of productive development, sustainable growth, improved living standards for the people, and reduced inequality. This path remains open and would require a strengthening of Latin American unity – a project formally shared by various strands of progressivism. Declarations in favour of this path dominate all meetings of progressive leaders – events that have facilitated the resurgence of the main organizations for autonomous regional action (CELAC and UNASUR).

However, widespread verbal support for integration has led to few concrete actions. Major initiatives for regional sovereignty – in the food, energy, and finance sectors – remain frozen. This paralysis contrasts with the seamless advancement of free trade agreements. Progressive governments have only made progress in some initiatives for the production and distribution of vaccines. They have not, however, created a Latin American state-owned lithium company, which would regulate supply and boost the local industrialization of this resource. It is true that there are projects to support de-dollarization, but governments in the region have not taken up the proposals to establish a Bank of the South or a common currency fund. Such foundations will be essential for securing real progress in monetary autonomy in interregional transactions.

The lukewarm approach of progressivism can only be overcome with the more decisive proposals and actions of the radical currents, which fight for an effective program of regional integration. They promote energy sovereignty through the creation of large interstate entities, they call for food sovereignty by controlling foreign trade, and they advance financial sovereignty by eradicating the tutelage of the IMF. They also call for initiatives to address social inequality, including the coordination of progressive tax policies to improve people's incomes.

These proposals of the Latin American left have been weakened in recent years by the deterioration of the Venezuelan economy, uncertainties in Bolivia, the harassment suffered by Cuba, and the adversities faced by the Bolivarian Alliance for the Peoples of Our America (ALBA). But, in a region that continues to stand as a clear leader of emancipatory projects, opportunities to adopt these grassroots initiatives persist.

STRATEGIES AND PLAYERS

The entire Latin American left supports shared pathways to reclaim sovereignty, overcome economic underdevelopment, and halt social decline. But the new geopolitical scene requires us to evaluate specific ways to both resist the domination of US imperialism and modify our dependence on China. These two pursuits demand fine-tuned strategies and well-defined programs. They are two distinct battles, yet they both involve constructing the same autonomous regional framework. This network should primarily serve to contain Washington's imperial interference. But it should also facilitate the development of the region by revisiting the agreements signed with Beijing. Being fully aware of both goals and seeking ways to pursue them jointly is a central objective of regional unity.

Without eliminating the covert presence of the US Marines and the blatant meddling of US ambassadors, Latin America cannot reshape its economy. But nor can the region overcome its underdevelopment without amending its fragmented agreements with China, which facilitate the plundering of its natural resources. Instead of accepting its subjection to US geopolitical mandates and Chinese trade priorities, Latin America could redefine its relationship with both world powers. To do so, it must regain its independence from the dominant force in the North and reorganize its agreements with Beijing, taking advantage of the flexibility of these agreements. The Belt and Road Initiative is just emerging; it has no previous foundations and is highly subject to the demands of its participants. Latin America has not explored any of these alternatives because it remains passive, honouring the deals the capitalist groups in each country make with China.

A new direction for the region that is favourable to the popular majorities requires their active participation. The study of Latin American reality must pay greater attention to the role of these subjects, moving beyond a focus solely on the behaviour of dominant groups. Battles between governments, powers, and their elites affect the future. But the future of Latin America will be determined by the actions and projects developed by its exploited, oppressed, and dispossessed.

FIGHTING FOR PEACE, PREPARING FOR WAR: THE BRITISH ANTIWAR MOVEMENT

LINDSEY GERMAN

The world passed a largely unremarked milestone in the spring of 2023 when the respected Stockholm International Peace Research Institute (SIPRI) announced that total global military expenditure had reached $2,240 billion in 2022.[1] This was an increase of 3.7 per cent in real terms over the prior year, with military spending growing for an eighth consecutive year. In Europe, moreover, the year-on-year increase in military spending for 2022 was an astonishing 13 per cent, a return to Cold War levels and a change of direction for many European states.

It's not hard to see why: the invasion of Ukraine by Russia has changed economic, military, and political calculations across Europe and further afield. The war has effectively led to a rearmament in Europe as states rush to donate weaponry and equipment to Ukraine while at the same time extending and enhancing their own weapons capacity, with the spread of military conflict more likely than it has been for decades. Germany is planning to double its spending on arms and the military, which will allow it to overtake the UK. In a particularly bizarre move, the EU peace fund – held jointly by the member states – is being used to buy artillery and other weapons for Ukraine.[2]

Beyond developments in Europe, there is also the dramatic increase in military tensions in the Pacific as relations between the US and China have deteriorated and the threat of conflict over Taiwan looms. The Hiroshima Summit of the G7 group of countries and allies in May 2023 marked a more confrontational approach to China. It was epitomized by the British Prime Minister Rishi Sunak declaring that 'China poses the biggest challenge of our age to global security and prosperity', adding that they are 'increasingly authoritarian at home and assertive abroad'.[3] The summit included reference to what was termed China's 'economic coercion' which, given the extensive imposition of economic sanctions on a range of states from Venezuela to

Russia by various of the G7 countries, smacks more than a little of diplomatic hypocrisy.

It is not out of order to suggest that we have entered the most dangerous period for the threat of international military conflict since at least the early days of the Cold War, and possibly since the ending of the Second World War and the use of nuclear weapons on Hiroshima and Nagasaki by the US in August 1945. While the Russian intervention in Ukraine has accelerated the potential for wider conflict, it has taken place at a time when imperialist rivalries between the leading world powers were already mounting and where military spending and alliances were expanding at an alarming rate.

At the heart of this growth has been the expansion of NATO, the post Second World War western military alliance designed, in the words of its first Secretary-General Lord Ismay, to 'keep the Soviet Union out, the Americans in, and the Germans down'.[4] In addition, recent developments in the Pacific region towards an expanding list of alliances are aimed at encircling China. These include the so-called AUKUS security pact which involves the US and UK providing Australia, a non-nuclear power, with nuclear powered submarines (to the fury of the French government with whom the Australians had a previous deal to build submarines). Further, in January 2023, the UK and Japan signed a defence agreement which commits the two countries to allow, among other things, 'the UK and Japan to deploy forces in one another's countries … [and] rapidly accelerate defence and security cooperation'.[5] This defence treaty may well involve committing UK troops to come to Japan's aid in the event of an attack. The role of NATO is growing in the Indo-Pacific and is contributing to the militarization of the region.[6]

Its expansion over recent decades in Europe has been relentless. The end of the Cold War from 1989 provided every reason for the military alliances that had dominated east and west Europe from the 1950s to disband. While that happened with the Warsaw Pact in 1993, NATO took the opposite direction, despite verbal assurances given to the then Russian leader Mikhail Gorbachev that its membership would not expand eastwards beyond the borders of the former DDR (the German Democratic Republic or East Germany).[7] In 1999, the three former Warsaw Pact countries – Hungary, Poland and the Czech Republic – were admitted as full NATO members, and only days later found themselves at war with their neighbour, Yugoslavia, through NATO's bombing campaign that prompted its dissolution as a state. That same year NATO developed a new strategic concept to include 'out of area' operations, in other words offensive military capacities to be deployed anywhere on the Eurasian land mass.

In 2004, another tranche of east European states joined, including Slovakia, Slovenia and the small Baltic States, added to in 2009 by Croatia and Albania, and in 2017 Montenegro became a member despite overwhelming popular domestic opposition. Today, NATO has member states stretching 1,000 miles east of the German border, including former Warsaw Pact countries such as Poland, and the Baltic States which were once part of the Soviet Union. In 2008 there was discussion among NATO members, led by the US, on the now-independent states of Ukraine and Georgia being allowed to apply for NATO membership. This was strongly opposed by Russia. However, in the present context, it is worth recalling that Ukraine has developed a very close military relationship with NATO in the past two decades, serving for example as part of the United Nations sanctioned (but NATO commanded) International Security Assistance Forces (ISAF) in 'Operation Enduring Freedom' (2001) in Afghanistan, and providing support for the US war in Iraq (2003) and subsequent occupation.[8]

The expansion of NATO caused severe diplomatic tensions with Russia, and the question of Ukraine's neutrality played a key part in the run up to the Ukraine war. The evolution of the war has been for Ukraine to increasingly become a proxy in the geopolitical conflict between NATO and Russia. This aspect of the war has further accelerated the process of NATO expansion, with membership extended to two previously neutral European states, Sweden and Finland, and with the de facto membership of Ukraine itself, whose military strategy is closely linked to that of NATO and whose armed forces rely on NATO weaponry and training. The war in Ukraine cannot therefore simply be reduced to a conflict between Russia and Ukraine, but is implicated in a larger geo-political struggle between NATO and Russia, and extends to the conflict between US and China, in which Ukraine has become one of the front lines. This war is escalating with the provision of increasingly offensive weapons from NATO, including British Storm Shadow cruise missiles with a 200km range,[9] German Leopard tanks, and now promised F-16 fighter jets. While the US is by far the largest arms supplier, a research brief for the British House of Commons notes:

> As the second largest donor, the UK has committed £4.6 billion in military assistance to Ukraine so far (£2.3 billion in 2022 and a commitment to match that funding in 2023). The UK is also hosting a training programme (Operation Interflex), which is supported by several allies, with the aim of training 30,000 new and existing Ukrainian personnel by the end of 2023. The UK has committed to training Ukrainian fast jet pilots but has

said that combat fighter aircraft will not be provided, at least in the short term. The UK is supplying long-range precision strike missiles.[10]

Given that both NATO and Russia are the leading nuclear armed powers, and that there have been comments from Putin that using 'tactical' nuclear weapons on the battlefield cannot be ruled out, the danger of major power direct conflict is real and possibly very close. The US and NATO are putting ballistic missiles with the capacity to add nuclear weapons in Romania and Poland, and more recently Russia has moved tactical nuclear weapons into Belarus.[11] The accumulation of nuclear warheads is one sign of the growing possibility of their first use by these powers.[12]

The background to this is not just a longer-term deterioration of relations but also the reversal of plans to reduce nuclear weapons. The withdrawal by US President George W. Bush from the Anti-Ballistic Missile Treaty in the aftermath of the 9/11 attacks led to this eventual deterioration of the US's relationship with its major nuclear rival. The more recent abandonment by the US of the Intermediate-range Nuclear Forces Treaty (INF) has further damaged moves towards disarmament and elimination of nuclear weapons. This is occurring at a time when new weapons technology from hypersonic missiles to artificial intelligence is developing. The ending of the INF treaty has been accompanied by the development of new weapons which can circumvent missile defence systems. New Russian nuclear capabilities such as its latest ICBM RS28 Sarmat and its suspension of the New Strategic Arms Reduction Treaty also point to a growing escalation of nuclear armaments on an international scale, something which will have implications much wider than those in Ukraine.

Faced with a war of the magnitude seen in Ukraine, the British antiwar movement, in the form of the Stop the War Coalition and other organizations such as the Campaign for Nuclear Disarmament (CND), has made clear its opposition to Russian aggression and invasion. Under existing standards of international law there can be no justification for intervening in another sovereign country as Russia did. This position is a starting point which enables the antiwar movement to engage in the wider debate inside the trade unions and the political process more generally. The antiwar movement has also insisted that the conflict did not begin in February 2022 but is part of the ongoing conflict within Ukraine itself, which has continued at different levels since 2014, and must be seen against the unsettled regional configurations of the past several decades since the end of the Cold War.

In addition to increasing tensions with Russia centring on NATO expansion, it is important to factor in the impact of the military interventions by the western states over this period: the first Gulf War, the Balkan wars, and the War on Terror following 9/11. In all these cases, it became clear that the US was using its newfound position as the only superpower to increase its influence and hegemony to discipline what it (and NATO) saw as 'rogue states'.

The American and NATO intervention in the Kosovo War in 1999 was particularly galling for the Russians in underlining their own reduced influence and power in the region. It brought a conclusion of the near decade long wars which resulted from the break-up of the former Yugoslavia, but it involved nearly three months of NATO bombing of Serbia, a close ally of Russia, and included a controversial direct hit on the Chinese Embassy in Belgrade. While the war was justified as a 'humanitarian intervention' to save the lives of the Kosovan people, it was clearly designed to shift the balance of military and hegemonic forces away from Russia and to assert western, especially US, might in the former Eastern Bloc states.

The war in Afghanistan, almost universally supported by governments internationally in the wake of 9/11, also involved NATO early on with the organization leading the ISAF from 2003 in a dramatic out-of-area operation. The invasion and occupation of Iraq which began in the same year was bitterly opposed by citizens and many governments alike, including millions marching on 15 February 2003 across some 600 cities globally. The obvious failures of both these wars led to even those who initially supported them changing their positions.

British and US troops eventually withdrew – ignominiously from Afghanistan after two decades of occupation and repression – but this did not signal a withdrawal from arms spending and conflict. Nor from further military incursions in other countries, although the nature of these changed from full blown invasion and occupation to air attacks, remote warfare via drones, and proxy armed forces. The bombing of Libya, for example, brought about regime change in 2011, and was initially backed by Russia and China at the UN Security Council as a humanitarian intervention. The NATO operation killed an estimated 30,000 and overthrew the country's president, Muammar Ghaddafi. The growing realization that this intervention was one of regime change and that it represented an expansion of NATO power meant that both China and Russia took this as a red-light blocking future support for similar military excursions. Russia felt sidelined over Libya, with its subsequent intervention and extensive – and bloody – bombing during the war in Syria an assertion of its power in the Middle East. The conflicts in Libya and in Yemen can also be seen as increasingly taking on a proxy nature between Russia, the west, and their respective regional allies.

The accumulated experience of these wars helped to create a dangerous and unstable international correlation of forces, a conjuncture where a new arms race with unprecedented destructive capacities drew in a whole number of countries, further exacerbating the instability. This is an unremarked contributory factor to the present crisis, but it is impossible for the antiwar movement to ignore it. It is inextricably tied to the changing relationship between the US and China as the latter emerges as an increasing challenge, both economically and politically, to the primacy of American power and imperialism – and thus NATO – in the world order.

THE STATE AND THE MEDIA

The antiwar movement has never expected or been provided a level playing field in terms of coverage or debate within the British media, or from government sources, because it is challenging basic assumptions about the role of the British state, its role in imperialism, and the actions of politicians and the military. But even by these standards the role of the state and media in pushing a certain narrative about the Ukraine war has been remarkable, whereas in the run-up to the Iraq war antiwar voices received at least some media attention. One national newspaper, the strongly working-class Labour-supporting *Daily Mirror,* opposed the war to such an extent that it made its own placards for the British part of the global demonstration of 15 February 2003. This time there has been little space for any such opinions either in broadcast or print media.

The calls for peace and a negotiated settlement – admittedly a minority view but one that is supported by nearly a quarter of the British public[13] – are simply not echoed in any major news outlet. There is no debate about whether the war is right or wrong, no discussion except the extent and type of the weapons to be sent to Ukraine, no analysis of the background to the war, the nature of the Ukrainian government, or whether NATO aggression might itself have played a part in the crisis. These will be dismissed as 'Putin talking points' and, thus, unworthy of further consideration.

It is impossible to know what exactly is happening on the ground in the war, given that both sides release only the information that they want us to know, and nothing more. The media coverage from Ukraine is under the control of government and military and so is at the very least self-censored. The same is true on the Russian side, including the state oppression of antiwar activists.

The most startling feature of all this is, perhaps, the role of various states in projecting soft power, and the close relationship between states and media as a result.[14] It is now a regular occurrence to see Ukraine's president,

Volodymyr Zelensky, addressing major political events around the world, either zoomed-in or in-person. The Ukrainian government has tried to extend these appearances to cultural and sports events such as the Oscars, the Qatar World Cup, and the Eurovision song contest. The latter, held in Liverpool in 2023 on behalf of the previous year's winners Ukraine, was awash with blue and yellow flags and featured the Princess of Wales on piano with the Ukrainian group.

The levels of state and media promotion of the war are extensive at both national and local levels in Britain – at Premier League football matches, sporting fixtures, royal funerals and coronations, among school children and university students, in pubs and town halls. There have also been extensive efforts to exclude Russian cultural and sporting figures – and even to prohibit recitals of Russian music. While there has been a minority prepared to stand up to this pretence of unanimity on the war, or to criticize the role of the British government, they have tended to be diffuse and somewhat fragmented, and those openly campaigning against the war and for peace talks find themselves operating against the stream, even if there is some audience for their ideas.

THE LEFT AND THE UKRAINE WAR

The left has traditionally been at the centre of the peace and antiwar movements in Britain, going back to the period before the First World War. A range of prominent left and Labour figures have been campaigners for peace, including Keir Hardie, Ramsay Macdonald, and George Lansbury. More recently, prominent Labour figures including Tony Benn and Jeremy Corbyn have supported Stop the War and CND, holding honorary positions in these organizations. The modern peace movement began with the founding of CND in the 1950s in response to the threat of nuclear weapons and the growing awareness of how deadly the consequences of nuclear war could be. This was at the height of the Cold War between the US and the Soviet Union, and very large numbers were mobilized for the organization's annual Easter marches to Aldermaston in the late 1950s and early 1960s around the slogan 'ban the bomb'.[15] CND has maintained itself ever since, reviving in the 1980s with the mass campaign against the siting of cruise missiles in Europe and becoming a partner of the Stop the War Coalition from 2003 onwards in opposing the war in Iraq.

In every major war since the 1990s, there have been those figures on the left who have shifted from opposition to previous conflicts to support for the present one. They have tended to remain isolated examples, useful to the pro-war media at the time but playing little part in left politics after the conflict subsides. Currently, however, the left is much more divided on the question of the Ukraine war and on the wider questions of attitude towards Russia and China. The assumptions made about previous wars in this century no longer apply in any simple or direct way. There is one obvious reason why this is the case. Those wars – in Afghanistan, Iraq, Libya – were asymmetrical wars, sometimes being waged against non-state actors, conducted by the British government in conjunction with the US and its other western allies. The current conflict started with the invasion of Ukraine by Russia, a major power, a permanent member of the UN Security Council and the possessor of nuclear weapons, who was the immediate aggressor. The fact that it's not 'our government' as direct aggressor makes a huge difference, because to the mass of public opinion it appears to be promoting peace. The fact that it is increasingly promoting war against Russia – and that the UK government under Prime Minister Boris Johnson did its best to scupper peace talks between Ukraine and Russia in April 2022 – is obscured.[16]

The lack of scrutiny of government motives by the media and politicians in Britain means that in most forms of public discourse there is no visible alternative to the dominant views. The extensive media reporting from the war in Ukraine means that, very differently from the wars in Afghanistan and Iraq, we see the terrible consequences of the bombing, artillery fire and drone attacks on the population, and the inherent sympathy for those suffering allows some who might be critical of the government on domestic issues to give it a free pass on the question of war.

These factors give the impression that there is near total unity of support for the war in Britain, an impression reinforced by the fact that there is effectively no opposition to the war policy within parliament or mainstream politics. The Labour Party is completely bipartisan on this question. Its leader, Keir Starmer, has moved the party in an increasingly pro-war and patriotic, flag waving direction since the invasion in February 2022. Just before it began, he demanded that eleven MPs from the left of the party remove their names from a statement organized by the Stop the War Coalition which opposed war and called for peace.[17] The MPs were threatened with losing the Labour whip if they did not do so. This would have meant being outside the parliamentary party and not being able to stand for Labour at any forthcoming election. In a sad day for Labour, all these MPs capitulated to Starmer's demand with indecent haste, and effectively agreed to keep silent on criticism of the war and any call for peace talks, despite the increasingly hawkish demands for more public spending on war and weaponry from Westminster. The only exceptions in terms of the UK parliament are from those MPs who have lost the Labour whip, Jeremy Corbyn and Claudia

Webbe, and one of the Sinn Fein MPs (who do not take their seats in the British parliament). Corbyn has maintained a longstanding commitment to antiwar and peace campaigning, and to international solidarity, throughout his 40 years as an MP. His hounding over these questions by Starmer since he became party leader is both extraordinary treatment of a former Labour leader, and evidence of the extent to which Corbyn's leadership threatened the dominant narrative on the foreign policy of the British state.

Support for that narrative has also come from Britain's Green Party, which has one MP in the Commons, Caroline Lucas, and a handful of members in the House of Lords. Lucas broke with Stop the War nearly a decade ago over its opposition to intervention in Syria. The Green Party voted at a recent conference – against all its previous policy – to support NATO, albeit in a 'defensive' role and with a commitment to no first use of nuclear weapons.[18] These would appear unlikely concepts given the nature and practice of the organization.

The line from a range of left politicians is that even talk of peace is regarded as a dangerous capitulation to Putin's aggression. This is a major setback, particularly for Labour. It is the first time in the party's history when there has been no prominent voice in parliament or in public life speaking out against war and for peace. It has a negative impact not simply on many of the MPs themselves but also on many thousands of Labour councillors and activists who are under threat of discipline if they speak out of line. One of the traditional key planks of labour movement policy has been removed.[19] This doesn't just lead to an absence of arguments for peace but to an increasingly positive endorsement of sending more offensive weapons to Ukraine and to increases in arms spending as a proportion of GDP. So, the traditional positions of the left have been effectively suspended, at least in the official labour movement, and in every individual union conference we see real divisions about how to respond to the Ukraine war.

There are those, moreover, who simply believe that Russia, together with its ally China, are the biggest danger to security in the world and must be defeated. To do so, the left must abandon its squeamishness about arms spending and, indeed, about trusting its own governments and do whatever it takes to win. The most prominent with this view is the commentator Paul Mason, erstwhile revolutionary socialist in a small group, whose political evolution has taken him, via respectable television correspondent posts on the BBC's *Newsnight* and on *Channel 4 News*, to support for Corbynism, disillusionment with Corbynism, cheerleading for the Keir Starmer leadership, and now the so far unsuccessful quest to find a safe seat at the next general election and become a Labour MP. Mason has become obsessive on the question of war and militarism, wanting to raise defence spending beyond the wildest dreams of most right-wingers in order to counter 'the Putin threat'[20] and denouncing those who oppose these plans as Putin apologists or 'tankies'. He even suggests an alliance between Stalinists and fascists is forming, seeing them both as threatening liberal democracy.

Others take less stark views than Mason, but end up in the same place. Their position is compatible with those of the major political parties as it implies no criticism of them or their military policy. Much of the debate here centres on the provision of arms to Ukraine by western governments, with many on the left arguing that the Zelensky government should be provided with whatever weapons it requests, regardless of the consequences for escalating the war. Some cite comparisons with the Spanish Civil War or the Easter Rising in Dublin in 1916 in their support. But the Russia-Ukraine war is both one between two sovereign states and a wider proxy war involving rival imperialist powers. It is not a civil war where the left is fighting a fascist uprising against a popular front government as in Spain; nor is it a rebellion against colonial oppression as it was in Ireland. Indeed, the Zelensky government has its own record of corruption, banning of trade unions and left groups, and neoliberal policies, as of course does Russia.

Nor is the nature of weaponry provided comparable. The German Kaiser sent support to the Easter Rising during the middle of the First World War in the form of one shipload of arms – 10 machine guns, crates of (mainly old) rifles, ammunition, and a few explosives. The Spanish Republic did obtain planes from the Soviet Union but had to pay for them. The scale and nature of weaponry being supplied to Ukraine today is of a totally different magnitude, quality, and effect, with offensive weapons now being supplied from NATO countries (as outlined above). While provision of such weapons was ruled out in the early stages of the war by the major powers, including the US, on the grounds that they might escalate the war and create wider conflict, every single supposed red line in weapons has now been crossed.

The justifiable arguments that Ukraine has the right to resist invasion, and that as a country it has the right to self-determination, should not be used to endorse arming what is not a resistance movement but a government with extremely close ties to western imperialism. It is very hard after a year and a half of fighting to see this war as contained within the borders of the protagonists, or to ignore the fact that the conflict has very much directly to do with NATO.

None of this is to endorse Putin's arguments. Russia is playing an aggressive and unjustified role, but this does not mean that the war should continue. The antiwar position is characterized sometimes as motivated by pacifism or naivety; and sometimes it is described by the pro-war left being of the 'my enemy's enemy is my friend' kind – that such is the dislike and distrust of US imperialism and its allies such as the UK, that any state designated their enemy should be supported. This is the commonplace that opposition to one's own ruling class must mean support for its opponents. But a cursory examination of antiwar movements this century will show that they have been aimed overwhelmingly at opposing our own governments, not at endorsing opponents of western states such as the Taliban or Saddam Hussein.

CHALLENGES FOR THE ANTIWAR MOVEMENT

One of the major challenges for the antiwar movement is the fragmentation of the left on the question of the Ukraine War. In terms of the wider population in Britain, there certainly is no great enthusiasm for the war, and there is a sizeable minority open to arguments against war and for peace. However, with the Labour Party firmly behind the war effort, the trade unions divided, and with opposition to war often tarred as apologism for Putin, it is hard to break through to gain a wider audience, and many challenges that make it harder to organize. Meeting venues have cancelled or refused bookings for antiwar meetings. Within the Labour Party, the effective prohibition on supporting Stop the War has had a chilling effect on those who might otherwise speak out but are faced with sanctions, possibly including expulsion, if they do so. The mainstream media blackout adds to the constraint on antiwar voices. In addition, the government has passed restrictive legislation aimed at protest and dissent, some of it directly focused on climate protestors, but which will be aimed at all sorts of groups protesting government policies, including foreign policy. Given the political climate outlined above, demonstrations against the war may well be met with higher levels of limitation or repression than they have seen so far.

There is another challenge facing the antiwar movement and that is the opposition to the Ukraine war which comes from the far right. There has always been an element of right-wing politics which has opposed previous wars, for nationalist or isolationist reasons. Over Ukraine, this has been an element of antiwar opinion, notably in countries such as Germany and Hungary, reflecting again levels of nationalism but also opposition to globalization and the 'global elite'. The existence of this strand allows those who support the war to denounce its opponents as 'far right and far left' – the extremes against the sensible majority, or as 'red-brown' alliance between Stalinists and fascists.

It is important for antiwar movements to reject this characterization but also to reject the logic of right-wing support for their cause. This is the approach antiwar organizers have taken in Germany, making it clear that the far right AfD would not be welcome on marches and their prominent members prohibited from joining it. This did not prevent German politicians from claiming that it was a march of far left and far right, but it was an important statement making it clear that the movement would not support the far right's agenda.[21]

Revulsion at the impact of globalization and the neoliberal agenda does not necessarily lead to left-wing outcomes. The far right has grown in many places by capitalizing on that sense of discontent with the global capitalist system; but its solutions are of necessity divisive, scapegoating different groups and stressing nationalist and protectionist measures. In particular, the right-wing narrative repeatedly blames migrants for the problems caused by global capitalism and advocates restrictions on freedom of movement between countries. The European right also stresses narrow values of family, the flag, and the Christian religion.

The antiwar and peace movements in Britain have, on the contrary, insisted that their agenda must include a broad internationalist approach, seeing refugees as in large part created by the wars of past decades, and to be welcomed rather than shunned as a problem. More fundamentally, accepting the narratives put forward by the far right would only help reinforce the views of our own government, and would strengthen its hand in terms of prosecuting the war.

How we deal with these challenges is not easy. It involves a combination of elements. The first point is to recognize that, given the present stalemate of the war and the terrible destruction and loss of military capacities in Ukraine, the US and NATO governments have entered a new phase of growing direct conflict with Russia and China. For the antiwar movement, this is a period of what might be called propaganda rather than mass agitation. It is one of disseminating sometimes quite complex arguments, on as wide a scale as possible, but particularly to those who welcome reasons to oppose the war. It is possible and necessary to conduct some agitation: demonstrations are always an important statement for the antiwar movement, but in the current moment mobilization of modest numbers could be expected.

The fight inside the trade unions is also historically central to the antiwar movement and here it is possible to find an audience even if it is not on a mass scale. The May 2023 annual conference of the UK-wide University and College Union (UCU) narrowly passed a motion opposing sending arms to Ukraine and calling for peace talks to end the war, alongside a second one talking more generally in terms of solidarity and support for refugees.[22] This caused a major furore in the union, with the general secretary and some of the union's national executive arguing it did not show solidarity, and various attempts to minimize or reverse the conference decisions. Although opinion is still deeply divided on the war, this decision illustrates that it remains important for the antiwar movement to take on open debate within unions.

However, the annual congress of the TUC, the body representing most British trade unions, also passed a motion in support of funding, including of military funds, and arguing that peace talks should be with the preconditions that Russia withdraw to pre-2014 borders. There was some opposition to this, with the Fire Brigades Union and Bakers' and Allied Food Workers' Union voting against; and UCU, the schoolteachers' National Education Union and the RMT (Railway, Maritime and Transport Workers) union abstaining. But the major unions voted for, falling in behind the GMB, a general union which has considerable membership in the defence industry. Interestingly, the TUC leadership put forward an 'explanation' of the resolution which argued that it did not put preconditions on peace talks, which rather contradicted it. Those arguing for it were forced to drop more open calls for sending arms to Ukraine, and couched the debate almost exclusively around humanitarian aid and solidarity, which are clearly uncontentious. [23]

It is possible to make progress on the arguments about the Ukraine war itself – and especially the contentions that there are underlying issues and background to the war, including the ongoing conflict in the Donbas since 2014, the expansion of NATO, and the dangers of nuclear escalation – by focusing on union conferences and union branch meetings. But there are also issues which make the connection with other questions that are of concern to trade unionists.

While there are a range of reasons for the recent increase in industrial combativity in Britain, one clear factor is the impact of the cost-of-living crisis on incomes, the fall in real wages across the working class, and the deterioration of public sector employment in terms of both wages and conditions. It is therefore possible to link support for industrial action to austerity in public services and the cost-of-living crisis, and from there to opposition to military spending and war. Placards and banners with slogans such as 'welfare not warfare' or 'wages not war' are well-received on most demonstrations around public services and support for strikes. There is considerable awareness that the Ukraine war itself is contributing to that crisis, in terms of higher energy and food prices (around 20 per cent for food inflation in the UK in the spring of 2023).

This is at a time when there is constant pressure from across the mainstream political spectrum to increase arms spending, and this is accompanied by an insouciance about the extremely costly arms packages going directly to Ukraine from politicians who object to any increases in public spending in other areas, including over the highly fraught and disputed issues of nurses' and teachers' pay. The British Trade Union Confederation (TUC) narrowly passed a resolution at its congress in 2022 calling for increases in 'defence' spending.[24] The argument put forth by the GMB union was that this would help provide jobs in the arms industry, an argument rejected by most of the public sector unions that opposed it. They understood that such an increase, regardless of its desirability, would mean further attacks on health and welfare spending. While there were very strong arguments against this position from several unions, the TUC's passing of the resolution was a significant retreat at a time when every other area of public spending is under attack and Britain has been in the midst of the biggest strike wave seen for a generation precisely over the lack of public sector funding for pay and staffing. There is clearly a lot of scope for challenging the UK's leading role in supplying arms into the Ukraine war, highlighting the dangers of such spending and the obvious need for social spending that is being denied.

There is also a healthy scepticism towards the British government given its record on wars. While the antiwar movement did not stop the Iraq war, the abject failure of the intervention has been clear and many of the arguments won in those years still resonate. The continuing UK involvement in the war in Yemen, including weapons and training; the aftermath of the western interventions in Afghanistan, Iraq and Libya; the devastation caused to the people of those countries, the destruction of the environment and the huge number of refugees caused by these wars – these past and present failures of British military intervention resonate with antiwar sentiments when the matter is debated and still present problems for those promoting new wars.

While for the British government and many supporters of the war there is a complete separation between these events and the war in Ukraine, it is the commonalities that emerge in all wars – brutal attacks on civilians, war crimes, bombardment of towns, ill treatment of prisoners of war – that are increasingly apparent. The nightly news coverage of the reality of war serves, on the one hand, to induce sympathy for the Ukrainian people but, on the other, it also creates revulsion against wars in general.

RESISTING IMPERIALISM

The antiwar and peace movements in Britain have never defined themselves as anti-imperialist, but have always argued to include those who oppose the wars but who are pacifists or do not share the anti-imperialist analysis.

While the Stop the War Coalition was formed with a number of anti-imperialists at its centre, holding such politics was not a prerequisite for membership. But such a perspective was very important in informing much of the debate, argument and orientation of the organization.

It allows organizers to recognize that these wars were not aberrations and that geopolitical conflicts are an integral part of the system of exploitation at the heart of capitalism. It also helps to explain rivalry between different powers and to consider the importance of economic resources (famously oil in the case of Iraq) but also the strategic aims of the imperialist states, and the US in particular.

The changes to the world system in recent decades are tending to make inter-imperialist conflict more likely and more deadly. The failures of the previous wars, the weakening of the US as the pre-eminent superpower, the emergence of a variety of economically and militarily important states, from India to Brazil, does not lessen but rather increases the likelihood of competitive rivalry between the leading powers. While it is true that the US still constitutes by far the biggest military power and is unique in its military bases and systems of alliance spread across the globe, it is also the case that China, Russia, India, and the UK are the next top military spenders (with Germany and Japan also pressing ahead). The strategic moves towards a growing number of competitive military alliances are indicative of the emerging economic tensions and military rivalries. On the one side, there are the western states whose chief aim is preventing China from operating freely in the Pacific. On the other side, there are China and Russia, alongside allies on their peripheries and in the Middle East. This is not to draw an equivalence between the US and the others: the US still represents almost 40 per cent of global military spending, three times that of China, and ten times that of Russia, with the US total GDP still much larger than China's (in dollar terms) and about fourteen times the size of Russia.[25] But it is to recognize that all the leading states have imperial interests (in protecting and expanding the internationalization of domestic capitals and protecting territorial spheres of influence), and the antiwar movement is right to insist that these geopolitical rivalries be accounted for in all military conflicts, not least in the Ukraine war.

China's astronomical rise industrially, economically, and militarily in recent decades has presented a growing problem for US imperialism as its relative economic pre-eminence declines and China catches up. While many on the left would balk at the designation of China as imperialist, there are ways in which its development is fitting into this pattern in the growing internationalization of Chinese capital and the capacity of the Chinese state to project its power internationally through military, institutional, and diplomatic means. The Belt and Road initiative of trading and investment with a whole range of countries, the investments and economic interventions in parts of Africa and growing levels of armament cannot be seen as purely defensive or altruistic moves. They are also strengthening the Chinese state and capital against its rivals, and as part of the competition for markets.[26]

While it is true that China has minimal direct military presence outside of its borders, with one base in Djibouti, that situation is changing. It has outposts also in Tajikistan and Pakistan, and there has been the supposed expansion of a naval base in Cambodia. With its naval capacity now approaching the US levels, in terms of number of ships, although not in terms of tonnage, more can be expected.[27] As a rising (state) capitalist power its already extensive military capacity is likely to increase considerably. Its main presence in terms of geopolitical competition has been in economic areas. But with growing pressure from the US through the AUKUS military pact and with South Korea and Japan as US regional allies, China is being pushed in a more military direction and is expanding its naval and other military capabilities accordingly. According to SIPRI: 'China remained the world's second largest military spender, allocating an estimated $292 billion in 2022. This was 4.2 per cent more than in 2021 and 63 per cent more than in 2013. China's military expenditure has increased for 28 consecutive years.'[28]

As an embedded process of the capitalist world system, imperialism locks state actors into both economic and military competition. While direct parallels between historical periods are always fraught, the situation today is reminiscent of the period before the First World War. Economic stagnation and instability, greater arms production, military alliances and treaties being struck, military conflict and flashpoints where major political forces are concentrated growing. In the words of a popular book on that conflict, the major powers are sleepwalking into a much bigger war.[29] Another global conflict will likely mean war between major powers in possession of nuclear weapons, which they may be tempted to use with unknown consequences.

The new weapons now available raise again the spectre of barbarism that Rosa Luxemburg warned about over 100 years ago as a potentiality always inherent in the logic of capitalist competition in the world market. Such an outcome, with the horrific destruction of populations and the surrounding ecology implied, should be unthinkable. That is the ultimate danger we are now facing, as the individual states in the emergent contesting military alliances engage in greater military and political competition, and as each imperial power appeals to a supposed national interest to unite the working class and trade union movements behind it. This was the case facing the socialists and working-class movements at the start of the First World War in 1914. The imperialist war had long been predicted and warned against, but the majority of the left in most belligerent countries backed their own 'national interest' and supported the war effort. It was a turning point for socialists. The socialist minority who opposed the war were isolated but recognized that one's own ruling class was the main enemy, in the words of the German socialist Karl Liebknecht.[30]

There are many differences between Liebknecht's time and today, but that principle holds. The antiwar movement opposes Putin and the intervention in Ukraine. But we also recognize that the actions of our own ruling classes are not in the interests of Ukrainian, Russian or British workers. Class struggle isn't just about what employers and government do over wages and conditions. It's also about what they do to the environment, to the health service, and the prioritization given to spending on arms and war. The importance of socialist arguments against war is greater than ever.

NOTES

1. Nan Tian, Diego Lopes da Silva, Xiao Liang, Lorenzo Scarazzato, Lucie Béraud-Sudreau and Ana Assis, 'Trends in World Military Expenditure 2022', Stockholm International Peace Research Institute, Stockholm, April 2023, available at: www.sipri.org.
2. 'Speeding up the delivery and joint procurement of ammunition for Ukraine', Council of the European Union, Brussels, 20 March 2023, available at: data.consilium.europa.eu.
3. Gregorio Sorgi, 'Sunak Ranks China As Top Challenge To Global Security', *Politico Europe*, 21 May 2023, available at: www.politico.eu.
4. This quotation is cited in 'Origins: NATO Leaders Lord Ismay' available at www.NATO.int.
5. Louisa Brooke-Holland, 'UK-Japan Defence Agreement 2023', Research Briefing, London: House of Commons Library, 13 January 2023, available at: www.commonslibrary.parliament.uk.
6. 'Regional Perspectives Report on the Indo-Pacific', NATO, 2022, available at: www.NATO.int.
7. This has become a highly controversial question in light of the Ukraine war and the question of NATO expansion. It would appear however that US Secretary of State James Baker, and later British prime minister John Major did give such assurances but that they were not written into treaties or formal agreements. For a brief summary of the claims and counter claims see: Patrick Wintour, 'Russia's Belief In NATO "Betrayal" – and why it matters today', *The Guardian*, London, 12 February 2022; an interesting take on this is Mary Elise Sarotte, 'A Broken Promise? What The West Really Told Moscow About NATO Expansion' in Grey Anderson, ed., *NATOpolitanism*, London: Verso, 2023, pp. 23-30.

8. For a full analysis of NATO expansion see: Grey Anderson, 'Weapon of Power, Matrix of Management', *New Left Review*, 140/141, March/June 2023.
9. James Gregory, 'UK Confirms Supply Of Storm Shadow Long-Range Missiles in Ukraine', *BBC News*, 11 May 2023, available at: www.bbc.co.uk.
10. Claire Mills, 'Military Assistance to Ukraine Since The Russian Invasion' Research Briefing, London: House of Commons Library, 23 May 2022, available at: www.commonslibrary.parliament.uk.
11. On these developments see for example: Daryl G. Kimball, 'Biden Policy Allows First-Use Nuclear Weapons', Arms Control Association, Washington, April 2022; and Shannon Bugos, 'US, Russia Discuss Threats Of Nuclear Use', Arms Control Association, Washington, 17 November 2022, available at: www.armscontrol.org.
12. For a recent assessment of this see: Paul Rogers, 'Nuclear Weapons On Rise In A World Where "Peace Through Deterrence" Is A Myth', *Open Democracy*, London, 15 June 2023, available at: www.opendemocracy.net.
13. Matthew Smith, 'One Year On, How High Is Support For Ukraine In Britain?', *Yougov*, London, 24 February 2023, available at: www.yougov.co.uk.
14. Joshua Rahtz, 'NATO's Fabulators', *Sidecar*, London, 5 May 2023, available at: www.newleftreview.org/sidecar; Serge Halimi and Pierre Rimbert 'Western Media As Cheerleaders For War', *Le Monde Diplomatique*, Paris, 8 March 2023, available at: www.mondediplo.com; Christian Perez and Anjana Nair, 'Information Warfare In Russia's War In Ukraine', *Foreign Policy*, Washington, 22 August 2022, available at: www.foreignpolicy.com.
15. For the history of CND see: Kate Hudson, 'CND: Now more than ever', London: Visipon, 2005.
16. Ian Sinclair, 'Did The UK Torpedo Peace Talks On Ukraine?', *Morning Star*, London, 17 November 2022, available at: www.morningstaronline.org.
17. The statement is entitled 'List of Signatories: Stop The War Statement On The Crisis In Ukraine', Stop the War, London 18 February 2022, available at: www.stopwar.org.
18. 'Peace, Security And Defence', Green Party Policy, Major Revision, Spring Conference 2023, available at: www.policy.greenparty.org.
19. The highest profile Labour left MP, John McDonnell, issued a statement in February 2023 on the anniversary of the war where he threw his weight behind calls for more arms to Ukraine and dismissed peace talks. John McDonnell, 'The Ukrainian Question For Socialists', *Labour Hub*, London, 21 February 2023, available at: www.labourhub.org.uk.
20. For an example of his views see: Paul Mason, 'As War Rages In Ukraine Rearming The UK Must Be A Proud Part Of Labour's Brand', *Labour List,* London, 27 February 2023, available at: www.labourlist.org.
21. Phillip Oltermann, 'Leaders of German Left Condemn Peace Rally Over Far Right Involvement', *The Guardian*, London, 24 February 2023, available at: www.theguardian.com.
22. The relevant motions are motions 5 and 6 on the 2023 conference agenda, available at: www.ucu.org.uk/media/13804/Congress-agenda/pdf/AGENDA_Motions_and_SOs.pdf.
23. Morgan Jones 'TUC Congress: Ukraine Solidarity Motion Secures Union Backing', *Labour List*, London, 12 September 2023, available at www.labourlist.org

24 Ben Chacko, 'The TUC Narrowly Votes To Back Higher Military Spending And Drop Defence Diversification Policy', *Morning Star*, London, 19 October 2022, available at: www.morningstaronline.co.uk.
25 Ashik Siddique, 'The US Still Spends More on Its Military Than 144 Nations Combined', Institute for Policy Studies National Priorities Project, 4 May 2023, available at www.nationalpriorities.org.
26 Lin Chun, 'China's New Globalism', in Leo Panitch and Greg Albo, eds., *Socialist Register 2019: A World Turned Upside Down?*, London: Merlin Press, 2018.
27 Azhar Serikkaliyeva, 'Chinese Overseas Military Bases: National Interests and Global Ambitions', Eurasian Research Institute, Akhmet Yassawi University, Almaty, April 2019, available at: www.eurasian-research.org.
28 Nan Tian et al., 'Trends in World Military Expenditure 2022', Stockholm International Peace Research Institute, Stockholm, April 2023, p. 4, available at www.sipri.org.
29 Christopher Clark, 'The Sleepwalkers: How Europe Went to War In 1914', London: Penguin, 2013.
30 Karl Liebknecht, 'The Main Enemy Is at Home', Leaflet, May 1915, Karl Liebknecht Internet Archive, 2002, available at: www.marxists.org.

'THE FIRST CRISIS OF THE ANTHROPOCENE': THE WORLD ECONOMY SINCE COVID

JAMES MEADWAY

The period since early 2020 has seen a challenge to humanity of a scale unknown for a century as Covid-19 swept across the world. The best estimate for mortality from SARS-CoV-2 at the end of 2022 stood at more than 14 million and, as new variants emerge and circulate, years of disruption lie ahead.[1] Already, at least 65 million people are estimated to be suffering from 'long Covid' in some form.[2] But if the human misery is clear, the long-run costs imposed on capitalism are only more slowly making their presence felt. Alongside the direct impacts, the indirect consequences have accelerated and reinforced the tendencies towards international conflict and the breakdown of the existing order, as well as the digitization of human life. The pandemic has made only too clear, even to those in the more protected developed world, the great pressures being placed on the earth's natural systems and the resulting ecological blowback.[3] If there was a 'metabolic rift' between humanity and nature forced open by capitalism, it is now being violently closed over our heads.[4]

As Adam Tooze described it in the first few months of the outbreak, Covid-19 is the 'first crisis of the Anthropocene'.[5] This essay takes the claim seriously: that the Covid pandemic is not merely an ephemeral event in human history, but the marker of a new and radically more ecologically-unsettled period for the whole planet. Typically, however, responses to the pandemic have viewed it only as a sudden radical discontinuity, with limited extended impacts, akin to the 1918 influenza pandemic.[6] Robert Brenner has characterized the initial years of the pandemic as 'escalating plunder', continuing a 'long epoch' of 'worsening economic decline' that has been met by 'political predation'.[7] This argument contains an essential element of truth, not least in the pure venality that much state Covid expenditure involved during the emergency response.[8] It develops a common line of argumentation from the Marxist left of an essentially unbroken decline in global capitalism since the mid-1970s. In this perspective, even the breakdown of the stable natural environment that we inhabit – of which increased epidemics and pandemics are a by-product – is secondary to the operations of the presumed falling rate of profit.[9]

But there is a far bigger issue at stake. As Mathew Lawrence and Laurie Laybourn-Langton put it with admirable clarity: 'All states, markets, economies, welfare systems, militaries, major religions, scientific breakthroughs, cultures, medical advances, wars, and the people that fought for them came about during a uniquely stable period of Earth's natural history. That era is now over.'[10] We enter this new and unstable period of natural history with the inheritance of human history: in particular, the transformational legacy generated over the last two hundred years of industrial capitalism, its accumulations of wealth and its social institutions.

While the stability of both global and national institutions, as well as the wider environment, opened up opportunities to extend capitalism's 'real subsumption' of both labour and nature,[11] the rising costs required even to maintain the system as it is today constitute a growing barrier to its further expansion. The account in this essay therefore emphasizes that the real barriers to productivity improvements that are emerging in the material base of the economy are decisive. These barriers to expansion are not 'fetters' on the forces of production arising from the relations of production, as in more orthodox Marxist accounts.[12] Rather, they are barriers in the forces of production that are imposing themselves on production relations. This end of 'cheap nature' is also the end of relative stability in the system's core and in its primary institutions.[13] To draw a schematic distinction with Robert Brenner and others, the primary barrier to profitability is not competition, but cost. The very material world we inhabit is undergoing what is for modern humans, an unprecedented shift into deep instability. It is this decay that overdetermines the conjuncture.[14]

THE END OF NEOLIBERALISM AND FINANCIAL HEGEMONY

Deglobalization and the end of US hegemony

For decades, the neoliberal playbook gave a robust set of policy prescriptions and guidelines for governments the world over, an ideological justification for those prescriptions (typically hinging on various claims about globalization, and the superiority of free markets and market-like institutions), and the institutional means for their enforcement, from bond markets to the IMF and the World Trade Organization (WTO). The result was a striking convergence of policy: the *pensée unique* that dominated how policy was supposed to be done.[15] Significant variations existed, but it could reasonably be argued, approaching the end of the 2000s, that these merely reflected differences in the distance travelled on the same common road towards the 'End of History'.[16] The 2007-08 crisis shattered this happy vision; although in reality the economies growing fastest in the years before the crash had deviated significantly from the pure neoliberal playbook, China most obvious amongst them, it was *after* the crash that the break with neoliberalism became strikingly apparent, both domestically and (crucially) internationally.

Crises, at least before 2008, had even seemed to reinforce the ideological claims of neoliberalism. The successful management of the 2003 SARS breakout led to over-confident declarations of a new 'post-Westphalian' global public health regime operating above and beyond nation-states, with the World Health Organization (WHO) as an effective global regulator.[17] Covid-19 exposed these pretensions. The WHO is dramatically underfunded, with a budget of just $4.4 billion in 2020, 'less than that of a single big city hospital'.[18] But as Covid revealed, it was also beset by internal rivalries and subject to the new dynamics of emerging 'great power' competition between the US, China and other states, leaving it in no position to impose itself on anyone.[19] Its plaintive appeals for the ending of intellectual property protections over vaccine technology, even when backed by some of the world's most populous states, fell on deaf or, at best, condescending ears in the Global North.[20] Its attempts to navigate between the desire of the Chinese government to impose strict controls over the reporting and investigation of the Covid outbreak, and the demands of the rest of the world for openness, resulted in some unsettling back-and-forth on questions of policy through the first years of the pandemic.[21]

In this, the WHO parallels other weak global structures that aim to achieve global public goods, most notably those associated with climate change.[22] While there have been important steps here, the pace of global transition into low carbon energy systems is far slower than would be ideal: neither the much-heralded 2015 Paris Agreement – a genuine breakthrough – nor the various scientific authorities charged with overseeing the disaster have the authority to set a direction for a world system facing increasing disorder.

As we move from a world where capitalism can impose itself on the planet, to one in which nature is imposing itself on capitalism, and therefore on all of us, the weakness of the structures we have in place to manage and resolve the conflicts that are inherent to a system of competing states and capitals will become more apparent. The global structures through which hegemony has operated over the last few centuries, through financial systems and international economic organizations, from the Casa San Giorgio to the World Bank, IMF and WTO,[23] continue to be irreparably weakened by ecological decay, and no parallel alternative structures have been created to replace them – nor, most likely, *can* they be created under capitalist conditions.[24] A world system built around the WHO, assorted climate change agreements and conflicting regulatory arrangements on data use,[25] rather than the financial and economic institutions of old, is a world system in a state of permanent, and potentially worsening, crisis.

The response of states around the globe, both to the ecological crisis and to rising state intervention by other governments, has been to push for more comprehensive government economic intervention than we have seen for decades. This was in evidence during the pandemic, when competitive emergency industrial strategy and quantity-led export controls were used to produce and distribute vaccines, but it has accelerated since, as, for example, Trump-era trade policy, aimed at breaking China's industrial capacities in critical industries like semiconductors, is now joined by Biden-era domestic government intervention. That, in turn, has sparked similar moves in the European Union, which is now preparing to tear up core neoliberal tenets like its state aid rules in the name of meeting state-supported competition elsewhere.[26]

Rising inequality and financialization

Such reforms are not necessarily making capitalism as a whole any more productive, nor, potentially, can they. The process of competitively-driven accumulation that gave capitalism its broadly productivity-improving dynamic for 200 years is, instead, being pushed towards forms of rent-seeking and the useless hoarding of wealth in place of increasingly costly and risky productivity-improving investment. The transfer of wealth upwards during the course of the pandemic was extraordinary. Oxfam estimated the ten richest men in the world saw their hoards more than double, from $700 billion to $1.5 trillion over 2020 and 2021. Concentrated in the essential (and monopolized) sectors of food, tech, energy and (of course) pharmaceuticals, the two-year period saw one new billionaire created every 30 hours.[27] Global inequality (between-countries) stopped falling in 2022 and is likely to have begun to increase. The same process of upwards wealth transfer observed in the Global North was hard at work in the South: the total number of billionaires in the Indo-Pacific grew by a third from March 2020 to November 2021, from 803 to 1,087, and their total wealth grew by 74 per cent.[28]

The previous model of financialization, in operation from the East Asian financial crisis of 1997-98 through to the global financial crisis a decade later, relied on exceptional 'financial elasticity' among the major institutions, overseen by central banks in the major economies and led by the US, that were willing (and indeed happy) to maintain exceptionally low real interest rates. Often incorrectly attributed to 'over-saving' by fast-growing East Asian economies, with China as the clear leader, the result was an extraordinary expansion of financial claims, and cross-border claims in particular, with the transatlantic relationships between US private sector institutions and counterparts in Europe of far greater weight on balance sheets than the transpacific.[29] The growth of credit in the older, developed core of the system, encompassing the richer states of North America and Europe, allowed a continual expansion of consumer borrowing that, in turn, helped finance the purchase of manufactured goods, especially from East Asia, with China's exceptional growth in this period the dominant new economic fact in the world.

In other words, the boom of the 2000s was the product of two distinct factors, rather than a single moment: the creation of a mass of financial claims in the West, through the 'excess elasticity' of its own financial systems (itself a proximate result of prior deregulation) and, on the other side, the expansion of material systems of production in the far East in particular, as the productive frontier of capitalism expanded and global value chains stretched further across the world, suppressing inflation. These two factors did not, as the 'global savings glut' thesis contends, have a strictly necessary economic relationship.[30]

The material realities of production *appeared* to matter less and less, at least from the viewpoint of the older core of capitalism: deindustrialization had shifted the geography of the world system, creating a vast, new working class in the developing world,[31] and shifting the material balance of resources consumed and carbon outputs generated – out of sight for the advanced economies, and out of mind. Meanwhile, the same processes of extended financializations allowed the expansion of an immense consumer bubble that, in turn, sustained continued, import-driven consumption in the advanced economies.[32]

When this financial bubble imploded over 2007-08, it was a failure generated in the core of the system, in the Euro-American banks, and it took national-level interventions by those major states to support the system as a whole.[33] But its *material* impacts were minimal: the balance of industrial production continued to shift from the historic core of the capitalist economy, as attested to by the extraordinary rise in CO_2 emissions since the 1992 Kyoto agreement.[34]

States and central banks to the fore

The period since the global financial crisis has seen central banks come to the fore in the management of the financial system, providing both exceptional levels of liquidity support to institutions and markets, while also overseeing tight new regulations on the actions of the major, private financial institutions themselves, including new forms of monitoring under the rubric of 'macroprudential regulation'.[35] This has had real-world impacts: the major (non-central) banks' balance sheets, globally, were far stronger entering the crisis in 2020 than they had been in 2007.[36] But the overall result, as the dust cleared from the initial conflagration, was to place central banks at the centre of economic management and to leave them, at least in the leading global economies, as the most important single economic institutions of contemporary capitalism – even forming a core element of a new 'state capitalism'.[37]

Originally justified during the global financial crisis as the necessary monetary response to the collapse of lending by financial institutions and an essential support for the broader economy, quantitative easing (QE) has become a key instrument of central bank power, and an important driver of rising wealth inequality. Banks and other financial institutions in receipt of QE money looked to exchange it for other higher-yielding assets, driving up their prices through this increased demand. This, naturally, worked greatly to the benefit of asset-owners, fuelling the rise of 'asset manager capitalism',[38] but had more muted impacts on the wider economy. And QE itself operated largely as a privilege of the richest economies with access to reserve currencies, primarily the US dollar, although the European Central Bank, the Bank of England, the Swiss National Bank and the Bank of Japan all exploited their ability to massively expand their own balance sheets through QE, with limited immediate repercussions.

With the pandemic, this mechanism shifted in two dimensions. First, QE and QE-like operations spread from the developed core of the world economy to a much broader group of economies, with the World Bank listing 18 less developed countries implementing such programs from 2020 onwards.[39] QE was no longer a privilege held only by the economies of the core; in an emergency, at least the larger, typically middle-income economies would also be able to use this mechanism.[40] Meanwhile, by the end of 2020, *all* major developed economies had implemented QE programs.[41]

Second, post-2008 QE was implemented as a monetary support to the wider economy, with bond-buying by central banks a necessary intermediary step, rather than the focus of the intervention. After 2020, bond buying became the focus of QE programs: with demand for government borrowing skyrocketing and major bond markets, including for US bonds, showing severe signs of strain in March 2020, central banks stepped in directly to sustain bond market functions. Although not admitted by central banks, this was a clear breach of the longstanding neoliberal injunction against 'outright monetary financing' of government debt. In conditions of lockdown, however, it resulted in a significant transfer of monetary savings to (typically better off) households who were unable to spend as they would usually wish. At the same time, it supported expenditures in those parts of the economy still able to function, resulting in the monopolistic profits and increased concentrations of wealth noted above.[42] Over 2020-22, these low interest rates and, in many cases, direct access to central bank money through Covid support schemes fuelled a wave of mergers and acquisitions, with US M&A spending rising to $506 billion in 2021, more than double the levels of 2019 or 2020.[43]

The growing influence of central banks has enabled the extension of the regime of major economy control, primarily through the development of 'swap lines'. These provide cheap access to emergency liquidity as a privilege from the world's major central banks to politically favoured subordinates. China has the largest single number of such swap lines, offering renminbi access to 38 central banks,[44] while the US Federal Reserve had opened 14 such lines by mid-2020, of which five are on a permanent basis.[45] In an internationalized financial system, such immediate support in non-domestic currencies, most obviously the US dollar, to domestic financial institutions facing possible insolvency is essential, since domestic central banks typically cannot provide such funding quickly and cheaply in an emergency.[46] But the provision of swap lines has been deeply politicized,[47] with favoured and otherwise privileged subordinate countries more likely to be offered such support than those who have fallen out of favour, for whatever reason.[48] This represents a specific form of power in the global system: on one side, a privilege for the recipient – but also an implied warning, since swap line provision is at the behest of the central bank. It can be provided, but it can also be taken away, and even the *threat* of this is a form of power.

This implied threat is increasingly being matched by the overt power of the state in the form of direct sanctions. Iran was a critical pre-Covid example, in which Iranian companies and banks were excluded from the dollar system by Washington fiat; far more dramatic were the sanctions imposed on Russia following its invasion of Ukraine in February 2022. The US and its close allies sought to exclude Russian entities from SWIFT, the global monetary messaging system used to facilitate cross-border monetary transactions, and to prevent the Russian Central Bank from selling its (substantial) reserves on international markets.⁴⁹ The direct targeting of a central bank to this extent was unprecedented,⁵⁰ but a rapid response by the Russian authorities, who had anticipated these moves by the Western powers, has limited their impact.⁵¹ Capital controls, rapid interest rate increases and the 'yuanization' of payments have all helped to cushion the blow.⁵² Taken together, the responses translate into a Russian economy gradually decoupling from the dollar-centred monetary system. However, of potentially greater importance over the longer-term is that other countries which are only weakly (if at all) aligned with the US now have the imperative to search for other sanctions-proof financial instruments and monetary systems. It is perhaps too early to claim that a new 'Bretton Woods 3' international monetary order is emerging,⁵³ given the continuing dominance of the dollar in trade and bond markets, but the direction of travel is clear. Initiatives like the expansion of the BRICS and the 'BRICS bank', the New Development Bank, reinforce the trend.⁵⁴

Ecological crisis as a driver

The pandemic acted as an accelerant of the tendency, evident since the 2008 crisis, toward a closer alignment of states and financial systems within the global hierarchy of currencies.⁵⁵ But if 2008 produced a strengthening of Washington's control within the global dollar system, the tensions that were already apparent burst through with the pandemic. Attempts to manage crises from Covid onwards tightened Washington's grasp on the dollar system, but in doing so reduced its global reach. Yet financial systems everywhere are becoming subject to shocks emerging far beyond their control, on account of the ongoing ecological crises. Insurers face catastrophic losses, retreating from once-valuable markets like Florida and California. Billions are tied up in assets now stranded by climate change and decarbonization.⁵⁶ The output losses and sheer destruction emerging from extreme weather events herald missed repayments and defaults from debtors: the 'climate Minsky moment' that former Bank of England Governor Mark Carney has highlighted.⁵⁷ Attempts by him and others to provide the institutional framework needed to manage a worsening situation have produced little beyond warm words, with major banks threatening a boycott of proposed legal structures.⁵⁸ The likelihood is that major shocks to the financial system will, as ever, rely on nation states to attempt emergency rescues and longer-term support.⁵⁹ Nor are the dangers confined to climate change: biodiversity loss also creates major new financial stability risks.⁶⁰

These shocks may become most evident at first in the Global South, where suppressed returns in the North after 2008 helped spur the expansion of debt. External public debt in low- and middle-income countries stood at $3 trillion by the end of 2023, double its 2010 level, of which 60 per cent was held by private creditors. Eighty of these countries were judged by the World Bank and IMF to be either in or at risk of debt distress, with ten already in distress.[61] There have been 14 'default events' reported by credit ratings agencies since 2020, across nine different countries, with five countries in default by the end of 2023 – a record high.[62] Critically, however, three-quarters of the countries at risk of debt distress are also those most vulnerable to the effects of climate change.[63]

The vice that is forcing financial systems and states into closer and closer alignment is being tightened by the ecological crisis, even as the world system itself is breaking apart under the same sets of pressures. If the 2008 crisis suggested hard *internal* limits to finance-led expansion, forcing states to intervene on an immense scale, the crisis of 2020 is the first point where *external* limits to the same expansion have become unavoidable for the system as a whole. It is the end, as Cedric Durand suggested,[64] of 'financial hegemony' as exercised during the neoliberal years, with the 'Dollar-Wall Street Regime' at its heart.[65]

THE DATA ECONOMY

Growing digitization

As lockdowns expanded, forcing much economic and social life online, the volume of internet traffic increased rapidly, by 48 per cent from 2019 to 2020.[66] Internet-heavy economies moved further online, while in the less developed world the frontiers of internet use expanded, with 782 million more people coming online in the two years since 2019 – the biggest surge in usage recorded for a decade.[67] Globally, the proportion of the world with an internet connection only surpassed 50 per cent in 2018. Today, two-thirds are online, albeit skewed towards high- and middle-income countries, where 85.5 per cent are online, compared to 27 per cent in low-income countries.[68]

The result of this expansion, inevitably, was to reinforce the dynamics of accumulation in the digital sector, with the value of the six big global tech firms surging by 38 per cent in the first six months of the pandemic, cementing their dominant position in the global economy.[69] As the initial waves of Covid receded, the ratchet effect became apparent: working from home and remote working in general has moved from an unusual situation for a few to a regular occurrence for many – though one typically skewed towards richer, older and whiter workers.[70]

The raw material and energy demands of the digital economy are a massive new source of increased (and rising) costs. Disguised by the extraordinary hype of 'Generative AI', in reality the technologies grouped around Machine Learning (ML) that make up the bulk of the AI investment bubble are best thought of as an extension of existing data-processing techniques, rather than a radical break with the past. As such, they are also dependent on existing hardware technologies alongside familiarly insatiable demands for analyzable data. This makes these technologies chronically, and notoriously, energy- and hardware-dependent: ChatGPT was trained with around 10,000 specialized Nvidia chips,[71] while its current application uses the energy equivalent of 30,000 US households daily.[72]

Meanwhile, precisely because the underlying technologies are an expanded use of what we already had rather than some radical breach with the past, the same hard barriers to their use and expansion in circuits of capitalist accumulation are apparent. The investment bubble in so-called AI over the last 18 months has resulted in supply shortages and bottlenecks throughout the digital industries, as companies try to grab limited server capacity, semiconductor supplies and energy resources. By early 2023, it was taking months for hardware manufacturers to meet this surge in demand. Amazon Web Services, Google, Microsoft and Oracle are among the server providers currently having to ration space to their AI customers.[73]

The great hope of AI is that it will unlock the potential for immense productivity gains across the economy, sufficient to overcome rising costs, for example in healthcare. But current technologies are wildly inefficient, creating unsustainable resource demands that rise exponentially with limited gains in computing power.[74] Moore's Law, that once-reliable source of productivity gains on the basis of computer power doubling roughly every two years, stopped operating around the mid-2000s, calling time on a relatively easy source of growth for capitalism.[75] Rising resource costs and limits present a hard barrier to growth through ML. Computers have been a disappointment for growth and productivity since their widespread adoption began over five decades ago and there are few reasons to assume a radical change in this regard.[76]

THE MATERIAL LIMITS TO CAPITALIST PRODUCTION

Soaring raw material demands

Despite the claims that that the new digital economy was 'weightless'[77] or that we would 'live on thin air',[78] the demand for hard, physical matter and energy has been enormously reinforced by its activities. Between 1970 and 2024, global annual material resource extraction rose from 31 to 104 billion tons, or 335 per cent.[79] Ed Conway notes that in 2019 'we mined, dug and blasted more materials from the earth's surface than the sum total of everything we extracted from the dawn of humanity to 1950'.[80] This expansion has been grossly inefficient: for example, the World Bank estimates that less than one-fifth of all global waste is recycled.[81] And as economies reopened over 2021-22, the surge in pent-up demand dislocated raw materials markets across the globe, causing surges in prices for commodities from tin[82] to epoxy resin,[83] and physical shortages of semiconductors.[84] These shortages have continued and, in some cases, worsened. Russia's invasion of Ukraine, a primary example of geopolitical disintegration under the Anthropocene, provoked exceptional increases in the price of food.[85]

It is here, too, that the interaction with the broader ecological crisis starts to become apparent. Efforts to decarbonize will further increase material demand as the switch from fossil fuels to renewables, and the necessary electrification of both infrastructure and personal consumption, creates heavy additional demands for exotic rare earth metals[86] and more mundane commodities like copper.[87] For example, 'renewable energy plants require on average 8–12 times more copper than fossil-based forms of power generation and [electric vehicles] 3–4 times more than an internal combustion engine vehicle'.[88] Global copper supplies are expected to fall short of even the (not especially dramatic) net zero 2050 targets.[89] Demand for lithium, essential to battery production, is expected to increase 40 times by 2040.[90] One projection suggests that a simple like-for-like switch of US cars from internal combustion to electric engines would require three times the current global production of lithium.[91] The 'commodity frontier' of capitalism is shifting;[92] the 'planetary mine' is deepening.[93]

Already these expanded demands for the raw materials of a 'decarbonized' economy are provoking new conflicts, both at the fault lines of the major powers, where zones of control are not yet established – and, in some instances, behind those fault lines as economies find themselves in unique (and perhaps temporary) positions of strength against the great powers. Potentially, at least, this disrupts not only the unipolar world of the 2000s, challenging the unambiguous hegemony of the US, but opens opportunities for those capitalist powers outside of the core economies to act independently. Moves by Chile and other South American countries to nationalize and otherwise claim greater control of raw mineral resources essential for future technological transformations, like lithium and copper, show the pattern of shifting relationships, with China as a major investor.[94] China's Belt and Road Initiative, which recently celebrated its tenth anniversary, has delivered over $1 trillion of investment, typically via loans and in transport and communications infrastructure, across 150 countries.[95] At a global level, initiatives by China and the other BRICS economies to expand the group are an as-yet-unrealized challenge to the US-centred economic system.

Older zones of great power contestation are being shaken up. In the Middle East, China and Saudi Arabia are developing increasingly close relations, with China brokering a rapprochement between the Saudis and the other major regional power, Iran, in early 2023.[96] The region's location as the majority source of the world's most important commodity is directly challenged by decarbonization; states in the region, with Saudi Arabia as the most dramatic example, are rushing to diversify their own economies, with varying degrees of success.[97] The US has unsubtly attempted to divest itself from its own diplomatic and military responsibilities in the Middle East and beyond,[98] withdrawing from Afghanistan and promoting the 'Abraham Accords' between regional despotisms and its long-standing ally, Israel; these were placed under, at the least, exceptional strain in autumn 2023 by the Israel-Hamas conflict.[99]

And new frontiers for conflict are emerging, as in the Arctic, where melting ice is reducing the cost of exploiting its fossil fuel resources and decarbonization is promoting the development of its vast critical mineral resources. Climate change further promises to make the Arctic sea-lanes a viable alternative for goods transport, dramatically reducing transport times and costs from East Asia to Europe. Control of all three – fossil fuel resources, critical minerals and Arctic sea-lanes – is now a direct point of great power confrontation,[100] the once-peaceful venue of the Arctic Council having fallen into abeyance following Russia's invasion of Ukraine[101] and with the US and China directly competing for access to the mineral resources of Greenland.[102] Large-scale extractive activities are conducted at the expense not only of the natural environment itself, but Indigenous groups and local residents, provoking protest and conflict.[103]

In addition to the reshaping of the geography of conflict (and potential conflict), climate change and the environmental crisis is also directly pressurizing supply chains. Biodiversity loss resulting from the global agrifood system[104] is placing the future of food supply under 'severe threat', according to the UN's Food and Agriculture Organization,[105] while climate change itself is expected to reorder the distribution of viable farmland.[106]

Meanwhile, extreme weather events impose severe disruptions on the production and transportation of food, resulting in shortages and price spikes.[107] Brazilian coffee, Belgian potatoes and Canadian yellow peas all suffered extreme weather price shocks in 2021,[108] followed by European sunflower and olive oil in 2022,[109] while 2023 has seen rice harvests in India badly affected by El Niño and a subsequent export ban imposed by the government. These idiosyncratic (but related) shocks are starting to overwhelm the cost advantages of globalized food supply chains, with every 1 per cent increase in the share of food production in global value chains being associated with a 2 per cent decline in prices – but an 8 per cent increase in price volatility.[110] The implicit trade-off in the globalized economy, of lower prices for greater exposure to risk, is breaking down. And the number of extreme weather events annually increased five-fold between 1979 and 2019. At the same time, the average cost of any given extreme weather event is estimated to have increased in real terms by 77 per cent over the same period.[111]

Even more fundamentally, global water systems are under huge strain. Already, a quarter of the world's population lacks access to drinking water, and 46 per cent lack safe sanitation.[112] From the point of view of capital accumulation in recent decades, these failures in basic provision could be mostly ignored. But climate change (on one side) and continued intensive use of water resources for production (on the other) are pushing shortages to the point of intrusion on capital's prerogatives for accumulation. Shortages for agriculture are becoming recurrent, with more than 80 per cent of the world's croplands expected to experience water shortages by 2050.[113]

More novel, however, are the water shortages now affecting the world's most advanced production process, the semiconductor supply chain. Vast quantities of water are needed to keep production lines clean, with a large fabrication plant typically using 10 million litres of water a day, equivalent to 300,000 households.[114] Taiwan Semiconductor Manufacturing Company (TSMC), producers of 90 per cent of the world's most advanced silicon chips, was reportedly forced to reduce production during a drought on the island in 2021, worsening the global chip shortage and pitting semiconductor plants directly against farmers in the contest for water.[115] Arizona, the site for two vast new government-subsidized TSMC plants,[116] each one using some 15 million litres of water a day,[117] is currently enduring its worst drought in 1,200 years.[118]

THE MONETARY DISLOCATION

The 2022-23 inflationary surge as first marker of the new regime

The post-pandemic period has been characterized by an extraordinary surge in inflation over 2022-23. Attributable in the first instance to Russia's invasion of Ukraine (itself prima facie evidence of the continued breakdown of Washington's global order), even as the inflationary shock of this major event has worn out, inflation across the developed world has remained stubbornly high. An older, monetarist argument has re-emerged in the last few years, attempting to explain this inflation as the inevitable consequence of 'excessive' monetary creation, with these excessive money balances chasing up the prices of scarce commodities. But the monetary explanation has great difficulty explaining the self-evidently *real* causes of rising prices for specific goods: it is not obvious why the Bank of England's balance sheet, for example, would cause Russia to invade Ukraine, or how the Federal Reserve caused El Niño, which has been strong so far this season,[119] impacting harvests around the world in complex interaction with climate change.[120] These specific real-world events hitting a credit money economy, necessarily biased towards excessive money creation under any circumstances,[121] create a tendency towards higher and more volatile inflation.[122]

As Grace Blakeley noted, in the first year of the pandemic the impact of the crisis was to accelerate the drive towards monopolization of critical industries and a greater concentration of wealth.[123] We have already seen how digitization gave a further boost to the handful of giant firms that dominate the data economy; similar processes of consolidation have accelerated in the critical sectors of food and energy supplies – notably, those that have experienced shocks since the pandemic.[124] Data technologies are actively facilitating concentration, with agribusinesses (for example) using data collection and analysis to facilitate vertical integration in the food supply system.[125] The 'concentration and centralization' of capital continues apace, and is increasingly directly aided by state intervention, with national governments intervening to support 'their' national firms. As interest rates have risen and monetary conditions tightened, the frenzy of cheap money-fuelled mergers and acquisitions has given way to more overt forms of state intervention, like the US' Inflation Reduction Act.[126] The post-pandemic bubble conditions that allowed speculative investment and disguised loss-making across the economy[127] have given way to a shakeout of the more exposed positions and assets.[128]

The process of concentration is directly fuelling generalized price rises and the redistribution this implies away from labour in general and toward specific monopolized sectors of capital. Isabella Weber and Evan Wasner's work details a mechanism by which market power of firms in key sectors, subject to shocks, can be translated into price surges – a phenomenon they label 'sellers' inflation'.[129] The implication is that while profits may rise in those key sectors, capital in general will be squeezed and, over time, as the shocks continue, this problem will worsen.

The presence of a 'double inelasticity' – inelastic demand for essentials and inelastic supply of those essentials – is the locus for a price surge, notably when firms in a sector are also able to exercise market power. As the material demands of capitalism grow, and as the ecological crisis raises costs across the system, these pressure points will worsen. The continuing presence of excess elasticity in the monetary system as a whole – whether delivered by private banking and finance, from the hoards of idle liquidity held by the wealthy and major corporations, or, under pressure of crises, the Federal Reserve and other central banks[130] – provides the means by which those price surges can be continually realized.[131] And the 'reaction function' of central banks across the world, geared as they are to an economic model in which raising interest rates undermines worker power through unemployment and therefore (in the model) reduces inflationary pressures, leans the whole system towards permanently higher nominal interest rates. Research is already starting to show how climate change impacts are feeding directly into developed economy inflation: as a result of the changing climate, a typical UK household is now spending over £600 more on food per year than two years ago.[132]

WORK AND NON-WORK

Labour

The dislocation caused by Covid lockdowns had a largely unanticipated side effect.[133] By clamping down on labour supply so severely – first through state-led restrictions, then in the decisions of many millions to remove themselves from the market for work – Covid has dramatically tightened labour markets. The result has seen an extraordinary increase in voluntary exits from employment, a sharp if uneven rise in (money) wages and, from spring 2022, the signs of a serious and sustained uptick in union organization and militancy in the developed world.[134]

The OECD, in a late 2022 survey, noted the tightening of developed world labour markets: 'Vacancy-to-unemployed rates have risen sharply in Australia, Canada and the United Kingdom. In other countries, such as France and Italy, labour markers have also tightened but from a situation of comparative slack at the beginning of the pandemic.'[135] These have occurred with some sectoral variations, with 'contact-intensive' services like care, and accommodation and food, particularly affected. Meanwhile, OECD members experienced a 'Great Resignation' with 'rising job vacancy rates [that] have gone hand-in-hand with rising quit rates'.[136] In the Global South, employment and labour participation have been slower to recover, reflecting 'more severe output losses and weaker protection' during the pandemic in the short term,[137] and, as we suggest below, longer-term structural problems for capitalism.

Some of these developed world impacts are likely to be purely cyclical in character, with rising demand for output as economies reopened creating more demand for labour. Some, however, will be due to 'structural factors', with the OECD following the IMF in focusing on a 'change in workers' preferences' as they are no longer so willing to accept 'low-quality jobs, that is, jobs characterized by low-pay, bad working conditions ... as well as poor social benefits'.[138] This shift in *subjectivity* engendered by the pandemic has clearly been important: the whiplash-inducing lurch from applauded 'essential workers' early in the pandemic to disastrous declines in real wages just a few years later has been for many workers in 'essential' industries a key motivating factor in recent strikes as well as decisions to quit.[139] And while not as polarizing, the realization that a better life might be had without work has been, for many older, asset-rich workers nearing retirement, a hefty inducement to quit. Redundancy payments during the pandemic, continually rising property prices in the developed world and (for strongly neoliberalized countries like the UK) relatively flexible pensions systems have all contributed as 'push' factors.[140]

But there is a much less happy *objective* element to the labour-market tightening, driven by Covid itself. The health impacts of Covid globally have been manifested in two dimensions. The first, which is relatively short term, is the secondary impact of the pandemic on wider health systems. With operations cancelled and more conventional medicine harder to get during the worst of the pandemic, and in some cases those with illness choosing to avoid healthcare, mortality and other negative health outcomes worsened in a number of cases globally.[141] Taken together, the immediate shock of the pandemic created populations that were not only more likely to sicken and die because of Covid, but also because of the second-order impacts resulting from the attempt to manage that Covid shock. These impacts should, at least, be of limited duration, but will be playing out in increased healthcare costs and reduced labour participation rates across the globe.

The second dimension will be longer term. Although research into the causes is ongoing, and currently points to multiple sources and symptoms under a common label,[142] 'long Covid' is serious enough to result in long term health impacts for its sufferers that, in turn, become difficulties in how and when they can work. The number of long Covid sufferers globally is unknown, although a recent estimate in *The Lancet* suggests around 45 per cent of those with Covid suffered some significant ill effects around four months after initial infection.[143] Survey evidence from 56 countries found that 45 per cent of self-reported long Covid sufferers 'required a reduced work schedule due to the illness' while a further 22 per cent reported that they were currently not working.[144] In the UK, 1.8 million people have reported suffering debilitating effects from long Covid, with the labour supply being reduced by around 110,000 being off sick per week.[145] In the US, 16 million working age adults (8 per cent of the workforce) are estimated to have long Covid, with two to four million removed from the workforce as a result,[146] accounting for perhaps 15 per cent or more of unfilled job vacancies.[147]

An increasingly elderly global population, with those over 65 expected to rise from 761 million in 2021 to 1.6 billion in 2050, is set to be concentrated in the Global North, with UN projections suggesting 25 per cent of developed world populations would be over 65 by this date.[148] The costs of 'social reproduction',[149] which the developed world had largely socialized over the previous century through extending state provision of education, healthcare and some limited post-working life income via pensions, could rapidly become unbearably large for capital. The BIS notes that:

> Estimates for [advanced economies] and [emerging market economies] suggest that age-related expenditures will grow by approximately 4% and 5% of GDP, respectively, over the next 20 years. Absent fiscal consolidation, this would push debt above 200% and 150% of GDP by 2050 in AEs and EMEs, respectively, even if interest rates remain below growth rates, as was the case in the pre-pandemic years.[150]

The costs of healthcare are expected to rise in line, particularly in the developed world but notably including China,[151] from $9.2 trillion in 2021 to $16.9 trillion in 2050.[152] Increased disease outbreaks are set to add to the burden, alongside the huge costs of non-communicable diseases,[153] with anti-microbial resistant strains already costing the US alone an estimated $55 billion, and this bill forecast to rise.[154]

Older, sicker and less productive is the future of the world's labour force.[155] If it becomes more expensive to sustain labour, to provide it with the essentials of life alongside a sufficient level of education, then the incentives for capital to divest itself from those costs naturally increase: it becomes necessary to reprivatize social reproduction, as far as possible, dumping the costs back onto families and households outside of national spheres of reproduction, as we see in the super-exploitation of migrant labour, and establishing expanded zones of informal and underpaid labour.

Perversely, the consequence of a reduced labour force in conditions of persistent, recurrent crises, may actually be to increase workers' power. The disruption of labour markets across the globe occasioned by the pandemic has led to the sudden re-emergence of labour as an independent political actor in society, from the 'Great Resignation' to conflicts over working from home, to what appears to be a brewing strike wave in core capitalist countries.

Rising prices have, as in the past, provided the motivation to strike; tighter labour markets the opportunity to make such actions effective.[156]

Blocked development and the digital alternative

This process is an acceleration of existing trends. Mike Davis highlighted, almost twenty years ago, how the expansion of 'urbanization' unfolded ahead of 'proletarianization', creating a 'Planet of Slums', arguing that 'urbanization has become decoupled from industrialization and subsistence from waged employment'.[157] But now, with just two degrees of warming, almost half of India's projected population by 2050 are at a risk of severe climate hazards.[158] In the standard IPCC 'business as usual'[159] scenario, 'India could become one of the first places in the world to experience heat waves that cross the survivability limit for a healthy human being resting in the shade, and this could occur as early as next decade'.[160] This would directly impact the capacity of those affected to work. Arriving on top of a legacy of colonialism, underdevelopment and poor infrastructure, the likelihood of India reaching the level of wide-scale economic integration achieved by China, its neighbour to the north, is being progressively diminished by worsening climate change. Alongside India, and suffering from similar, longstanding legacies of colonialism and underdevelopment, are a spread of highly exposed countries across sub-Saharan Africa.[161] The ecological crisis is hugely reinforcing the tendency towards creating a 'relative surplus population'.[162]

Under these circumstances, the classic Lewisian model of growth, in which 'surplus labour' generated from agriculture is absorbed into the modern sector,[163] faces rising and potentially insurmountable barriers. This does not mean some investment cannot take place: clearly, in recent years, it has, with China in particular making very substantial infrastructural investments across the Global South.[164] But the integration of surplus labour into the wider economy becomes harder the heavier the costs of climate change and wider ecological disruption become. The result is 'combined and uneven development', worsened by the ecological crisis, with a few leading industries and sectors surrounded by an underdeveloped economy. In a recent survey, the World Bank was gloomy about the prospects for the future development of low- and middle-income countries, citing precisely these ecological and geopolitical barriers to growth.[165] And with developed economies, notably including the US, refusing to make serious, mandatory commitments to 'loss and damage' financing for climate change impacts, the prospect of significant reparations being paid from the richer North to the poorer South seems to be, at present, minimal.[166]

Instead, deeper integration into the digital economy for labour in the Global South is more likely than the classic model of capitalist development. While fuller integration into the global division of labour will remain barred by a combination of past underdevelopment alongside present and future ecological shocks, the presence of a robust digital infrastructure allows the precariously and informally employed access to an extensive digital economy – turning their data into a new 'frontier commodity'.

The number online, estimated at 5.3 billion as of 2023,[167] is significantly larger than the International Labour Organization's estimate for the numbers employed globally, at 3.2 billion – of which two-thirds, or around 2 billion, are in any case informally employed.[168] This huge digital population is a source of value not only (or even) in the conventional manner of steady integration into the abstractions of the labour market but as a potential source of data acquisition and integration into consumption systems. Notoriously, Big Tech relies on an army of underpaid and grossly exploited workers, typically in the Global South, to maintain its systems, from providing content moderation[169] to, more recently, the guided 'training' of large-scale machine learning systems.[170] But beyond this, especially as developed markets reach saturation point, there are new continents of human material to be digitally mined: not only exploited as labour, in the conventional fashion, but also dragged into the immense infrastructure of data collection and analysis. The gains per new developing world user are lower, since the disposable income of any given user is typically lower, but as saturation in developed markets is reached, these new frontiers become viable.[171]

End of cheap labour, cheap nature

What we are witnessing now starts to resemble something like the 'end of cheap labour' resulting from the 'end of cheap nature'. Covid, in this scenario, was both an immediate shock, and an acceleration of trends that were otherwise becoming more apparent. The interaction between the two is critical. It was the ecological conditions created by pre-industrial development that opened up the path to a world of 'cheap labour'. Shaping and conditioning 'cheap labour' at the peak of its application was a global financial system that allowed the extension, to a planetary scale, of supply chains tying production across many places with final consumption somewhere wholly different, creating a global working class to match a global consumer society.[172] Those supply chains are now directly threatened by their own ecological consequences, occurring in conditions of (and reinforcing) geopolitical instability.

Where once the systemic processes all worked in the same direction, the lines of capitalist control being established by and reinforcing each other through the formation of a financial system, a trading system, a monetary system and, ultimately, something closely resembling a global labour market, the same processes are now running against each other. The end of the cheap world means the breakdown of financial systems, the failure of trading systems and the dissolution of a global labour market.

And yet, simultaneously, the raw experience of the Anthropocene is emerging as the decisive moment of commonality amongst us all. By analogy, if the arrival of modern economic growth was prepared by the 'unification of the globe by disease',[173] its conclusion is being heralded by the 'unification of the proletariat by disease',[174] with the conditions of the pandemic providing a common experience of crisis. These are Ajay Singh Chaudhary's 'exhausted of the earth', echoing Frantz Fanon's 'wretched': all those brought together by the compounding crises of the Anthropocene.[175] The scope of the struggles engendered by a changing world reach beyond the 'economistic' confines of the historical labour movement and more immediately into those zones of contestation that John Bellamy Foster has rightly described as 'revolutionary' when they emerge: 'community, health, and the environment'.[176] None of these by themselves need present an incipient and radical challenge to the system, but the conditions of the crisis are such that each will arrive entangled in the others, opening the route to broader solutions than only single-issue demands.

'End of the month, end of the world: same logic, same struggle'[177]

The disorder at the start of the Anthropocene is terminating the conditions whereby a compromise between state, capital and labour was viable. Conflict, along broader parameters than in the past, will be the result. A capitalist world economy in which nature, rather than capital, is moving to dominate is one moving out of the familiar patterns of accumulation of the last two centuries. The emerging patterns of economic life, in which 'natural' events intrude and shake up our own human activities on a regular basis, are not those which can sustain reformist politics based on consistent growth and stable employment – certainly not in the core countries, which are typically less exposed to immediate ecological shocks but for whom future shocks could, therefore, be more politically destabilizing as a result.

The politics of compromise with capital were built on a tamed and controlled nature and premised for more than a century since its arrival on a version of economic growth in which the proceeds of growth are shared and the conditions of social reproduction provided for. These conditions no longer apply. Incipient signs of this failure in the historic core of the system are already evident, in the miserable performances of the historic social democratic parties and the rise of 'populist' far right political formations and individuals. The latter are so far proving typically better at exploiting our worsening conditions and the conflicts they engender. There are no guarantees that the fusion of crises under the Anthropocene will automatically lead to desirable political conclusions.

More direct conflicts are spreading to the core of the system: for example, since October 2022, thousands of protestors have mobilized against the construction of 16 '*megabassines*' in western France.[178] These vast reservoirs, with each *megabassine* on average the size of ten football pitches, are intended to keep water-intensive farming viable even as shortages threaten it. But diverting water to high-intensity agribusinesses means starving smaller farmers and local residents of the same supplies. Protests, up to 30,000 strong, have been met with violent police repression, but represent a new frontier in the climate struggle, acting (in the words of Andreas Malm) as 'the first social protests around adaptation to climate change'.[179]

Sometimes hidden, sometimes open, this form of politics will overdetermine other concerns. A capitalist economy with limited growth, beset by crises, unable to provide secure conditions for production and reproduction is one in which the efforts at crisis management themselves become the structuring principle of struggle – El Niño causes rice harvest failures across India; attempts by its government to manage shortages through export bans spark further price rises across the world,[180] which then provoke demands for protection against inflation.[181] 'The total movement of the whole disorder is its order':[182] the logic of an essentially endless, open-ended crisis is for capitalism to continually reproduce its own failed resolutions to the crises and, with that, the enforced unity of those being forced to carry the cost of its failures.

A new mass politics is essential. In outline: redistributive, from the dead wealth at the top of society to living labour elsewhere. The demand for wage rises (on one side) or controlled prices (on the other) are fundamental here. The old rhetoric of a 'moral economy' is central. Prefigurative, acting today to create the conditions required for collective survival in the Anthropocene, at whatever scale can be made viable – an occupied workplace, a local community park, a regional government. And internationalist, as the shared conditions of ecological collapse and geopolitical conflict create the possibility of uniting a broader collective to act in the name of common humanity against social and ecological collapse.

NOTES

1. William Msemburi, Ariel Karlinsky, Victoria Knutson et al., 'The WHO estimates of excess mortality associated with the COVID-19 pandemic', *Nature*, 613, 2023, pp. 130-37.
2. Hannah E. Davis, Lisa McCorkell, Julia Moore Vogel and Eric J. Topol, 'Long COVID: major findings, mechanisms and recommendations', *Nature Reviews Microbiology*, 21, 2023, pp. 133-46.
3. John Bellamy Foster, Brett Clark and Hannah Holleman, 'Capital and the ecology of disease', *Monthly Review*, 1 June 2021, available at: www.monthlyreview.org.
4. Jason W. Moore, 'Metabolic rift or metabolic shift? Dialectics, nature, and the world-historical method', *Theory and Society*, 46(4), 2017, pp. 285-318.
5. Adam Tooze, 'We are living through the first economic crisis of the Anthropocene', *The Guardian*, 7 May 2020. See also his *Shutdown: how Covid shook the world's economy*, New York: Viking, 2021.
6. Brian Beach, Karen Clay and Martin H. Saavedra, 'The 1918 influenza pandemic and its lessons for COVID-19', NBER Working Paper 27673, Cambridge, MA: National Bureau of Economic Research, August 2020.
7. Robert Brenner, 'Escalating plunder', *New Left Review*, 123, May/June 2020, pp. 5-22.
8. CMI-U4, 'Covid-19 and corruption', blog, available at: www.u4.no.
9. From different versions of this perspective, see for example: Robert Brenner, 'The Economics of Global Turbulence', *New Left Review*, 229, May/June 1998; Michael Roberts, *The Long Depression: how it happened, why it happened, and what happens next*, New York: Haymarket Books, 2006; Chris Harman, *Zombie Economics*, London: Bookmarks, 2009.
10. Laurie Laybourn-Langton and Mathew Lawrence, *Planet on Fire*, London: Verso, 2021, p.1.
11. Karl Marx, 'Draft of Capital, Book I: the process of production', 1863, ch. 6, available at: www.wikirouge.net; see also: Soren Mau, *Mute Compulsion: a Marxist theory of the economic power of capital*, London: Verso, 2023, ch. 11 especially.
12. Karl Marx, 'Preface', *A Contribution to the Critique of Political Economy*, 1859, available at: www.marxists.org; G.A. Cohen, *Karl Marx's Theory of History: A defence*, Princeton, NJ: Princeton University Press, 1978.
13. Jason W. Moore, *Capitalism in the Web of Life: Ecology and the Accumulation of Capital*, New York: Verso, 2015.
14. Alex Callinicos, *The New Age of Catastrophe*, Cambridge: Polity Press, 2023, p. 11. Adam Tooze has popularised the term 'polycrisis', in an effort to summarize the uniquely grim combination of multiple, overlapping crises. I am here, like Callinicos, attempting to demonstrate a structure to the conjuncture, rather than a formless whirl of competing causes and 'multiple determinations'.
15. David Harvey, *A Brief History of Neoliberalism*, Oxford: Oxford University Press, 2005.
16. Francis Fukuyama, *The End of History and the Last Man*, New York: Free Press, 1992; Perry Anderson, *A Zone of Engagement*, London: Verso, 1992.
17. David P. Fidler, 'SARS: political pathology of the first post-Westphalian pathogen', *Journal of Law, Medicine and Ethics*, 31, 2003, pp. 110-15; see also: Theodore M. Brown, Marcos Cueto and Elizabeth Fee, 'The World Health Organization and the

Transition From "International" to "Global" Public Health', *American Journal of Public Health*, 96(1), 2006, pp. 62-72.
18   Tooze, *Shutdown*, p. 32.
19   Colin Kahl and Thomas Wright, *Aftershocks: Pandemic Politics and the End of the Old International Order*, New York: St Martin's Press, 2021.
20   Ashleigh Furlong, Sara Anne Aarup and Samuel Horti, 'Who killed the covid vaccine waiver?', *Politico*, 10 November 2022.
21   On declining public confidence, see: Chaou Guo et al., 'The effect of COVID-19 on public confidence in the World Health Organization: a natural experiment among 40 countries', *Global Health*, 18(77), 2022.
22   The notion here of a 'global public good' as an essential component of a functioning hegemony is taken from: Charles Kindleberger, *The Great Depression 1929-1939*, London: Allen Lane, 1973.
23   Giovanni Arrighi, *The Long Twentieth Century*, London: Verso, 1994, p. 112
24   James Meadway, 'Neoliberalism is dying – now we must replace it', *openDemocracy*, 3 September 2021.
25   Nigel Cory and Luke Dasoli, 'How cross-border barriers to digital trade are spreading globally, what they cost, and how to stop them', Information Technology and Innovation Foundation, 19 July 2021, indicates that the 'number of data-localization measures in force around the world has more than doubled in four years'.
26   Irina Trichovska, et al., 'The European Commission loosens State aid rules to foster energy transition and prevent the flight of green technologies from Europe', *Insight Alert*, White & Case, 27 March 2023, available at: www.whitecase.com. The mechanism whereby one state competitively forces state intervention within others is well-described in: Nikolai Bukharin, *Imperialism and the World Economy*, Moscow, 1915/1925, available at: www.marxists.org.
27   Oxfam, 'Food and energy billionaires pocket a $453bn windfall…', press release, 23 May 2022, available at: www.oxfam.org.uk.
28   Emma Seery, 'Rising to the Challenge: the case for permanent progressive policies to tackle Asia's coronavirus and inequality crisis', Briefing Paper, Oxford: Oxfam International, 12 January 2022.
29   Claudio Borio and Piti Disyatat, 'Global imbalances and the financial crisis: link or no link?', BIS Working Papers no.346, Geneva: Bank of International Settlements, 2011.
30   As determined by the balance of net claims between different economies: if one country is running a surplus, another must, by accounting identities, be running a deficit. A decisive challenge to this view is provided by Borio and Disyatat, 'Global imbalances', who note that this view looks only at net claims, rather than analysing the gross flows of financing that hold the key to understanding the financial system in general and the 2008 crash in particular.
31   In 1990, the total potential labour force of the older industrialized world, covering all those aged between 20 to 64, was 685 million. In China and Eastern Europe, it was 850 million. By 2014, it was 763 million in the former, but a staggering 1,120 million in China and Eastern Europe. Charles Goodhart, and Manoj Pradhan, 'Demographics will reverse three multi-decade global trends', BIS Working Paper 615, Geneva: Bank of International Settlements, August 2017, p. 5

32 Robin Blackburn, 'The Subprime Crisis', *New Left Review*, 50, March/April 2008, pp. 63-106; and a comment by Geoff Mann, 'Colletti on the Credit Crunch: A Response to Robin Blackburn', *New Left Review*, 56, March/April 2009, pp. 119-27.
33 Adam Tooze, *Crashed*, New York: Viking Press, 2018.
34 'In the last 30 years, the amounts of CO_2 emissions have increased at a rate faster than ever before in history', with half of all CO_2 emissions have been produced since 1990. See: Thorfinn Stainforth and Sarah Pepinster, 'CO_2 emissions need to be reduced twice as fast as the rate they have gone up since 1990', Institute of European Environmental Policy, 19 October 2022, available at: www.ieep.eu.
35 Samuel G. Hanson, Anil K. Kashyap and Jeremy C. Stein, 'A Macroprudential Approach to Financial Regulation', *Journal of Economic Perspectives*, 25(1), 2011, pp. 3-28.
36 Tooze, *Shutdown*, p. 114.
37 Martin Sokol, 'Financialisation, central banks and "new" state capitalism: The case of the US Federal Reserve, the European Central Bank and the Bank of England', *Environment and Planning A: Economy and Space*, 55(5), 2022, p. 1305-24.
38 Benjamin Braun, 'Asset Manager Capitalism as a Corporate Governance Regime', Max Planck Institute for the Study of Societies, March 2021.
39 'Asset purchases in emerging markets: unconventional policies, unconventional times', *Global Economic Prospects 2021*, Washington, DC: World Bank, January 2021, ch. 4.
40 Elina Ribakova et al., 'Credible emerging market central banks could embrace quantitative easing to fight COVID-19', *VoxEu*, Centre for Economic Policy Research, 29 June 2020, available at: www.cepr.org/voxeu.
41 Jongrim Ha and Gene Kindberg-Hanlon, 'Financial Market Effects of Asset Purchase Programs in Emerging Markets: An Early Assessment', Mimeo, Washington, DC: World Bank, 3 February 2021, available at: https://ssrn.com/abstract=3825293.
42 In the US, these lockdown 'excess savings', held primarily by better-off households, reached a peak of $2.1 trillion in August 2021. They have since been paid down rapidly to $190 billion by June 2023, helping to account for the sustained growth of the US economy. Across the 'advanced economies', the savings rate during the pandemic rose by a factor of two or more, with similar but more modest increases in (already higher) savings rates in emerging economies. In both advanced and emerging economies at around 8 per cent of GDP in mid-2021, before declining, with US households spending down more rapidly than most. See: Hamza Abdelrahman and Luiz E. Oliveira. 'The Rise and Fall of Pandemic Excess Savings', Federal Reserve Bank of San Francisco Economic Letter 2023-11, 8 May 2023, available at: www.frbsf.org; Hamza Abdelrahman and Luiz E. Oliveira, 'Excess no more? Dwindling pandemic savings', *SF Fed Blog*, 16 August 2023, available at: www.frbsf.org; Francois de Soyres, Dylan Moore and Julia Ortiz, 'Accumulated Savings During the Pandemic: An International Comparison with Historical Perspective', *FEDS Notes,* 23 June 2023, available at: www.federalreserve.gov.
43 'Amid Russia's war, America Inc reckons with the promise and peril of foreign markets', *The Economist*, 12 March 2022.
44 Hector Perez-Saiz and Longmei Zhang, 'Renminbi Usage in Cross-Border Payments: Regional Patterns and the Role of Swaps Lines and Offshore Clearing Banks', Working Paper 2023(77), Washington, DC: International Monetary Fund, 2023.
45 'Federal Reserve Board announces the extensions of its temporary U.S. dollar liquidity swap lines and the temporary repurchase agreement facility for foreign and

46   international monetary authorities (FIMA repo facility) through March 31, 2021', Federal Reserve, press release, 29 July 2020, available at: www.federalreserve.gov.
46   China's most active swapline provision, over the last few years, has been to the central bank of Argentina, which has used the cheap renminbi funding available to fund currency operations, intended to support the peso, and, over summer 2023, to meet repayments for IMF loans. Vincent Arnold, 'Argentina: Emergency Liquidity Support Through Chinese Central Bank Swap Line and Qatari SDR Loan', Yale School of Management, Program on Financial Stability, 30 August 2023, available at: som.yale.edu.
47   John Michael Casetta, 'The Geopolitics of Swaplines', M-RCBG Associate Working Paper Series No. 181, Mossavar-Rahmani Center for Business and Government, Harvard Kennedy School, April 2022, available at: www.hks.harvard.edu.
48   Close analysis of Federal Reserve board minutes has found such political calculations have swayed decision makers against rewarding the Reserve Bank of India with its own dollar swapline, for example. See: Aditi Sahasrabuddhe, 'Drawing the line: the politics of federal currency swaps in the global financial crisis', *Review of International Political Economy*, 26(3), 2019, pp. 461-89.
49   European Commission, 'Joint statement on further restrictive economic measures', 26 February 2023, available at: https://ec.europa.eu.
50   The Central Bank of Iran had been subject to weaker sanctions since 2011. For parallels being drawn with the management of the Greek crisis by the Troika in 2015, see: James Meadway, 'How Europe learned to use central banks as a weapon', *Jacobin*, 28 February 2022.
51   Max Seddon and Polina Ivanova, 'How Putin's technocrats saved the economy to fight a war they opposed', *Financial Times*, 16 December 2022.
52   Alexandra Prokopenko, 'How Sanctions Have Changed Russian Economic Policy', Carnegie Endowment for International Peace, 9 May 2023, available at: www.carnegieendowment.org; Richard Disney, 'How have the forecasts on the effect of sanctions on Russia held up a year on?', *Economics Observatory*, 26 April 2023, available at: www.economicsobservatory.com.
53   Zoltan Poszar, 'Bretton Woods III', Credit Suisse, 7 March 2022.
54   Michael Stott, 'Brics bank strives to reduce reliance on the dollar', *Financial Times*, 22 August 2023.
55   Stefan Murau, Fabian Pape and Tobias Pforr, 'International monetary hierarchy through emergency US-dollar liquidity: A key currency approach', *Competition & Change*, 27(3-4), pp. 495-515.
56   Ian Smith, 'Insurers rack up $50bn in losses from natural catastrophes this year', *Financial Times*, 9 August 2023; Gregor Semieniuk et al., 'Stranded fossil-fuel assets translate to major losses for investors in advanced economies', *Nature Climate Change*, 12, 2022, pp. 532-38; Advait Arun, 'The doom loop: insurance markets and climate risk', *Phenomenal World*, 22 November 2023, available at: www.phenomenalworld.org.
57   Mark Carney, 'Breaking the tragedy of the horizon - climate change and financial stability', Speech at Lloyd's of London, 29 September 2015; see also: Hugh Miller and Simon Dikau, 'Preventing a "climate Minsky moment": environmental financial risks and prudential exposure limits', London: Grantham Research Institute on Climate Change, 2022.
58   'Major US banks threaten to leave Mark Carney's climate alliance', *Reuters*, 21 September 2022.

59   Felicia Khoo and Jeffrey Yong, 'Too hot to insure – avoiding the insurability tipping point', FSI Insights 54, Geneva: Bank of International Settlements, 20 November 2023.
60   Katie Kedward, Josh Ryan-Collins and Hugues Chenet, 'Biodiversity loss and climate change interactions: financial stability implications for central banks and financial supervisors', *Climate Policy*, 23(6), 2023, pp. 763-81.
61   Ivana Vasic-Lalovic, Lara Merling and Aileen Wu, 'The Growing Debt Burdens of Global South Countries: Standing in the Way of Climate and Development Goals', Washington, DC: Centre for Economic Policy Research, October 2023.
62   'Sovereign defaults are at a record high', Fitch Ratings, 29 March 2023, available at: www.fitchratings.com.
63   Vasic-Lalovic et al., 'The Growing Debt Burdens…'.
64   Cedric Durand, 'The end of financial hegemony?', *New Left Review*, 138, Nov/Dec 2022, pp. 39-55.
65   Peter Gowan, *The Global Gamble: Washington's Faustian bid for global dominance*, London: Verso, 1999.
66   TeleGeogrpahy, *The State of the Network 2022*, Washington, DC: TeleGeography, 2022, p. 12.
67   'As Internet user numbers swell due to pandemic, UN Forum discusses measures to improve safety of cyberspace', press release, United Nations, 7 December 2021, available at: www.un.org.
68   'Internet Use', Facts and Figures 2022, International Telecommunications Union, 30 November 2022, available at: www.itu.int.
69   James Meadway, 'Covid-19 and the case for a digital commons', press release, Institute of Public Policy Research, 6 August 2020, available at: www.ippr.org.
70   Mariya Brussevich, Era Dabla-Norris and Salma Khalid, 'Teleworking is Not Working for the Poor, the Young, and the Women', *IMF blog*, 7 July 2020, available at: www.imf.org.
71   Zoe Corbyn and Ben Morris, 'Nvidia: The chip maker that became an AI superpower', *BBC News*, 30 May 2023.
72   Peter Cohan, 'As ChatGPT and other AI tools increase energy demand, here's what investors need to know', *Forbes*, 9 November 2023.
73   Aaron Holmes and Anessa Gardizy, 'AI Developers Stymied by Server Shortage at AWS, Microsoft, Google', *The Information*, 7 April 2023, available at: www.theinformation.com.
74   Thompson et al. demonstrate that with current ML technologies, marginal gains in computational power are only obtainable with exponential increases in energy and resource use, constituting a hard barrier to further progress. Neil Thompson et al., 'The computational limits of deep learning', pre-print, July 2022, available at: https://arxiv.org/pdf/2007.05558.pdf.
75   Neil Thompson, 'The economic impact of Moore's Law and when it faltered', working paper, January 2017, available at: https://ssrn.com/abstract=2899115; Neil Thompson, Shuning Ge and Gabriel F. Manso, 'The importance of (exponentially more) computing power', pre-print, June 2022, available at: https://arxiv.org/pdf/2206.14007v1.pdf.
76   See, for example: Robert Solow, 'We'd better watch out', *New York Times Book Review*, 12 July 1987; James Meadway, 'It's more fun to compute', *Pandemic*

Capitalism, 20 September 2021; Giles Wilkes, 'A blob-chart way of dissecting Britain's economic future', *Freethinking Economist*, 28 September 2023, available at: www.freethinkecon.wordpress.com.
77   For example: Diane Coyle, 'The weightless economy', *Critical Quarterly* 39(4), 1997, pp. 92-8.
78   Charles Leadbeater, *Living on Thin Air*, London: Penguin, 2000.
79   'Global trends of material use', *MaterialFlows*, n.d., available at: www.materialflows.net.
80   Ed Conway, *Material World: a substantial story of our past and future*, London: WH Allen, 2023.
81   Silpa Kaza et al., *What a Waste 2.0: A Global Snapshot of Solid Waste Management to 2050*, Washington, DC: World Bank, 2018.
82   Tom Daly, 'Tin surge worsens supply chain woes for electronics, solar and auto firms', *Reuters*, 6 December 2021.
83   Jacki Pedersen, 'Plastic Resin Prices 2021–Resin Shortage & Cost of Plastic Explaine', Summit Packaging, 21 July 2021, available at: https://summitpackaging.com/
84   'Supply chain issues and autos: when will the chip shortage end?', *JP Morgan Research*, 18 April 2023, available at: www.jpmorgan.com.
85   Lotanna Emediegwu, 'How is the war in Ukraine affecting food security?', *Economics Observatory*, 30 March 2022, available at: www.economicsobservatory.com.
86   International Energy Authority, *The Role of Critical Minerals in Clean Energy Transitions*, Paris: IEA, 2021.
87   'World copper deficit could hit record; demand seen doubling by 2035', S&P Global, 14 July 2022, available at: www.spglobal.com. Such efforts won't be enough, obviously: a recent paper pointed out that the 1.5 degree warming target could only be hit if *all* carbon-intensive infrastructure was phased out from 2018 onwards. Christopher J. Smith et al., 'Current fossil fuel infrastructure does not yet commit us to 1.5°C warming,' *Nature Communication*, 10(101), 2019, pp. 1-10.
88   Karolin Schaps, 'Copper shortfall's "dramatic impact" on energy transition drives search for answers', International Bar Association, 15 December 2022, available at: www.ibanet.org.
89   Justin Lin, 'The Copper Conundrum: three factors of supply and demand', *Global X*, 24 March 2023, available at: www.globalxetfs.com.au.
90   International Energy Authority, 'The Role of Critical Minerals in Clean Energy Transitions', World Energy Outlook Special Report, March 2022, available at: www.iea.org.
91   Nina Lakhani, 'Revealed: how the US transition to electric cars threatens environmental havoc', *The Guardian*, 24 January 2023.
92   Jason W. Moore, 'Sugar and the Expansion of the Early Modern World-Economy: Commodity Frontiers, Ecological Transformation, and Industrialization', *Review (Fernand Braudel Center)*, 23(3), 2000, pp. 409-33.
93   Martin Arboleda, *The Planetary Mine: territories of extraction under late capitalism*, London: Verso, 2020.
94   China has spent almost $16 billion bn on lithium mining and processing facilities in Chile since 2018. Daniel A. Peraza, 'Lithium monopoly in the making? China expands the 'Lithium Triangle', *Geopolitical Monitor*, 25 August 2022, available at: www.geopoliticalmonitor.com.

95 Christoph Nedopil Wang, 'China Belt and Road Initiative (BRI) investment report 2023 H1', Green Finance and Development Centre, Fanhai International School of Finance, Fudan University, Shanghai, 1 August 2023, available at: www.weforum.org.
96 Maria Fantappie and Vali Nasr, 'A New Order in the Middle East?', *Foreign Affairs*, March 2023
97 For a qualified success, on its own terms, see: 'Saudi Arabia: staff report for the 2023 Article IV consultation', Washington, DC: IMF, 7 July 2023.
98 Philip Shetler-Jones, 'The strange case of America's Indo-Pacific strategies', London: Chatham House, 14 March 2022, available at: www.chathamhouse.org.
99 Branko Marcetic, 'Forget "peace," did Abraham Accords set stage for Israel-Gaza conflict?', *Responsible Statecraft*, 20 October 2023, available at: www.responsiblestatecraft.org.
100 See, for example, the US Department of Defense's 2019 assessment of the changing Arctic as 'a potential avenue for expanded great power competition and aggression'. Office of the Under Secretary for Defense Policy, *Report to Congress: Department of Defense Arctic Strategy*, Washington, DC: DoD, June 2019, p. 5.
101 As of March 2023, it has begun meeting again with Norway chairing, but without Russian participation, leading to fundamental questions about its purpose. See: Brett Simpson, 'The rise and sudden fall of the Arctic Council', *Foreign Policy*, 31 May 2023.
102 Sou-Jie van Brunnersum, 'China failed its Arctic ambitions in Greenland', *Politico*, 22 October 2022.
103 Ksenija Hanaček et al., 'On thin ice - The Arctic commodity extraction frontier and environmental conflicts', *Ecological Economics*, 191, 2022.
104 Tim G. Benton et al., 'Food system impacts on biodiversity loss: three levers for food systems transformation in support of nature', research paper, Royal United Services Institute, February 2021.
105 'The biodiversity that is crucial for our food and agriculture is disappearing by the day', press release, United Nations Food and Agriculture Organization, 22 February 2019, available at: www.fao.org.
106 UN FAO, *Climate Change and Food Security: risks and responses*, Geneva: UN FAO, 2015.
107 Speculation, inevitably, has added to the volatility. But it is the nature of speculation to *amplify* rather than *cause* the underlying price volatility. See recent evidence in: UNCTAD, *Trade and Development Report 2023*, Geneva: UN Conference on Trade and Development, 2023, ch. 3.
108 Camilla Hodgson and Steven Bernard, 'Food prices remain high into 2022 on shortages due to extreme weather', *Financial* Times, 8 January 2022.
109 European Commission, 'Agricultural production – crops', 17 October 2023, available at: https://ec.europa.eu/eurostat/statistics-explained.
110 Covering global prices for the period 2000 to 2015 – that is, before recent increases in price volatility. Bernhard Dalheimer, Marc F. Bellemere and Sunghun Lim, 'Global agriculture value chains and food prices', working paper, 5 June 2023, available at: www.marcfbellemare.com.
111 Jessica Whitt and Scott Gordon, 'Gloomy forecast: the economic costs of extreme weather', Barclays Corporate and Investment Bank, 4 May 2022, available at: www.cib.barclays.

112 UNESCO, *UN World Water Development Report 2023*, Paris: United Nations Educational Cultural and Scientific Organisation, 2023.
113 Xingcai Lui et al., 'Global Agricultural Water Scarcity Assessment Incorporating Blue and Green Water Availability Under Future Climate Change', *Earth's Future* 10(4), 2022.
114 Dexter Johnson, 'Scarcity dives fabs to wastewater recycling', *IEEE Spectrum*, 25 January 2022, available at: https://spectrum.ieee.org.
115 Raymond Zhong and Amy Chang Chien, 'Droughts in Taiwan pit chipmakers against farmers', *New York Times,* 8 April 2021.
116 Emma Kinery, 'TSMC to up Arizona investment to $40 billion with second semiconductor chip plant', *CNBC*, 6 December 2022.
117 Justine Calma, 'Water shortages loom over future semiconductor fabs in Arizona', *The Verge*, 18 August 2021.
118 Marcello Rossi, 'How Tucson, Arizona is facing up to a megadrought', *BBC*, 31 October 2022.
119 'El Nino/Southern Oscillation Diagnostic Discussion', Climate Prediction Centre, National Oceanic and Atmospheric Administration, 12 October 2023.
120 Bin Wang, et al., 'Historical change of El Niño properties sheds light on future changes of extreme El Niño', *Proceedings of the National Academy of the Sciences*, 116(45), 2019, pp. 22512-17.
121 Claudio Borio, 'On money, debt, trust and central banking', BIS Working Papers No 763, Geneva: Bank of International Settlements, January 2019.
122 James Meadway, 'The economic mainstream is getting inflation wrong', Progressive Economy Forum, 19 January 2022, available at: www.progressiveeconomyforum.com.
123 Grace Blakeley, *The Corona Crash*, London: Verso, 2020.
124 Stephen Disla, 'Consolidation in the food system', blog, T. Colin Campbell Center for Nutrition Studies, 9 November 2022, available at: https://nutritionstudies.org/consolidation-in-the-food-system.
125 International Panel of Experts on the Food System, *Too big to feed: Exploring the impacts of mega-mergers, concentration, concentration of power in the agri-food sector*, Brussels: IPE-Food, 2017, pp. 62-4.
126 Anirban Sen and Anousha Sakoui, 'Dealmakers see rebound after US activity buoys global M&A volumes', *Reuters,* 29 September 2023.
127 The so-called 'Everything Bubble' of 2020-2022. See: James Mackintosh, 'The Fed pricked the Everything Bubble', *Wall Street Journal*, 14 June 2022.
128 For example, the failures across the US mid-size banks, most notoriously including Silicon Valley Bank. See: Frank van Gansbeke, 'The Silicon Valley Bank and the polycrisis', *Forbes*, 12 March 2023. China's property bubble is undergoing a similar shakeout. See, for example: Engen Tham, Julie Zhu and Claire Jim, 'How Evergrande's downfall signalled China's property crisis', *Reuters*, 31 August 2023.
129 Isabella M. Weber and Evan Wasner, 'Sellers' Inflation, Profits and Conflict: Why can Large Firms Hike Prices in an Emergency?', Working Paper 2023-2, Amherst, MA: University of Massachusetts, 2023, available at: https://scholarworks.umass.edu/econ_workingpaper/343/.
130 It is striking that attempts to directly reduce liquidity through 'quantitative tightening' (i.e., central banks selling bonds they hold in exchange for money) has provoked significant financial dislocation. There is a hard barrier on the extent to which any such process can be carried out without directly intruding on central banks' primary

130 function of preserving financial stability. See, for example: Raghuram G. Ragam and Viral V. Acharya, 'Where has all the liquidity gone?', *Project Syndicate*, 7 October 2022, available online at: www.project-syndicate.org.
131 Note that this implies a reversal of the causality found in the conventional quantity theory of money: here, we have price rises causing money to circulate, rather than money in circulation causing prices to rise.
132 ECIU, *Climate, Fossil Fuels, and UK prices: 2023*, London: Economic and Climate Intelligence Unit, 27 November 2023, available at: www.eciu.net.
133 Not completely unanticipated. James Meadway, 'Coronavirus is the greatest challenge capitalism has ever faced: will a new system result?', *New Statesman*, 23 March 2020.
134 'Wages are surging across the rich world', *The Economist*, 13 October 2021. The surge in money wages has continued, but until very recently prices were rising well ahead of them.
135 Orsetta Causa et al., 'The post-COVID-19 rise in labour shortages', OECD Economics Department Working Papers No 1721, Paris: OECD Publishing, 2022, p. 8.
136 Causa et al., 'The post-COVID-19 rise', p. 16.
137 IMF, *World Economic Outlook*, Washington, DC: International Monetary Fund, October 2023, p. 1.
138 Causa et al., 'The post-COVID-19 rise', p. 17; Romain Duval et al., 'Labour market tightness in advanced economies', IMF Staff Discussion Notes, SDN/2022/001, Washington, DC: International Monetary Fund, 2022.
139 The OECD demonstrates a clear correlation between low pay, pre-pandemic, and rising post-pandemic quit rates. Causa et al., 'The post-COVID-19 rise', fig. 9.
140 House of Lords Economic Affairs Committee, 'Where have all the workers gone?', 2nd Report of the Session 2022-23, December 2022, ch. 3.
141 For a global survey: Vahid Mogharab et al., 'Global burden of the COVID-19 associated patient-related delay in emergency healthcare: a panel of systematic review and meta-analyses', *Global Health*, 18(58), 2022.
142 'Large study provides scientists with deeper insight into long COVID symptoms', press release, Washington, DC: National Institutes of Health, 25 May 2023.
143 Lauren L. O'Mahoney et al., 'The prevalence and long-term health effects of Long Covid among hospitalised and non-hospitalised populations: a systematic review and meta-analysis', *The Lancet*, 55(101762), 2023.
144 Hannah E. Davis et al., 'Characterizing long COVID in an international cohort: 7 months of symptoms and their impact', *The Lancet*, 38(101019), 15 July 2021.
145 Tom Waters and Thomas Wernham, 'Long covid and the labour market', IFS Briefing Note BN246, London: Institute for Fiscal Studies, July 2022.
146 Katie Bach, 'New data shows long Covid is keeping as many as 4 million people out of work', Brookings Institution, 24 August 2022, available at: www.brookings.edu.
147 Katie Bach, 'Is "long covid" worsening the labour shortage?', Brookings Institution, 11 January 2022.
148 UN Department of Social and Economic Affairs, *World Social Report 2023: leaving no-one behind in an aging world*, Geneva: UNDESA, 2023, p. 3.
149 Tithi Bhattacharya, ed., *Social Reproduction Theory: remapping class, recentering oppression*, London: Pluto Press, 2018.
150 Bank of International Settlements, *Annual Economic Report 2023*, Geneva: Bank of International Settlements, 2023, p. 56.

151 For a representative example of discussion about China, see: Pak Yiu et al., 'China's aging population threatens a Japan-style lost decade', *Nikkei Asia*, 22 March 2023, available at: https://asia.nikkei.com.
152 Institute for Health Metrics and Evaluation, *Financing Global Health 2021*, Seattle: University of Washington, 2023, p. 61, available at: www.healthdata.org.
153 Estimated to reach a cumulative output loss of $47 trillion over 2010-2030. D.E. Bloom et al., *The Global Economic Burden of Non-communicable Disease*, Geneva: World Economic Forum, 2011.
154 Porooshat Dadgostar, 'Antimicrobial Resistance: Implications and Costs', *Infectious Drug Resistance*, 12, 2019, pp. 3903-10.
155 Radiohead, 'Fitter Happier', *OK Computer*, 1997.
156 James Meadway, 'Covid reshaped the global labour market – these strikes are just the start', *openDemocracy*, 17 February 2023.
157 Mike Davis, *Old Gods, New Enigmas: Marx's lost theory*, 2018, London: Verso, p. 17; see also the earlier Mike Davis, *Planet of Slums*, London: Verso, 2006
158 Harry Bocott et al., 'Protecting people from a changing climate: the case for resilience', New York: McKinsey Global Institute, 8 November 2021, available at: www.mckinsey.com.
159 'Representative Concentration Pathway 8.5', indicating no significant abatement measures. For a description, see: 'Explainer: the 'high emissions' RCP8.5 global warming scenario', *Carbon Brief*, 21 August 2019, available at: www.carbonbrief.org.
160 Jonathan Woetzel et al., 'Will India get too hot to work?', New York: McKinsey Global Institute, 25 November 2020.
161 David Eckstein, Vera Kuenzel and Laura Schaefer, *Global Climate Risk Index 2021*, Bonn: Germanwatch, January 2021, available at: www.germanwatch.org.
162 David Neilson and Thomas Stubbs, 'Relative Surplus Population and Uneven Development in the Neoliberal Era: Theory and Empirical Application,' *Capital and Class*, 35(3), 2011, p. 451.
163 W. A. Lewis, 'Economic Development with Unlimited Supplies of Labour,' *The Manchester School*, 22, 1954.
164 Under the Belt and Road Initiative, between 2013 and 2021, China provided at least $331 billion in development financing to Global South countries, with countries in Africa alone receiving $91 billion. Kevin P. Gallagher et al., *The BRI at Ten: maximising the benefits and minimising the risks of China's Belt and Road Initiative*, Boston, MA: Boston University Global Policy Development Unit, 11 October 2023.
165 Annette de Kleine Fege, Eric Lacey and Habiburahman Sahibzada, 'It's become a middle-income world, but increasingly hard to join the club', World Bank, 16 March 2023, available at: blogs.worldbank.org.
166 Sara Schonhardt, '"Take it or leave it": Acrimony flares amid tenuous agreement on climate aid', *Politico*, 4 November 2023.
167 As of Q3 2023. Datareportal, 'Digital around the world', n.d., available at: https://datareportal.com/global-digital-overview.
168 International Labour Organisation, *World Employment and Social Outlook: Trends 2023*, Geneva: ILO, p. 12.
169 Billy Perrigo, 'Exclusive: OpenAI Used Kenyan Workers on Less Than $2 Per Hour to Make ChatGPT Less Toxic', *Time*, 18 January 2023.

170 Adrienne Williams, Milagros Miceli and Timnit Gebru, 'The exploited labour behind AI', *Noema*, 31 October 2021, available at: www.noemamag.com.
171 The parallel with David Ricardo's classic description of declining returns in agriculture should be clear, in which the most productive farmland is brought into use first, followed by steadily less and less productive farmland is brought into use as investment grows.
172 Beverley Silver, *Forces of Labour: Workers' Movements and Globalisation since 1870*, Cambridge: Cambridge University Press, 2003.
173 Emmanuel Le Roy Ladurie, 'A concept: the unification of the globe by disease', in *The Mind and Method of the Historian*, Chicago: University of Chicago Press, 1981; see also: Alexander Anievas and Kerem Nisancioglu, *How the West Came to Rule: the geopolitical origins of capitalism*, London: Pluto Press, 2015.
174 James Meadway, 'Covid reshaped the global labour market – these strikes are just the start', *openDemocracy*, 17 February 2023.
175 Ajay Singh Chaudhary, *The Exhausted of the Earth*, London: Repeater, 2024, p. 222.
176 John Bellamy Foster, 'Capitalism, exterminism and the long ecological revolution', *MR Online*, 24 December 2017, available at: www.mronline.org.
177 From the April 2019 'Final Appeal' of the 'Assembly of Assemblies' of the gilets jaunes, agreed by 235 delegates from local groups. Simon Fairlie, 'End of the world, end of the month', *The Land*, 25, 2019, available at: www.thelandmagazine.org.uk.
178 Matine Valo, 'Les mégabassines, symbole d'un agrobusiness intenable ou réponse adaptée aux sécheresses?', *Le Monde*, 3 November 2022.
179 Quoted in: Nicolas Celnik, 'Andreas Malm: 'Cibler les SUV ou jets privés peut aider les luttes'', *Reporterre*, 28 March 2023, available at: https://reporterre.net.
180 Pratik Parija, 'India Seen Keeping Rice Export Bans Into 2024, Holding Up Global Prices', *Bloomberg*, 19 November 2023.
181 Roman Royandoyan, 'Philippines' Marcos announces cap on rice prices', *Nikkei Asia*, 1 September 2023.
182 Karl Marx, 'Lohnarbeit und Kapital', Marx-Engels Werke, 6, my translation, available at: https://marxwirklichstudieren.files.wordpress.com/2013/11/lohnarbeit-kapital.pdf.

FROM GLOBALIZATION TO GEOPOLITICS – A WAY BACK, NOT FORWARD

BIRGIT MAHNKOPF

There is some evidence to suggest that the globalization pushes at the end of the nineteenth century and in the second half of the twentieth century were expressions of comparable phases of a cycle of expansion and integration. As after that first phase of globalization, which ended with the decline of the British Empire at the beginning of the twentieth century, so today we are moving back to geopolitical confrontation between sovereign nation states and to hot and cold wars. The globalization surge before World War I was followed by a period of world economic contraction and disintegration in the interwar period. At its peak in the 1930s, this phase provoked a devaluation after the Great Depression and gave impetus to purely nation-state oriented, outwardly aggressive policies of autarky. Therefore, the question is whether these cycles of globalization, including dangerous relapses into protectionism and autarkic policies as in the 1930s, and a new shift from geoeconomics to geopolitics, are again possible 100 years later. Today, there are indeed many signs that a strengthening of neo-nationalist forces against neoliberal globalization is on the agenda. As in the past, these forces aim at the preservation of national security, the establishment of military supremacy and facilitating investors' access to coveted 'strategic resources'.

GOALS AND INSTRUMENTS OF SOFT AND HARD POWER

With the return of geopolitics after more than three decades of neoliberal geoeconomics, the economic logic of achieving maximum profit is complemented by the territorial logic of extending power into the sovereign space of other states. Admittedly, it cannot be argued that this development is in contrast with supposedly 'peaceful competition' among market participants according to globally accepted rules and norms, and instead a throwback to the binary logic of foes and friends. For even at the height of the latest phase of globalization, more wars were fought than during the decades of Cold War. Nevertheless, the use of military means to enforce economic and political interests is part and parcel of a new geopolitics.

In the geoeconomic realm, competitors are not enemies: competitiveness is a basic characteristic of – more or less – free trade. Where industries are unable to compete, they instead rely on protectionism and the informal economy. This has been the subject of trade conflicts between the highly developed, old industrialized countries and the newly industrializing countries of the Global South for many years. However, especially since the rise of the neoconservatives in the US and their 'America-first' ideology, trust has not solely been placed in peace-making trade. For the US, neoliberal market freedom has always gone perfectly well with the use of military power to secure the strategic supply of territorially-bounded raw materials, especially fossil fuels, and the US has never hesitated to assert its interests, 'if necessary', with military force.

Within neoliberal discourse, there is no opposition between market and power as the two are viewed as complementary. However, opening, linking and dominating markets during recent decades was done primarily, though not exclusively, through the use of 'soft power': the informal extension of power by setting norms and rules – for example, technical norms, but also human rights standards – or through indirect control over the rules of the world trade system. Equally important was the influence Western industrialized countries exercised through international organizations and a variety of informal groups, including both business communities and NGOs. In this way, the goals of geoeconomic competition were enforced through the establishment of quasi-monopolies, the exercise of power beyond the territory of individual nation-states, control of system-relevant infrastructures and, above all, privileged access to natural resources of all kinds – particularly to oil, as the 'blood' of modern industrial capitalisms.

Today, the same goals are increasingly pursued through geopolitical means. And by no means is this about a historically powerful confrontation between the 'free West' and 'reactionary Russia', nor is it about the global defence of a fictitious 'norm-led foreign policy' against autocratic rulers of all hues. The current linking of territories through power politics is again about the control of geographical spaces through expansion into the sovereign territories of other states – in the air, on land and in the sea. This is happening with the aim of maximizing both economic and military power. Dominion over territory is a defining feature of nation-state sovereignty and is based on a very broad understanding of 'national security'. This includes defence against migration flows, the fight against organized crime and protection against spying and surveillance systems commissioned or utilized by foreign powers. Above all, at the core of national security is securing the supply of energy and raw materials for a state's own industries and population.

The means used to achieve such goals are partly the same as those previously used under the banner of globalization, such as norm-setting through financial and developmental levers. However, in doing so, less and less reliance is placed on the power of the most competitive market actors to determine the norms and rules for technical standards, prices, exchange rates and the rules of the world trade regime.[1] Heretofore, the dominant dynamic in the world economy was that less competitive market players had to behave as 'standard takers', where they either succeeded in holding their own in the market (for example, through wage dumping and undercutting global standards by violating labour and human rights), or they were pushed into the 'informal economy', that is if they did not disappear from the market altogether. Today, it has become possible that the West and not just 'the rest' could be forced to 'take standards' and rules made by someone else, most probably Chinese firms. As a result, 'hard power' instruments have increasingly come to dominate, though some such tools (such as export or import bans) occupy a grey area between hard and soft instruments of foreign economic policy.

At the same time, however, genuine 'hard power' instruments of state power are increasingly on the agenda again. These include military intervention in the sovereign space of other states, which can take place both with or without a declaration of war. This includes the conquest, control and defence of territories in proxy wars, as well as 'regime change' and the consolidation of governments controlled from outside a state's sovereign territory, usually through the financial, informational and/or military support of selected population groups. Increasingly, this also takes place through the killing of disagreeable representatives of a foreign power using remote-controlled drones.

However, the financing, planning, and construction of large infrastructure projects (or alternatively their blocking) – particularly those necessary for the extraction and transport of fossil fuels and often in ways that are linked to credit – have always been an important means of opening up the ability for a far away power to exert control in the sovereign territory of other states. Both the construction and prevention of new energy pipelines has always been a geopolitically hard-fought process. This is because a pipeline extends the reach of state power and influence, ensuring that government and business at one end can exert control over their counterparts at the other. It allows a state to control remote production areas, but at the same time pipelines represent high-risk and very expensive investments that only pay off with long-term contracts. But pipelines and other transport facilities for oil and gas can also be instrumentalized to put political pressure on states that are strategically important for their transit. Extraterritorial powers can bring about the termination of a long-term business relationship between states at either end of a pipeline through diplomatic pressure, military action, or both, as happened in February 2022 with the Nord Stream gas pipelines between Russia and Germany under pressure from the US.[2] In September 2022, Russia also took an active decision to terminate supply through Nord Stream I, in response to the sanctions imposed by the Western allies.

In the future, transcontinental power grids will also become especially important for geopolitical strategy. States, especially rich countries in the West, will seek to secure future energy security, a basic prerequisite for modern industrial capitalism, through as extensive a process of electrification as possible for transport, industry and housing, but also for waging war, even though the latter will still ultimately depend on access to oil for the mobility it allows. To achieve energy security primarily through electricity, however, grids must be expanded on an enormous scale, both nationally, transnationally and even trans-continentally. As a result, the access, availability and use of electricity sources and flows will become strategic goals for national energy security policies, as will the export of power facilities and components.

The overarching goals and objectives in today's geopolitical confrontation are difficult to narrow down, because a multitude of concerns are often amalgamated. In most cases, however, it is a matter of preserving national security, establishing military supremacy and/or gaining access to strategic resources for investors. In this context, access to fossil fuels remains at the top of the agenda, because modern industrial capitalism is essentially addicted to them. At the same time, certain minerals are increasingly required for the production of renewable energy technologies, electromobility, advanced medical technology and, most importantly, for the digitalization of industry, infrastructure and modern warfare. Since in the 'digital age' of capitalism seemingly any new technology with civilian uses either has its origin in military development or can be used for military applications, both the geopolitical objective of preserving national security and the establishment of military supremacy include the need to establish and defend 'technological sovereignty'.

'ENERGY AS A WEAPON' IN THE NEW GEOPOLITICS

Only rich and highly equipped states are in a position to actually pursue a policy of 'energy security'. For this requires the ability to influence supply and demand, especially for oil and gas and in the future perhaps for electricity flows, and thus necessitates the ability to control the price of resources, transport logistics and the routes of distribution for raw materials from producing to consuming countries. In the past, this power held by rich countries has rightly been described as 'oil imperialism', and its use has served to increase economic inequality in the world. Today, we might instead call it 'resource imperialism', since minerals are becoming equally important for national sovereignty in a world of friends and foes.

Most oil and gas deposits have long since exceeded their peak production levels; only in 'rogue states' such as Iran, Venezuela and Russia, as well as in the Arab Gulf states, is this not yet the case. For all newly discovered oil and gas fields, the so-called harvest factor has been steadily decreasing since the mid-2000s. However, as demand has continued to rise, the extraction of oil from unconventional sources such as the deep sea or tar sands, as well as the extraction of gas through the technically complex – and, in ecological terms, exceedingly harmful – method of blasting open rock through 'fracking', has become profitable. Due to the fracking boom, the US has effectively been self-sufficient in gas for some time now, and as such has been trying to take geopolitical advantage of this.

After the US forced the 'turning off' of the Nord Stream 2 pipeline from Russia to Germany in February 2022, an ever more stringent sanctions regime was set in motion by the EU member states and six Western allies (US, Canada, Japan, South Korea, New Zealand and Australia).[3] Framed as punishment for Russian aggression and the invasion of Ukraine, the sanctions have so far not had a particularly negative impact on Russia, but rather on EU member states themselves, as discussed below, and even more so on developing countries who are struggling with secondary effects such as inflation, currency depreciation and supply chain shortages.

The 'economic war' which cannot be named is putting the brakes on the European Green Deal (EGD) even before it actually gets off the ground.[4] After Russia cut off gas supplies to Europe in retaliation for Western sanctions, it was decided that more coal may be burned in the EU for a period of 5-10 years, and that coal will now be imported into the EU from Australia, South Africa and Colombia instead of Russia – sources with significantly longer supply routes and correspondingly higher transport costs and emissions. In addition, nuclear energy is now being vigorously expanded in a series of European states – Hungary, Czechia, Slovakia, Belgium, France, the UK and even Sweden – even though it can be demonstrated that nuclear power lacks both 'technical and economic foundations'[5] and that European countries will still rely on Russia, alongside China, as the biggest suppliers of enriched uranium, the key fuel used in nuclear power plants.

In its 'RePowerEU' programme, the EU Commission assumed that only €210 billion would be needed for 'energy independence from Russia' by 2027, and that this could easily be raised through a combination of public and private funds. A large part of this was to go to the development of renewable energy sources and only €12 billion was earmarked for oil and gas supplies.[6] However, EU member states have since earmarked billions more in 2022 alone for new fossil fuel infrastructure and private investment, alongside the recommissioning of coal-fired power plants in Germany and the Netherlands, followed by further investments in oil and gas supplies in both 2022 and 2023. In March 2023, the European Commission approved $750 billion in state support for businesses affected by the sanctions regime imposed on Russia and for measures under the 'NextGenerationEU' program at the heart of the EGD. In addition to pipeline gas from Norway, liquefied natural gas (LNG) imports from the US increased two-fold, inputs from Qatar 23 per cent, and (ironically) LNG imports from Russia went up 12 per cent during the last year.[7]

Furthermore, representatives from the EU are travelling around the world in order to source additional LNG supply from states such as Qatar, Azerbaijan and Egypt, states which adhere to Western notions of 'liberal democracy' as little as Russia, and they have even started to persuade governments in Senegal, Nigeria and Mozambique to commit to new gas projects. EU efforts to replace former supplies of cheaper gas from Russia with more expensive LNG has led numerous countries of the Global South to step back from LNG and burn more coal, as they are unable to pay the higher prices that have resulted from the so-called 'gas war' between the West and Russia. In fact, to free itself from Russian gas and oil, which in the future will be piped to the south and east, EU-based oil and gas majors such as BP, Shell, Eni and TotalEnergies are among those which have increased their global upstream oil and gas investment. Each of the almost 200 new fossil fuel projects planned as of 2022 would result in at least a billion tonne of $CO2$ emissions over their lifetime; in total this is the equivalent to about 18 years of current global $CO2$ emissions. A group of journalists from *The Guardian* has coined this phenomenon as the building of new 'carbon bombs'.[8] What's more, the EU bloc is now competing with larger Asian states such as China, Japan and India for LNG supplies on volatile global energy markets, and thus might have to face the doubling or even tripling of prices in the future.⁹

A significant nail in the coffin for a 'greener' EU will be the economic and technological 'lock-in effects' resulting from the expansion of gasification, transportation and reliquefaction infrastructures for LNG in Germany, Spain, France and Italy, accompanied by corresponding projects in the UK and Turkey. Already during Donald Trump's presidency, the large German gas market became a desirable target for the growing US fracking industry, and thus there was already considerable diplomatic pressure in 2018 to build up LNG infrastructure in Germany in parallel with the construction of LNG terminals from Texas to Philadelphia. Today, Germany – which had no LNG import capacity before 2022 – is now one of the heaviest investors in additional LNG infrastructure among EU member states.

Obviously, the state-subsidized construction of LNG infrastructure in both the US and Europe, as well as the connection of new pipelines to the existing gas network, comes at a high cost for both the public sector and private investors. The latter are therefore keen to ensure that the plants will be in use for as long as possible, seeking to accomplish this through long-term contracts of at least 20 years to avoid their investments becoming 'stranded assets'. But this can be expensive for the public purse. What's more, import capacity in Europe as currently planned will exceed 400 billion cubic metres by 2030, yet demand could shrink to just 150 billion cubic metres due to renewable energy sources of electricity forming an increasingly larger share of Europe's energy mix if their development proceeds as planned in the EGD.¹⁰

Thus, due to the weaponization of energy supplies in the course of the war in Ukraine, the EU has enabled the expansion or initiation of almost 50 fossil fuel infrastructure projects, while mobilizing considerable sums for energy-intensive industries and the electricity sector. The financial and social costs that could result from a migration of European companies to the US, where energy prices are significantly lower, cannot even be estimated. This development would also give rise to a whole series of further problems, all of which would make an energy transition through the massive expansion of renewable energy sources in Europe difficult, if not impossible.

NEXT TO THE 'GAS WAR' A LOOMING 'NEW OIL WAR'?

With the geopolitical use of 'energy as a weapon', for which only Russia has received blame so far, we are experiencing not only a so-called 'gas war', but also facing the potential for a new oil war due to escalating conflict over its price. Conflicts in capitalism always revolve around 'paper oil', 'paper gas' and 'paper minerals', i.e., their prices as generated through international futures exchanges by private traders for the probable demand of tomorrow – and the currency in which these are invoiced. In this respect, the year 2022 probably ushered in a 'turning of the tides' – with further increases not just in prices for fossil energy, but also for many other non-fossil minerals. This has also led to the stabilisation of the dollar, which had been battered in recent years, as it is the currency in which not only the lifeblood of capitalism, oil, is traded but also most other goods and services worldwide. And since the debt crisis of the 1970s, we all know that the state of the dollar is not just a problem for the US, but also for the rest of the world, as Larry Summers once noted. This is the background against which we must view the ongoing battle over the new energy order.

The wealth of industrialized countries, particularly that of the US, is based on abundant and cheap fossil energy – the basis of 'energy security'. This term, according to the dimensions found in the 2001 'Cheney Report of the National Energy Policy Development Group', encompasses strategic control over oil and gas resources across the globe, including logistical aspects such as pipelines, tanker routes, refineries and storage; influence on supply and price formation, partly through controlling demand; and, finally, the determination of the currency in which oil and gas transactions are settled. Strategic control can be reached by means of diplomacy and the establishment of 'special relations', as between the US and Saudi Arabia for some 80 years. It can also be achieved through indirect pressure towards allies, as seen between the US and other NATO members, or by means of subversion, as in Latin America and Africa. Finally, it can be sought using direct military force, as in Iraq and in Afghanistan, or via proxy wars, such as in Libya. With the 2017 US National Security Strategy, the expansion of the fossil fuel industry, and the building and maintaining of energy infrastructure for export purposes, became important pillars of US strategy, in alignment with Donald Trump's aspiration for the US to become a major global vendor of fossil fuels, to match its current position in the world's arms industry.[11]

But since 2022, cracks have begun to appear in the pact with Saudi Arabia, the most influential member of the OPEC+ countries, an alliance which has been beneficial to the US for decades. The pact has been based on the principle that Saudi Arabia receives military support from the US and in exchange it imposes within OPEC+ an oil price that suits American interests. This desired price is one high enough to keep US domestic production of unconventional oil lucrative, but that is not so high as to endanger the supply of cheap gasoline from abroad, especially when elections are imminent, as is the case in 2024. Yet, Saudi Arabia seems increasingly willing to disregard US desires for increased oil production in order to bring down prices.

Instead, OPEC+ has cut oil output twice in recent years, once in autumn 2022 and again in April 2023, aiming to shore up prices. Not only has this been good for Russia amidst the war in Ukraine, but it has also generated revenue for financing Saudi Arabia's huge energy transition investment projects, a transition they have termed 'Saudi Vision 2030'. What's more, China is already partnering with Saudi Arabia in this area, with the potential for even more cooperation in the future. Should oil prices continue toward the $100 per barrel mark, as desired not just by the Arab states but also by Russia as a member of OPEC+, US strategy – no matter who wins the 2024 election – will be thrown into turmoil, since 'paper oil' and 'paper gas' act as an important a geopolitical constraint as the physical availability of fossil fuels themselves do.

Furthermore, the role of the US in the geopolitical 'great game' of the 21st century, including its position as a hegemon already facing erosion of its position and authority, will not be determined solely by its still-superior military strength, but also depends to a significant extent on whether the dollar continues to function as the dominant oil currency. For decades, the US has had almost unlimited credit in global capital markets, thus being able to turn the dollar into the world's 'oil currency', as well as the denomination in trade for other strategic resources. This means that when the US central bank turns on the printing presses to print dollars, it by extension makes a rich source of oil bubble up. As long as the US dollar comprises approximately 60 per cent of worldwide central banks' currency reserve holdings, the US can buy the much-wanted 'black gold' almost without limit.[12]

But alternatives to the dollar as the oil currency are emerging. On the path away from the geoeconomic enforcement of interests and back to the geopolitical exercise of power, where 'security partnerships' decide on economic relations and a 'charmed circle' of highly developed industrialized countries tries to impose its will on other states more by sticks than by carrots, efforts are growing among many states to diversify the basket of currencies in which oil is transacted. It seems possible that in the longer term the renminbi (presumably as a digital currency) could prevail as an alternative to the dollar for both international trade and cross-border investment. Already today, the oil trade is being conducted in currencies other than the dollar, not just in the renminbi but also in the rouble, the rupee, the UAE dirham dollar, and, in Iran's case, non-dollar backed stablecoins (a crypto-currency pegged to a commodity or currency).

Such developments, of course, frighten both the US and its friends in Europe, who fear that if 'predictions about a coming multipolar currency order are correct, the US will undergo a meaningful decline in its power base and in its ability to project power, with broader implications for international stability and order'.[13]

THE FIGHT FOR 'TECHNOLOGICAL SOVEREIGNTY' AND KEY MINERALS

In the battle between the US and China for future global hegemony, it is not only physical strategic resources and the role of the dollar as world and oil currency that are important, but also the ability to set standards for future technologies, such as in mobile phone networks, the development of particularly powerful algorithms and supercomputers, and the digital technologies necessary for modern warfare.[14] This includes the mastery of closed value chains for the production of all so-called 'clean technologies', particularly electric vehicle batteries, solar panels, wind turbines and, increasingly, the technology involved in carbon capture and storage.

Against this backdrop, the new US industrial policy, based on the Chips and Science Act (CSA) and the Inflation Reduction Act (IRA) of 2022, must be viewed as a geopolitical attack against China which nevertheless also hits US allies in Europe and Asia alike. These acts build a particular ring of protectionism around the US. The CSA aims to address the fact that the expected 'new golden age' of technological innovation will be entirely driven by 'dual use technologies' such as sensors, image recognition, satellite communication, robotics, 'big data' tools and powerful computers. The latter will be applied not only in advanced manufacturing, mobility, energy production and many other ostensibly civilian areas, but also most importantly in modern weapons and warfare. Today, semiconductors are a matter of national security, as large swathes of the economy increasingly rely on the functionality they provide. Moreover, modern wars simply cannot be fought without cutting edge semiconductors, cloud computing, sophisticated artificial intelligence (AI) algorithms and equipment for autonomous driving, flying and killing.

There is thus an all-out struggle for AI-dominance in the tech industry, and it seems clear that the biggest winner will be the companies making the weapons that will be used by all combatants – those that dominate the market for training large AI models, and those that produce graphical processing units (or GPUs). However, even if the US remains the global leader in 'breakthrough' AI innovation, China has become the world's top high-tech manufacturer and a serious competitor in key technologies, already leading in AI implementation while perhaps surpassing the US in quantum communication. This is obviously a significant challenge in light of the dual use nature of these technologies. Therefore, while the main aim of the CSA is to fund semiconductor research, it also includes 'guardrails' intended to prevent companies from building chip factories in China.[15] Nevertheless, US self-sufficiency in chip production seems to be an illusion, since at the same time that it wants to compete with China in advanced chip production it would have to increase its production of the low-value chips it currently imports.[16] In response to the declaration of an open 'chip war',[17] triggered by US export restrictions, China is concentrating on less miniaturized chips, which can find wide use in the 'Internet of Things', 5G telecommunication equipment and the growing market for electric vehicles.

Parallel to the race for chips is a race for telecommunication technology, with many (but not all) European countries following US advice to ban the Chinese market leader Huawei on security grounds. Nevertheless, having set the 5G standard, Huawei is on the way to setting the next generation 6G standard as well. Meanwhile, China has retaliated against the sanctions on Huawei and the smaller firm ZTE by edging Sweden's Ericsson out of its huge domestic market. Thus, it becomes possible that in the near future we may face two versions of tomorrow's mobile telephony – which would indeed be a strong sign of a deglobalizing world economy, especially since this development would take place alongside growing tensions over the control of physical infrastructure that involves Chinese companies, or that directly connects the US to mainland China or Hong Kong, such as subsea telecommunication cables.

Subsidy packages from the CSA and IRA seem to fall squarely in line with the tradition of 'military Keynesianism' pursued by the US during the Cold War period.[18] But at the same time, this program is also reminiscent of the US under Roosevelt preparing for its participation in the war against Hitler's Germany under the famous slogan, 'America's Answer! – Production', popularized via the great 1942 propaganda poster by French graphic designer Jean Carlu.

US INDUSTRIAL POLICY IMPACT ON 'CLEAN' ENERGY PRODUCTION

Through the Inflation Reduction Act, the Biden Administration aims to end the deindustrialization of the past decades and to make the US the world's 'preeminent manufacturing power again'.[19] US companies, as well as those in allies such as the EU, Australia, Japan, South Korea and India, are to be encouraged to move the production of valuable component parts to the US – be it semiconductors, display screens, batteries, sensors, semiconductor wafers or solar cells – in order to reduce dependence on all sorts of Chinese-assembled parts.

However, in the manufacturing state of solar panels globally, China's share exceeds 80 per cent which is more than double its share in global demand;[20] 65 per cent of batteries for electric vehicles are produced in China and almost 80 per cent of cathodes are manufactured in the country. The wind industry's supply chain and production of infrastructure upgrades such as cables are also concentrated in China. In some of the specialized materials used in batteries and in other niche products, China's market share is even close to 100 per cent. Furthermore, many of the metals needed to produce modules, semiconductor wafers and cells are extracted and/or produced by Chinese firms both inside and outside of China.[21] Thus, for either the US or the EU, self-sufficiency in battery cells and solar module production in the near future seems to be quite improbable, no matter how many billions the big producers are currently subsidized with.

During the last decade, China has invested ten times more in new solar photovoltaic (PV) supply capacity than the EU, the former 'leader' in renewable energy technology. As a result, today its share in all solar PV manufacturing equipment already exceeds 80 per cent.[22] Furthermore, these investments in China have helped to bring down costs for solar PV for the EU, the US and indeed many poorer countries in the Global South that, without these imports, would have to rely on far more environmentally damaging energy sources such as wood and coal.

When solar production costs were declining, EU member states simply did not invest, while the US showed only a minor increase in its investments. No wonder then that in 2021, investment in renewable energy technology in China was 20 per cent higher than investment in the US and the EU combined. In the meantime, prices for important inputs for renewable energy technologies such as critical minerals, semiconductors and even bulk material like steel and cement have risen, leading wind turbines to cost 35 per cent more today than they did three years ago. In 2022 China capped off its enormous spending on 'low-carbon' energy transition technologies with an impressive investment of $546 billion, including a huge amount invested in electromobility. This investment comprises nearly three quarters of the amount investment by the remaining nine of the top ten renewable energy investing countries combined, with the result that half of the world's spending in this sector now takes place in China.[23]

Given these constraints, it does not seem particularly plausible to avoid the cheap offers 'made in China' and insist again on a strategy of 'do it at home', now referred to as 're-shoring' or 'de-risking'. With a growing energy infrastructure, demand for high-voltage electric cables to connect offshore wind projects in European countries is rising fast, while European-controlled supply has been delayed. This is in part due to the scarcity of raw materials such as copper, but it is also due to a lack of converter stations and skilled labour to lay the cables at the bottom of the sea. Thus, it a matter of 'energy security' to rely on Chinese companies to provide the raw materials for high-voltage cabling and converter stations, instead of excluding, as planned, the involvement of these firms in critical national infrastructure projects. Even with European production of semiconductors slated to double (particularly in Germany), no solar panel nor wind turbine consists of these components alone. Meanwhile, the EGD agenda will shrink entirely into wishful thinking if it is to be accomplished without cheap components from China (or Chinese owned companies located in Vietnam and Malaysia).[24]

THE RACE FOR 'CRITICAL RAW MATERIALS'

It is not possible within the scope of a single essay to elaborate in detail upon all the geopolitical consequences which will arise from the intensifying 'scramble' for scarce minerals, necessary for all sorts of 'clean' or 'green' technologies, including those with dual-use civilian and military purposes. But it is surely not an exaggeration to state that the control of supply chains for the raw and processed minerals – such as copper, lithium, cobalt, nickel, rare earth elements, iron, uranium and aluminium – needed for chip production, renewable energy technologies, military equipment and even just the basic infrastructure of modern industrial societies will likely become as important as secure access to cheap oil and gas. A shortage of just one or two important raw materials or components can today disrupt entire value chains, thus reducing the resilience of advanced industrial economies to an extent which was unthinkable at the height of fossil fuel capitalism.

In an economic sense, raw materials become 'critical' when foreseeable demand drives up their price so much that companies fear they will no longer be able to keep up because they cannot continue to pass on rising prices to end users – as is the case today with many minerals. Studies by the German Energy Agency as well as the World Bank demonstrate the trajectory of demand for these materials: because the rich countries of the Global North, first and foremost those in the EU, are committed to transitioning to 'clean' (i.e. low carbon) technologies, the demand for graphite, lithium and cobalt could increase by 450 per cent in the period from 2018 to 2050. For basic materials such as aluminium, copper, iron, zinc and nickel, the percentage increase is expected to be less dramatic, but in absolute terms the projected demand remains huge. Depending on how extensive this transition turns out to be, global demand for mineral raw materials alone could rise from 40-50 million tons in 2020 to 1.8-3.5 billion tons in 2050.[25]

This does not even include the material demand for the required infrastructure (such as power grids), the necessary conversion of traffic routes, factories and residential buildings, nor for the frames and chassis of electric cars. The latter are known to require six times more of these critical raw materials than a conventional vehicle, consisting of up to 800 kg of aluminium. In order to extract this raw material, without which even large wind turbines could not be made, entire villages in countries such as Ghana are resettled, or the inhabitants are simply driven out. Bauxite is then mined to be processed into aluminium, until the mine is exhausted and what then remains is usually a gloomy moonscape with contaminated groundwater. The mining of copper in countries such as Chile or Indonesia, a material needed in huge quantities for the generators, gearboxes and cables of wind turbines, is hardly less destructive to nature. It is often funded through credit commitments from rich industrialized countries. And for neither copper nor aluminium does the World Bank expect that even exorbitant increases in recycling quotas could cover even half of the growing demand.

The mining and processing of minerals is usually a rather dirty business, from which European and US companies have withdrawn in recent years to concentrate on the higher-value (ergo, more lucrative) steps in the value chain. Against this backdrop, it proves to be a great advantage for China that it extracts many of the raw materials needed both for the electrification and digitalization of economic and military activities in its own country, while importing the remainder. Today, China is able to turn 'critical minerals' extracted in mines it controls mostly in Asia and Africa into intermediate products, thus using all its options to incorporate them into higher-value end products. This is increasingly upsetting the order of the previous global division of labour.

At present, many political leaders at both the national and the European level, following the lead of the US, give the impression that Western states will be able to subsidize without limit the firms which are needed to build up strategically critical supply chains. As a precondition for this, mining and processing of all 'critical minerals' would have to be rapidly restarted and expanded either domestically or in 'like-minded countries' of the Global South. But where extraction of coveted commodities such as lithium for battery production is envisaged within Europe, for example in the rural north of Portugal or in Serbia, the process is associated with considerable environmental damage and massive protests immediately arise from the local population. What is possible in the vastness of the Mongolian desert, where Rio Tinto and Chinese companies disregard environmental and human rights standards while extracting raw materials for use in solar modules and wind turbines, can hardly be realised in densely populated Europe or the US.

It is indeed puzzling how the interests of the rich Western countries, who want to shirk their responsibility for the global ecological catastrophe with an 'energy turnaround', could be implemented while in a confrontation with China rather than through cooperation. China accounts for between 60 and 100 per cent of global refining capacity for most of the minerals needed to realize this clean tech vision. China controls mines in Africa and Mongolia; it has financed and built highways, railroads and harbours across Eurasia and huge parts of Africa to export raw materials for processing in China; and it is itself home to many of the most needed minerals.

THE NEW BATTLE FOR THE 'HEARTLAND' OF THE WORLD

Geopolitical conflicts still revolve around the same regions as at the beginning of the 20th century. Back then, the British geographer Halford MacKinder described the huge land mass comprising Europe, Asia and Africa as the great 'island of the world', encompassing the three adjoining continents and representing the 'heartland' of the world.[26] This is where the last major resources and the last suspected reserves of conventional and thus less expensive fossil fuels are located today[27] – and by far the largest quantity of minerals and metals needed for all civil and military technologies of digitalization. These materials will also be needed for the production of energy from renewable sources and its use in electromobility, for industries such as chemicals and aviation, and for the medical equipment used in modern industrial societies.

As is well known, this huge Afro-Eurasian landmass has been the focus for a decade of a project by an actor with enormous financial and technological power. China's Belt and Road Initiative aims to create 'the largest market with unparalleled potential' through the construction of a tricontinental network of railways, oil and gas pipelines, and industrial infrastructure – including, above all, power plants, ports and electricity grids – according to President Xi Jinping in a 2013 speech at Nazarbayev University in Kazakhstan.[28] At the same time, China is securing access to many 'strategic' raw material deposits in this region through the expansion of its state-owned companies. Road and rail links across this heartland could, once completed, enable much faster transport of goods between East and West compared to shipping, as well as from Africa to Europe and Asia. These transport routes would also be less exposed to the dangers of a blockade by the US and its allies than the waterways now being used. Because China has never treated the African continent as a 'sideshow', unlike the old imperial powers of

Europe and the US, the People's Republic could succeed in doing what all hegemonic world powers have tried to do for 500 years: dominate the tricontinental landmass on which more than 70 per cent of the world's population lives.

Eurasia, however, also remains vital for Europeans, especially with regard to energy security. As Zbigniew Brzezinski, influential advisor to US administrations from Ronald Reagan to Barack Obama, once wrote, whoever dominates this huge landmass dominates the world. Therefore, as has been the credo of American foreign policy since the early 1990s, no power should be allowed to gain the ability to drive the US (geographically far from the continent!) out of Eurasia. This purpose is served by the approximately 750 US military bases in 80 countries that have created an 'iron ring' around Afro-Eurasia today including the expanded 'pivot area' of the Indo-Pacific region. The 2017 US National Security Strategy, makes this unmistakably clear that in a 'competitive world ... China and Russia challenge American power', forcing them to fully develop all their economic and technological potential in order to put a stop to China's striving for world domination.[29]

Because the availability of energy sources plays a key role in this, China is seen as the main adversary, but Russia is equally targeted as an energy supplier. From this point of view, Europe serves on the one hand as a military bridgehead to Eurasia, a 'typical' great power that is supposed to fulfil its conventional and nuclear alliance obligations, i.e., it must be able to wage war itself in the future and not simply – Germany in particular – 'enjoy the spoils of world export championships'. On the other hand, the EU is also seen as a large market that can be conquered either by US or Chinese (tech) companies. Against this backdrop, the aggressive 'tech-geopolitics' of the US government becomes quite reasonable.

THE RENEWAL OF GEOPOLITICS AND CLIMATE ENDGAME

Cheap energy remains a decisive prerequisite for the production of cheap food; it is needed for machines, fertilizers and pesticides, the transportation and storage of food, and increasingly for the artificial irrigation of cultivated land. However, it can be assumed that energetic and non-energetic agricultural raw materials will never again be available as cheaply as they were in past decades. This will lead to considerable distribution conflicts and force workers to change priorities in their personal lifestyles, but at the same time – and under much more difficult conditions – to demand their fair share of the profits generated by the extractive sector in the pursuit of critical minerals. Alongside this, they will not be spared the fact that the 'new normal' is to get by with fewer 'energy slaves'.[30] Against this background, the war in Ukraine is proving to be a trigger for a secular energy crisis. The return to an imagined 'normality' of cheap energy, however, is out of the question. It is for this, and not for the now-accelerated militarization of the EU, that the term 'turning point' is wise to use.

Worst of all, we are today faced with a 'climate endgame'[31] instead of socioecological transformation. The climate negotiations at winter 2021's COP26 in Glasgow and the announcement of a 'Green Deal' for Europe and 'Clean Deal' for the US – which are definitely not the same – have sent a strong signal to investors that fossil fuels will not be profitable in the longer term and so it would be wise to invest in renewable energy sources and related infrastructure as soon as possible. But today, in parallel with the growing demand in Europe for bombs for since the outbreak of the war in Ukraine, huge new 'carbon bombs' are also being built. The geopolitical moves that started in recent years offer little cause for optimism: in response to the war in Ukraine, both coal and nuclear power plants are increasingly being kept in operation and even expanded, not only in Europe but across the world. New oil and gas projects are being launched everywhere. This can only be described as an open declaration of war on the bio-physical systems of the Earth. If this war on the planet is not stopped immediately, we will catapult ourselves back to temperatures last seen during the Eocene, about 50 million years ago, long before man's appearance in the Holocene.

In times of a climate catastrophe that is already being experienced in many places and growing existential hardship, an increase in violent intra- and inter-state conflict must be expected. In the near future, 'synchronous failure' is to be expected, which could spread globally through countries and systems – comparable to the domino dynamics that set the 2007-09 global financial crisis in motion. But once a certain threshold of chaos is reached – which in everyday language means an excess of disorder, but in the scientific sense above all the unpredictability of processes – the synchronous collapse of ecological and social systems threatens civility in the way people interact with each other even before their civilization comes to an end.

It is foreseeable that the geopolitical dominance of the US will be consolidated on the basis of its 'digital-military-industrial complex' and its ruthless pursuit of great power interests, but with the complete neglect of an environmental agenda. It is also quite likely that Russia will be economically weakened, at least in the longer term, and turn south and east in a subordinate role to China. In the process, the country will not only have to sell off its raw energy materials as well as many agricultural and mineral resources at dumping prices, but also – just like Ukraine – disregard all of its ecological obligations.

There is still the possibility that China could one day become a central pivot of the geopolitical relations of the Afro-Eurasian region, MacKinder's great 'island of the world'. However, this presupposes that the US does not seek an imminent military conflict in light of this possibility, while its naval forces for now are still superior to those of China. Moreover, China could only become a new hegemon if it finds a sustainable solution for the threatening nexus of energy-water-food supply in its own territorial space.

Particularly bleak, however, is the picture that Europe presents. Through 'self-imposed vassalage',[32] it is tied into the Atlantic alliance and will emerge from its military and economic engagement with Ukraine very much weakened economically, particularly as a result of its hasty and ill-conceived withdrawal from energy links with Russia and through to its misguided spending on rearmament, which, together with inflation and supply bottlenecks, will drastically reduce the competitiveness of European industry. Moreover, a deep recession could also bring a decline in the value of the euro. And, worst of all, the fate of the 'non-OECD world' remains of no concern to any of the 'big players'.

At the bottom of these attempts to defend the status quo of the world's most powerful forces, which can pursue their interests no matter the cost for other nations and people, we are confronted with the secular problem of 'peak production' of nearly everything which modern capitalist industrial societies depend on: cheap fossil fuels, cheap minerals, cheap land and cheap water – all of which are necessary for modern technologies such as renewable energy, batteries for electro-mobility, consumer electronics and the tools of modern warfare. Thus, we are faced with, in the words of Michael Klare, a 'race for what is left',[33] which we call the 'renewal of geopolitics', while ignoring that we are confronted with the limits of our civilization as such.

NOTES

1   Elmar Altvater and Birgit Mahnkopf, *Grenzen der Globalisierung*, Münster: Westfälisches Dampfboot, 1999; Elmar Altvater and Birgit Mahnkopf, *Las limitationes de la globalización*, México, D.F: siglo veintiuno editores, 2002; Elmar Altvater and Birgit Mahnkopf, *Globalisierung der Unsicherheit*, Münster: Westfälisches Dampfboot, 2002; *La Globalizacíon de la Inseguridad,* Buenos Aires: Paidós Entorno, 2008.
2   President Donald Trump already put European allies under pressure with punitive tariffs because of their gas imports from Russia. But it was only his successor, Joe Biden, who was able to announce to the press on 2 February 2022 – so before Russia invaded Ukraine – that the commissioning of the Nord Stream 2 pipeline from Russia to Germany would be prevented by the USA. Since then, nothing has stood in the way of the expansion of the liquefied natural gas infrastructure on both sides of the

Atlantic – and the markets for much more expensive US fracked gas in Europe and Asia are secured for decades to come.

3   These include freezing Russia's central bank reserves; disconnecting major Russian banks from SWIFT; restricting foreign currencies; placing sanctions and asset freezes on more than 10,000 individuals, entities, vessels, aircraft; export controls on dual-use goods; an oil-price cap; a ban on gold imports from Russia; superyacht confiscations; travel bans; and the exodus of many western firms from Russia.

4   Birgit Mahnkopf, 'Nebelkerze Green New Deal', *Blätter für deutsche und internationale Politik*, 6, 2021, pp.75-84.

5   Other technologies are expected to offer a significantly better cost-performance ratio with fewer economic, technical and military risks. See: Christian von Hirschhausen, et al., 'Energy and Climate Scenarios Paradoxically Assure Considerable Nuclear Energy Growth', *DIW-Weekly Report*, 45-49, 2023, pp. 293-301.

6   Under the plan, the EU increased the renewable energy target from 40 to 45 per cent of power generation by 2030, which translates into more than 200 GW in additional capacity.

7   Institute for Energy Economics and Financial Analysis, 'Over half of Europe's LNG infrastructure assets could be left unused by 2030', 21 March 2023, available at: www.ieefa.org.

8   Damian Carrington and Mathew Taylor, 'The "Carbon Bombs" Set to Trigger Catastrophic Climate Breakdown', *The Guardian*, 11 May 2022.

9   In August 2023, the prospect of strikes at LNG projects in Australia were enough to drive the price for LNG up by 40 per cent.

10 IEEFA, 'Over half of Europe's LNG infrastructure assets could be left unused by 2030'.

11 Barney Jopson, 'Donald Trump hails new era of US "energy dominance"', *Financial Times*, 29 June 2017; Steve Ciala, 'Who Loses From Trump's Pursuit of "Energy Dominance"? You, the Taxpayer', Energy Policy Institute at the University of Chicago, 29 August 2017, available at: epic.uchigago.edu; Michal Klare, 'Militarizing America's Energy Policy', *TomDispatch.com*, 11 February 2018, available at: www.tomdispatch.com.

12 At the same time, however, the US has always used its currency, with the devaluation and revaluation strategies pursued by the Fed, as a means of coercion with which it could enforce its interests within the 'international order' as an alternative to the use of military power.

13 Carla Norrlöf, 'The Dollar Still Dominates: America Financial Power in the Age of Great Power Competition', *Foreign Affairs*, 21 February 2023; and Nouriel Roubini, 'A bipolar currency regime will replace the dollar's exorbitant privilege', *Financial Times*, 5 February 2023.

14 It seems that the war in Ukraine has become a 'test bed' for new dual-use technologies such as drones, facial recognition systems and satellite communication. See: Mareitje Schaake, 'Businesses scent a tech opportunity in Ukraine war', *Financial Times*, 16 August 2023.

15 When it comes to spending on R&D, the US is no longer the undisputed leader that it was in the post-WWII era. Its share of global GDP spent on R&D has fallen since the turn of the millennium (from 40 per cent in 2000 to 31 per cent in 2020), while

R&D's share of GDP in China has risen (from only 5 per cent in 2000 to 25 per cent in 2020). See: Karen Kornbluh and Julia Tréhu, 'The New American Policy of Technology', Policy Report, German Marshall Fund, March 2022.

16 Gary Clyde Hufbauer and Megan Hogan, 'Chips Act will spur US production but not foreclose China', Policy Briefs 22-13, Peterson Institute for International Economics, October 2022; available at: www.piie.com.

17 Chris Miller, '*Chip War: The Fight for the World's Most Critical Technologies*', New York: Scribner, 2022.

18 Grey Anderson, 'Strategies of Denial', *Sidecar*, 15 June 2023, available at: newleftreview.org/sidecar.

19 Ro Khanna, 'The New Industrial Age: America Should Once Agan Become a Manufacturing Superpower', *Foreign Affairs*, Jan-Feb 2023, pp. 141-54.

20 International Energy Agency, *Special Report on Solar PV Global Supply Chain*, July 2022; *Global EV Outlook 2023,* April 2023; *World Energy Investment 2023*, January 2023. All available at: www.iea.org.

21 International Energy Agency, *Energy Technology Perspectives 2023*, January 2023, available at: www.iea.org.

22 Certainly, the manufacturing process of solar PV (and also other renewable energy technologies, not to mention the production of all sorts of digital devices) consumes a lot of energy, which presently is generated in China by coal power plants. However, as the IEA correctly points to in its *Special Report on Solar PV Global Supply Chain*, solar panels only need to operate for 4-8 months to offset their manufacturing emissions. Thus, a frequently formulated accusation against China does not stand up to scrutiny – at times, the protectionist legislation of the US is justified because it promises truly 'clean' technologies, while China's 'green' technologies are criticised for not being 'clean' due to their reliance on coal-powered electricity. Another criticism of the 'clean' character of the 'green' technologies produced in China is characterised by obvious double standards. The German foreign minister Annalena Baerbock, like her prompters in the US, misses no opportunity to point to violations of human rights and core labour standards in the factories in Xinjiang, where most parts for China's renewable energy technologies are produced. But never does one hear from these advocates of a 'value-based foreign policy' a simultaneous criticism of forced labour in US prisons or the use of child labour (mostly from Nigeria) in Italian agriculture, which is often carried out under intolerable conditions for less than half of minimum wage.

23 BloombergNEF, *New Energy Outlook: China Report*, 30 May 2023, available at: www.bnef.com.

24 Giovanni Sgaravatti, Simone Tagliapietra and Cecillia Trasi, *Cleantech manufacturing: where does Europe really stand?*, Brussels: Bruegel, 17 May 2023, available at: www.bruegel.org.

25 DERA (Deutsche Energie und Rohstoffagentur), *Wirtschaftsmächte auf dem metallischen Rohstoffmarkt – Ein Vergleich von China, EU und USA*, Berlin: DERA, 2020, available at: www.dera.org; Kirsten Hund, Daniele La Porta, Thao P. Fabregas, Tim Laing and John Drexhage*, Minerals for Climate Action: The Mineral Intensity of Clean Energy Transition*, Washington: World Bank, 2020, available at: www.worldbank.org.

26 Halford John Mackinder, 'The Geographical Pivot of History', *The Geographical Journal*, 23(4), 1904.

27 Conventional oil and gas resources have a much higher 'energy return on energy invested' (EROI) than so-called unconventional oil and gas, be it from on- or offshore territories. See: Elmar Altvater and Birgit Mahnkopf, 'The Capitalocene: Permanent Capitalist Counter-revolution', in Leo Panitch and Greg Albo, eds, *Socialist Register 2019: A World Turned Upside Down*, London: Merlin, 2018.

28 Ministry of Foreign Affairs, People's Republic of China, 'Speech by Xi Jinping, President of the PRC, at the Nazarbayev University, 8 September 2023', available at: www.worldipn.net.

29 *National Security Strategy of the United States of America*, Washington, DC: The White House, December 2017, p. 2.

30 This term, going back to Buckminster Fuller in 1944, clarifies that economic, technological and ultimately social progress since the beginning of the Industrial Revolution has been based on 'energy doing the job for us'. Even poor people living in rich industrialized countries, but especially their middle classes and even more the very rich people of this world – of which there are more and more in all regions of the world – maintain whole armies of 'energy slaves'. These armies would have to be considerably reduced, even if a switch to renewable energy sources instead of fossil fuels were to succeed.

31 Luke Kemp, Chi Xu, Joanna Depledge and Timothy M. Lenton, 'Climate Endgame: Exploring catastrophic climate change scenarios', *PNAS*, 119(34), 1 August 2022.

32 Michael Klare, 'The Ukraine War's Collateral Damage', *TomDispatch.com*, 22 May 2022, available at: www.tomdispatch.com.

33 Michael Klare, *The Race for What's Left: The Global Scramble for the World's Last Resources*. London: Picador, 2012.